D0960050

# ALL THE NATIONS
# UNDER HEAVEN

■

COLUMBIA HISTORY OF URBAN LIFE

*Kenneth T. Jackson, General Editor*

COLUMBIA HISTORY OF URBAN LIFE

Kenneth T. Jackson, GENERAL EDITOR

Deborah Dash Moore. *At Home in America: Second Generation New York Jews.*   1981

Edward K. Spann. *The New Metropolis: New York City 1840–1857.*   1981

Matthew Edel, Elliot D. Sclar, and Daniel Luria. *Shaky Palaces: Homeownership and Social Mobility in Boston's Suburbanization.*   1984

Steven J. Ross. *Workers on the Edge: Work, Leisure, and Politics in Industrializing Cincinnati, 1788–1890.*   1985

Andrew Lees. *Cities Perceived: Urban Society in European Thought, 1820–1940.*   1985

R. J. R. Kirkby. *Urbanization in China: Town and Country in a Developing Economy, 1949–2000 A.D.*   1985

Judith Ann Trolander. *Professionalism and Social Change: From the Settlement House Movement to the Present.*   1987

Marc A. Weiss. *The Rise of the Community Builders: The American Real Estate Industry and Urban Land Planning.*   1987

Jacqueline Leavitt and Susan Saegert. *From Abandonment to Hope: Community-Households in Harlem.*   1989

David Hamer. *New Towns in the New World: Images and Perception of the Nineteenth-Century Urban Frontier.*   1989

Andrew Heinz. *Adapting to Abundance: Jewish Immigrants, Mass Consumption, and the Search for American Identity.*   1990

Chris McNickle. *To Be Mayor of New York: Ethnic Politics in the City.*   1993

Clay McShane. *Down the Asphalt Path: The Automobile and the American City.*   1994

# ALL THE NATIONS UNDER HEAVEN

■

*An*
*Ethnic*
*and*
*Racial*
*History*
*of*
***New***
***York***
***City***

*Frederick M. Binder*
*David M. Reimers*

COLUMBIA UNIVERSITY PRESS **NEW YORK**

Columbia University Press

New York    Chichester, West Sussex

Copyright © 1995 Columbia University Press

All rights reserved

Library of Congress Cataloging-in-Publication Data

Binder, Frederick M.

All the nations under heaven : an ethnic and racial history of New
York City / Frederick M. Binder, David M. Reimers.

p.   cm.

Includes bibliographical references and index.

ISBN 0-231-07878-1 (alk. paper)

1. Ethnology—New York (N.Y.) 2. New York (N.Y.)—Ethnic
relations. 3. New York (N.Y.)—Race relations     I. Reimers, David
M. II. Title.

F128.9.A1B45   1995                           94-45085

305.8'009747'1—dc20                           CIP

Casebound editions of Columbia University Press books
are Smyth-sewn and printed on permanent and durable
acid-free paper.

Printed in the United States of America

c 10 9 8 7 6 5 4 3 2 1

*To
Corky
and
Teri*

# Contents

Preface      *ix*

1 ▪ *Multiethnic from the Beginning: New York City,*
 *the Colonial and Revolutionary Years*      *1*

2 ▪ *Dynamic Growth and Diversity:*
 *The City and its People, 1789–1880*      *33*

3 ▪ *Diversity in Action: Irish and German Immigrants*
 *in a Growing City, 1789–1880*      *59*

4 ▪ *Old and New Immigrants in Greater*
 *New York City, 1880 to World War I*      *93*

5 ▪ *Jews and Italians in Greater*
 *New York City, 1880 to World War I*      *114*

6 ▪ *Ethnic New Yorkers from the Great War*
 *to the Great Depression*      *149*

7 ▪ *A Time of Trial: New Yorkers During*
 *the Great Depression and World War II*      *176*

8 ▪ *A Better Time: New York City, 1945–1970*      *197*

9 ▪ *Truly a Global City: New York,*
 *1970 to the Present*      *225*

Afterword      *259*

Notes      *263*

Selected Reading      *315*

Index      *319*

*Preface*

**W**hile the Netherlands initially sought to establish Manhattan as a
Dutch colony and trading center, from its beginnings the emerging city
of New York became home to a variety of ethnic and racial groups. For
most of its history, people of European and African origin have constituted the largest numbers. In recent years, however, New York's population has become truly global in origin, and today those of European
background are in the minority.

Ethnic diversity is not unique to New York. Much has been written
about the nation as a whole being a refuge for millions of people from
all corners of the globe. The fact remains, however, that it has been
through New York's port that until recently the majority of immigrants

entered the United States and within New York City that so many of them established initial residence. Yet, even though New York has long stood as the symbol of America's immigrant heritage, there exists no general ethnic and racial history of the city.

*All the Nations Under Heaven* is primarily a narrative and analytical history of ethnic and racial New York, from its beginnings as a Dutch trading outpost until the present, when new Third World migration has made the city's population global in character. The book centers on the development of New York's pluralism. This focus inevitably deals with the experiences of groups as they entered the city, adjusted and accommodated to the ever changing urban environment, and faced tension and hostility. It is concerned with the process by which they modified their own cultures and transformed that of the city. New York prides itself on the diversity of its seven million inhabitants and a climate emphasizing toleration and accommodation. Yet the establishment of such a climate was not easy and even today is not fully realized. Now, as in the past, ethnic and racial conflict is ever on the surface of New York City's life.

It is not possible in a book of this length to deal with all of the many ethnic and racial groups that have come to New York City. Nor can we give equal attention to those we discuss. Rather we highlight those groups which, because of their numbers, time of arrival, and significance, illustrate clearly the major themes in our story. Hence, French Huguenots—a relatively small colonial migration—are included because they demonstrate how some groups assimilate rapidly. On the other hand, blacks—present in New York from its earliest days—have never been permitted full participation in the life of the city. Thus we devote much space to black New Yorkers because of the importance of racism in the city's history.

Nor is it possible to cover all aspects of those we do include. We have concentrated on the public sphere and patterns of settlement. Thus we focus on neighborhood development, work, organized religion, politics, and some but not all of the great variety of organizations immigrants and migrants created to deal with life in New York City. We leave to others to provide in-depth treatment of such important topics as family life, the experience of children, and the roles of women.

The authors wish to thank several conferences for inviting them to present their ideas. David Reimers gave a paper on the "Asian Impact

■

on New York City," at a conference on Asian Americans at Hofstra University in 1990. He also discussed recent developments in New York City as part of the Commonwealth Lecture at the University of London in February 1989, and at a conference sponsored by the New-York Historical Society in 1986. A paper resulting from these lectures was published in William Pencak, Selma Berrol, and Randall Miller (eds.), *Immigration to New York* (Philadelphia, 1991). A paper by Reimers on the post-1945 New York Irish is included in Ronald Bayor and Timothy Meagher (eds.), *The New York Irish* (Baltimore, forthcoming). Both authors have presented some of the main themes in "New York as an Immigrant City," in Silvia Pedraza and Ruben Rumbaut (eds.), *Making an American: Immigration, Race and Ethnicity in the United States, Past and Present* (Belmont, Ca., 1995).

We have received assistance from many persons and several institutions. Both New York University and the College of Staten Island proved necessary sabbaticals for research and writing. The staffs and the libraries of New York University, branches of the City University of New York, Columbia University, Fordham University, and the New York Public were indispensable. We have included a brief reading list at the end, but the main sources we used are indicated in the footnotes. At an early stage Tom Kessner read several chapters and an outline and made constructive comments that prompted us to make considerable changes. The anonymous readers for Columbia University Press also provided us with important criticism. Carl Prince read the last half of the manuscript in a different form and was helpful in reorganization. Three persons, Leonard Dinnerstein, George Lankevich, and Phil Hosay, read a draft and gave us extensive comments. Len also read early chapters, discussed the project as it progressed, and gave us the benefit not only of his criticisms but also his extensive knowledge of American ethnic history. It was also helpful that Len is a native New Yorker and was able to convey to us his own experiences in the city. George Lankevich read the manuscript and also used his pen freely on matters of style as well as content. Because he has written a general history of New York City, he was especially helpful. One could not ask for better friends and critics than George and Len. One could not ask for a better (or more patient) editor than Kate Wittenberg of Columbia University Press. It was a pleasure working with her again as well as with Leslie Bialler and others at the press.

■

In the end, whatever mistakes and interpretations we made are our own and not those of our pre-publication readers. Our wives, to whom the book is dedicated, did no research, no editing or proofreading. They have not read the text. But without their help, support, and patience in so many other areas, the work could not have been completed.

Frederick M. Binder
David M. Reimers
Lake Dunmore, Vermont
September 1994

■

# ALL THE NATIONS
## UNDER HEAVEN

■

*Multiethnic*

*from the*

*Beginning:*

*New*

*York*

*City,*

*the Colonial*

*and*

*Revolutionary*

*Years*

The heterogeneous ethnic character for which New York City has long been famous began to emerge on April 17, 1524, when the first European vessel sailed into the harbor. The ship *Dauphine* was under the command of an Italian captain, Giovanni da Verrazano, hired by King Francis I of France to search out a western sea passage to the Orient. Verrazano sighted the "great river [Hudson]" and most likely Manhattan Island as well, but he went no further; instead, he sailed up the rugged northern coast of America before returning to France. A similar objective and a similar outcome marked the second recorded voyage into the harbor in January 1526. This time it was a black Portuguese explorer, Estaban Gomez, who commanded a ship flying the colors of

Spain. He too sighted the mighty river, named it the San Antonio and sailed off to other places.[1]

Because neither Verrazano nor Gomez sought to find the path to the Orient on the river flowing northward, the glory of discovery went to the man who did. Up to a point Henry Hudson fit the mold of his predecessors, a man from one country—he was English—sailing under the banner of another—he was hired by the Dutch East India Company— to discover an all-water route to the Far East. But Hudson's curiosity was apparently aroused as he sailed the *Half Moon* into New York Bay in September 1609. He landed on Manhattan Island, traded with Indians for furs, and sailed up and mapped the river later named for him as far as the site of present day Albany.[2]

More significant for the future than Hudson's curiosity and sense of adventure was the nation for which he sailed. Seventeenth-century Netherlands was the great mercantile center of Europe and "Almost alone of the European states . . . seemed to recognize the commercial possibilities of the New World."[3] Private merchant traders quickly took advantage of the fur trade opportunities New Netherland represented. Profitable trading ventures and competing English claims to the territory ultimately convinced the States General of the necessity of establishing a more secure presence in the land Hudson had claimed for the Dutch nation.[4]

While Dutch commercial interests determined the purposes for the founding of the colony, it was another related Dutch trait that determined the ethnic makeup of New Netherland. No nation of Europe was as tolerant of religious refugees, ethnic and linguistic minorities, or political exiles. Thousands of these flocked to Amsterdam and other Dutch cities, where they often played significant roles in commercial activities. The largest group consisted of Protestant refugees from oppressive Spanish rule in the southern provinces of the Netherlands, French-speaking Walloons and Dutch-speaking Flemings. But there were many others. A recent study documents both the ethnic diversity of seventeenth-century Netherlands and the economic success achieved there by many refugees. Citing a 1631 tax assessment in Amsterdam, the author reports "of the 685 wealthiest individuals no less than 160 were Flemish or Walloon, 30 were German, and numerous Italian, English, and Scandinavian names dotted the list."[5]

Not all refugees were able or willing to sink permanent roots in

■

Dutch soil. The story of the Pilgrims' stay in Leyden and their ultimate decision to leave for New England is familiar to every school child, and the Dutch overseas empire offered promise to other emigres. In 1602, the East India Company received a charter from the States General giving it a monopoly of Dutch trade east of the Cape of Good Hope and west of the Strait of Magellan. Ultimately the company established colonies and dominated trade in Malaya, Indonesia, Ceylon, and the Spice Islands. In 1621, a newly formed West India Company obtained a similar charter granting it a 24-year monopoly of trade with West Africa, North and South America, the coast of Australia, and the West Indies. Its commercial prospects appeared promising: gold, ivory, and slaves from West Africa, sugar from Brazil, salt from Venezuela, a wide variety of products from the West Indies, and furs from New Netherland.[6]

It seems most appropriate that New York City's origins were part and parcel of a corporate venture. It is equally appropriate that a major portion of the first settlers on Manhattan consisted of refugees seeking security and economic opportunity. In 1621, a group of Walloon refugees had petitioned the legislatures of the Dutch states of Holland and West Friesland for assistance. They described themselves as "diverse families of all manner of manufacture who, having solicited the English to be transported to Virginia, would now prefer to be employed by the West India Company."[7] When the petition finally passed on to the company in 1623, the directors were prepared to act. Settlers under the company's auspices would help check independent fur poachers in New Netherland and help secure the Dutch claim to the territory against the encroachments of Britain and France.

The company offered attractive terms to prospective colonists. In return for a pledge to remain in New Netherland for six years, the settler was granted the right to own and sell land, to conduct trade within the colony for profit, to hunt, to fish, and to search for precious metals and gems. While public conformity to the Dutch Reformed Church was required, freedom of conscience in private worship was guaranteed. The settler, in turn, had to assist in the construction of military structures and public buildings and to serve in the militia in times of war.[8]

And so, in May 1624, as recorded by the seventeenth-century Dutch historian Nicolaes Van Wassenaer, "a company of thirty families, mostly Walloons" reached the Hudson River aboard the *Nieu Nederlandt*, dropping anchor north of Manhattan. Under the command of Cornelius

Jacobsz May of Hoorn they constituted the colony's first permanent settlers.[9] The West India Company's development plan envisioned fur trading posts at the head of navigation on the Hudson, Delaware, and Connecticut rivers, with Walloons expected to devote themselves to farming in support of these posts. In accordance with these objectives several river settlements were established and a fort was begun on Governor's Island in New York Harbor.[10] The following year a second expedition under the leadership of Willem Verhulst brought approximately one hundred additional Walloons along with livestock and provisions. Verhulst began a process, later fully implemented by his successor Peter Minuit, of evacuating outlying posts, removing all women and children from the largest settlement at Fort Orange (near present-day Albany), and resettling them on Manhattan Island. The costs of maintaining a number of scattered settlements against Indian threats and the need to establish a centrally located headquarters for the colony were factors in the decision.[11]

Under director-general Peter Minuit, son of Walloon refugees from Westphalia, Germany, the town of New Amsterdam took shape on the southern tip of Manhattan. Following company instructions to secure its claim to Manhattan, Minuit began negotiations with the Canarsie Indians shortly after his arrival in 1626. The resultant purchase of the island for 60 guilders or roughly 24 dollars has marked Minuit in the minds of generations of schoolchildren as one of history's shrewdest dealers. However, in point of fact, the Canarsie title to Manhattan was without substance; they did not own it. Their homes were on Long Island, and they merely used Manhattan as a hunting and fishing ground. In later years, as they sought to secure full land rights, the Dutch made additional land purchases from Native Americans living in the upper reaches of the island.[12]

Once the company's dubious title to the land was secured, Minuit gathered settlers onto Manhattan. Construction of thirty log houses, Fort New Amsterdam, a stone countinghouse, and a large mill whose upper loft would be used for church services soon marked the first of what would be many city construction booms.[13] The Verhulst/Minuet decision to evacuate most settlers from the outlying posts might possibly have prevented the elimination of the Walloon presence in New Netherland. These French-speaking Calvinists were apparently ill suited for life in a wilderness outpost. Many of them had been only part-

■

time farmers in Europe, devoting considerable time to income-producing weaving or lace-making. More than half of those settled at Fort Orange had left even before the evacuation order of 1626, and there is evidence of a continuing exodus from the colony following resettlement in Manhattan. A 1628 report found "A portion of the Walloons are going back to the Fatherland, either because their years have expired, or else because some are not very serviceable to the Company."[14] Nevertheless, a goodly number of Walloons did find developing opportunities in New Amsterdam to their liking, for they constituted an estimated twenty percent of the town's increasingly heterogeneous population as late as 1650.[15]

Historian Jon Butler describes New Amsterdam's French-speaking populace as exhibiting "little inclination towards exclusivity," as neither being encouraged to nor apparently desirous of setting up a separate French-speaking congregation. He contrasts Manhattan's Walloons to French settlers on Staten Island, where Walloons were joined between 1650 and 1660 by a number of Waldensians, a persecuted religious brotherhood from eastern France. The Staten Island French apparently were far more interested than their brothers across the harbor in maintaining their heritage; they appealed to the governing body of the Dutch Reformed Church in Amsterdam, the Classis, for a minister who could preach in French as well as Dutch.[16] Manhattan's Walloons were ultimately relegated to a minority as the company's expansion in New Amsterdam led to an influx of non-French artisans, clerks, traders, and sailors.

New Amsterdam's Walloons must have felt themselves overwhelmed as both the numbers and the ethnic variety of the townspeople increased without a significant rise in French-speaking immigration during the remaining years of Dutch rule. In 1643, Father Isaac Jogues, a Jesuit missionary who had escaped from Mohawk captivity and journeyed to New Amsterdam, reported that as many as eighteen languages were spoken in the town of approximately a thousand residents. He was also struck by New Amsterdam's religious diversity: "No religion is publicly exercised but the Calvinist, and orders are to admit none but Calvinists, but this is not observed, for besides the Calvinists there are in the colony Catholics, English Puritans, Lutherans, Anabaptists, here called Mnistes [Mennonites], etc."[17] Father Jogues was by no means favorably impressed with what he observed: "The arrogance of Babel

■

has done much harm to all men; the confusion of tongues has deprived them of great benefit."[18]

Father Jogues's antipathy to ethnic and religious diversity was undoubtedly shared by the Dutch Reformed clergy of New Amsterdam. At the time of the arrival of Manhattan's first minister, Domine Jonas Michaelius, in 1628, religious toleration was not generally viewed as a virtue in either Europe or its colonial outposts. But, clergy aside, the Dutch nation had reasons to be an exception in these matters. In addition to a sensitivity nurtured by years of victimization by Spain, what made the Dutch in old Amsterdam and New Amsterdam so receptive to diversity was their commercial prosperity, which was greatly dependent upon toleration. The polyglot population of New Amsterdam was a result of the West India Company's desire to attract colonists at a time when life in the Netherlands was quite satisfactory to most Dutchmen. Out of pure necessity the company continued in America policies that had proven so successful at home. It granted official status, financial support, and declarations of conformity to the Reformed church while it permitted freedom of conscience and opportunities to worship in private to nonconformists.

The fine balance between toleration and conformity came close to being undermined during the director-generalship of Peter Stuyvesant (1645–1664). An able administrator, although arrogant and authoritarian, the religiously orthodox Stuyvesant believed that maintaining the established church was an essential ingredient in creating an orderly community. In Dominies Johannes Megapolensis and Samuel Drisius, copastors of the New Amsterdam church, Stuyvesant found willing partners in the defense of orthodoxy. In 1653, when Lutherans petitioned Stuyvesant for permission to hold public services, a crisis ensued. Significant numbers of the non-Dutch inhabitants of the colony had originated in Lutheran regions of Germany, Scandinavia, and Schleswig-Holstein.[19] The troika of Stuyvesant, Megapolensis, and Drisius saw the petition as a threat to the established order. The director-general, apparently fearing discord in the colony no less than the challenge to his church, passed the petition on to the company in Amsterdam, while the pastors quickly sent a letter urging the Classis to bring pressure upon the company to deny the Lutherans' request. The alternative, they insisted, would "tend to the injury of our church, the diminution of hearers of the Word of God, and the increase of dissensions."[20] As might be expected, the company's response reflected its overriding interest in attracting settlers to New Netherland regardless of their ethnic background or religious affiliation. Unprepared to challenge the Classis yet determined to defuse religious controversy, the West India Company simply told Stuyvesant not to accept any more petitions of that sort but to reject them "in the most civil and least offensive way."[21] In 1656, after Stuyvesant fined and imprisoned Lutherans on Long Island for holding public services without an approved Reformed minister, the company again ordered him to be less zealous and more flexible in his religious policy. The controversy ultimately ended when the company permitted the Lutherans to worship publicly in Reformed churches after making certain adjustments in their catechism. Neither the pastors in New Amsterdam nor the Classis in the Netherlands were pleased with this compromise, but company policy won out in the end.[22]

Evidence abounds that traditional Dutch toleration far outweighed Stuyvesant's reputation as a religious zealot and attracted settlers to New Netherland. Religious refugees from Puritan New England, among them Anne Hutchinson, made up a substantial part of the population of Dutch Long Island, including the present-day borough of Queens.[23] Most troubling to Peter Stuyvesant was the presence of English Quakers, members of the Society of Friends, who were at that time welcomed in no American colony. Quakers might have found shelter in the Dutch settlement if not for those visible practices and principles which seemed to breed hostility. Seventeenth-century Quakers were far more determined to call attention to themselves and to publicly express their innermost feelings than would be true in later years. For example, when the first Quakers landed in New Amsterdam in August 1657, two women among them attracted a large crowd when they suddenly engaged in shaking, quaking, and rolling on the ground in spasms of religious ecstasy. These women were quickly banished from the colony, but others took refuge among the English settlers on Long Island. There followed incidents of public preaching and refusal to show deference to authority on the part of the Quakers and, in response, torture, banishment, and ordinances discouraging further Quaker settlement and religious gatherings instituted by Stuyvesant. One reaction to Stuyvesant's persecution was the Flushing Remonstrance, a document signed by thirty-one English residents of Flushing, proclaiming their support of

■

religious toleration. The consequences for the leading signatories were arrest, trial in New Amsterdam, and, for one of the leaders who refused to recant, banishment. News of the goings on in New Netherland reached the company directors in 1663, in the form of a lengthy protest written by a former colonist, the Quaker John Browne. The corporate response was predictable: Stuyvesant was told, though it would be desirable to keep "these and other sectarians" away, the consequences of such efforts might well impede immigration "which must be favored at so tender a stage of the country's existence. You may therefore shut your eyes, at least not force people's consciences, but allow everyone to have his own belief, as long as he behaves quietly and legally, gives no offense to his neighbors, and does not oppose the government."[24]

More significant than the experiences of the Lutherans and Quakers in illustrating the uniqueness of the Dutch in dealing with minority ethnic and religious groups is the story of the establishment of the first Jewish community in New Amsterdam. Today New York has a Jewish population larger than that of any city in the world, a population tracing its beginnings back to the last decade of Dutch rule on Manhattan. The Netherlands welcomed Sephardic Jews from Spain and Portugal even before that nation had achieved its independence. The common experience of having suffered under Spanish tyranny likely contributed to the Dutch willingness to accept these refugees, many of whom were Maranos—Jews who had been forced to convert to Christianity but who secretly adhered to the tenets of Judaism. In Amsterdam by the 1590s, a visible community of Jews existed and enjoyed a high level of toleration and prosperity. Beginning in 1635, Ashkenazic Jews from Germany joined their coreligionists in the Netherlands as refugees from the destruction and anti-Semitism spawned by the Thirty Years War (1618–1648). After 1648, Polish and Russian Jews, victims of the Chmielnicki Cossack uprising, also arrived, and by the mid-seventeenth century Amsterdam was a center of Jewish religious and secular scholarship.[25]

Jews figured prominently among those who took advantage of the expanding Dutch commercial empire, both as investors and as colonizers. When the Dutch captured Recife, Brazil, from the Portuguese in 1630, a sizeable group of Maranos who had been living there emerged to proclaim their adherence to Judaism. They were soon joined by hundreds of Jews from the Netherlands and later arrivals from a half dozen

■

other European lands. During twenty-four years of rule by the Dutch West India Company the Jewish community of Recife grew to almost five thousand people; religious life flourished; and Jews prospered as merchants, traders, brokers, planters, and refiners.[26]

All this was not to last. The Portuguese took advantage of Dutch pre-occupation with their war with Britain (1652–1654) to recapture their Brazilian colonies, and Recife fell in 1654. What had been a haven for Jews now became a place of danger, for where the Portuguese were, so too was the Inquisition. Under the terms of surrender the Jews were permitted to leave in peace. Most returned to the Netherlands, but many scattered to the French and British West Indies and particularly to Dutch Surinam and Curacao. One group of twenty-three Racife Jews arrived in New Amsterdam aboard the French ship *St. Charles* during the first week of September 1654.[27]

The distinction of being the first Jew in New Amsterdam probably belongs to Jacob Barsimson, who arrived from the Netherlands on August 22, 1654, either as one of a group of settlers sponsored by the West India Company or possibly as an agent of Dutch Jews sent to determine the feasibility of future Jewish settlement in New Netherland. Whatever Barsimson's purpose, he received little attention from the authorities. Such was not the case with the *St. Charles* arrivals. The two dozen emigres were both Jewish and impoverished, having paid dearly for their four-month journey from Brazil. Even after selling most of their personal goods at auction, the group was indebted to the captain of the *St. Charles* to the sum of 495 guilders. Only after assurances in court that funds from the Netherlands would arrive to indemnify them were two of their number released from civil arrest.[28]

The Jews' first winter in New Amsterdam must have been extremely difficult. They were forced to depend upon the Dutch Reformed Church for support, and the charity was not granted with great enthusiasm. A letter from the Reverend Megapolensis to the Amsterdam Classis on March 18, 1655, reveals: "It would have been proper that they [the Jews] should have been supported by their own people, but they have been at our charge, so that we had to spend several hundred guilders for their support."[29]

More than charity reluctantly granted caused discomfort for the Jews, and more than their poverty produced the hostile reception by New Amsterdam's authorities. There is ample evidence that Peter

Stuyvesant and the Reverend Megapolensis were extremely bigoted toward Jews, perhaps even more so than toward Lutherans and Quakers. Shortly after their arrival the director-general wrote to his superiors in Amsterdam, "we have, for the benefit of the weak and newly developing place and the land in general, deemed it useful to require them in a friendly way to depart . . . praying also most seriously . . . that the deceitful race—such hateful enemies and blasphemers of the name of Christ—be not allowed further to infect and trouble this New Colony."[30] Megapolensis was no less virulent in his communiques to the Classis. Reporting the arrival of additional Jews from the Netherlands in spring of 1655, he described them as having "no other God but the uprighteous Mammon, and no other aim than to get possession of Christian property." He urged "that these godless rascals, who are no benefit to the country, but look at everything for their own profit, may be sent away from here."[31]

Fortunately for New Amsterdam's Jews, their coreligionists in the Netherlands responded to pleas for assistance and lobbied the directors of the West India Company on their behalf. Their memorial to the directors pointed out the advantages to the colony of additional loyal, productive, tax-paying citizens and reminded them "that many of the Jewish nation are principal shareholders of the Company."[32] The directors' letter to Stuyvesant on April 25, 1655, was very much in keeping with their handling of the earlier Lutheran issue and would be echoed later during the Quaker controversy. It began on a note of understanding of and even agreement with Stuyvesant's attitude regarding the Jews and their presence in New Amsterdam, but once more the directors made it quite apparent that their primary concern was turning a profit. The director-general was reminded of the financial losses attending the fall of Recife and of "the large amount of capital" the Jews had "invested in the shares of this company." He was instructed "that these people may travel and trade to and in New Netherland and live and remain there, provided the poor among them shall not become a burden to the company or to the community, but be supported by their own nation."[33]

This response by the directors guaranteed the Jews the right to remain in New Amsterdam but could hardly temper the continued hostility of the town's civil and religious authorities. Numerous municipal impediments were placed to prevent the Jews from enjoying the

■

full benefits of citizenship. Over the next years, at times as individuals and at times as a community, they petitioned for relief from discriminatory taxation and to gain the rights and responsibilities granted to other residents. When Stuyvesant and the New Amsterdam Council rejected their pleas, they turned to the directors of the company, who in most cases offered them at least limited support. For example, when in December 1655, Salvador Dandradj, a Jew, petitioned New Amsterdam authorities for the right to purchase a home, his application was "for pregnant reasons declined."[34] Ultimately the matter was resolved by the company directors who instructed Stuyvesant to permit home ownership but with the added stipulation that "they must without doubt endeavor to build their houses close together in a convenient place on one or the other side of New Amsterdam—at their choice— as they have done here."[35] What the good gentlemen were in effect proposing was the establishment of a residential ghetto on Manhattan Island. However, their proposal was never implemented. Two-and-one-half centuries would pass before a nearly exclusively Jewish neighborhood appeared on the city's Lower East Side.

In similar tedious fashion the Jewish community won privileges previously denied them: to trade with the Indians on the Delaware and Hudson rivers; to sell at retail; to stand guard as members of the Rattle Watch; and the rights of burghership (1657). They were permitted to become butchers in order to provide kosher meat, but were prohibited from engaging in other crafts. Public religious services remained forbidden to them as they were forbidden to all dissenters. A number of the original Jewish refugees from the *St. Charles* did leave New Amsterdam for the more comfortable and less hostile atmosphere of the Netherlands, but those who remained probably knew that, despite obstacles, they experienced more toleration in New Netherland than they likely could in any other colony in North America. Perhaps no other act symbolized the planting of Jewish roots in Manhattan as did the establishment of New Amsterdam's first Jewish institution, "a little hook of land situated outside of this city for a burial place"(1656).[36]

The insistence by the West India Company that a degree of toleration be extended to Jews and Protestant religious dissenters was in keeping with its long standing efforts to transform New Netherland into a profitable venture. Unfortunately, the tolerant policies of the company did not extend to Native Americans. During the first years of the colony settlers had traded with Indians who frequently appeared in New Amsterdam. But relations soon deteriorated, especially under Governor-General Willem Kieft, who displayed a total lack of understanding of Indian culture and sensitivities. A series of provocations beginning in 1639 culminated in the full-scale Kieft's War of 1643–1645. In the end the Indians were brutally and totally vanquished.[37]

Kieft's War set the stage for future relations between Europeans and Native Americans. As the settlers moved farther north and onto Long Island and Staten Island, the Indians were pushed out; they would play only a tiny role in the development of the city. As one historian put it: "the line of demarcation between the European and Indian communities became clearly defined."[38] Many Europeans came to accept the view of one Dutch minister who reported in 1628, "As to the natives of this country, I find them entirely savage and wild, strangers to all decency, yea, uncivil and stupid as garden poles, proficient to all wickedness and godlessness; devilish men, who serve no body but the Devil."[39] Dutch toleration did indeed have its limits.

1645 was a fateful year for New Amsterdam and the colony of New Netherland. It saw the end of the devastating Indian war and the appointment of Peter Stuyvesant as director-general. Though bigoted, Stuyvesant was a capable administrator following a line of less than able predecessors. His reign lasted until the British conquest in 1664, and saw New Netherland's population increased from 2,500 to more than 6,000, while New Amsterdam's rose from under 1,000 to over 1,500.[40] With the expanding population came an expanding economy. Livestock raising supplemented farming and fur trading on Manhattan Island. Ships from the Netherlands brought the kinds of provisions necessary to support a settled, increasingly affluent community: leather boots, books, woolens and duffles, agricultural tools, pearl handled looking glasses, lace, and perfumed soap.[41]

More than Peter Stuyvesant's guiding hand accounted for New Netherland's increasing prosperity. The colony assumed greater importance to the Dutch government and merchant community during the 1650s. The loss of the Brazilian enclave to the Portuguese led to a reassessment of the potential value of the North American colony. New Amsterdam's central location held out the promise that the fur trade with the Indians could be augmented by increased commerce with Virginia for tobacco and with New England for fish and barrel staves. As

■

Dutch commercial rivalry with Britain increased, New Netherland took on added strategic importance as well. The exclusion of Dutch vessels from British ports caused the First Anglo-Dutch War, 1652–1654, and only an increased population, particularly an increase of Dutch colonists, would provide safeguard against possible attack from New England. A secure colony could possibly circumvent a restrictive British navigation policy to inhibit Dutch coastal trade with New England and Virginia.[42]

During the last decade of Dutch rule in New Netherland both the West India Company and the government in Amsterdam launched intensive propaganda campaigns in which New Netherland was described in the most glowing terms, "the epitome and most noble of all climes, a maritime empire where milk and honey flowed."[43]

Just how significant a role propaganda played is questionable, but during the last years of Dutch rule in New Netherland trade flourished and population rose. Authorities were particularly pleased with the increase in the number of native Dutch citizens emigrating from the United Provinces. Also conducive to the desired stability of the colony was a marked change in the character of the new settlers. Records of arrivals from the Netherlands for the period 1657 to 1664 show a substantial decline in the number of the single males, previously the bulk of immigrants, as nearly 70 percent of the new colonists came with their families. The majority were young people with one or two small children, but also included was a sizeable number of middle aged parents of four or more older children.[44]

The Europeans who emigrated to New Netherland were for the most part of humble origins. Ship passenger manifestos for arrivals in New Amsterdam between 1654 and 1664 list occupations for 177 individuals. "Of that number, one-third were farmers, more than one-quarter were soldiers, and another quarter were craftsmen. The remainder were farm laborers, servants, fishermen, and laborers."[45] Yet from such beginnings did the legendary New York Dutch families of wealth and standing emerge. The first Schuyler was a baker's son who emigrated from Amsterdam in 1650. Frederick Philipse of Philipsburg Manor fame arrived in the city in 1647 as a carpenter. The founder of Van Cortland Manor settled in New Amsterdam in 1637 as a soldier and eventually established a brewery in the town. Only the land-rich von Rensselaers, patroons of the Hudson Valley since the 1630s,

■

were exceptions to the rags to riches story of the colony's Dutch contingent.[46]

While extreme wealth was obtainable for only a few in New Amsterdam, opportunities for improvement through trade, commerce, and crafts were considerable during the expansion of the 1650s and 1660s. New opportunities for status through political office opened up on February 2, 1653, when Director-General Stuyvesant "grudgingly proclaimed a grant of municipal government similar to that in the Fatherland."[47] Two burgomasters (mayors), five *schepens* (aldermen), and a *schout* (sheriff) together with Stuyvesant constituted the first municipal council in North America. A further sign of the growth of the city was the granting of great and small burgher rights in 1657, "restricting trade to residents so endowed, the local citizens gained the monopolies and privileges customary in European municipalities at the time."[48]

The arrival of yet another group of people during the last years of Dutch New Netherland began the troubled history of race relations in New York. On September 15, 1655, the ship *Witte Paert* docked at New Amsterdam with a full cargo of 300 African slaves. Although slaves had appeared in New Amsterdam as early as 1626, they had previously come in relatively small parcels from the Dutch West Indies. The *Witte Paert's* arrival signaled the inauguration of New Amsterdam as a port of destination in the transatlantic slave trade. Many more such voyages followed as the West India Company added slave trading to the list of commercial ventures by which a most enterprising colony could prosper. Many of the slaves were trans-shipped and sold in Virginia and Maryland, but enough remained to give New Amsterdam a black population estimated between 20 and 25 percent of its total by 1664.[49]

Neither the Dutch government nor the Dutch West India Company had moral scruples about buying or selling slaves or using slave labor. While the company had not intended to develop an elaborate slave society, the Dutch, as did the English who followed them, suffered from a shortage of labor necessary for the growth of the colony. The Dutch preferred white servants to black, but when the former were not readily available they turned to imported slaves.[50] Most African slaves who remained in New Amsterdam worked for the West India Company as agricultural laborers or in unskilled tasks essential for the colony's expansion and fortification against Indian and foreign attacks. Some individuals also owned slaves, while others leased them from the com-

■

pany.[51] On the eve of England's seizure of New Amsterdam in 1664, 30 of 254 persons on the tax list were slave holders. About half of these 30 were among the wealthiest individuals in the colonial city, but the remainder were scattered throughout the income levels.[52]

Slavery under the Dutch was not as tightly defined as it would be under the English, and some individual slaves had substantial latitude in their movements. The Dutch West India Company provided their bondsmen with medical care, food and housing, and granted "half freedom" to those who had rendered particular service. Those with this status were conditionally manumitted and given papers that certified them to be "free and at liberty on the same footing as other free people."[53] Such individuals apparently had considerable freedom in finding their own housing and employment, but they had to work for the company when their labor was required, and their children were deemed company property.[54] Along with "half freedom" a few slaves received land grants on the condition that they settle just outside the colony, a human buffer against the Indians.[55] Still others won outright manumission; thus free blacks existed in the city alongside slaves.[56]

Unlike the slaves in the system then beginning to emerge in Virginia, New Amsterdam's slaves had the same standing as whites in the courts. They could even testify in cases involving whites, and they were not subject to special punishments as slaves. Moreover, the Dutch armed their bondsmen and allowed them to serve in the militia during emergencies. Indeed, during the crisis year of 1663 "half free" blacks petitioned the company, offering assurances of loyalty in return for the removal of all restrictions on their liberty. The company, facing food shortages and the threat of English invasion, complied with grants of full freedom for the petitioners.[57] While "half free" blacks for very practical reasons were granted full freedom in 1664, nearly seven hundred of their fellow Africans in New Amsterdam remained in bondage in that year.[58]

The existence of a fairly loose system of servitude should not lead anyone to assume that slavery was unimportant to the Dutch. While some slaves were granted "half freedom," this status was not automatically passed on to their children, who still remained in bondage unless colonial authorities decided otherwise.[59] Nor should the reader assume that the Dutch believed in racial equality. The system of white over black, as manifested in black slavery, became a tragic legacy the English willingly continued when they replaced the Dutch as rulers of New Netherland.

■

The New Amsterdam that fell to the British in the summer of 1664 was the most ethnically and racially diverse city in America, but it was also without question a Dutch city. A majority of its citizens were Dutch, and Dutch language, culture, and political and religious institutions were dominant. The Dutch Reformed Church had remained throughout the period the established church of the colony, but, as historian Joyce Goodfriend points out, "admission to the Dutch Reformed Church was not confined to persons of Dutch nationality." It played an "integrative role" which "in some respects may have compensated for the divisiveness associated with a heterogeneous population."[60] Ethnic diversity in the city was also countered to some extent by a considerable number of intermarriages. Records indicate that as many as 25 percent of the marriages in the final Dutch years were exogamous.[61]

Architecturally too New Amsterdam was very much a Dutch port city with 300 step-gabled houses, bowling greens, windmills, and even a canal spanned by bridges.[62] The crews who manned the ships of the English conquerors found New Amsterdam to their liking, a sailor's town with established inns (English, Dutch, and French) where drinking, gambling, and socializing with the opposite sex could be enjoyed.[63]

Undoubtedly the appearance of the English fleet of four frigates in the waters off New Amsterdam on August 26, 1664, was a most unpleasant sight to the town's Dutch burghers. Yet, Peter Stuyvesant found few among them ready to join him in resisting the impending invasion. While the director-general tore up one surrender demand after another, New Amsterdam's leading Dutch citizens, including Stuyvesant's son, busied themselves preparing a petition calling for capitulation in order to prevent the "absolute ruin and destruction" of the city. With only four hundred company troops at his disposal, Stuyvesant was forced to accede to the wishes of the citizens. He yielded to the demands of the British commander, Colonel Richard Nicolls, without a shot having been fired. By October 20th all the citizens of the city—Dutch and non-Dutch alike—had pledged their allegiance to the English king, and both New Amsterdam and New Netherland were renamed New York.[64]

Historians speculate that it was more than fear of physical destruction and certain defeat that motivated New Amsterdam's citizens in their reluctance to offer even token military resistance. After all, strict-

■

ly speaking they were not surrendering Dutch rule for British rule. The Dutch West India Company and not the government of the Netherlands had controlled the city and colony from the very beginning, and even during the most prosperous years of the Stuyvesant administration the burghers understood that their interests were secondary to those of the company's stockholders back home. Allegiance to an English king rather than to a Dutch company would not be too heavy a burden to bear, particularly considering the commercial and trade opportunities available within a rich and expanding British empire. Furthermore, despite wars stemming from commercial rivalry, England and the Netherlands historically had strong cultural, economic, and political ties; briefly, during Queen Elizabeth's reign, the Dutch states had been a British protectorate. "Although Oliver Cromwell's 1650 suggestion that the two nations be rejoined in a permanent union was rejected by the Dutch States General, the two peoples still tended to view each other as 'Neighbors, both of one religion and one belief.' "[65]

Certainly the generous terms of capitulation offered by Colonel Nicolls must have been reassuring. All citizens were informed that their property and goods would be secure; they would be permitted to continue to follow Dutch practices in matters of inheritance, would be free to continue worship at the Dutch Reformed Church, and would not be required to bear arms against any foreign army. Moreover, current Dutch authorities were to remain in office for a year with political liberties promised the residents beyond that period. And anxious merchants were told that, in addition to being granted the right to trade with England and her colonies, direct commerce with the Netherlands would be permitted for six months. In fact, it continued uninterrupted for another four years.[66]

Under such terms it is understandable that no mass exodus followed British occupation of the city, though Nicolls's articles of surrender permitted emigration. A few employees of the Dutch West India Company did leave, and the scarcity and increasing cost of agricultural land on Manhattan encouraged a number of young men to seek their fortunes in the Hudson Valley.[67] But "out-migration from New York City was not a dominant force in reshaping the city's social structure."[68] Even Peter Stuyvesant, stripped of his office, returned to New York after personally delivering his final report to the directors of the Dutch West India Company in Amsterdam.

■

Despite their secure position in English New York, the Dutch community did welcome the reconquest of the city by Netherland forces in 1673. They had not suffered in any material way under the English, but they had in the realm of the emotions. The reestablishment of Dutch control over a city renamed New Orange meant a return of *schout, burgomasters*, and *schepens* in place of the sheriff, mayor, and aldermen of British rule. Citizen declarations of loyalty and affection were no longer made to an English duke or even to the Dutch West India Company but to the States General and to the Prince of Orange.[69]

However, the history of New Orange was less than two years. Defeated in its war against England, the Dutch agreed to a treaty of peace signed on February 9, 1674, under which the Duke of York regained his colony. English influences returned to dominate government forms and practices, the names of streets, and economic and social life. As if to impress upon his Dutch New Yorkers that their future was to be as English subjects, the new governor general, Edmund Andros, required an oath of allegiance to the crown which no longer contained exclusions from military service against the foreign enemies of Britain. Dutch ships were no longer permitted to partake of the commerce of the colony. When the appointive positions of sheriff, mayor, and aldermen were reinstituted, English names as well as Dutch were prominent among the office holders.[70]

But post-1674 English control did not immediately destroy the Dutch presence and influence in New York. Numerically the Dutch would remain the dominant ethnic group in New York City throughout the seventeenth century. Though political control had fallen into English hands, several years would pass before the Dutch residents would loose their preeminent position in the city's cultural and economic life. The presence of a cohesive Dutch community undoubtedly made New York less attractive to prospective English settlers than other new colonies. Not until the last decade of the century would New York's English establish religious and cultural institutions commensurate with those of the Dutch.[71]

James, Duke of York, had no intent to exclude the New York Dutch from politics or commerce but was determined to have them play by English rules within an English world. In the arena of trade this put merchants at an initial disadvantage, since they lacked the contacts within the British market system possessed by newly arriving English.

■

In the realm of politics there was direct governmental manipulation as Englishmen were appointed to municipal offices as a deliberate colonial policy. Given the differences in legal traditions, governmental forms, and languages, tensions existed on all levels. At least twice during this period ethnic hostility became so pervasive on the constable's watch that warnings of punishment were addressed to those who "shall presume to make any quarrel upon the watch upon the account of being of different nations."[72] Ethnic politics had come to New York, and over the next three centuries the city would perfect its operation. The situation existing at the outset of the 1680s in New York City—English rule over a predominantly Dutch population—pleased neither party. To the chagrin of the English, New York was still largely a Dutch city in population, language, and the very architecture of its buildings. More important, the Dutch possessed a monopoly of those institutions which are significant in defining an organized community. The Dutch Reformed Church and the schools and charitable organizations it sponsored, though no longer maintaining the official status they had under West India Company rule, continued to flourish. The English, on the other hand, failed to develop a truly cohesive community until the end of the century. The constant movement into and out of the city by soldiers, government officials and civil servants, as well as those seeking economic success, impaired social stability. There was great diversity of religious affiliations among the English—Anglicans, Quakers, Congregationalists, Presbyterians, and even a few Catholics—and, except for a small Quaker meeting and the military chapel at Fort George, no English church existed in the city until Trinity Church opened for services in 1698.[73] Only then, thirty-four years after the initial English conquest, did Trinity supply "a measure of organizational coherence to the New York City English community."[74]

For the Dutch residents of New York City the last two decades of the seventeenth century were crucial. At the outset they could feel a sense of security in the knowledge that, regardless of the British flag flying over Fort George, in numbers and culture the city remained quite Dutch. As late as 1687 Governor Thomas Dongan reported that since 1680 "there has not come into this province 20 English, Scotch, or Irish families."[75] Rather it was the arrival of Huguenots during these decades and increasing numbers of New Englanders migrating to the city that gradually reduced the Dutch majority. By 1698, English and

■

French together accounted for approximately 40 percent of the 4,937 inhabitants, and growing affinity between these groups in matters of marriage, religion, business, and politics did not bode well for continued Dutch dominance.[76] Dutch influence was retracting. Until 1664 only members of the Dutch Reformed Church were permitted to worship publicly, but the English accorded this privilege to Lutheran, Quaker, and Jewish, as well as Anglican and Huguenot congregations during the late seventeenth century. Along with its exclusive right of public worship the Dutch church also lost its near monopoly over charitable and educational activities as each of the religious bodies established its own institutional network. The Dutch lost ground in the economic sphere as well. While they still predominated in the middle-class craft occupations and controlled the highly remunerative field of flour processing, they had been replaced by the English and French in the single most lucrative and socially prestigious category: merchant. By 1703, English and French merchants outnumbered their Dutch counterparts by almost two to one.[77]

The frustration of declining Dutch dominance in economic affairs was exacerbated by an act of James II that severely diminished the political significance of their numerical superiority. New York, the Jerseys, and the New England colonies were merged into the Dominion of New England with Joseph Dudley and later Sir Edmund Andros serving as governor.[78] The capital of the Dominion was Boston, a reality which transformed New York politically from a provincial capital to an outlying city. Only the Glorious Revolution of 1688 and the landing in England of William, Prince of Orange, on March 1, 1689, brought renewed hope for Dutch New Yorkers. When hope gave way to impatience, a group of predominantly Dutch citizens led by Jacob Leisler seized control of the city in the summer of 1689. They thought themselves agents of the new Dutch king of England and believed he would surely be responsive to their resentments and aspirations. That "Leisler and his followers appealed to those longing for older, better days" was symbolically reflected in their renaming Fort George Fort Amsterdam.[79]

As self-proclaimed spokesmen of King William and Queen Mary, the Leislerites also eagerly declared themselves defenders of the Protestant faith against the Catholicism of James II. Rumblings of anti-Catholicism had been heard during the administration of Governor Thomas

Dongan (1683–1688). As a Catholic he attracted co-religionists to the city, appointed a Catholic collector of the port, and permitted Jesuit priests to conduct public masses for the first time in Manhattan. In proclamations and letters Leisler portrayed his enemies as furthering the "diabolical designs of the wicked and cruel Papists," who "did threaten to cut the inhabitants' throats," and to burn the city. For decades afterwards New York remained an uncomfortable place for Catholics to reside.[80] The downfall of Jacob Leisler and his hanging as a traitor who had illegally usurped power was largely the work of those who had prospered under King James and Andros, including a number of wealthy Dutch merchants and landowners who had accommodated themselves to English rule.[81] "Unable to assail the [Glorious] revolution and the ideology behind it which had placed William on the throne, the opposition assaulted the . . . revolution by focusing on the person of Leisler."[82]

Though the city's political battles continued to be fought along Leislerian–Anti Leislerian lines for more than twenty years after Leisler's death on May 16, 1691, by the turn of the century an increasing number of New York City's Dutch citizens had become reconciled not only to English rule but also to the increasingly English character of the city. If few followed Nicholas Bayard and Stephen Van Cortland into the Anglican Church, a goodly number among them were willing to withdraw opposition to the Ministry Act of 1693, which provided for the public support of an Anglican minister, "in exchange for a charter guaranteeing legal security for the Dutch Reformed Church."[83] The driving force to attain the charter (awarded in 1696) was Hendricus Selyns, a Reform minister who believed the best way to maintain ethnic identity was through a secure church able to strengthen the Dutch language and Reform religion even in the face of an Anglican establishment.[84]

The eighteenth century would see the hopes of Selyns end in failure. In 1701 younger members of the Dutch community demonstrated in their voting patterns a waning attachment to the "good old days" nostalgia associated with Leislerian politics.[85] Drawn primarily from the upper strata of society, their allegiance to ethnic culture was balanced with mastery of the customs and language of the ruling group, the English. A pattern was thus offered that would be followed down the centuries by other minority groups, first biculturalism, ultimately

■

acculturation. As the century progressed, demands began to be heard within the Dutch Reformed Church that religious services be conducted in English. By 1726, the consistory of the Dutch church acknowledged the need for schooling in the English language "in order properly to carry on one's temporal calling."[86] Increased contact between youth of the Dutch and English communities led to increases in exogamous marriages in which English often became the language of the home. Though elders of the Reformed church decried such tendencies and held off demands for English language services until 1763, they could not hold back the conditions that led to them.[87] Success in business and social life in New York City required mastery of English.

A study of New York City residential patterns in 1730 reveals how ethnic-religious factors played a significant role in determining where people lived. Dutch church members generally resided in the northern part of the city, which extended not far beyond Wall Street. "Trinity [Church] drew particularly heavily from the East River Wards, and especially, from the southern most tip of the island." Jews clustered in the South and Dock ward areas, and Presbyterians and Huguenots concentrated in the East Ward.[88] Yet, significantly, the author also took note of methodological problems in his analysis, pointing out that "there were significant potential advantages for those of Dutch origins to shift basic allegiance towards the English community, to the point of effectively becoming English themselves in habits and alliances. Therefore, to assume that all who retained Dutch-style names can be denoted as part of the Dutch ethnic\cultural community may well be particularly hazardous."[89]

The process of waning Dutch influence in the city was attested to by eighteenth-century commentators. Jean de Crèvecœur in the early 1770s "found Dutch neatness, combined with English taste and architecture." Dr. Alexander Hamilton observed in his 1744 visit to the city that Dutch language and customs had "pritty much [begun] to wear out." The Swedish scientist Peter Kalm found in 1748 that most young people spoke English and preferred to be considered Englishmen rather than Dutch. On his arrival in Manhattan in 1753, Thomas Pownall, newly appointed secretary to the royal governor, saw a city with the "general appearance of a Dutch town," but the newer buildings, he noted, had been "built in a more modern taste, & many of the Gable-ends of ye old houses, just as is done in Holland," were "new fronted in

■

the Italian Stile."Visitors also noticed a growing tendency among young Dutch New Yorkers to affiliate with the Anglican church.[90] By 1776, they had a choice of three English churches, as St. George's and St. Paul's had been constructed to accommodate the growing Anglican community.[91]

Visitors to New York may not have stayed long enough to discover that acculturation never meant the total abandonment of things Dutch for things English. Numerous Dutch pastimes became part of the New York scene: bowling, coasting, sleighing, Easter eggs, Saint Nicholas— later called Santa Claus—dispensing gifts at Christmas. "And, of course, many Dutch words such as boss, cookie, cruller, and stoop became part of the English language."[92] Furthermore, the very heterogeneity of the city, which in the end overwhelmed Dutch domination, was in large measure the result of a tradition of broad toleration instituted by the Dutch and continued by their conquerors. This, more than customs and language, was perhaps the greatest Dutch contribution to the shaping of New York City.

If New York gradually lost its Dutch character, New Amsterdam's racial and ethnic diversity was not affected. The heterogeneous ethnic and religious character of the city which had been so apparent to visitors to New Amsterdam continued to fascinate new arrivals to New York. William Byrd of Virginia, visiting the city in 1685, described the population as "about six eighths Dutch, the remainder French and English."[93] Thomas Dongan, who had arrived as governor in 1683, commented in 1686 on the variety of religious groups he found. Aside from Dutch and French Calvinists "Here bee not many of the Church of England; few Roman Catholiks; abundance of Quakers preachers men and Women especially; Singing Quakers; Ranting Quakers; Sabbatarians; Antisabbatarians; Some Anabaptists some Independants; Some Jews; in short of all sorts of opinions there are some and the most part of none at all."[94] Dongan was by no means happy with the religious situation he found or with the fact that foreigners constituted the "most prevailing part" of the city's population. Similar sentiments were expressed in 1692 by an English citizen who informed the members of the Royal Society that "Our chiefest unhappyness here is too great a mixture of Nations, & English ye least part."[95]

One important group adding to this diversity after England conquered New Amsterdam was the Huguenots, a small portion of the estimated 200,000 French Protestants who fled persecution in the years immediately preceding and following the revocation of the Edict of Nantes in 1685. Among the Protestant nations of Europe receiving the Huguenot refugees was England, which absorbed between 20,000 and 30,000 of these highly skilled artisans, merchants, shopkeepers, and cloth-trade workers between 1680 and 1695. The Huguenots received a mixed reception in England. Welcomed by the Protestant population as victims of Catholic persecution, they also aroused fears of competition among English weavers. Anglican churchmen were wary of a possible alliance between the Huguenots and native Dissenters and from the very outset pressured Huguenot churches to incorporate into the Church of England. Refuge in England, particularly for the young and least skilled among the refugees, provided neither material prosperity nor freedom from pressure to conform in matters of religion. Some 5,000 left to seek these objectives in England's North American settlements.[96]

The Huguenots who came to New York City built the core of a distinct French community, something the Walloons who had preceded them had failed to achieve. They clustered their homes together, most living in the city's East Ward, and by 1682 the refugees had obtained a minister, Pierre Daille, who formed a congregation that worshipped in the Anglican chapel at Fort George. With the arrival of another minister, Pierre Peiret, a second congregation was established, which built the French Church on Petticoat Lane in 1688. By 1692 the church added a gallery to accommodate its growing membership. That same year Huguenot services ceased to be held at Fort George, when its congregants en masse joined the Petticoat Lane church. By 1695, New York's French Church with 200 families was second in size only to the 450 family Dutch Reformed Church. The Anglican congregation, since 1693 the officially established church of New York City, had but 90 families worshipping at Fort George.[97] In 1703, the French parish numbered between 700 and 800 members, and it was determined that a larger church was necessary, the current structure being "to small to Conteine them."[98] On Staten Island the Huguenot community numbered 36 French families by the mid 1690s and existed affably with the island's 40 English and 44 Dutch families. These Huguenots even employed a minister to lead a congregation already a decade old.[99]

Because of New York's liberal treatment of refugees, affluent Huguenot newcomers could enter easily into the city's economic and political life. Numbers of them became particularly successful as merchants and in the maritime trades, thanks in no small measure to familial contacts in England and in the Netherlands. The wealthy Huguenot merchant Stephen De Lancey won election as assistant alderman in 1691, and by 1700 other Huguenots had achieved victories at the polls as candidates for positions as constables, tax assessors, and tax collectors.[100] But if established Huguenots were overrepresented on the highest rungs of the city's economic ladder in terms of their percentage of the total population, members of their community were also overrepresented at the bottom.[101] Younger and poorer emigres required time to establish themselves, but an expanding economy and their own skills and enterprise ultimately rewarded their efforts.

As individuals the Huguenots' assimilation into the economic, political, and social spheres of New York City was remarkably successful. Their dissolution as a distinct ethnic-religious body was no less dramatic. As the eighteenth century progressed and the city became even more heterogeneous in makeup and its religious life more varied, the French Church, once a bastion of Huguenot cohesiveness, weakened to the point of collapse. Quite simply, the push to assimilate overwhelmed the bonds of ethnic loyalty. For example, Huguenot parents saw advantages to their sons if they were apprenticed to English masters rather than to Huguenot craftsmen. More significant was the rate of exogamous marriages between Huguenots and Dutch and English spouses; the 41 percent rate of the 1690s more than doubled to 87 percent by the decade 1750–1759.[102]

Such marriages did not necessarily bring with them abandonment of the French Church. Under the leadership of a strong minister like Pierre Peiret (1687–1704), the French Church flourished as Huguenots who had married exogamously brought their children there to be baptized. But Peiret proved exceptional, and during Louis Rou's long tenure in the pulpit (1710–1750) dissatisfaction with his personal life style and indifferent leadership drove a considerable number of congregants into the Dutch Reformed and Anglican churches. Internal squabbling, periods of years without a full-time minister, and proselytizing efforts by the Anglican Society for the Propagation of the Gospel in Foreign Parts spurred the process. Staten Island's Huguenot minister, David de Bonrepos, encouraged cooperation with the English church to the point of urging his parishioners to attend Anglican instruction

■

and services. Bonrepos died in 1734. The next year the elders closed the doors of their church, and its members joined with their fellow Huguenots who had previously affiliated with Staten Island's Anglican, Dutch Reformed, and Moravian churches. New York City's French Church, the last nonconforming Huguenot congregation in the province, finally closed its doors in 1776. It reopened with a small congregation in 1796, only to affiliate with the Protestant Episcopal Church in 1803. In effect, the Huguenot chapter in New York City had come to an end.[103]

While Huguenots assimilated into English culture, the Jewish settlement managed to remain a separate community. The seeds of Jewish institutional life planted during Dutch days took root under English rule. The community remained small, "accounting for slightly less than two percent of the total white population in 1703," but it did survive.[104] A continuing trickle of new immigrants, particularly of Ashkenazic origin, offset those lost by assimilation. Only approximately one half of the Jewish community in 1700, by 1750 the Ashkenazi were overwhelmingly in the majority.[105]

Legally and socially, Jews were tolerated in colonial North America. No ghetto walls hemmed them as they did in much of Europe, but restrictions on their religious life and economic and political practices followed them to the New World. In New York City, however, these did not prove unduly harmful to the wellbeing of the Jews. Guild restrictions excluding Jews from crafts remained officially in effect after the British conquest but were largely ignored in a city where craftsmen were in short supply. Prohibitions against Jews engaging in retail businesses persisted longer as did restrictions on exercising the franchise. But Jews did eventually open retail shops, though there were cases in the late seventeenth century where the letter of the law was applied. Jews did vote, and one of their number won election to the office of constable as early as 1718. Yet in at least one contested election, for the Assembly in 1737, they were specifically forbidden to cast ballots. Throughout the eighteenth century restraints were officially lightened on individual Jews, and the Naturalization Act passed by Parliament in 1740 further encouraged a more liberal approach to the granting of citizenship rights. It provided that a foreigner who became a citizen of one colony automatically would become a citizen in all the English colonies. The applicant was required to have lived in a colony for seven

■

years, to take the oath of supremacy, and to have received the sacraments administered by the Anglican church. The religious requirement was modified specifically to permit the naturalization of Jews and Quakers.[106]

By and large New York Jews prospered during the eighteenth century as retailers and wholesalers, as craftsmen, and as importers and exporters. Some, like the merchants Jacob Franks and Lewis Gomez, could be counted among the city's wealthiest inhabitants. By mid-century Peter Kalm believed that Jews enjoyed "all the privileges common to the other inhabitants of this town and province."[107]

Progress in the Jews' religious life in many ways paralleled their socioeconomic experiences. Under the Dutch the right of public worship had been a monopoly held by the Reformed Church, but Jews and dissenting Christians were permitted to worship in private. The Jews had some reason to believe that English rule might prove even more liberal in religious matters. In 1674 the Duke of York had instructed Governor Andros to "permit all persons of what religion so ever, to inhabit" the province without harassment "for and by reason of their differing in matter of religion."[108] In 1685, Jews of New York petitioned Governor Dongan for permission to practice their religion freely and publicly. The governor referred the petition to the city's Common Council which ruled "That noe publique Worship is Tolerated by act of assembly, but those that professe faith in Christ, and therefore the Jews Worship not be allowed."[109] And yet by 1695 twenty Jewish families had established a public synagogue in a rented room on Beaver Street, naming their congregation "Shearith Israel" (Remnant of Israel). In 1730 the congregation dedicated a newly erected synagogue in the center of Jewish settlement on Mill Street, the first to be built in North America.[110]

Despite the predominance of Ashkenazic Jews in the congregation by that date, the worship service continued to adhere to the Sephardic rite of its founders. Since New York Jews had no ordained rabbi until the nineteenth century, religious leadership was exercised by the congregation's *hazzan* (reader), who also bore the title of "minister." In addition to leading the services, the *hazzan* was responsible for the religious training of the congregation's children. His educational duties became more rigorous after 1755, when the congregation established a school combining secular and religious subjects, including Hebrew,

■

Spanish, English writing, and arithmetic; a professional teacher was hired in 1762. Also in the employ of the synagogue was a *shoket*, who performed the ritual slaughter necessary for koshering meat. In 1758 a burial and mutual aid society was formed at Shearith Israel, a type of organization that would become common among New York Jews in the years ahead.[111]

During the American Revolution the synagogue's minister, Gershon Mendes Seixas, and a goodly number of its congregants left the city, taking with them the Scrolls of the Law. When the British evacuated, Seixas and the others returned, and Jewish religious and communal life revived. Reminders of colonial New York are few in a constantly changing metropolis, yet Shearith Israel, popularly known as the Spanish-Portuguese Synagogue, survives to this day in Manhattan at 70th Street and Central Park West.[112]

Africans were not so fortunate as Jews or Huguenots under English rule. Shortly after the conquest of Manhattan, the English authorities confirmed all titles to slave property. In the ensuing years conditions for blacks were worsened by provincial legislation making manumission more difficulty to implement, placing restrictions on former slaves freed during the Dutch era, and, in 1706, declaring the slave status of blacks would not be affected by their conversions to Christianity.[113] Most colonists believed that blacks were inferior to whites and that their proper place was as slaves, and the transfer from Dutch to British control only increased the use of slave labor. Like the Dutch, the English had a labor shortage, especially after 1720 when the city's economy grew rapidly. A few thousand European immigrants did arrive in New York, but until the 1760s their numbers proved inadequate to meet the colony's labor needs. Imported slaves under a tight bondage system filled the gap, and from 1730 to the 1750s the black population grew faster than the white. By 1746 one in five New Yorkers was an African American, but as the city received significant numbers of white immigrants, the black proportion of the population declined. Nevertheless, at the time of the American Revolution the figure was still about 16 percent. In neighboring Kings County (Brooklyn), bondsmen made up about one third of the population at mid-century with more than half of the white citizens owning slaves.[114]

In New York slave owners typically possessed two or three blacks, who usually lived and worked in their masters' homes, laboring as household

■

domestics. One member of the city's elite, William Smith, utilized twelve slaves to run his household.[115] Yet black slaves also worked as coopers, tailors, bakers, tanners, carpenters, sailmakers, masons, and candlemakers among other occupations; some masters even permitted skilled bondsmen to hire out their own labor.

As the city became more dependent upon black labor, its white citizens grew fearful of slave uprisings. New York's colonial legislature enacted severe restrictions upon the slaves, and the courts interpreted these laws in a harsh manner. A 1677 decision, for example, established the principle that all blacks brought to trial were presumed to be slaves.[116] The English had no system of "half freedom" as had existed under the Dutch, and English masters increasingly defined their bondsmen as property with few or no rights. Yet despite restrictions, slave families continued to be maintained. Slaves who hired out their own labor had possessions and cultivated their own gardens. Elias Neau of the Society for the Propagation of the Gospel in Foreign Parts operated a school for slaves. Although he mainly taught religion, students there also learned to read and write, practices frowned upon by most white New Yorkers.[117]

Details of colonial slave life are not abundant, but it is certain that blacks desired freedom and were prepared at times to rebel against their plight. Slave holders chronically complained about runaway bondsmen and the failure of colonial authorities to exercise strict controls over slavery. According to the newspaper ads for runaways, mostly young males made the break for freedom.[118] Runaways frequently headed to Long Island where they sometimes found sanctuary among friendly Indians.

The greatest fear harbored by the city's white population was that slaves would burn buildings and rise up in rebellion. Wooden structures and an inadequate fire service made arson especially dangerous. In 1712 a slave rebellion began with arson and ambushing of whites who fled the burning building along with several others who had come to their aid. Governor Robert Hunter swiftly called out the militia and alerted the city's inhabitants to the uprising. Authorities quickly suppressed the rebellion, captured those suspected of being involved, indicted 39 slaves for murder or as accessories to murder, and convicted 23 of them. All were sentenced and most were hanged, but three were burned to death, at least one by slow fire.[119]

■

The 1712 "uprising," for so it was termed by fearful white citizens, led public officials to impose new restrictions upon all black inhabitants of New York. Even free blacks were seen as a menace, and among the new ordinances were those making manumission more difficult to effect.[120]

The city experienced another wave of hysteria over slave insurrection in 1741. Whether slaves really planned a rebellion then is unclear, but many city officials and citizens believed such a plot existed. They retaliated in a panic, not only against dozens of slaves but also against several whites suspected of being part of a ring of thieves, arsonists, and potential supporters of the rebels. Before the hysteria subsided, the court, using dubious evidence, convicted dozens of accused slaves and sentenced them to death.[121]

As white labor became more plentiful in the late eighteenth century, and as the spirit of the American Revolution joined with religious doubts about human bondage, slavery came under increasing attack. Moreover, the British promised freedom for those slaves who served in the Loyalist cause. Since New York was occupied by British forces during the greater part of the war, many slaves flocked there in search of freedom. After 1781, Loyalists evacuated many of these blacks, some of whom ended up enslaved in the West Indies. Those who were left behind were perhaps more fortunate, for in 1784 the New York legislature granted freedom to slaves abandoned by the departed Loyalists.[122] Some slaves won their freedom for service to the patriot cause, and many New York slave owners, caught up in the Revolution's rhetoric of freedom, emancipated their bondsmen. In 1771 New York City reported 3,137 slaves, but fifteen years later the number had fallen to 2,103.[123]

In 1785 antislavery advocates organized the New York Manumission Society to work for the gradual abolition of slavery. When the legislature met that year, those opposed to slavery had a clear majority in both houses, yet they could not agree on the future status of New York's blacks. While many favored the abolition of slavery, few were willing to grant newly freed black New Yorkers equal civil rights. A handful of radicals argued for complete equality along with emancipation, but when they were unable to convince others of their view and efforts at compromise proved fruitless, abolition failed.[124] The New York Manumission Society then concentrated on improved laws to foster individual emancipations and to outlaw the slave trade. But further efforts to enact an abolition bill were unsuccessful. Black slaves would have to wait another generation for their emancipation.

In large measure the years of British colonial rule were marked by growth, peace, and prosperity for the free residents of New York City. Historians have noted that even the exaggerated fears of slave uprisings tended to unite the white population and thus deemphasized ethnic differences.[125] But the most effective checks on potential interethnic disharmony were time and general wellbeing: "as time passed ethnic distinctions were blurred by the familiar agents of intermarriage and acculturation. In times of economic or political stress, ethnic or religious loyalties could still be reinvigorated in the city, but these responses became less automatic with each succeeding generation."[126]

The city's economic development during the eighteenth century was remarkable in terms of both expansion and diversity. From the outset, mercantile activity dominated the business life of the town as products from England, the West Indies, and neighboring colonies poured into the port, and New York flour, wheat, and meat were exported. But the crafts, retail trade, and light manufacturing also flourished, and when, following the war, the city's brokers formed an organization for buying and selling government securities, the foundation of the city as the nation's financial center was laid. No less dramatic was the city's population growth. New York City claimed 5,000 residents in 1700 and 25,000 on the eve of the American Revolution. During the Revolution large numbers of citizens fled the British occupation. But many quickly returned, and thousands of newcomers joined them. The city numbered 33,131 in 1790.[127]

For all the growth and change that marked New York City during the eighteenth century, the characteristic that had always been its most distinctive remained constant—the ethnic, racial and religious heterogeneity of its population. While French and Dutch immigration had all but ceased as the eighteenth century wore on, English, German, Scot, and Irish settlers arrived in substantial numbers. At the outset of the American Revolution at least twenty-two houses of worship representing at least twelve denominations existed.[128] When Major Samuel Shaw of Boston visited the city in May 1776, he described its people as "a motley collection of all the nations under heaven."[129] Thus, Shaw echoed sentiments expressed as early as 1643 by Father Isaac Jogues. What these men apparently could not foresee was that out of this

■

"Babel" and from the efforts of this "motley collection" would emerge America's premier city.

By the time of Independence a broad tolerance had developed. During the Revolutionary era the Anglican Church was disestablished and all creeds, including the Roman Catholic, were accorded full freedom of worship. Catholics had not been welcomed in most English colonies, and, other than during the Dongan administration, New York was no exception. Few Catholics lived in New York City prior to the Revolution, and those who did could not worship publicly. However, by 1776 Ferdinand Steinmeyer, a Jesuit Father, journeyed frequently from Maryland to help Catholics celebrate mass in their homes, and a few years later, in 1785, the first Roman Catholic parish was founded.[130]

Toleration did not come immediately to all who landed in Manhattan over the nearly two centuries of colonial history. But it is striking how short-lived and relatively mild was the intolerance leveled at such groups as Quakers, Lutherans, and Jews. Equally striking was the relative ease and rapidity with which acculturation occurred. As noted, New York's climate of interethnic harmony was surely promoted by the fact that it contributed to economic wellbeing as well as made for sound colonial policy. Also likely helpful was the fact that, though representatives of "all the nations under heaven" came to dwell there, they arrived in rather small numbers—a handful of Jews, a few hundred Huguenots. Yet within a few decades after the new nation was established, Manhattan's shores were to be buffeted by massive waves of immigrants different in language and religion from the majority of the city's residents. Then New York's reputation for toleration and adaptability would be tested as never before.

■

*Dynamic*
*Growth*
*and*
*Diversity:*
*The City*
*and Its*
*People,*
*1789–1880*

Postwar New York was first confronted with the problem of assimilating newcomers during the 1790s, when its population jumped from 33,131 to 60,489.[1] Immigration along with natural population growth and a sizeable influx of people from rural New York and from out-of-state accounted for this spurt. Of the sending nations Britain—particularly its Irish counties—France, and the German states led the way. The successful culmination of the American Revolution as well as the potential for economic improvement served to inspire downtrodden Irish, who constituted the largest immigrant group during the first ten years of peace. After a decline beginning in 1794, the failed 1798 Irish rebellion once more sent boatloads of refugees from Erin to New York.[2]

Rebellions also contributed to the increase in New York's French population. The vicissitudes of the French Revolution encouraged both republicans and monarchists at various times to seek refuge on Manhattan island. The slave revolt in France's Santo Domingo colony beginning in 1793 added an estimated 4,000 refugees to the city's population. While most of these newcomers established permanent residence, a number sought temporary refuge and would eventually return to France. Among the latter were a few who went on to achieve considerable notoriety, including Louis Philippe, Francois Rene Viscount de Chateaubriand, and Charles Maurice de Talleyrand. One sign of the vitality of New York's French community during the decade was the appearance of numerous advertisements in French in the city's newspapers. In 1795 French exiles established a bilingual newspaper, the *French and American Gazette*, which lasted one year before being transformed into the monolingual *Gazette Française*. This journal was published for three years before it was forced to give up the ghost.[3] The French immigrants failed to form a vital ethnic community, and they generally assimilated into the larger white society. One of their number, John Dubois, would become the city's Catholic bishop in 1826.[4]

Among the newer members of New York's German community were a few veterans of the mercenary force employed by the British during the American Revolution.[5] They were soon joined by immigrants from the Fatherland, several of whom possessed the craft skills for which Germany was noted. An item in the New York *Gazette* of January 20, 1797, noted that many also arrived carrying a burden of debt: "40 German Redemptioners, Just arrived in the ship Minerva . . . from Hamburg, consisting of carpenters, joiners, blacksmiths, and bricklayers, etc. . . . Their times to be disposed of. For further particulars, enquire of the captain on board."[6]

A pattern of earlier immigrants coming to the assistance of recently arrived countrymen was visible by the first full decade of American independence. For example, the Friendly Sons of Saint Patrick, a society initially formed during the colonial period and revived in 1784, aided Irish immigrants. In 1785 German-born residents of the city had founded and taken steps to incorporate a German Society "for encouraging emigration from Germany; relieving the distress of emigrants, and promoting useful knowledge among their countrymen."[7]

■

As in the past members of the established community did not always welcome the newcomers. The application for incorporation by the German Society, while approved by the legislature, was vetoed by the state Council of Revision on the ground that such action would encourage other ethnic groups to establish similar societies. Such a consequence the council deemed "productive of the most fatal evils to the state" for it would bring to our shores hordes of immigrants who were "ignorant of our Constitution, and totally unacquainted with the principles of civil liberties."[8]

Religious and political prejudices affected how New Yorkers responded to natives of Ireland and France. During the late nineties, the years of the undeclared naval war with France and the Alien and Sedition acts, Federalists in particular looked askance at French republicans and Irish political refugees residing in New York City. Thus, for example, in 1798 bookseller and printer Hugh Gaine wrote in his journal, "too many United Irishmen arrived here within a few days," and a letter to the *Commercial Advertiser* warned against "the commodious instrument of the agents of France."[9]

On the other side of the ledger, when the political climate was less hysterical, New Yorkers proved they could be quite charitable toward newcomers in difficulty. Such was the case when city residents raised thousands of dollars in support of needy refugees from Santo Domingo and opened a hospital facility on Vesey Street to care for their sick. Such was also the case in 1794, when prominent citizens organized the New York Society for the Information and Assistance of Persons Emigrating from Foreign Countries. Finally, it should be noted that the German Society, acting as an unincorporated body after being rebuffed by the Council of Revision, was at last awarded a charter by the state in 1804.[10]

Hostility toward political refugees subsided with the end of the undeclared war with France. Congress allowed the Alien and Sedition laws to lapse after 1800, and New Yorkers turned their attention to domestic affairs. At the outset of the nineteenth century there were indicators aplenty of the kind of city New York would be in the years ahead. The multiethnic makeup of its citizenry had been firmly established during the colonial period, and there was no reason to believe that this would be reversed. The city's commitment to commercial enterprise was also unquestioned. By 1810 it had overtaken its chief

■

competitor, Philadelphia, and led the nation in both population and the value of its imports and exports.[11] The wars in Europe had been a boon to New York shipping interests, a boon stalled by the Embargo Act of 1807, ended by the War of 1812, but resumed once again when peace returned in 1815.[12] New York's favored geography and the initiative and daring of its business leaders extended the city's primacy over Boston, Philadelphia, and Baltimore. Taking the lead in developing and employing steamboats and in instituting regularly scheduled packet service to England, New York merchants came to dominate both coastal and oceanic shipping, and the completion of the Erie Canal in 1825 established the city as the principal center of trade with the nation's interior.[13]

While commerce held sway over the economic life of the city in these years, manufacturing was rapidly rising in significance. During the first quarter of the century artisans dominated trade from their small shops, yet by the late 1820s a shift from shop to factory, from small scale to large scale manufacturing was already in evidence in such fields as shipbuilding, sugar refining, and musical instrument production. The establishment of George Opdyke's ready-to-wear clothing factory in 1832 was an important step in the development of what was to become New York's major industry, employing nearly 30,000 people by mid-century.[14] By 1860, not only was New York the leading garment center, it also was home to almost one-third of the nation's printers and publishers. Machine and engine manufacturing joined the list of important larger industries, and light industries produced everything from soap to cigars, furniture to billiard cues. That year there were thirty-three firms devoted exclusively to producing pianos.[15]

The spectacular growth of industry and particularly of commerce contributed to New York City's emergence as the financial center of the nation. Foreign and domestic trade brought a need for banks, insurance companies, auction houses, and a permanent stock exchange. By the century's fourth decade Wall Street had become the center of the city's financial district, described by an English visitor in 1838 as the most "concentrated focus of commercial transactions in the world. . . . The whole money-dealing of New York is here brought into a very narrow compass of ground, and is consequently transacted with peculiar quickness and facility."[16] From Wall Street, as one historian has aptly put it, New York's mercantile leaders with "the backing of British cap-

■

ital . . . were able to provide the credit and loans on which American domestic trade and economic development came increasingly to depend."[17]

New York's success acted as a magnet that drew in people from within and without the United States.[18] Until 1820 the leading roles in the city's mercantile affairs had been played primarily by descendants of the original English and Huguenot settlers, with the Dutch tending to seek their fortunes in real estate. During the 1820s, however, these old "Knickerbocker" families were overwhelmed by an influx of New Englanders from Connecticut, Rhode Island, and New Bedford, Nantucket, and Cape Cod in Massachusetts. Names like Tappan, Macy, Grinnell, Fish, Dodge, Phelps, King, and Whitney dominated New York's financial and mercantile houses, shipping firms, and shipbuilding industry into the late years of the century.[19] These sons of New England's Puritans altered the very tone of New York's business life. Unlike the more "laid back" longstanding residents, these newcomers were, as one contemporary described them, "more conservative in character, more grave in temperament, and at the same time, more enterprising, and more insistent in action."[20]

"Enterprising" and "insistent in action" are terms that could well describe many of the European business people attracted to an expanding New York. Many arrived with modest resources, but almost all were intent upon settling permanently in the United States and making their fortunes. Among the most successful of these entrepreneurs were merchant princes John Jacob Astor from Germany, Scotsmen Archibald Gracie and Robert Lenox, and Alexander T. Stewart from Ulster. Others came as representatives of European financial and manufacturing houses, often staying on to become permanent residents and citizens. Perhaps the most well known today is August Belmont, who arrived in New York representing the House of Rothschild, married into the Perry family of naval fame, and ultimately established himself as one of the city's premier financiers.[21]

Included among the nations of origin of New York's foreign-born merchant leaders were France and France's lost Santo Domingo possession, the Netherlands, Switzerland, and Spain. But, as the city's principal sister-in-trade-and-finance was Liverpool, it is not surprising that the British constituted the largest grouping of foreign businessmen.

These newcomers to the city played a significant role in business, but

■

their numbers were not large enough to quantitatively affect the ethnic character of the metropolis. As late as 1835 only 10.2 percent of the city's population of 207,089 was foreign born. Yet, by 1860 47 percent of its 813,669 residents had been born abroad.[22] The story behind that change, the story of mass migration, introduces the real drama of New York's ethnic history during the nineteenth century.

The years between roughly 1815 and 1880 have traditionally been labeled the era of the "Old Immigration," with most of the newcomers arriving from northern and western Europe. Hundreds of thousands of Irish and Germans as well as lesser numbers of English, Scots, Welsh, French, Swiss, Scandinavians, Dutch, and Belgians came to New York in the decades preceding and immediately following the Civil War. However, in the nation's premier port at mid-century an English visitor was able to find representatives of numerous other countries walking its streets, "in short, a few of all the nations upon the earth."[23]

Although the "Old Immigration" lasted nearly sixty-five years, it varied yearly in size and ethnic makeup of the immigrant groups. Readjustments and downturns in the economies of Europe fostered emigration, while similar crises in the United States could temporarily retard the process.[24] Religious and political persecution acted to spur emigration as did dramatic spurts in population growth. On both sides of the Atlantic wars discouraged and the return of peace encouraged migration.

Historian Richard B. Stott offers a useful summary of the general background and motives of the immigrants arriving in New York City during the antebellum years. He points out that they were young (50 percent between the ages of fifteen and thirty), the majority were male (though the percentage of females steadily increased, rising from 23 percent of the total during the five year period 1821–1825 to 43 percent during the years 1855–1860) and rural (people who, "though poor by American standards, were from the middling ranks of the peasantry"). However, as Stott states, "artisans were overrepresented among immigrants choosing to remain in New York City."[25]

In some cases religion was the main reason for emigration. Intolerance drove members of minority sects to seek the freer religious atmosphere to be found in the United States, among them Prussian "Old Lutherans," Jews from Bavaria and Wurtemberg, Swiss Methodists and Baptists, Norwegian Quakers, and Swedish Jansonites. The political cli-

■

mate also contributed its share of emigres, with the arrival of Germans, Poles, Hungarians, and Italians—leaders of, and participants in the failed uprisings of the 1830s and 1848 in behalf of republican government and/or national liberation. Probably more numerous than these idealists were the young men who escaped to America in order to avoid compulsory military service in the armies of rulers they had no role in choosing.[26]

For the vast majority of emigrants, however, it was economic causes that led them to choose a new beginning in America. Subsistence farmers were driven off the land by landlords seeking more efficient and profitable use of their holdings or by devastating crop failures, most notable of all the potato blight of the mid 1840s which victimized hundreds of thousands of Irish and German families. The process of industrialization, ever more efficient machinery and larger factories, cost numerous urban craftsmen and rural weavers their livelihoods. Exacerbating these conditions was a dramatic rise in population throughout the British Isles and in most of continental Europe during these years.[27]

Though the mostly young men who undertook the journey to America certainly came with hopes of improving their lot, in most cases neither the decision to leave home nor the goal of economic well-being were matters involving the emigrants alone. In their native lands they were participants in a family-based agrarian economy. Stott points out that "often the decision to emigrate was made not solely by the individual but as part of a *family* decision."[28] And the *family's* welfare was the prime consideration determining the outcome of the discussions. Testifying to this process were the millions of hard-earned dollars sent back home from America by the immigrants to help their families get by as well as to provide passage for others to emigrate.[29]

From Liverpool, from Havre, London, Bremen, and Hamburg they sailed to the United States; of the 5,457,914 who arrived between 1820 and 1860, fully two-thirds, 3,742,532, debarked in New York City.[30] The flood halted temporarily during the Civil War, but afterwards numbers rose again with the same ratio arriving through New York City. In the early years of the century the emigrant could not be certain of the availability of space, sailing dates, or cost of the voyage and so worked out individual arrangements for passage. However, establishment of regularly scheduled packet service soon ended this practice,

■

and commercial houses on both sides of the Atlantic, recognizing that profits could accrue from human baggage, brought system and order to the emigration process beginning in the late 1820s. These firms contracted for ship's space and set rates for passage. Some even established their own passenger lines, engaged in propaganda to encourage emigration, and offered assistance in transmitting passage money from immigrants in America to their families back home. Advances in marine technology also contributed to easing the difficult journey. Beginning in the late 1850s steamships entered the immigrant carrying trade, cutting voyage time from six to eight weeks down to less than two by the 1880s.[31]

Improved services could only make a most difficult experience a bit less onerous. The twenty to sixty dollars a steerage ticket cost during this period usually got one across the ocean but rarely without major trauma. Passengers were subjected to the possibility of seasickness, overcrowding, dirt, hunger, stench, disease, and even death brought on by shipwreck, typhus, cholera, smallpox, or malnutrition. The mortality rate aboard immigrant ships, however, is estimated to have averaged about two percent or less except during epidemic years, when it rose precipitously (c. 10 percent in 1817–18 and 1831–34; c. 20 percent in 1847).[32]

Finally sailing through the Narrows and into New York's harbor was undoubtedly a heartening experience for the immigrants. However, particularly during the first decades of this period, the arrival could prove as harrowing as the journey. Prior to 1882, when the federal government took control, processing immigrants through the port of New York fell under the jurisdiction of state and city governments, which until 1847 did very little to accommodate the newcomers. Those with communicable diseases were sent into quarantine at the marine hospital on Staten Island. Others, who were sick or became ill soon after arriving, had to make their own way to the city's almshouses or public or private hospital charity wards. Even a sound body and coins in one's pocket were not sufficient to provide a pleasant transition from ship to shore. After facing the medical officers, they encountered the "runners," agents of boardinghouse operators and of companies that specialized in transporting immigrants by boat or rail to the interior. These runners usually were of the same nationality and spoke the same language as the immigrants they greeted. Their goal was to win the migrants' trust, often misinform them regarding employment opportunities in or beyond the city, and then proceed to bilk them of as much cash and\or property as possible in return for overpriced travel tickets, baggage transport at exorbitant rates, and boardinghouse accommodations at highly unfair rents.[33]

To mitigate these conditions became a goal of such organizations as the German Society, Irish Emigrant Society, St. George's Society (English), and St. Andrew's Society (Scottish). High on their agenda was encouraging immigrants to migrate out of the city, an endeavor that met with only limited success. But their lobbying efforts to have the state play a more active and productive role in the immigration process bore fruit in 1847. That year the legislature in Albany passed a bill establishing the Board of Commissioners of Emigration. The members of the board, all serving without pay, consisted of six gubernatorial appointees, the mayors of New York and Brooklyn, and the presidents of the German Society and the Irish Emigrant Society. They were given both the power and the funds to inspect incoming ships and provide aid, information, and employment assistance to the immigrants. In addition to the marine hospital at Staten Island, which continued to treat contagious cases, a new facility was established on Ward's Island at Hell Gate to serve immigrants as a hospital, dispensary, and place of refuge for the infirm. A state law enacted in 1848 regulated boardinghouse rates and practices.

The serious problem of runners remained, however. With immigrants disembarking at several different piers, it was impossible to keep these extortionists at bay. To thwart this, in 1855 the Board of Commissioners of Emigration designated Castle Garden as the central landing station for all immigrants. Located at the Battery at the foot of Manhattan, this former fort, former amusement hall, and recent aquarium served as immigrant entrepot until replaced by Ellis Island in the 1890s. Here newcomers received aid, advice, and services from honest brokers and agents, city employees, and representatives of the various immigrant aid societies.[34]

With more than two thirds of the immigrants arriving in the United States after 1820 debarking in New York, the city's foreign-born population steadily rose. In the single decade of the 1850s over two million immigrants landed in Manhattan. But, even though New York's Irish and German populations had grown immensely, the fact remains that by 1860 the city held but 9 percent of the nation's immigrant Germans and a bit over 12 percent of its Irish.[35] Who did stay in the city? Edward K. Spann provides a concise but accurate answer, "the ablest and most ambitious on the one hand and the poorest and most unwanted on the other."[36]

Responding to rapid population and economic growth, the boundary of the city's settled area pushed ever northward. In 1815 it had extended but two miles from the island's tip at the Battery, yet ten years later the city limits had reached 14th Street. By 1865, paved and graded streets reached to 42nd Street, while housing was already available in sections of the east fifties. Beyond that frontier line were found the suburban Manhattan villages of Harlem, Bloomingdale (what is now the Upper West Side), and Yorkville (now the east eighties). During the 1830s and 40s more and more of the buildings in lower Manhattan were converted to commercial use as residents moved uptown or to Brooklyn. So was born the commute to work, a journey made possible by advances in mass transportation. First came twelve-passenger omnibuses, followed by horse-drawn railways which more than doubled the carrying capacity. In 1832 the New York and Harlem Railroad was inaugurated with service from Prince Street to 14th. By 1838 the line extended all the way north to Harlem.[37]

Lower Manhattan as an area of residence was left to the thousands of immigrants pouring into the city. Lacking the funds to pay for uptown housing and the costs of daily transportation to work, they had to live within walking distance of their jobs at the East River docks, shipyards, and warehouses or the inland shops, factories, and commercial houses. To accommodate these people and to reap the huge profits stemming from ever-rising land values and skyrocketing rents, existing single family homes were converted into multiple dwelling apartments housing three or four families.[38] A city inspector's report in 1834 found "many mercenary landlords who only contrive in what manner they can stow the greatest number of human beings in the smallest space."[39] By the mid-forties a more "efficient" style of multifamily dwelling made its appearance in the city and rapidly replaced the converted apartments. This was the tenement, which would provide housing for most immigrants. By 1864 the Council on Hygiene reported that there were already 495,592 people living in 15,309 tenements in New York City, and their numbers continued to grow after that.[40]

■

Tenements came in a variety of sizes, but most were dreadfully cramped with "300–400 square feet of floor space and two to four rooms."[41] A report by the Council on Hygiene described a typical midcentury tenement as "a structure of rough brick, standing on a lot twenty five by one hundred feet; it is from four to six stories high, and is so divided internally as to contain four families on each floor—each family eating, drinking, sleeping, cooking, washing and fighting in a room eight feet by ten, and a bedroom six feet by ten."[42] Though indoor plumbing, central heating, and gaslight had begun to appear in better housing as early as the 1840s, not until the 1860s could tenement dwellers expect the luxury of one water spigot per floor, and that was only in the newest structures. Prior to the 1860s, and long after for most tenement dwellers, water had to be carried up from street pumps or from wells located in the yards close by the outdoor privies. Beginning in 1852 a popular philanthropic endeavor was to establish public bath houses in the congested immigrant districts of the city. The first of these was the People's Washing and Bathing Establishment on Mott Street.[43]

Tenement rental charges depended on the amount of light and ventilation available. Apartments with windows could rent for as much as thirteen dollars a month, while single rooms in the dark interior of the building could be had for as little as seventy-five cents a week. Most primitive of all tenement accommodations were the cellar apartments, where in 1850 more than 29,000 newcomers to America dwelt.[44]

Investigations of tenement house conditions by city and state bodies, the private Citizens' Association of New York, and the New York Association for Improving the Condition of the Poor (AICP) documented appalling conditions and called for reform legislation. Then as now, however, a good number of concerned citizens believed that poverty was a consequence of character deficiency, and they were wary of assisting those considered undeserving.[45] Reform-minded religious women, for example, set up missions in the emerging immigrant slums to teach the poor proper work habits and inculcate them with Protestant moral values.[46]

At the same time, the more active AICP and the enlightened Council on Hygiene understood that overcrowded tenements also contributed to destitution. Such crowding, declared the AICP "breaks down the barriers of self-respect, and prepares the way for direct profligacy."[47] Their efforts to aid the poor immigrants led to the enactment of the Tenement House Law of 1867, a measure with low standards but one that did represent a first step toward housing reform. The city enacted subsequent laws in 1879, 1887, and 1895, but no truly effective legislation appeared prior to 1901.[48]

Housing reform was not the only program pushed by native New Yorkers who were beginning to see the environmental roots of poverty. Charles Loring Brace and his followers in the Children's Aid Society focused on the growing number of homeless children, called "street arabs." Brace believed their numbers would grow because "immigration is pouring in its multitudes of poor foreigners." These children, if not helped he insisted, "will soon form the great lower class . . . (and) poison society all round them."[49] From the 1850s until the program's demise in the 1890s, the Children's Aid Society placed thousands of such children in homes in the West, where it was hoped they would receive proper moral training.[50]

Catholics were convinced that Brace's Children's Aid Society was sending Catholic children to homes where they would be converted to Protestantism. To ensure that Catholic children be placed in Catholic homes, the Catholic Protectory of New York was organized in 1863. While its plans for placement failed, the New York Foundling Hospital, established six years later by the Sisters of Charity of St. Vincent de Paul, took up the task of child placement. Under the leadership of Sister Irene Fitzgibbon, the Hospital sent thousands of New York City children to new homes in the West.[51]

These reforms, unfortunately, had little impact upon the poverty of tenement life. During the 1840s in the heavily Irish Fourth and Sixth wards almost 45,000 people were packed into a quarter of a square mile with enough room for one person per 140 square feet. By 1860 commercial development in the Fourth Ward had reduced the amount of residential space by a third, while the total population remained about as it had been fifteen years earlier.[52] In the Sixth Ward close by City Hall was the most notorious slum area of all, Five Points, formed at the juncture of Anthony Street (Worth Street today), Orange Street (today's Baxter Street), Cross Street (Park Street today), Mulberry Street, and Little Water Street (no longer extant). Symbolizing the horror of this district was the Old Brewery, converted into a tenement in 1837 and housing as many as a thousand residents at a time before being torn down in 1852.[53] Charles Dickens described what he observed during his visit to Five Points in 1842:

> This is the place, these narrow ways, diverging to the right and left, and reeking everywhere with filth. . . . Here too, are lanes and alleys, paved with mud knee-deep . . . ruined houses, open to the street, whence, through wide gaps in the walls, other ruins loom upon the eye . . . hideous tenements . . . all that is loathsome, drooping, and decayed is here.[54]

In the Sixth Ward the deathrate in 1863 was three times that of the entire city. Residents of other tenement districts fared hardly better, existing in the most crowded, unsanitary conditions imaginable and subject to periodic outbreaks of diseases brought on by filth and impure water: typhoid, dysentery, typhus, and, what historian Charles Rosenberg terms "the classic epidemic disease of the nineteenth century," cholera, which struck the city in 1832, 1849, and 1866.[55] During the first cholera outbreak in 1832, before the scientific bases of that and other diseases were discovered and made known, it was widely assumed that its victims were the recipients of God's punishment for their intemperate ways. Their poverty was their fault as were the consequences of their poverty, including disease. Such is the inference of a Board of Health report on the epidemic that stated "the low Irish suffered the most, being exceedingly dirty in their habits, much addicted to intemperance, and crowded together into the worst positions of the city."[56]

Though cholera was not restricted to the city's immigrant population, it did bear the brunt of the outbreaks. And among the immigrants the Irish, being the most numerous, the weakest upon arrival in the city, and comparatively poorer, suffered the most. In the 1849 cholera year Irish-born residents represented more than 40 percent of the city's death toll from the disease.[57] In the ten years between 1849 and 1859, 85 percent of the foreign-born patients admitted to Bellevue Hospital were Irish. The 1855 census reveals that the Irish constituted 53.9 percent of the city's foreign-born population.[58]

The reality of having grown from small town to major metropolis in just a few decades unfortunately was not reflected in municipal services. Prior to 1866 roaming hogs served as the city's principal garbage collectors. Not until the completion of the Croton Aqueduct in 1842 did clean water begin to flow into the city, and not until 1849 did the

■

government begin to build a municipal sewer system. A uniformed police force first appeared on the streets in 1853; and, despite a devastating "Great Fire" in 1858, which destroyed a seventeen block area south of Wall Street, a professional city fire department was not established until 1865. Even after municipal services were instituted, it often took years before the improvements were felt in the poorer districts. For example, in 1857 the sewer system served but 138 miles of the city's nearly 500 miles of streets.[59] When in 1865 45 of 90 tenants of a First Avenue building contracted typhoid fever, it was found that the tenement's outdoor privies "were less than six feet from the house, not connected with a sewer" and, according to the investigating police surgeon, "in the 'worst possible condition.'"[60]

To help make ends meet, immigrant families often made space available in their cramped quarters for paying boarders, usually unattached young men and women. But even more popular, particularly for single men, were a multiplicity of boardinghouses.[61] For the young person fresh off the boat and with little money there were the lodging cellars in the lower wards, where for pennies a week boarders had the privilege of sleeping on the floor and receiving a meager diet. However, most boardinghouses were considerably more comfortable and, though hardly luxurious, were generally clean, with decent food, the companionship of fellow boarders, and a degree of privacy. Rent in better boardinghouses was usually higher than that charged by families who took in boarders. An 1857 description of one such establishment for eighty male boarders indicates that the living quarters were cramped but clean and that the food was plain but abundant. A Sunday dinner there included meat, potatoes, cabbage, and squash eaten in an atmosphere of joviality. Saturday evenings were given over to cards, board games, and dominoes, and once a year the lodgers held a dance, complete with orchestra.[62] As a general rule the residents of boardinghouses shared a common language, so that there were German boardinghouses, French boardinghouses, and those where Irish, Scots, and other English-speaking immigrant workers lodged.[63] Yet, as might be expected in this diverse city, in 1855 one Sixth Ward house owned by a German couple housed twenty-one male lodgers, including fourteen Germans, three Irish, two Dutch, one French, and one Hungarian.[64]

During this period most people lived within walking distance of where they worked, and though there was a growing tendency for the

■

more affluent to commute from home to job, few wards lacked a population of the well-off. In 1865 the Council of Hygiene reported that in the Sixth Ward "two-thirds of the population is composed of the lowest grades of the laboring poor, and of the vicious classes; the remaining third is made up of better classes of people who live upon wages."[65] Among the latter were skilled and semiskilled workers, businessmen and professionals directly or indirectly tied for their livelihood to the factories and shops located there.[66]

New York's East Side was where most of the working class, and consequently the immigrants, who constituted a majority of that population, lived. During the 1820s a core of Irish settlement developed in the Sixth Ward, and during the same years the Tenth and Eleventh wards had heavy enough concentrations of Germans to earn the appellation *Kleindeutschland* (Little Germany). With the huge influx of immigrants after 1840, however, neither the Irish nor the German neighborhoods were able to absorb all their recently arrived countrymen. There was no ethnic homogeneity in New York wards; the Sixth Ward, for example, in 1855 held "approximately fourteen thousand Irish, fifty-two hundred Germans, twelve hundred English and Scotch, one thousand Italians and Polish, and fifteen hundred persons of other nationalities."[67] The New York State Census of 1855 demonstrates that of the city's twenty-two wards the largest percentage of foreign-born residents resided in the Fourth and Sixth wards, yet even there 30 percent of the population was native born.[68]

Nonetheless, the numbers of German and Irish immigrants were so great that their presence was strongly felt in certain wards. In 1855 the Irish constituted 46 percent of the population of the First Ward, 45.6 percent of the Fourth Ward, and 42.4 percent of the Sixth Ward, while the Germans dominated the Tenth, Eleventh and Seventeenth wards with 30.3 percent, 33.6 percent, and 27.3 percent respectively. Irish and Germans workers were present in sufficient numbers to sometimes populate entire boardinghouses and tenements, and even whole streets.[69]

Though the heaviest concentrations of Irish and Germans were on the East Side of Manhattan, their numbers were too great to exclude them from any of the city's wards. By the 1850s settlements of both of these groups had spread across New York City's East River border. The Germans were particularly mobile. They constituted two-thirds of the population of Brooklyn's Williamsburg. In Queens's Astoria, and

■

Brooklyn's Flatbush, German farmers had already developed market gardens to feed Manhattan's wants. By the 1860s Manhattan's German population was following the brewers uptown to Yorkville and turning Brooklyn Heights into a heavily German neighborhood.[70]

By 1860 the Irish (203,740) and the Germans (118,292) were the dominant immigrant groups of the city. The third largest contingent of newcomers during this era was from the remaining regions of the British Isles—England, Scotland, and Wales—but their numbers seem minuscule (37,187) when compared with the masses of Irish and Germans.[71] Sharing both the English language and Protestant religion with the majority of the city's native-born residents, they had little difficulty assimilating. Unlike the many destitute Irish, they possessed skills that they could use in the rapidly expanding city. British immigrants appear to have favored the Hudson River wards, particularly the Eighth, but they were found scattered throughout the city.[72]

Despite the advantages of language, religion, and skills, British immigrants, like those from other lands, were not immune to the hardships imposed by the city's business cycles. Some found themselves penniless and living in the almshouse or as charity cases in the city's hospitals. Also, in true immigrant fashion, Scottish, English, and Welsh immigrants sought out their countrymen in the city. Scots drank their ale and ate food at taverns like John O'Groats's House, the Lady of the Lake Tavern, the Burns House, and the Blue Bonnet. During the 1840s they read the *Scottish Patriot*, which carried news of home. When military companies composed of native-born New Yorkers refused to admit them, Scottish men organized their own military companies, the Scottish Guard and the Highland Guards. As they had in Scotland, members of New York's Scot's community attended Presbyterian churches. When the Reformed Presbyterian Church opened its doors in 1833, it shortly became known as "the Scotch church," reflecting the national origins of its members.[73]

Welsh New Yorkers were eager to preserve the language and customs of their native land. The first Welsh newspaper published in the United States, *Cymro American*, appeared in New York in 1832, and others followed in the 1850s. By the 1830s several small Welsh congregations existed in the city. They provided places for worship for these immigrants and sponsored singing competitions, for which Wales had long been famous. The main secular organization devoted to promoting

■

Welsh affairs and to preserving the Welsh language was the St. David's Society, which sponsored an annual St. David's Day festival.

English immigrants, too, formed their own institutions. They mostly joined the city's established Methodist and Episcopalian churches, but a few felt the need to organize their own Anglo-American Free Church of St. George the Martyr in 1840. The elite among New York's English celebrated Queen Victoria's birthday and organized several London-style social clubs, the most esteemed being the St. George's Society. Those less high up in the social order found conviviality at one of the handful of English style pubs. A few newspapers were established for English immigrants, but they could not compete for long with the city's main line English language press.[74]

Irish Protestants, called Orangemen for their allegiance to the Protestantism of William of Orange, who had assumed the English throne in 1689, did not wish in any way to be identified with the city's growing number of Irish Catholics. These Protestant Irish, mostly from Ulster, brought the Orange order to the city as early as the 1820s, and they organized separate lodges in the 1860s.[75] Ulstermen celebrated Boyne Day on July 12. The holiday marked the anniversary of William of Orange's victory over King James II at the Battle of the Boyne in 1690 that insured Protestant ascendancy in Great Britain and Ireland. To show their displeasure of Irish Catholics, on Boyne Day in 1824 they marched in a predominately Irish Catholic neighborhood with Orange banners waving. This particular demonstration resulted in a street brawl between the two factions of Irishmen.[76]

Yet that clash and several others following were minor compared to the Orange riot of 1871. The Orangemen insisted on a holding a parade celebrating that year's Boyne Day. Tensions had been rising for years, as many Orangemen, along with other New York Protestants, claimed that Catholics threatened American values and were undesirable citizens. Rumors of violence and threats by both Irish Protestants and Catholics prompted the city and state to provide police and military protection for the marchers. When the parade, with its military accompaniment, reached the west twenties along Eighth Avenue, shots were fired and rocks thrown. Panic ensued as the militia lost control and fired indiscriminately; the death total was sixty-two, mostly Irish Catholics killed by militia bullets.[77] Boyne Day celebrations continued for a few more years, but the 1871 riot was the last of the major riots

■

pitting Irish Catholics against Irish Protestants. Many Orangemen joined nativist organizations like the American Protective Association and the Order of United American Mechanics in the 1870s and 1880s, and continued to argue that Catholicism was a menace to their city.[78]

Immigrants from France and other countries, as had those from Great Britain, settled throughout the city. The poorer among them were more likely to be found in the lower wards of the East Side, while the more comfortable moved north along the West Side. Thus, by 1860 the 8,074 French, who constituted the city's fourth largest immigrant group and who had few laborers or destitute among them, were found in greatest numbers along the Hudson River wards, Washington Square, near Fifth Avenue in the fifties, and on the East Side above Tenth Street.[79]

In the years after 1830 small numbers of immigrants arrived from Switzerland, the Netherlands, Bohemia, and the Scandinavian countries. These people tended to locate in the East Side wards, some of them in areas dominated by other national groups with similar linguistic roots: French-speaking Swiss among the French, German-speaking Swiss and Dutch among the Germans.[80]

The city's immigrants even included a few from those ethnic groups who would dominate migration patterns by the turn of the century. The first Greeks, for example, arrived as refugees from the turmoil of the Greek War for Independence in the 1820s and were followed by merchants who settled in lower Manhattan after 1870.[81] Poles also numbered among the early arrivals. By 1852, there were enough to create a Polish Democratic Club with 200 members. More arrived in the 1870s, establishing a notable colony in the Williamsburg-Greenpoint section of Brooklyn near where the Williamsburg Bridge would eventually connect Brooklyn and Manhattan. It was during the 1870s that Polish Catholics organized their first church, dedicated to St. Stanislaus.[82]

The small Italian colony that established roots in the city during the early decades of the century had by 1880 grown to approximately 20,000, of whom 12,000 were foreign born. The first arrivals, mainly from Northern Italy, found housing in the Five Points and other nearby slum blocks. Even before the late-century mass migration, the area around Mulberry Bend in lower Manhattan was commonly referred to as "Little Italy."[83]

Many of the Italians of the early decades were unskilled laborers, forced into jobs at the bottom of the economy and often depicted by

■

native New Yorkers in such unflattering terms as "a vagabond but harmless class of organ grinders, rag-pickers ... and the like."[84] But Italy also sent New York a goodly number of the skilled workers for which its northern regions were noted: chefs, stonecutters, mosaic makers, carpenters, and cabinet makers. These people were generally warmly received, as were the Italian merchants who by 1830 had established shops on Bleecker, MacDougal, Sullivan, and Thompson streets, just south of Washington Square.[85] As one New Yorker noted:

[The Italian grocer takes] great pride in the artistic arrangement of fruit so that they will attract the eye; the Italian barber has transformed the appearance of the barber shop and has made it clean and attractive, displaying the sign of "Tonsorial Artist"; while the boot-black, beginning with a tiny box, rises to the established chair . . . , sparing no effort in his attempt to render satisfactory service and in making himself affable and agreeable. There is absolutely no doubt about this class being a permanent population, and it may be observed that their business success is notable and that they have brought their trade to a higher level than that in which they found it.[86]

The political upheaval of an Italy striving for unification and independence from foreign domination "fueled the flight to New York" of intellectuals, musicians, composers, and men of letters. Vicenzo Botta, formerly a member of the Sardinian parliament, became a professor of modern languages at New York University and served as president of the Union League Club. E. P. Fabbri, a partner of J. P. Morgan, was instrumental in endowing the Italian School that opened on Leonard Street in 1855. In 1879, Luigi Palma de Cesnola, who won the Congressional Medal of Honor for service as a brigadier general in the heavily Italian Garibaldi Guard during the Civil War, became director of the Metropolitan Museum of Art. Among the pioneers of opera in antebellum New York City were Ferdinand Palmo, who invested and ultimately lost his baker-business fortune in a lavish opera house on Chambers Street; Luigi Arditi, composer of *La Spia* based on James Fenimore Cooper's novel *The Spy*; and Alavatore Patti, who as co-director helped make the Astor Place Opera House, erected in 1847, the city's most successful opera venture yet.[87]

In 1879, on the eve of what was to be termed the "New Immigration," the New York Association for Improving the Condition of the

■

Poor declared that "no more peaceable, thrifty, orderly neighbors could be found than these Italians. They do not beg, are seldom or never arrested for theft, are quiet, though quick to quarrel among themselves, are equally ready to forgive."[88]

The city's first Chinese immigrants also appeared during this era, but their numbers were not large. A census taken in 1855 recorded thirty-eight Chinese men who lived in lower Manhattan. Some were sailors, other operators of boardinghouses, proprietors of small businesses, peddlers, or cigar makers.[89] Some of these male settlers married Irish women, and a few even became American citizens. By 1873 the *New York Times* reported some 500 Chinese were living in New York, about half in the emerging Chinatown of lower Manhattan.[90]

Immigrants from all lands shared a variety of experiences: the crossing, the landing, the tenement and boardinghouse, the poverty. They all formed organizations like the St. Andrew's Society, the St. George's Society, the Irish Emigrant Society, and the German Society to aid newcomers at the docks, while ethnic newspapers and fraternal organizations kept them informed of affairs of interest to immigrants. And when the Civil War broke out, many of the foreign born flocked to the colors. Among the volunteer units organized by the city's ethnic groups were the German 8th Regiment, the Polish Legion, the Cameron Rifle Highlanders, the Guard de La Fayette, the Netherlanders' Legion, and the Garibaldi Guard, which was made up of Hungarians, French, Spaniards, and Croats as well as Italians.[91]

By 1860 it had become obvious that New York City had been reshaped by the coming and settling of this immigrant wave. It wasn't simply the newcomers' vast numbers or their ethnic variety that accounted for this. Of utmost importance was the fact that the metropolis became numerically dominated by immigrants from Ireland and Germany. These people were so different in so many ways and present in such large numbers that they could not be ignored, nor could they fail to make a significant impact. Of the 813,669 residents of New York City in 1860, 383,717 were of foreign birth, but almost six of seven of these were from Germany and Ireland.[92] Their experiences in the city must provide the primary focus of our discussion of immigration and ethnicity during these years and will be considered in the next chapter.

Before moving on, however, it is important to recall that race as well as ethnicity or nationality was a vital factor in New York. All native-

■

born white citizens and newly arrived immigrants came in contact with, affected, and were affected by the city's black residents. We have noted how the city's anti-slavery society, formed in 1785, failed to convince the state's white residents to abolish slavery, and in fact during the decade following the adoption of the Constitution the number of bondsmen in the city actually increased. This was in part due to the influx of French emigres fleeing the slave rebellion in Haiti; a number of these refugees brought their slaves with them. Members of the New York Manumission Society, some of whom themselves owned slaves, achieved a limited victory with the passage of the Gradual Manumission Act of 1799, a law that freed males born after that date at age twenty-eight and females at age twenty-five.[93] A few unscrupulous owners subsequently sold their slaves rather than waiting to give them freedom, a practice the Manumission Society successfully fought in the state legislature. In 1820 the census takers found only 518 black bondsmen in the city, and in 1827 legislation emancipating all slaves in the state took final effect. By 1830 there were no slaves in New York.[94]

Emancipation did not bring equality, nor is there much evidence of great improvement of life for black New Yorkers now living in freedom. During legislative debates over the abolition of slavery, white New Yorkers made clear their belief that blacks should not have equal civil rights. A few abolitionists wanted to grant blacks equal suffrage, but even this proposal was omitted from the state's new constitution in 1821. Moreover, on three occasions the state's white voters rejected an equal ballot for black males; not until the nation ratified the Fifteenth Amendment (1870) did they finally obtain that right of citizenship. Voters in New York City were more opposed to black suffrage than those elsewhere in the state. This was in part due to hostility by the black's chief competitors on the bottom of the economic and social ladder, the Irish and the Germans.[95] Ugly comments were made during the attempts to secure black voting. One Democratic paper warned of potential interracial sex and of black arrogance if the proposition passed. "The negroes of Five Points long for the day when they will be privileged to take to their arms the palefaced beauties of the Caucasian race in the city of New York. Already the waiters and whitewashes and bootblacks have grown impudent in anticipation of the bright prospect before them."[96]

Due to the virulent racism of the nineteenth century, black New Yorkers found themselves limited largely to low paying and menial

■

employment opportunities. During slavery many bondsmen had worked as household servants, and they continued to labor at these jobs after emancipation, because few other occupations were open to them. In 1797 the New York Manumission Society found that most blacks were employed as domestics and laborers with only a few small traders and mechanics.[97] State census takers subsequently reported similar occupational patterns, and in 1855 revealed that 75 percent of employed blacks were still common service workers. Black women were even more restricted than men in their opportunities; they usually worked as household employees or as laundresses.[98]

For those fortunate few who learned a trade, chances to ply it were limited. Remarked one white affiliated with black education, "A few have obtained trades of the following description: viz. Sail Makers, Shoemakers, Tin Workers, Tailors, Carpenters, Blacksmiths, etc. . . . In almost every instance, difficulties have attended them on account of their color, either in obtaining a thorough knowledge of the trades, or, after they have obtained them, in finding employment in good shops."[99] Moreover, the embryonic labor movement before the Civil War virtually ignored black workers. When New York barbers decided to organize for higher prices, whites insisted on establishing separate black and white associations.[100]

Yet despite all these impediments, a small black elite did emerge in the nineteenth century. In the 1850s black New York boasted nine doctors and four lawyers, but most in the professional category were teachers in black schools or clergy serving black churches.[101] In the 1790s, the most famous black tradesman was Samuel Fraunces, owner of Fraunces Tavern where George Washington bid farewell to his troops. Most blacks working in the food industry, however, did not own taverns but rather were waiters and porters in hotels and restaurants.[102] Blacks worked as barbers, and a few even owned their own shops. Lacking capital and clientele to expand, tradesmen generally ran small shops but were hindered by a reluctance of city officials to grant them licenses. In 1835 and again the next year, for example, two blacks were denied licenses to become cartmen.[103]

The arrival of waves of immigrants after 1830 helped the city grow rapidly, but to black New Yorkers the newcomers hardly represented a blessing. Immigrants desperate for work took whatever jobs were available, often at the expense of blacks. Though the numbers of blacks were

■

too small to offer much competition to immigrants, in some occupations the two groups clashed. Conflict occurred over securing positions as house servants, barbers, porters, stevedores, brick makers, coachmen, and whitewashes.[104]

Both blacks and immigrants, especially the Irish, believed that each stood in the way of the other's opportunities, and the occasional use of black strikebreakers aggravated a tense situation. In 1854 employers replaced striking white longshoremen with blacks only to discharge them when the strike failed.[105] A few years later economic conflicts with racial overtones led to violence in Brooklyn. One tobacco factory there employed a mixed labor force, while a second factory hired only blacks. Racial tensions aroused by the latter situation led to the burning of the factory by an angry mob of whites.[106] In 1863 long standing economic hostility and the association of blacks with the suffering of the Civil War combined to make them the primary victims of the predominately Irish mob action of the New York City draft riots.

Given the limited incomes of black New Yorkers, it is not surprising that they lived in the city's worst housing. Manhattan had no distinct racial ghetto before the Civil War, so blacks and whites frequently resided side by side in the same blocks and sometimes occupied apartments in the same tenements. On occasion black families took in white boarders.[107] If there was a core of black settlement, it was north of Chambers Street up to Houston Street and on the West Side of Manhattan between 23rd and 40th streets.[108] But if blacks did not live in a distinct racial neighborhood, they usually occupied the most inferior housing. Charles Dickens described their dwellings as "leprous houses," "hideous tenements," and "cramped hutches," places, "where dogs would howl to lie, women, and men and boys slink off to sleep, forcing the dislodged rats to move away."[109]

Under such crowded and unsanitary conditions it was not surprising that black residents suffered from poor health. Typhus fever, small pox, tuberculosis, pneumonia, and bronchitis were all too common among the city poor, black and white. The death rate among blacks was probably the highest in the city.[110]

Neither the state nor the city of New York passed codes segregating their black citizens. Yet blacks found themselves segregated or barred from using privately owned public facilities. Blacks did use the city's horse-drawn street cars at times, but treatment varied. Some companies

■

refused African Americans permission to ride, while others allowed them to travel on a separate outside platform, regardless of the weather.[111] Angered by their treatment, individual blacks organized a Legal Rights Association and took transit companies to court. After Elizabeth Jennings, a black woman on her way to church, was injured when she was forcibly ejected from the Third Avenue omnibus in 1854, she sued and won damages. Her counsel was Chester Arthur, future President of the United States. Similar suits against the Sixth and Eighth avenue lines won changes in transit policy, so that by the time of the Civil War, most of these public conveyances admitted blacks.[112]

During the antebellum period, blacks were regularly ejected from the ferry connecting Manhattan and Brooklyn and kept out of most theaters, restaurants, and places of public amusement. Frederick Douglass said that on the Hudson River steamers blacks were "compelled sometimes to stroll the deck nearly all night, before they can get a place to lie down, and that place frequently unfit for a dog's accommodation."[113]

Even the churches of New York City segregated black congregants. Those attending white churches were seated in the rear, in an "African corner," or "Nigger pew." Others abandoned white churches entirely to found their own congregations. The independent black church movement began in Philadelphia in 1787, when the Rev. Richard Allen led a group of black worshippers out of a predominately white congregation, where they were unwelcome, to organize the African Methodist Church. African Americans founded similar black independent churches in New York City, among them Episcopal, Congregational, Presbyterian, and Methodist.[114] When the black St. Philip's Protestant Episcopal Church, organized in 1819, petitioned the Episcopal diocese of New York in 1846 to be received into the diocese's convention, white churchmen rejected the request. A majority report declared that blacks "are socially degraded, and are not regarded as proper associations for the class of persons who attend our convention."[115] Not until 1853, after repeated applications for entry, did the white Episcopalians finally admit St. Philip's to the convention. The Episcopal church's General Theological Seminary, on the other hand, consistently refused to accept black applicants.[116]

New Yorkers largely segregated their public and private schools, though a few black children did attend white schools. The Manumission Society founded the first African Free School in 1787 and organized several others for newly freed blacks before transferring their control and management to the privately operated New York Public School Society in 1834. During the 1850s these "colored schools" became part of the city's newly created public school system. Through these years the schools continued to teach basic elementary education, stressed moral uplift, and operated on a racially segregated basis. Blacks also operated several schools of their own from time to time, but these ventures lacked adequate financing to survive.[117]

In Brooklyn blacks apparently attended some mixed schools until the 1820s. Then segregation became more rigid, and black Brooklynites established their own schools. When a public school system was created, black schools were placed under white control, but continued to employ black teachers.[118] In both New York and Brooklyn black public schools were underfunded and black teachers paid lower salaries than their white colleagues. Prejudice dictated that black education, no matter how thorough, did not lead to good jobs, and so most students left at an early age to seek employment. A black New Yorker commented in 1859, "It is a common complaint of colored teachers that their pupils are taken from school at the very time when their studies become most useful and attractive."[119]

Black New Yorkers, though generally poor and few in number, nonetheless founded and supported their own institutions. During the anti-slavery struggle, African-American New Yorkers organized an anti-slavery society, took an active role in the abolitionist movement, and ran charities for orphans. Their clergy not only gave spiritual comfort but also provided leadership to the black community. The Rev. Samuel Cornish served for 20 years on the executive committee of the American Anti-Slavery Society, while other ministers joined similar anti-slavery groups.[120] Cornish, along with John Russwurm, also founded the nation's first black newspaper, *Freedom's Journal*.

The birth of the anti-slavery Republican party and the coming of the Civil War and the Reconstruction Era brought new hope for New York's black residents. As southern slavery ended and as black troops fought well in the war, a growing number of whites accepted the notion of some equal rights for black citizens. The passage of the 13th, 14th, and 15th amendments reflected this emerging national consensus, though exactly what rights black Americans would actually attain remained in doubt.

■

When the widow of a black soldier was ejected from an Eighth Avenue street car reserved for whites, the Union League rallied to her support and prepared to take her case to court. The company, however, capitulated, and consequently such discrimination on public cars in the city ended.[121] Finally, in 1873 the state legislature enacted a civil rights law prohibiting discrimination because of race or color on public conveyances, in theaters, inns, and other public amusements. The law was not rigorously enforced, however, and African-American New Yorkers continued to face a depressing racism in the late nineteenth century.[122]

The degraded condition of African-American New Yorkers prompted some observers to equate their plight with those of the incoming Irish. Both groups occupied miserable tenement housing, lived lives of wretched poverty, and faced virulent prejudice. But no white group, not even the Irish, suffered so much for so long as did the blacks. Nonetheless, among European immigrants entering the city during the nineteenth century, the Irish did encounter the most difficulties and were subject to the most hostility by native-born citizens. Their experiences and those of the German immigrants will be discussed in some detail in the chapter that follows.

■

*Diversity*

*in Action:*

*Irish and*

*German*

*Immigrants*

*in a*

*Growing*

*City,*

*1789–1880*

# i

It is a truism to assert that the Irish, the largest of the era's immigrant populations, were probably the least suited by experience, training, and culture for city life. As a consequence, they provide the story of America's first highly visible urban, poor-white minority group. While not all the immigrant Irish were impoverished and unskilled, so many of them were that as a group they received less of the good and more of the bad that life in New York City offered. As early as the 1790s observers noted the poverty of the city's Irish Catholics. A majority of the victims of the yellow fever epidemic in 1795 were Irish, and so many poor Irish appeared in the 1790s that the Friendly Sons of St. Patrick could scarcely find funds to assist them.[1] Years later, in describing his flock, New York's Bishop John Hughes wrote that they were "the poorest and most wretched population that can be found in the world—the scattered debris of the Irish nation."[2]

Carole Pernicone's study of the heavily Irish Sixth Ward found that, according to the 1855 census report, 51.2 percent of the ward's 1,116 families arrived in the city as family units. She also revealed that, in addition to family unit migration, often a single family member would emigrate and ultimately raise enough money to send for the remainder.[3] In contrast to the Germans, the number of Irish women emigrating exceeded the number of men. Some were widowed heads of families who lacked skills to obtain an adequate income, or else faced discrimination in finding decent paying jobs.[4] Once here, the leading contribution to female-led families was probably the high rate of industrial accidents. Irish men dominated the ranks of unskilled laborers employed in dangerous work on the docks and in the construction trades, and many died on the job.[5] For the widows and children of these victims, starvation and homelessness could be avoided only through income-producing work.

Even in male-headed households, laborers' salaries were so low that extra income was essential for survival. Whether we speak of the low salaries, industrial accidents, and seasonal unemployment common among the unskilled male workers or the few extra pennies earned by women who took in one or two boarders or did needlework in the home for twelve cents for each day's labor, we are speaking about extreme poverty. The majority of Irish immigrants experienced its reality for at least a portion of their years in New York.[6]

Irish immigrants were most apt to live in the crowded tenement districts where they encountered poor sanitation and epidemics. More comfortably placed Irish, especially a number of young and single women, managed to escape the worst aspects of immigrant slum living. Some of these became Catholic nuns and served in the diocese's expanding network of charitable agencies, schools, and hospitals. Most others, after the 1820s, dominated domestic service in New York City; by 1855, 74 percent of domestics were Irish, and in 1880 44 percent of Manhattan's and Brooklyn's servants were still Irish.[7] So common a stereotype was "Bridget," the serving woman, that one guide book, *Advice to Irish Girls in America* by the Nun of Kenmare, simply assumed

■

that all Irish women who worked would enter domestic service.[8]

While life was not all roses for the city's "Bridgets"—They worked long hours, and a few suffered abuse by their employers—most lived in middle-class homes, where they benefitted from a healthy diet; and, because room and board were free, they were able to save part of their wages for their dowries. Historian Christine Stansell tells us that between 1819 and 1847 these young women accounted for between one half and two thirds of the savings accounts opened by unskilled workers at the New York Bank for Savings.[9]

Not all single Irish women entered domestic service. The needle trade drew some, and for a few others a way "of getting by, of making the best of bad luck" was through prostitution. One study of the city's prostitutes in 1855 revealed that 35 percent were Irish and 12 percent German.[10]

As the Irish often were blamed for their poverty, so too were they castigated for the means by which they sought a measure of relief from its effects. There seemed to be no end of drinking establishments in the immigrant districts. For the first generation of Irish in particular the saloon was the center of a relatively inexpensive social life, just as the pub had been back home. In 1864 the Sixth Ward alone had one drinking establishment for every six people. At Peter Sweeney's saloon, for example, one could gain entry for ten cents and quaff whiskey at three cents a glass. The saloon keeper was a respected figure in his community and by the Civil War had become a key figure in local politics. Yet to many a well meaning reformer the saloon represented both a den of immorality and a prime cause of poverty among the Irish.[11]

The Irish immigrant life style did indeed differ in many respects from that of the native, white Protestant American. Politically, economically, and culturally oppressed in their native land, competing for the most menial jobs, and experiencing prejudice on all fronts in their new setting, what William Shannon terms the "two-fisted aggressiveness of the Irish" is not difficult to understand.[12] During the mid-nineteenth century New York City was an arena of rivalry, competition, and violence between ethnic and racial groups. Often unemployed and seeking excitement, young Irish men organized into street gangs, whose names reflected a variety of old and new country loyalties. The Bowery B'hoys, Dead Rabbits, Kerryonians, True Blue Americans, Plug Uglies, and O'Connell Guards, among others, provided their members

■

opportunities for raucous sociability and plenty of two-fisted action. So too did the city's many volunteer fire companies, more adept at fighting each other than at effectively extinguishing fires.[13]

After 1830 the city witnessed an unusually large number of street riots and brawls, even by modern urban standards. Irishmen were prominently involved in many of them, a circumstance which appeared to confirm that they were indeed a belligerent people. A closer examination of some of those outbreaks reveals more about the Irish condition in New York than merely the propensity of bully boys to do their thing. In 1837, for example, it was actual hunger that drove Irish workers to break into and loot grain warehouses in what became known as the Flour Riot.[14] The Irish often vented their rage and violence against New York's blacks, fellow victims of prejudice, yet often competitors for low level unskilled jobs as waiters, coachmen, and dockworkers. In their hostility to blacks the Irish adopted racial attitudes expressed by New York working people as early as the colonial period and reflected as recently as July 1834 in an eight-day, anti-abolitionist riot which ravaged black homes and churches.[15]

Anti-black sentiments were not part of the baggage brought from Ireland, but anti-English sentiments certainly were. They account to a considerable degree for the Irish gangs' participation in the famous Astor Place Riot of May 1849, which stemmed from the rivalry between British actor William Macready and the darling of the American stage, Edwin Forest. Both men were appearing at the same time in rival productions, and ethnic pride and anger were deeply involved. The riot involved more than 10,000 workingmen, native and immigrant alike, and led to thirty-one deaths.[16]

Finally there were instances of street brawls that pitted Irishmen against Irishmen in seemingly senseless fits of violence. The biggest such battle occurred on July 4th and 5th, 1857, between the Dead Rabbits and the Bowery B'hoys. Nearly 1,000 gang members were involved, and before two regiments of state militia finally quelled the melee, ten men lay dead and at least 80 suffered wounds. However, even this riotous affair was related to broader events. New York's condition of inadequate police protection had reached a point of near lunacy that summer with two competing forces in the city, the reputedly corrupt Municipal Police under the control of Mayor Fernando Wood's Democratic administration and its supposed replacement the Metropolitan

Police, created by the Republican-controlled state legislature. Mayor Wood's refusal to disband the Municipals led to open combat between the two forces on June 16th and contributed to a climate of lawlessness that continued into July. Such was the resentment against the state-appointed police force that two weeks later a crowd largely made up of Germans—not generally known for violent behavior—battled Metropolitans in the Seventeenth Ward.[17]

The allegiance of the Bowery B'hoys to Mayor Wood and the Municipal Police reveals a good deal about ethnicity and politics as well as street violence in New York City during the antebellum years. The Bowery B'hoys were Irish and in the First, Fourth, Sixth, and Fourteenth wards so too were the majority of Municipal policemen.[18] A Democratic mayor claimed the loyalty of the Municipals, and the Irish citizens of the city were overwhelmingly and fiercely loyal Democrats.[19] Wood's election in 1854 was secured largely by the Irish of the Sixth Ward, who conjured up 400 more votes for him than there were registered voters in the district. Continued Irish support for Wood in the 1856 election was strengthened by such factors as the mayor's opposition to prohibition, his granting of city lands to facilitate the construction of a new St. Patrick's Cathedral, and most certainly for his appointments of Irishmen to city jobs, particularly on the police force. While the Irish adherence to the Democratic Party was indeed secure, no individual politician—not even Fernando Wood—could count on that support continuing indefinitely. In the mayoral elections held in December 1857, Tammany Hall, under the leadership of its new head, the notorious William Marcy "Boss" Tweed, decided to run Daniel Tieman against Wood, the "regular" Democratic candidate, who had committed the unpardonable sin of ignoring Tammany when he appointed heads of executive agencies. In a campaign marked by violence, Tweed's successful wooing of the Bowery B'hoys and other Irish gangs was crucial in Tieman's victory over Wood by 2,300 votes.[20]

The loyalty of the Irish to Tammany Hall and the Democratic party, which seemed almost ordained by nature in later years, had in fact evolved over time. In its early days as it was transformed from a fraternal lodge to a political machine, Tammany Hall claimed to represent the interests of the city's workingmen against both aristocratic privilege and foreign competition. Such competition included immigrant labor-

■

ers as well as imported goods. By the 1820s politics was changing in a more democratic direction, and when New York's constitutional convention of 1821 did away with the property requirement for white, male voters, it enabled increasing numbers of poor Irishmen to become potential voters capable of swinging municipal elections. The Jacksonian democratization of politics, notably illustrated by the selection of a mayor by popular election beginning in 1834, along with the rising tide of immigration led Tammany to shift away from its nativist stance. Irish immigrants were not simply to be accepted by the Democratic party; they were actually to be wooed.[21] As shop gave way to factory and as unskilled and semiskilled labor replaced the craftsmen as the numerically dominant representatives of the working class, urban politics also changed. Richard Stott has described how:

> A new and distinctively working-class style of politics began to emerge in the 1840s and 1850s. Related to change taking place in working-class life, it paid attention less to ideology than to the personal qualities of political leaders. At the same time pugilists came to dominate working-class politics in the city, and elections themselves became stormy, brawling affairs. At the same time, also, the saloon emerged as central to the city's political life.[22]

The Irish immigrants were hardly passive pawns to be manipulated by political leaders. Unlike the Germans who, at least until the arrival of political refugees in the late 1840s, appeared rather indifferent to politics, the Irish came to America with a tradition of political involvement. Popular demonstrations, mass meetings, and other forms of political action on behalf of Irish Catholic causes provided experiences readily applicable to New York City politics.[23] The Irish in New York knew well how to use their saloons and their street gangs for Tammany's causes. In return, Tammany delivered assistance in expediting naturalization; protected saloon keepers from overzealous enforcers of closing laws; expressed strong anti-nativist and anti-prohibition positions; hosted picnics, balls, river excursions, and other social events; and, most important of all, provided jobs for "lamplighters, fire wardens, meat inspectors, and policemen."[24]

In time politically activist-minded Irish found such rewards to be not enough. They demanded more substantial pieces of the action—

political office and/or a place among the Democratic leadership. The most successful of these early zealots was Mike Walsh, an Ireland-born journalist who in 1840 formed his partisans into "the Spartan Band," and three years later established a weekly newspaper, *The Subterranean.* Having considerable talents as a public speaker, Walsh called for more attention to workers' rights and wider participation for workingmen within the Democratic party. He acted the gadfly at political meetings, virtually forcing himself on Tammany's leaders, who, in 1846, finally nominated and helped elect him to the state assembly. In 1850 Walsh won election to the U.S. House of Representatives, where he remained until his death in 1859.[25]

As Irish and other ethnic populations of the city grew, so too did their role in the Democratic party. In 1856 two Irishmen and a German won election to the City Council, and an Englishman served as alderman from the First Ward. With the ascendancy of Tweed as head of Tammany, the Irish came extremely close to the apex of power. Though of Scotch-Irish, Protestant origins, Tweed had strong ties to the city's Irish Catholic community in most everything but religion, in which he professed no affiliation. He had been a member of an Irish street gang and an Irish volunteer fire company. His closest political associates were Irishmen Peter Sweeney and Richard "Slippery Dick" Connolly.[26]

When the corruption of the Tweed Ring was finally exposed in 1871, journalists and cartoonists were quick to point to the close ties between the Boss and his Irish followers. Certainly Tweed's active support of Irish Catholic efforts to prevent the Orange parade celebrating the Battle of the Boyne contributed to his downfall. The order of Tweed's police commissioner forbidding the Protestant Ulstermen from marching was rescinded by Governor Hoffmann. For Tweed, the subsequent riot, erupting just days after public disclosure of Ring corruption, was another nail in his coffin.[27]

Ironically, Tweed's downfall permitted Irish Catholics to finally attain the highest seats of political power in the city. In 1871 John Kelly assumed the leadership of Tammany Hall, and in 1880 shipping magnate William R. Grace was elected mayor. Neither was really a man of the masses of the city's Irish. Kelly, basically conservative, was more interested in attracting wealthy businessmen and professionals to Tammany than in serving the city's hard pressed, working-class communities. As for Grace, he proved an able mayor but hardly qualified as a true

■

New York Irishman. He made his fortune in the shipping business while a resident of Peru and continued to be interested in that country's affairs when he moved to New York after the Civil War.[28]

Writing of the urban Irish in America of 1870, Lawrence H. Fuchs states that the "most important communal organization . . . , next to the church itself, was the Democratic Party, and for Irish men, the party probably was more important than the church. In and through the party they found sociability, jobs, and a way to claim American identity." [29] What they had failed to claim in New York City by that year, however, was control of the top positions in Tammany and the Democratic Party. Even while William R. Grace was serving his second term as mayor in 1884, one estimate found 58 percent of the positions of power within the Democratic Party still held by "old stock" Americans against only 29 percent by Irish and 10 percent by Germans. "Yet the Irish and Germans made up over three quarters of the city's population in 1880."[30]

If the Irish failed to fully control the Democratic party by 1880, there is no doubt of their influence over what Fuchs saw as their most important communal organization; Irish men and women totally dominated the Roman Catholic Archdiocese of New York. The growth of the church in New York City had been phenomenal since 1820, when there were but two churches to serve the city's Catholic population of approximately 30,000. By 1840 the church had established eight new parishes as the Catholic population reached close to 90,000, and in 1865 somewhere between 300,000 and 400,000 Catholics attended thirty-two churches. In the United States the Catholic parishes were generally organized along ethnic-language lines. Thus, of the thirty-two New York churches, eight were German-speaking, one was French-speaking, and twenty-three were English-speaking, which in effect meant their parishioners were overwhelmingly Irish.[31]

The figures above reflect the course of immigration into the city. The Irish arriving after 1820 were, with few exceptions, Catholic, while the Germans were a religiously heterogeneous lot. By 1860, as Jay Dolan informs us, "for every German Catholic there were six to seven Irishmen." Naturally enough, "the principal authority in the city, the bishop, was an Irishman."[32] The "Irishman" Dolan referred to was John Hughes, who succeeded the Frenchman John Dubois as bishop of New York in 1838. Hughes became archbishop in 1850, when Pope Pius IX raised the diocese of New York to the position of archdiocese,

■

and continued in office until 1864. His successor, the Irish-American John McCloskey, in 1875 became America's first cardinal.[33]

Under Hughes's dynamic leadership the Roman Catholic Church in New York moved from weakness to vast power. In 1841 the diocese had but ten churches, one priest for every 8,000 people, and $300,000 in debts. "Within fifteen years, however, [Hughes] succeeded in establishing doctrinal unity, in paying off the debts, in tripling the number of churches, and in creating a variety of charitable, social, and educational organizations that became a strong basis for Irish Catholic community life in New York."[34] Perhaps most symbolic of the changed status of the church was its formal administrative center. When Hughes assumed the bishop's chair, old St. Patrick's Cathedral was located on Mulberry Street on the Lower East Side. At the time of his retirement and as a result of his efforts a new, grand and Gothic St. Patrick's was under construction on prestigious Fifth Avenue between 50th and 51st streets, where it is still to be found.[35]

The cathedral would have many residents, but no Catholic prelate in New York, before or after, ever exerted the influence that Bishop Hughes did among the city's Irish. No Irishman in politics or business during the antebellum period achieved power comparable to that which Hughes held within the church. Furthermore, whether Irish Catholics attended church regularly or not—and many did not—in terms of self-identity, birth, and heritage they remained Irish and Catholic. This melding of nationality and faith had been forged in Ireland in the face of English-Protestant attempts to subvert both. In America nativist hostility and evangelical Protestant assertiveness only served to strengthen that alloy. Hughes's responses to these challenges had much to do with his popularity within the Irish community and with the respect he earned among those without.[36]

Bishop Hughes's refusal to advocate a passive, defensive position for American Catholics made him, in his own way, as confrontational as any Bowery B'hoy or Dead Rabbit. As spokesman for the city's growing Irish Catholic population whose votes no political leader could ignore, he might not be loved by Protestant America, but he also could not be taken lightly. He demonstrated his potential political power and influence in a battle that erupted almost immediately after he took office as archbishop. In 1840 New York City lacked a public school system. The bulk of the state's school funds earmarked for the city went to

■

the Public School Society, a chartered philanthropic organization founded by Protestant laymen to provide elementary schooling for poor children and governed by a self-perpetuating board of trustees. Though nondenominational, the climate and orientation of its schools were such that most Catholics could not in good conscience enroll their children. Their objections included the recital of Protestant prayers and hymns, exclusive use of the King James Bible, and the employment of religious, literary, and historical texts displaying anti-Catholic biases, including the frequent use of the derogatory term "popery." With many Catholic parents boycotting the society's schools and with a paucity of Catholic schools, large numbers of New York City's children were totally without the benefits of education.[37]

The election of William Henry Seward to the governorship in 1838 on the Whig ticket had drastic consequences on the school situation in the city. Sympathetic to the Irish condition here and abroad and hopeful of breaking the Democrats' hold on New York City's Irish vote, Seward openly proposed that public money be used to support Catholic schools. Bishop Hughes responded enthusiastically to these sentiments and, working closely with the governor and his aides, petitioned the city's Common Council for a share of the state school funds for Catholic schools. In the face of opposition from the Public School Society, anti-Catholic nativists, and citizens sincerely concerned about a perceived threat to church-state separation, the council on two occasions rejected Hughes's request. Political action then moved to Albany, where the state legislature, in receipt of anti-Catholic petitions, editorials, and tracts, hesitated to support the Hughes-Seward cause. Determined to get favorable action, Bishop Hughes decided to impress legislators with the potential power of the city's Irish voters. Under his leadership, for the first and only time in the city's history, a Catholic political party was established to contest the 1842 state legislative race. Ten assemblymen who supported the Hughes school aid position ran on both the Catholic and the Democratic slates, and they won election. Three nonsupportive Democrats were opposed by Catholic party candidates and were defeated. Although no separate Catholic slate candidates succeeded, Bishop Hughes had made his point: New York's Irish Catholics had enough power to tip the balance of power in city-wide elections. Bowing to that political reality, the Democratic-controlled legislature prepared to enact a school law for New York City.[38]

■

The measure that was finally passed did not by any means provide everything Hughes desired. It established in the city a district public school system in which "no religious sectarian doctrine or tenet should be taught, inculcated, or practiced."[39] Public funds would not be forthcoming to support Catholic schools or religious teachings, but Catholic children attending public schools in their neighborhoods would no longer be subjected to teachings explicitly critical of their faith. The failure to gain governmental funding for the kind of schools he wished moved Hughes in a new direction. He began to build a separate, privately financed parochial school system. During the remainder of his tenure and afterward the number of parochial schools and the number of children attending them grew considerably. In 1840, almost 5,000 children attended Catholic schools. By 1870 the parochial school population reached 22,215. Yet, whereas the 1840 figure represented 20 percent of the city's total school population, the 1870 figure represented but 19 percent. Ethnic population growth simply outpaced the church's ability to pay for school expansion.[40] Furthermore, an improved religious climate in the public schools made them inexpensive alternatives to parochial schools for most Irish parents. In heavily Catholic districts Irish Catholics won strong representation on the school boards and among the faculty. Jay Dolan notes that as early as 1843 the elected school board in the Sixth Ward "read like a roll call for the Hibernian society and included two trustees of the parish."[41]

Bishop Hughes's decision to promote the growth of a separate parochial school system not surprisingly fed nativist, anti-Catholic propaganda mills. It also was criticized by some who had traditionally been among his friends and supporters, including Horace Greeley and the old-stock American convert to Catholicism, Orestes A. Brownson. They objected to what they believed were anti-assimilationist tendencies inherent in the move and undoubtedly were correct in their perception.[42] But if Bishop Hughes displayed a siege mentality and a desire to keep the Irish strong and separate behind the protective barrier of the church, it is perhaps understandable, given Irish history and the intense American nativism during the antebellum years. Foreigners of every nationality felt the sting of nativist barbs, particularly during election campaigns or periods of economic downturn. For example, during the municipal election campaign of 1844 the *Daily Plebian* in a single paragraph spoke of German and Irish "thieves and vagabonds," Eng-

■

lish and Scotch "pickpockets and burglars," "wandering Jews" using "their shops as receptacles for stolen goods, encouraging thievery among our citizens. Look at the Irish and Dutch [German] grocers and rum-sellers monopolizing the business which properly belongs to our native and true-born citizens."[43] But if the net was widely tossed, the Irish by far bore the brunt of these attacks. They arrived in the greatest numbers, were the poorest, and were willing to work for the lowest wages. Wages for all laborers dropped during decades of high immigration, among unskilled labor from a dollar a day in the early 1830s to seventy-five cents a day in the 1840s. The huge Irish influx of the 1840s helped make "possible the full introduction of factory production" and the consequent lowering of status among workingmen.[44] The causes of decline in the living standards of the working class were more complex than merely the result of mass immigration, but as Douglas T. Miller points out, "the immigrant often served as a convenient scapegoat for a variety of frustrations."[45]

That the Irish became the primary target of religious bigots was a consequence of their near universal allegiance to the Roman Catholic Church and the growing Irish domination of the priesthood and clerical offices of the church in the United States. The historical enmity toward Catholics was directed more at the church politic and "popery" than to purely religious teachings and practices. Nativists charged that the church politic was the enemy of democracy, of social reform, and of the nonsectarian, Protestant values traditionally promoted in the public schools.[46] In 1850, in response to oft repeated charges that his church threatened to displace the dominant place of Protestantism in American society, Archbishop Hughes declared in a speech entitled, "The Decline of Protestantism and Its Causes," that Protestantism was a sterile religion in contrast to dynamic Catholicism. As for Catholic intentions:

> Everybody should know that we have for our mission to convert the world, including the inhabitants of the United States, the people of the country, the officers of the Navy and Marines, commanders of the Army, the legislatures, the Senate, the Cabinet, the President, and all.[47]

As one historian put it, "Rather than pour oil on troubled waters, Hughes preferred to ignite the oil."[48] Even native-American Catholics

■

felt uncomfortable with and voiced objections to Irish dominance of the church. Orestes Brownson, who had strong disagreements with Hughes's anti-assimilationist policies, wrote in 1856, apparently referring to Catholicism in New York City, "In the parts of the country where the prejudices against Catholicity are the strongest, it seems to be *Celtic rather than Catholic*; and Americans have felt, that to become Catholics, *they must become Celts*, and make common cause with every class of Irish agitators, who treat Catholic America *as if it were a province of Ireland*."[49]

The success of the Democratic party in winning the allegiance of the Irish Catholics led to success of the Irish in gaining municipal jobs in return for their loyalty. But Irish association with Tammany Hall's corrupt politics provided further grist for nativist mills. While the Democrats found their Irish supporters a highly valuable political asset, their opponents in the city used anti-foreign, anti-Catholic sentiment to attract the votes of native Americans. During the school controversy the city's Whig politicians resorted to appeals to nativist sentiments, but separate nativist parties had emerged even earlier. In 1835, for example, a short-lived Native American Democratic Association appeared in close alliance with the Whigs, who had seen their attempts to win the Irish vote in 1834 come to naught. Later, in 1844, the nativist American Republican Party elected its candidate, James Harper, mayor of New York City, while in 1855 the Know Nothing movement candidate for mayor, James Barker, came in second in a four-man race, losing by a mere 1,500 votes.[50] Nativist campaigns traditionally played upon the fears and prejudices of the electorate and urged restriction of office holding to native-born citizens, a twenty or twenty-one year naturalization law, deportation of foreign-born criminals, the exclusion of Catholic influence in public life, and reading of the Protestant King James Bible in the public schools.[51]

Some political leaders used an anti-Irish, anti-foreign stance in order to achieve other, unrelated ends. There was a strong reform, anti-corruption factor in the American Republican movement of the 1840s, while the New York Know Nothing Party of the 1850s preserved the pro-slavery, pro-Millard Fillmore, anti-Seward wing of a disintegrating Whig Party. But if nativist sentiment was strong enough to periodically attract politicians, its staying power wasn't very great. Nervous reaction to the Philadelphia nativist riots of 1844 dampened nativist politics in New York for several years, and the Know Nothing Party was ultimately drowned out by the growing sectional slavery crisis. Yet, so long as they were associated with Tammany Hall and until a new wave of immigrants began pouring into the city in the 1880s, the Irish remained the main targets of nativists. The post–Civil War anti-Tweed crusade of *Harper's Weekly* and its cartoonist Thomas Nast focused on the strong Irish support for Tammany, but it failed to point to the presence of Irish Americans among those who exposed the ring's crimes, including the chief prosecutor in the Tweed trials, Charles O'Connor.[52]

Generations of oppression in Ireland and decades of intolerance and poverty in the United States were part of the legacy of New York City's Irish in the years following the Civil War. The war itself proved to be a mixed bag of hope, opportunity, and frustration for the Irish. At the very least it deflated the nativist movement, since the incessant demand for troops provided opportunity for the city's ethnic groups to demonstrate their loyalty to the Union and their personal worth. No regiment was more renown for bravery and sacrifice than the predominantly Irish 69th.[53]

But if the Irish who volunteered were motivated by patriotism or by a desire to prove their loyalty to America, they had not enlisted in a struggle to free the slaves. Antebellum New York's shipping, banking, and manufacturing economy was strongly tied to the slave South, and prior to the outbreak of war sentiment in the city had been strong for compromise. Its citizens rejected Lincoln by 30,000 votes and overwhelmingly defeated a measure that would have granted equal suffrage for blacks.[54] Irish laborers in particular feared the possibility of freed slaves flocking northward to threaten their livelihoods. During the war Archbishop Hughes warned Secretary of War Cameron that Catholics would fight for the nation and the Constitution but not to free the slaves: "indeed they will turn away in disgust from the discharge of what would otherwise be a patriotic duty."[55] As one New York City black put it, it is "well known by both white and black that the Most Rev. Archbishop do hate the black race so much that he cannot bear them to come near him."[56]

By the summer of 1863 the patriotic fervor that had motivated Irish enlistees in the early days of the war had lost a good deal of its intensity, while Lincoln's issuance of the Emancipation Proclamation enraged many Irish New Yorkers. Tension gave way to violence during the week

■

after Saturday, July 11th, the day New York drew names under the Conscription Act of 1863. That first draft list contained 1,236 names, the majority of whom were poor Irishmen unable to afford the $300 required to purchase an exemption. To Irish workingmen it seemed that the war to preserve the union had become a crusade to uplift African Americans at the expense of their blood. Antiwar politicians and newspapers fed this resentment. For example, Benjamin Wood of the *Daily News* argued that the draft "would compel the white laborer to leave his family destitute and unprotected while he goes forth to free the negro, who, being free, will compete with him in labor."[57]

On Sunday a mob attacked the registry office. On Monday, as drawing was scheduled to resume, full-scale rioting broke out. For four days a predominantly Irish mob virtually controlled the streets of Manhattan. It "assaulted and killed Negroes, burned the Colored Orphan Asylum . . . , sacked the homes of antislavery advocates, intimidated peaceful workers and forced them to leave their jobs, and plunged into an orgy of robbery and pillage" before police, soldiers, and armed civilians finally restored order.[58] Estimates of the death toll in the rioting run as high as 1,200, including at least eighteen blacks who were lynched. Illustrations of the rioting published in *Harpers Weekly* on August 1, 1863, leave no doubt in the viewer's mind that the mob was Irish.[59]

Yet another side of Irish involvement was revealed in an editorial appearing in the August 1 edition of *Harper's*:

> It must be remembered . . . , that in many wards of the city, the Irish were during the late riot staunch friends of law and order; that Irishmen helped to rescue the colored orphans in the asylum from the hands of the rioters; that a large proportion of the police, who behaved throughout the riot with the most exemplary gallantry, are Irishmen; that the Roman Catholic priesthood to a man used their influence on the side of the law; and that perhaps the most scathing rebuke administered the riot was written by an Irishman—James T. Brady. It is important that this riot should teach us something more useful than a Revival of Know-Nothing prejudices.[60]

That such sentiments should have been expressed in a publication traditionally hostile to Tammany Hall and its Irish followers is noteworthy. *Harper's* editors wrote in awareness that not only had Irishmen acted on the side of law and order during the riots but also that, one

■

week before the riots began, Irish soldiers of New York's 69th Regiment had suffered grievous losses at Gettysburg. Eight years later, in its attack on the Tweed Ring, *Harper's* would revert to the stereotypical depictions of the Irish so common on the vaudeville stage. But in fact by the 1870s the Irish of New York City could not be fit into a single mold. Continued immigration of poor Irishmen, spurred on by a famine in 1879, contributed to maintaining the image of "shanty" or "tenement" Irish as the poorest of the city's white ethnics, but there were already among earlier Irish immigrants and their children those who had prospered mightily. That generational reality will be discussed in later chapters.

## ii

When the German episode in New York is examined, one immediately sees how the skills, experiences, and culture amassed in the mother country determined what life would be like in the new land. Because the contrasts between the Irish and the Germans in these matters were considerable, there were great contrasts in how the two groups were perceived by native New Yorkers and how they adapted to life in New York City. Language was a great divider, and not since early colonial days, when Dutch vied with English in the streets and marketplaces of New York, had the sounds of a minority tongue been heard with such frequency. As much as the Irish detested their English oppressors, their years under British domination made Anglo-Saxon dominated New York far less strange to them than it was to the Germans. Yet, in fact, it was the Germans who more rapidly and in greater numbers seem to have adapted to and prospered in New York City, even while standing apart socially and culturally from the English-speaking residents. They had arrived in America with more money, more skills, and a higher rate of literacy than had the Irish.[61]

This is not to say that Germans did not know poverty. Many did. There were those, for example, who earned their living as rag pickers and bone gatherers and who lived in the Eleventh Ward's "Rag Pickers' Paradise," a miserable slum despite its name.[62] But to balance the ledger, after 1845 Germans were increasingly prominent among the city's artisans and skilled tradesmen. "By 1855, Germans were already a majority of tailors, shoemakers, cabinetmakers, and upholsterers, bakers, brewers, cigarmakers, locksmiths, paperbox makers, potters, textile workers, gilders, turners, and carvers. Over the next two decades they came to dominate most other skilled trades as well."[63]

German men largely monopolized the skilled trades. German women were expected to stay at home and care for the family. Of course, circumstances forced them to search for employment outside their homes, but apparently not in such numbers as Irish women. In the heavily female occupation of domestic service, in 1880 there were only 5,800 Germans employed compared with 24,000 Irish. Yet as was the case in so many immigrant families, the women brought in badly needed funds by working at home. Historian Dorothee Schneider tells us, "German women tried to avoid wage labor outside home. Taking in boarders, sewing, taking in wash, or making cigars were the ways of earning additional dollars while officially retaining the status of housewife."[64]

Germans also experienced the stings of nativism. Many New Yorkers accused German workers of driving down the wages of American craftsmen and of contributing to the increase in cheaply made and priced goods, particularly furniture. During the 1850s their fellow immigrants, the Irish, accused Germans of acting as strikebreakers who threatened their dominant position on the city's docks. Native Americans castigated them for not speaking English, for being clannish, for loving beer, and for treating the Sabbath as a day of relaxation and recreation. Bigots hated German Catholics for being Catholic, and others depicted the small group of intellectual refugees from the revolutions of 1848 as "red republicans," "agnostics," and "freethinkers." Newspapers that were quick to see an immigrant-criminal identity found German names prominent among the safecrackers, counterfeiters, and fences of New York.[65]

Certainly nativism along with cultural differences encouraged German separateness and retarded their assimilation. Yet, even as victims of nativism the Germans suffered less intense hostility directed at them than did the Irish. Because Germans rarely formed street gangs or participated widely in the raucous activities of the city's fire companies, they were not associated with street and gang violence. Unlike the Irish, only a portion of the Germans were Catholics, and few of them held power in a church politically dominated by Irish clerics. And statistically German names were considerably less prominent than those Irish ones on the city's charity roles and on its police blotters.

■

If Germans faced criticism for their cultural clannishness, their limited participation in the city's seamier political life served to protect them from nativist criticism directed at Tammany Hall. Most Germans did vote Democratic, but a number of them, active in abolitionist circles, felt more comfortable in the Republican party. Germans were not connected in the public mind with corrupt city politics, though they were perceived as being associated with radical political movements, which were at times considered dangerous. And overcoming all the negative stereotypes directed at them, the Germans received plaudits for being hard workers, skilled in crafts and shrewd in businesses.[66] No equivalent of the commonly displayed "No Irish Need Apply" notices greeted them.

Heavy German concentrations in the city's Tenth, Eleventh, Thirteenth, and Seventeenth wards earned the area a number of appellations. Non-Germans most often referred to it as Dutch Town, but to its German residents it was *Kleindeutschland* (Little Germany). By 1875 the four wards were more than 64 percent German American, representing approximately half of the city's German population.[67] At the outset of the 1870s *Kleindeutschland* consisted of some 400 city blocks:

> Tompkins Square formed pretty much the center. Avenue B, occasionally called the German Broadway, was the commercial artery. Each basement was a workshop, every first floor was a store, and the partially roofed sidewalks were markets for goods of all sorts. Avenue A was the street for beer halls, oyster saloons and groceries. The Bowery was the western border (any thing further west was totally foreign), but it was also the amusement and loafing district. There all the artistic treats, from classical drama to puppet comedies, were for sale.[68]

Far more isolated from the general population by virtue of language and culture than were the Irish, the Germans also displayed a greater desire to remain apart. For them separateness or self-segregation not only protected them from nativist hostility and the difficulties of coping with a foreign language but also maintained their positive identification with things German. And when allegiance appeared to waiver, there were those in the community who warned of the dangers. For example, German Catholic priests insisted that maintenance of the German language was essential lest communicants abandon their reli-

■

gion. "Language saves faith," was an oft-heard slogan in the parish churches of *Kleindeutschland*.[69]

German separateness was not exclusively a matter of Germans vs. non-Germans, since prior to the establishment of a unified German nation in 1871, German immigrants rarely identified themselves chiefly as Germans. They were Bavarians or Brandenbergers or Hessians or Swabians or Prussians. Particularism among *Kleindeutschland*'s population was reflected in speech dialects, loyalties, institutional structures, and residential patterns. In his detailed study of the area, Stanley Nadel found that regional origin played a key role in determining in what neighborhood one lived, and that, along with religion, it was an important factor in the selection of marriage partners. Thus, in 1860 72 percent of Bavarians were married to other Bavarians, and another 18 percent chose spouses from adjoining regions of southwest Germany.[70]

In matters of religion also the pattern of German separateness from the English-speaking community and divisions within the German community persisted. Among Catholics and Protestants alike language and religious traditions of their homeland fostered a desire for national churches. For Catholics, who constituted the largest group of religiously affiliated Germans, this required the sympathy and cooperation of the Irish-dominated hierarchy, something not always forthcoming. Not without cause, German Catholics resented Irish dominance and believed that Archbishop Hughes was far more concerned with the spiritual needs of his own fellow Irishmen than those of other ethnics. As one Irish priest put it in 1865, referring to the German Catholics, "our ordinary authorities almost ignore their existence."[71]

The incentive to establish German national parishes initially came from laymen, who usually led the fundraising, supervised the construction of the church, and, only upon completion of the structure, applied to the bishop for a German-speaking priest.[72] While Hughes had little recourse but to comply with such requests, since the parish had in effect already been established, he was not always willing to endorse other nationalist ventures. In 1850, for example, he adamantly opposed the efforts of the German parishioners of Most Holy Redeemer Church to found a cemetery in land they owned in Williamsburg. The parishioners claimed that German burial parties at the official Catholic cemetery had persistently met with insults from Irish onlookers. When the Germans continued to use the Williamsburg cemetery after Hughes's insistence that there be only "one cemetery for Catholics of all nations," the bishop threatened to close down Most Holy Redeemer. Needless to say, Hughes won that battle.[73]

Despite limited support from the city's Irish-led church authorities, German Catholic parishes prospered. The first, St. Nicholas, had been established in 1833 on Second Street between Avenue A and First Avenue and reluctantly accepted by the diocese nine years later. By the Civil War there were seven German parishes, and the number continued to increase during the following decades.[74] The founder of St. Nicholas and the leading figure in the movement for German national parishes was the Austrian-born Rev. Johann Stephen Raffeiner. Father Raffeiner employed his considerable personal wealth and his skills in fundraising to serve the German Catholic communities of Manhattan and Brooklyn; his own money helped found Holy Trinity Church in Williamsburg and St. Francis of the Fields Church in Brooklyn. He succeeded in bringing over from Bavaria the Sisters of St. Dominic to serve Holy Trinity, encouraged German priests to emigrate to New York, and inspired young German Americans to enter the priesthood. Even Archbishop Hughes was impressed, and in 1853 he named Father Raffeiner vicar-general for Germans of the archdiocese. Upon Raffeiner's death in 1861 the position of vicar, much to the displeasure of German Catholics, remained unoccupied until 1875, when the Bavarian-born priest Michael May was named to the post.[75]

Father Raffeiner's later activities had centered in Brooklyn, so spiritual leadership of Manhattan's German Catholics fell increasingly into the hands of German priests of the Redemptionist order, led by Rev. Gabriel Rampler. Feuds with parishioners of St. Nicholas Church led Rampler, with Bishop Hughes's permission, to establish in 1844 Most Holy Redeemer parish on Third Street. The parish's prosperity was marked seven years later by the erection of an impressive new stone church structure. The popularity of Most Holy Redeemer was in no small part due to the intensive missionary activities of the Redemptionists, well beyond that typical of Irish Catholic churches in New York. They held "fire and brimstone" revival meetings, of the type associated with evangelical Protestantism, and the parishioners warmly received their particular emphasis upon Marian devotion. Furthermore, the parish set a pattern for other German Catholic churches by sponsoring a wide variety of social, cultural, and charitable societies

■

(*vereine*) to meet competition offered by Protestant churches and secular bodies within the German community. Beginning with St. Joseph *Verein*, a relief society established by Father Rampler in 1843, Most Holy Redeemer went on to sponsor mutual aid societies, youth groups, and singing societies. Physical protection of church property from Know-Nothing attacks was provided by a militia company, the *Jager-compagnie*, and a second company, the Henry Henning Guards, was later established. Both military groups were splendidly uniformed, took part in parades, sponsored picnic outings and shooting contests, and generally fostered a strong sense of religious and ethnic pride. The units, incidentally, helped counter the influence of regionalism.[76]

Beyond parish activities, the interests of German Catholics were served by Catholic newspapers like the *Katholische Kirchenzeitung, Die Aurora*, and the *Katholische Volksblatt*. Following the Civil War the New York Central *Verein* provided a city-wide Catholic organization devoted to assisting German Catholic immigrants when they landed at the Port of New York.[77] German Protestants were no less inclined than their Catholic countrymen to establish ethnic churches, but there the similarity ended. As Protestants in a Protestant nation they felt far more welcome and had no Irish hierarchy to contend with. Most churchgoing German Protestants affiliated with one form or other of Lutheranism, but several other Protestant denominations also supported German congregations. As early as 1839 the city had six Protestant German congregations: two Lutheran, one Dutch Reformed, one Evangelical Reformed, one Episcopalian, and one Christian (*Algemeine Christliche*). As more Germans arrived in New York, the variety of denominations came to include Baptist, Presbyterian, and even Mormon. Lutheran growth was most impressive. By 1865 all but two of New York's twenty-four Lutheran congregations were German, and the heavily Prussian and north German immigration of the following two decades added substantially to the numbers. Immigrants from German-speaking Swiss areas, from Baden, Wurttemburg, Darmstadt, and from the Dutch border regions helped establish the German Dutch Reformed Church as the second largest denomination among New York's German-American Protestants.[78]

Individual Germans chose among Protestant denominations or among churches within the same denomination often on the basis of the dynamism of the minister. Church membership thus tended to be

■

rather fluid. Whatever their denominational affiliation, German Protestant churches showed a desire to foster Germanism and discourage assimilation by providing ethnic schools, clubs, and cultural and social activities. Unhampered by a non-German hierarchy, the Lutherans in particular achieved great success in assisting newly arrived immigrants.[79]

The general tone of German Protestantism in metropolitan New York was conservative. During the 1840s German pastors railed against the liberal republican movements in their homeland; during the post Civil War years most of them enthusiastically supported the Bismarkian drive for German unification. Anti-assimilationist laymen and clerics saw the religiously and ethnically diverse population of Manhattan as a constant threat to German separatism. Beginning in the 1850s, therefore, and continuing for the next two decades, many of them helped establish German communities in Brooklyn and neighboring Long Island districts.[80]

German Americans of nominally Protestant background, constituting the majority of German immigrants during the final three decades of the century, were far less likely to formally join a church then were their Catholic brethren. Estimated figures of church membership for 1860 report 8,000 Protestants, 28,000 Catholics, and 7,000 Jews out of a population of 85,000 Germans in New York City. Twenty-one years later, when the German-American population of the city exceeded 280,000, Protestant church membership stood at somewhere between sixteen and twenty-one thousand.[81]

Since the 1840s an alternative to church affiliation, particularly among the city's German intellectuals and social reformers, were the *Frei Gemeinden*, the Freethinkers. Anti-clerical, often openly hostile to religion, such groups devoted themselves to promoting ethical principles derived from rational rather than spiritual sources. Despite their nonreligious stance, Freethinkers organized themselves along lines similar to mainline religion, holding "meetings" on Sunday mornings and conducting Sunday and day schools. Their membership never exceeded a few thousand, but the numbers of distinguished German Americans among them heightened their influence, particularly during the 1840s and 1850s. The *Frei Gemeinden* approach to ethical behavior continues to be espoused today by the Ethical Culture Society, founded in 1876 by Felix Adler, a member of New York City's German-Jewish community.[82]

■

The waves of immigrants that made Christian New York very much a multiethnic affair had a similar impact on the city's Jewish community. The descendants of the Spanish and Portuguese Jews of colonial days were joined by coreligionists from throughout northern and western Europe. To an overwhelming degree, however, the largest sending nation during this period was Germany, which in 1820 was home to about 10 percent of the world's Jewry.[83] Most emigrating German Jews came from the rural areas of Bavaria, Wurttemburg, and the Palatinate, where their occupations as merchants, peddlers, artisans, grain and hop dealers, and money-lenders tied them closely to the regions' peasant economies and made them sufferers of the decline in those economies. But for Jews economics never provides the entire explanation for emigration. For centuries the Jews of Europe had been victims of prejudice, living under conditions that ranged from bare toleration to brutal persecution. German Jews in particular had benefitted from liberal ideals of the Enlightenment. Napoleon's troops tore down ghetto walls, and many of the inhabitants rushed out to participate in the larger German community. But the defeat of Napoleon brought with it reaction and the return of political and economic repression. The failed revolutions of 1848 similarly caused upheaval in the German states and subsequent intolerance toward Jews.[84]

Between 1846 and 1886 it is estimated that the German-Jewish population of New York City grew from 7,000 to 85,000. The impact on the city's Jewish religious life of this influx along with those from other lands was considerable. Until 1825 New York City had only a single synagogue, Shearith Israel, where the Sephardic ritual continued to be followed even though Ashkenazic Jews had long been in the majority. That year English, Dutch, German, and Polish Jews founded the first Ashkenazic synagogue, B'nai Jeshurin. In 1828 a group broke off from B'nai Jeshurin to establish Anshe Chesed, which by the early 1840s had become a purely German synagogue. Nationality-based synagogues were by no means a monopoly of the Germans. Among the twenty-six synagogues founded between 1825 and 1860 were English, Bohemian, Dutch, French, and Russian-Polish congregations.[85]

Not only was the Jewish religious community divided along lines of national origin, but also the founding of Temple Emanu-El in 1845 signalled the beginnings of a religious division between Orthodox and Reform Jewry. Throughout the nineteenth century, Reform Judaism

■

was almost exclusively a German affair, representing an effort to adapt ancient Jewish practices to modern times, to make them more compatible with Enlightenment ideals and American religious practices. Influential in the founding of Temple Emanu-El was Leo Merzbacher, the first ordained rabbi to serve New York City's Jewish community. Prior to his move to Emanuel, Merzbacher held a joint appointment as rabbi of Orthodox congregations Anshe Chesed and Rodeph Shalom. Among the more dramatic changes instituted at Emanu-El were the use of German (later English) along with the traditional Hebrew in its abbreviated worship service, the introduction of sermons, organ music, and the seating of men and women together. Most profound was its emphasis on the ethical teachings of the prophets and the diminished adherence to Jewish law and traditional ritual. In truth, more than matters of religious practice separated the members of Emanu-El from their Orthodox fellow Jews. By 1860 the Reform synagogue was identified with the social cultural, and economic elite among New York's German Jews.[86]

Like their fellow immigrants of Christian origins, the majority of New York's German Jews were not affiliated with a religious body. Yet, for Jews religion was but one aspect of being Jewish. For centuries, resulting from a mixture of choice and proscription, the Jews of Europe had existed as communities within the larger Gentile communities. A sense of peoplehood existed among most Jews that neither the Enlightenment nor the apparent absence of overt anti-Semitism among New York's German Americans of the period could extinguish. Thus, there existed a distinct German-Jewish community within *Kleindeutschland.* There were Jewish fraternal organizations, most notably B'nai B'rith, founded in 1843, and the Free Sons of Israel, founded in 1849, both of which ultimately became national in scope. In addition, as did other German groups, Jews formed mutual aid societies, burial societies, literary societies, and a variety of other forms of *Vereine.* There were some Jews who cut themselves off completely from Jewish communal life, but this was not common. Rather, as Nadel explains, "Many of *Kleindeutschland*'s Jews participated in the broader-based German political and cultural organizations, but may have turned to the Jewish *Vereine* for more social activities."[87]

German was the language spoken by the German Jews of New York, and with their compatriots they promoted its inclusion in the city's pub-

■

lic schools. They gloried in German culture and admired German education. The wealthy among them often sent their sons to Germany for university training and to obtain wives. But even for the most affluent of the German-Jewish community, "a need was still felt for the ministrations of religion and the organization of specifically Jewish institutions."[88]

The regional and religious varieties among New York's German Americans were but two manifestations of the numerous divisions that marked this ethnic group during the nineteenth century. Perhaps this heterogeneity is most dramatically illustrated by the flourishing of so many newspapers and magazines within the German-American community. The most influential German-language paper was the secular, pro-Democrat *New Yorker Staats-Zeitung*, established in 1834, and followed the next year by the Whig-leaning *Allgemeine Zeitung*. The emerging Republican party of the 1850s had the support of the *Demokrat* and the *Abendzeitung*, while during the post-Civil War decades the socialist *Volks-Zeitung* challenged the *Staats-Zeitung*'s position as leader in total readership.[89] It seems as if there was a German-language paper for just about every taste and interest: literary newspapers; humor and sports papers; journals of commerce; newspapers promoting the causes of reform, socialism, abolitionism, and freethought. The *Neue Zeit*, a women's weekly, fostered feminism while more traditional views on family values and sex roles appeared in the *Illustrierte Welt*, *Familienblatter*, and the *Illustrierte Zeitung*. In one two-year period, 1850–1852, 28 German-language papers could be found in New York City. Many of these lasted only a short time, succumbing to competition, fluctuating political fortunes, and changing tastes. Yet, even as late as 1890 there were twelve flourishing German-language dailies competing for readership.[90]

Whatever their slant or persuasion, the German-American editors, led by the *Staats-Zeitung*'s Oswald Ottendorfer, generally stood in support of the maintenance of a distinct German society and culture, and that certainly is what existed in New York City. The Germans were by no means unique among ethnic groups in establishing lodges, benevolent and mutual aid societies, militia companies, and nationality-based drinking establishments. But the number of Germans, their language, and most of all the scope and variety of their community-based activities made them appear the most ethnic of the ethnics, even including the Irish. Certainly the Irish had their grog shops aplenty, but what

■

could compare in color or conviviality to the German beer gardens and the beer served in them? In 1848 Ferdinand Maximilian Schaefer introduced lager beer in the city, and its popularity soon spread beyond German neighborhoods. The beer gardens were establishments in which whole families gathered. Some held as many as three thousand people drinking, eating, listening to and singing German music, and gazing nostalgically at large wall murals depicting romantic scenes of the Fatherland. Here the spirit of *Gemutlichkeit* reigned. Of course there were other, smaller drinking establishments in *Kleindeutschland*, among them the traditional, male-dominated "standing only" saloons, and the *Lokale* that catered to families and provided tables and chairs.[91]

Professional theatrical entertainment became available to the residents of *Kleindeutschland* on a permanent basis with the opening of the Stadttheater on the Bowery in 1854. Particularly in the decades following the Civil War, German high culture became increasingly a part of the city scene. During the 1878–1879 season alone the drama *Faust* received 223 German-language performances in the metropolitan area. For Germans and non-Germans alike symphonic and operatic music in the city was dominated by German musicians, vocalists, and conductors performing works of German composers.[92]

At the very heart of German social life in New York City were the vast numbers of fraternal lodges and *Vereine* sponsored by occupational groups, by German regional organizations (*Landsmannschaften*), or, as noted earlier, by churches. The variety of *Vereine* was staggering. Most common were the sickness and benefit societies, but there were also singing associations and literary associations, *Vereine* to sponsor amateur dramatics, and *Vereine* to promote shooting contests (*Schutzenvereine*). Political refugees of the 1848 revolutions sponsored gymnastic societies, *Turnvereine*, which combined physical fitness with active support of the free soil and abolitionist movements. Socialists among the Forty-Eighters established the *New Yorker Socialistischer Turnverein*, which added the promotion of Marxism and trade unionism to the agenda.[93]

The activities of the various societies were not limited to their members. The Sunday performances of singing and dramatic groups attracted hundreds, while the *Volksfests* (folk festivals) held at Jones' Wood on the East River above 60th Street or across the Hudson in New Jersey drew tens of thousands. These *Volksfests* featured orchestral and choral performances, parades and dances, athletic and shooting contests,

■

speeches, dramatic readings, poetry recitals, and, of course, abundant food and drink. The Scots, the Welsh, and the Irish also had their field days, but these German *Volksfests* were truly special. What could match the *Plattdeutscher Volksfest* of 1875 which began in Tompkins Square Park, moved across the Hudson by ferry boats, and involved 150,000 participants?[94]

The distinctive German-American culture of New York City was by no means restricted to evenings and weekends, to religion and relaxation. In the world of work the strong German presence in the skilled trades has previously been noted. But, even here regional origin and occupation were closely related. For example, Nadel points out that in 1860, 75 percent of *Kleindeutschland's* grocers were born in Hannover, while in 1870, one third of all German-born shoemakers were from Baden, though Badenites constituted but 15 percent of the German-American labor force. Tailoring had by the late 1870s "developed into a Prussian preserve."[95] Yet Nadel also reveals that in many instances regional dominance of a particular field was short lived; by 1870 the Hanover-born grocers had virtually disappeared, as many became wine and liquor dealers or saloon keepers.[96]

Opportunities provided by an expanding economy enabled a number of German Americans from rather humble artisan or merchant backgrounds to make spectacular advances. "Brewer princes" like Jacob Ruppert and Max Schaefer, piano manufacturers Henry Steinway and his sons, and rubber magnate Conrad Poppenhusen became prominent before 1860. Many German-Jewish financiers, including names like Straus, Guggenheim, Kuhn, Loeb, and Lehman, arrived in America with limited financial resources and started out as peddlers and merchants. Some enterprising dry goods peddlers invested their earning in retail clothing stores and later turned to manufacturing inexpensive, ready-to-wear clothing. Substantial profits from uniform manufacturing during the Civil War added capital for the further expansion of this industry.[97]

Paralleling the success stories of some was a growing awareness, not at all limited to German Americans, of a widening social and economic gap along class lines in the city. Perhaps the most dramatic example of a totally German class conflict was the Steinway piano strike of 1870, brought on by Henry Englehard Steinway's attempt to cut the wages of workers by almost a third. In this instance the strikers, assisted

■

financially by German trade unionists from throughout the city, gained a victory. "There was no evidence of non-German union help to the strikers."[98]

Separate German trade unions had their origins in the 1850s, resulting from language difficulties and the hostility of native-born and Irish workers toward Germans. Early in that decade, while the economy was booming, there had been considerable cooperation among the various ethnic workers as they struck for higher wages and shorter hours. During the massive tailors' strike of 1850, for example, there was class unity between German and Irish workers. However, a downturn in the economy beginning in 1854 and culminating in the Panic of 1857 proved disastrous to organized labor and exacerbated ethnic and racial tensions.[99]

Conflicts between labor and capital within the German community during the antebellum period attracted the attention of promoters of a variety of radical, utopian philosophies. Among the more prominent was Wilhelm Weitling, who arrived in New York in 1847. Two years later his *Arbeitbund* (Workers' League) was organized to promote a brand of communism strongly influenced by Charles Fourier, the French utopian socialist. Weitling's utopianism envisioned a rather complex system of producer and consumer cooperative schemes, advocacy of public schooling, religious and moral preaching, and anti-nationalism. By 1852 New York's German artisans had grown weary of Weitling's notions, which seemed far removed from addressing their immediate interests in higher wages and improved working conditions. The idea of producer cooperatives, however, did have considerable appeal in *Kleindeutschland*, and some were actually launched. It was the less than enthusiastic support of such projects by non-German trade unionists combined with a lack of capital and managerial skills that doomed the movement.[100]

More lasting in its impact on New York's German workers was the Marxian socialism introduced into the city by Forty-Eighter refugees, most notably Joseph Weydemeyer. After arriving from Germany in 1851, Weydemeyer worked closely with German trade union leaders to establish the *Allgemeiner Arbeitbund* (later *Amerikanisher Arbeitbund*), a party whose platform combined the goals of socialism with those of trade unionism. Wisely, he added objectives particularly dear to German sensibilities, such as resistance to "Sunday" laws and temperance legislation. When Weydemeyer left the city to settle in the Midwest in 1856,

■

the movement was salvaged by Frederick Sorge, a refugee who had fought in the 1849 uprising in Baden. Sorge formed a Communist Club in Manhattan and shortly thereafter brought the organization into Marx's International Workingmen's Association. In 1868 he led a Social Party of German workers into the city's municipal elections, but it was unsuccessful at the polls. Yet socialism's influence was maintained by a continuing stream of class conscious German immigrants and by social-ist-leaning German-language newspapers like the *Arbeiter Union*. As the German-American trade union movement expanded with American industrialization, socialist leaders and Marxian ideals remained promi-nent. The New York Cigarmakers Union and the United Cabinetmak-ers were perhaps most fervent in their attachment to socialism, and both organizations experimented with cooperatives. But, like their English-speaking counterparts, German-American workers depended upon traditional union tactics like the strike to attain their immediate goals. German Americans did introduce socialism to America, but they gained far more respect from fellow workers for their skill in union organizing. In time this respect helped erode old prejudices, and after the 1860s greater worker cooperation was achieved.[101]

German businessmen no less than German workers displayed a strong tendency toward ethnic solidarity. Among the products of their cooperative ventures were the German Savings Bank (1859), the Ger-man-American Fire Insurance Company (1857), and a German hospi-tal formed in 1866.[102] When faced with growing union strength dur-ing the last years of the Civil War, German employers responded by forming trade associations. The first of these, the Boss Cabinetmakers in 1863 and the Merchant Tailors' Association in 1864, initially hoped to break the unions; but, failing to accomplish this, their purpose became to present a united, industry-wide front against union demands.[103]

Perhaps the most creative attempts by German businessmen to ensure labor peace and at the same time to maintain strong ties to Ger-man culture in the New World were the separate German towns they founded in Queens County beginning in the late 1860s. By 1880 Col-lege Point had become a German-American industrial town dominat-ed by the Conrad Poppenhusen Enterprise Works, the Hugo Funk Silk Mill, the Samuel Kunz Mill, the I. B. Kleinert Rubber Company, and the Germania Ultra Marine Works. The largest employer (11,000 workers) and leading personality in College Point was the rubber mag-

■

nate Conrad Poppenhusen, who presided over factory and town like a benevolent despot. Poppenhusen's benevolence made him a founder of the Germania Life Insurance Company; his Poppenhusen Institute provided College Point residents with a kindergarten and free classes in the arts and crafts; he paid to build a causeway between College Point and Flushing, and his private funds employed a teacher to ensure the continuity of the German language in his town. Poppenhasen's efforts kept German language and culture dominant in College Point for more than thirty years.[104]

Piano manufacturer William Steinway developed the second of Queens's German industrial towns. Steinway left Manhattan in the late 1860s because he needed more space for his expanding business, but there was another motivating factor:

> we wished to escape the anarchists and socialists who even at the same time were constantly breeding discontent among our workmen and inciting them to strike. They seemed to make us a target of their attacks and we felt that if we could withdraw our workingmen from contact with these people, and with other temptations of city life in the tenement districts, they would be more content.[105]

In Astoria it was the piano magnate who, like Poppenhasen in College Point, dominated the community. Steinway erected a huge industrial complex with housing for his workers and contributed public parks and baths to the town. Also following Poppenhasen, he paid the salary of the public school German teacher, who it was hoped would provide a solid grounding in the native language to the children of the 81 percent of his workers who were German.[106]

Thus, metropolitan New York saw two very different but very German responses to industrialism. In College Point and Astoria, in the spirit of Prussia, authority was obvious. In very much the same mold as Alfred Krupp's factory towns in Germany, workers lived, labored, played, and prayed in a German atmosphere created and guided by industrialist patrons. Back in Manhattan, however, the German radical strain was most in evidence as workers sought a better life through socialist/union activism.

New York City's German Americans simply did not fit into a single mold. Not all German unionists were socialists by any means; not all German nonsocialist workers were Democrats any more than all German financial and industrial leaders were Republicans. Wide religious, regional, and class differences among the Germans made their politics very hard to predict during the antebellum years. The party support Tammany could count on among the Irish was impossible for Germans. As a consequence German-American New Yorkers never received the political rewards that strict party loyalty earned for the Irish. However, the tendency of Germans to act as an ethnic bloc within varied political organizations provided them with no small amount of clout in different venues. At election time Germans had to be wooed.

During the 1850s strong free soil and anti-slavery sentiment among German Forty-Eighters gave Republicans hope of making significant inroads in New York's German community. Well-attended rallies in support of Republican presidential candidate John C. Frémont held in *Kleindeutschland* during 1856 were addressed by leaders of the *Turnverein* movement. Some of the most notable members of the city's Forty-Eighter refugee population became Republicans, but in the end the majority of German Americans voted for the eventual winner, James Buchanan. The Democratic party's traditional pro-immigrant, anti-nativist stance on the one hand and on the other the association of some city Republicans with temperance, Sunday observance, and nativism dictated the outcome.[107] Germans active in Democratic politics—saloon keepers, professionals, and journalists, most notably Oswald Ottendorfer of the *Staats-Zeitung*—were adept at forging alliances within the party that gained them the greatest possible influence. For example, when in 1857 Mayor Fernando Wood broke with Tammany and established his Mozart Hall organization, most German party activists went with him. And, while most of Wood's Irish supporters returned to Tammany in 1858, the Germans remained loyal and reaped the patronage benefits of Wood's 1859 electoral victory. With the onset of the Civil War Wood's pro-Southern sentiments cost him heavily in the German community, and the Republicans once again had cause for optimism. The German-Americans leaders did leave Mozart Hall in 1861, but not to support the Republican mayoral candidate. Tammany had nominated Godfrey Gunther, the son of German immigrants, for mayor, and a German Democratic Union Party was hastily established to endorse him. Republican George Opdyke won a

■

narrow victory, but Gunther outpolled Wood, thanks to massive support in the German wards. In 1863 the German Democrat Union again nominated Gunther and, with the support of a splinter group of Irish Tammanys led by "Honest John" Kelly, won the mayoral prize.[108]

Ottendorfer and his fellow German-American Democratic leaders used their organizational skills and the power of the press brilliantly. In alliance with native American reformers and with the power of the *Staats-Zeitung* and the *New York Times* behind them, they played a major role in breaking the stranglehold the Tweed Ring held over Tammany Hall. In 1872 a German Reform Party, led by Ottendorfer and his colleagues August Belmont and William Steinway, nominated William Havemeyer for mayor. With broad support from reform elements throughout the city, Havemeyer achieved victory.[109]

The 1872 election was the highwater mark in the political careers of Ottendorfer and his circle. Despite his own German antecedents, Mayor Havemeyer proved insensitive to the political aspirations of his German supporters and avoided the immigrant community generally when filling patronage jobs. The sugar magnate even filled traditionally ethnic-held positions with old-stock Americans. Frustrated in their attempts to deal with Havemeyer, the German Reform Party named Ottendorfer its mayoral candidate in 1874. However, by this time a clean government element led by "Honest John" Kelly had gained control of Tammany and subsequently won back the city's reform-minded citizens. A revived Tammany, promising patronage jobs to ethnic supporters, overwhelmed Ottendorfer, who lost all but one of the city's heavily German wards.[110]

The era of separate German parties ended for the most part in 1874. Despite the theoretical attachment of many workers to socialism, the majority of the city's German Americans were, like the Irish, increasingly aligned with the Democratic party and remained so as Tammany enacted tenement legislation and served other immigrant causes. Furthermore, the growing German-American population—from 15 percent to 28 percent of the city's total between 1860 and 1890—assured greater political influence and patronage for the community. The number of custom house jobs held by German Americans, for example, rose from 23 in 1861 to 54 in 1884.[111] For Ottendorfer and a number of his political colleagues defeat in 1874 left a bitter taste for democratic politics. "By 1877 they had reached the conclusion that the only way to end municipal corruption and high taxes was essentially to disenfran-chise anyone who didn't pay taxes on property worth over $500 or a rent of $250 a year."[112]

Lawrence H. Fuchs tells us that, after a short time in the United States, German Americans in the nineteenth century "went through a process of reconfiguration of their ancestral identity. Immigrants of dif-ferent backgrounds found it was to their advantage to establish a new identity as ethnic-Americans, although the term obviously had not been invented."[113] As years passed there was increased participation in religious, political, economic, and charitable life as German Americans rather than as Bavarians, Prussians, Hessians, etc. Bismarck's successful campaign between 1864 and 1871 to forge a unified German Empire fostered so great a sense of nationalism among the residents of New York City's German neighborhoods that even a great many Forty-Eighter republicans overcame their hostility to the Prussian monarchy. The Franco-Prussian War, which broke out on July 19, 1870, found the vast majority of New York German Americans enthusiastically sup-porting the Fatherland.[114]

Yet, the "reconfiguration" from German particularism to ethnic unity as German Americans was far from complete. In 1880 a resident of *Kleindeutschland* might well belong to a "German" union, church, or political club along with those from a wide variety of German regions; nonetheless, localism remained a potent force as memberships in regional associations, choices of marriage partners, and the persistence of regionally-based German neighborhoods testify. Continuing Ger-man immigration, which reached its peak in 1882, served to strength-en localism. These newcomers were themselves evidence that, despite unification, the German Empire was still very loosely held together, particularly in the realms of culture, religion, and dialect. But localism was by no means limited to newcomers. Regional loyalties were effec-tively passed on to American-born children who continued to join and participate in the activities of *Landsmannschaft* associations and to sub-scribe to German dialect newspapers like the *Plattdeutsche Post* and the *Schwabbisches Wochenblatt*.[115]

Separated from one another by differences in religion, class, and regional loyalties and separated from the larger American society by a strong adherence to cultural continuity, the German-American com-munity of nineteenth-century New York was, nonetheless, immensely

■

dynamic and flourishing. This community was also on the move, as during the post-Civil War years affluent Germans were leaving the older neighborhoods of *Kleindeutschland* for homes in uptown Manhattan. By 1880 Yorkville was emerging as the new center of German-American culture in New York.

The movement of Germans, and to a lesser extent the Irish, from lower Manhattan marked a stage in the history of New York City's immigrant groups. As they prospered, they sought better housing away from their first areas of settlement. This was a process repeated again and again by others. The living quarters they left behind were not left empty, for after 1880 New York continued to grow economically and geographically and to attract new waves of immigrants, this time from other regions in Europe.

■

*Old and*

*New*

*Immigrants*

*in Greater*

*New York*

*City,*

*1880 to*

*World*

*War I*

As the twentieth century approached, New York maintained its position as the nation's largest city. For a brief period Chicago, rapidly recovering from its famous fire, appeared to be a viable challenger. But with the merger of Manhattan with its four outlying boroughs to form Greater New York City in 1898, the city easily outdistanced its midwest rival. Consolidated New York contained more than three million inhabitants, and on the eve of World War I housed a population twice as large as Chicago's.[1]

New York also remained America's leading port. While the city slipped from its commercial high point of 1850, when 70 percent of America's exports and imports went through its harbor, nearly half of the nation's shipping came through New York at the turn of the century. And about two of every three new immigrants entered the United States through Ellis Island, just off shore of Manhattan's southern tip, after it opened as a reception center in 1892.[2]

World commerce gave the city financial supremacy as well. Led by J. P. Morgan & Co., New York was home to the nation's leading banks. The New York Stock Exchange anchored Wall Street, and giant law firms emerged after the Civil War to serve the needs of the metropolis and the nation.[3] These enterprises required the employment of large numbers of professional and other white collar workers, who, in turn, further contributed to the city's growth.

While shipping, commerce, and finance gave New York a preeminence among American cities, they did not necessarily attract new immigrants as settlers. Laboring jobs and manufacturing, which usually did not require a knowledge of English and a high level of skill, provided that lure. Rapid industrial growth characterized New York from 1815 to 1880, after which crowded streets and high rents hindered development of most space-demanding industries. Meat packing and steel located in cities like Pittsburgh and Chicago, while light manufacturing flourished in New York. Publishing, metal working, food processing and the manufacture of clothing and luxury items required a large-scale labor force that the incoming immigrants helped provide. Overall the number of wage earners in industry doubled between 1880 and 1910.[4]

Of all the industries attracting immigrants, clothing was by far the leader. Prior to the 1890s the ready-to-wear clothing industry was, with the exception of women's cloaks, primarily producing menswear. Technological progress, however, led to a spectacular rise in the manufacture of women's suits and shirtwaists by the 1890s. During the final decades of the century much of the finishing work on garments—final trimming and basting and making buttonholes—was farmed out to Yiddish-speaking subcontractors. They, in turn, recruited mostly unskilled immigrants to labor in their homes or in tenement-flat workshops, which became universally known as "sweatshops." There as many as twenty men, women, and children were crammed together, peddling on machines, cutting, and hand sewing with needles and thread they had to supply themselves for eighty-four hours or more per week. Long hours, seasonal unemployment, child labor, barely subsistence wages,

■

and airless flats; these were the conditions under which thousands of newly arrived immigrants labored.[5]

After 1880 New Yorkers intensified efforts to improve living conditions of the city's working class residents. Established groups like the New York Association for Improving the Condition of the Poor and the Children's Aid Society continued to assist poor immigrants and their offspring, though the Children's Aid Society no longer placed children in western homes. A new private agency, the settlement house, appeared in 1889 when the Henry Street Settlement opened its doors under the leadership of Lillian Wald. White social worker Mary Ovington was instrumental in founding the National Urban League, which helped blacks find jobs and housing. Other voluntary groups formed to assist specific minorities.[6]

Not content with voluntary efforts, New York progressives turned to the state and city governments to improve the urban environment. A citizens' group led by Lawrence Veiller was largely responsible for the passage of the Tenement House Law of 1901.[7] Reformers also persuaded municipal agencies to build new playgrounds and public baths, improve sanitation and make city agencies more efficient. While some reform attempts, such as those aimed at closing saloons and censoring movies, annoyed many immigrants and while reform legislation was not always effectively enforced by oft-corrupt public officials, the efforts of concerned citizens did contribute to alleviating conditions in tenement neighborhoods.[8]

After settling the political fight over aid to parochial schools in the 1840s, New Yorkers did build more public schools. These were mostly elementary, but in 1897 the city opened three new high schools.[9] Educational reformers criticized the city's schools, arguing that they were unprofessional, dirty, and overcrowded, that they failed to prepare immigrants for jobs and for citizenship, and, with their local-based authority, were subject to mismanagement and even corruption. Advocates of change sought to bring efficiency and honesty to the system through centralized control, and were rewarded for their efforts in 1896, when a bill to that effect was passed by the state legislature.[10] Though hailed as great improvement for the city's public schools, the bill's immediate results were by no means clear as overcrowding and other poor conditions continued.[11] New York taxpayers were either unwilling or unable to erect buildings quickly enough to enroll the

■

fast-growing immigrant population. By the time of World War I, nearly three-quarters of a million youngsters attended the public schools. Because of crowded conditions many received only part time instruction, and thousands of others were turned away because the buildings could not accommodate them. The Compulsory Education Act of 1895, mandating attendance until the age of twelve or through the fifth grade, could not be fully enforced for years. Classes of sixty pupils were not uncommon, and only a small minority contained fewer than forty students. And the system's problems were compounded because so many of the new pupils were foreigners or the children of immigrants who entered school with English language deficiencies.[12]

Also at the state level, legislators enacted laws providing pensions for widowed mothers with children and instituting workmen's compensation benefits. Largely through the efforts of Frances Kellor, the first state-controlled employment bureau opened in 1911. In addition, Albany legislators responded to New York City's disastrous Triangle fire of 1911 that claimed the lives of 146 workers, most of them young, immigrant, Jewish women. The Triangle Shirtwaist Company had ignored existing fire regulations and had maintained unsafe, though not illegal, working conditions. Pressure by union workers, led by the dynamic Rose Schneiderman and an aroused public opinion, resulted in the passage of new factory safety regulations.[13]

As the job mix of New York altered, so too did the ethnic composition of the city's workforce. After 1880, Germans and Irish still settled in the city. For example, 55,000 Germans arrived in the 1880s and twice that number in the next decade, making them the largest ethnic group in New York.[14] But by the turn of the century immigration from Great Britain, Germany, and Ireland ebbed as the economic and social climates in those countries generally improved. The trickle of "New Immigrants" from southern and eastern Europe, who had begun to increase their numbers around 1880, became a flood after 1900.[15]

Meanwhile, those who arrived as part of the "Old Immigration" continued their struggles to achieve upward mobility, some with considerable success. German immigrants and their descendants found prosperity in the city's expanding economy, and a substantial white collar middle class—and even a social and economic elite—emerged by the 1880s. Oswald Ottendorfer, publisher of the influential *New Yorker Staats Zeitung*, was listed, along with some other Germans, in the city's

■

*Social Register.* Germans also founded their own elite ethnic organizations like the *Deutscher Verein* and the *Liederkranz* singing society. Rising anti-Semitism precluded German Jews from inclusion among the city's upper crust, and none were in the *Social Register* at the turn of the century. Prosperous Jews were also barred from the socially prominent German organizations, and so increasingly they turned to their own societies such as the *Harmonie*, the Progress, and the Fidelio.[16]

The move out of *Kleindeutschland* continued as Germans prospered. By World War I, the old area was a shadow of its former self, while Yorkville in Manhattan's east eighties became the center of German residence and culture.[17] Harlem, in upper Manhattan, attracted middle class German Jews and Protestants. Still other German New Yorkers left Manhattan entirely and found homes in the outer boroughs, especially in Brooklyn. In 1900 about 60 percent of the city's Germans resided in Manhattan but only 42 percent could be found there ten years later. Two thirds of the second generation resided outside of Manhattan in 1910.[18] These new areas of settlement were made accessible by the city's continuing transportation revolution. Faster electric street cars and elevated lines replaced the old horsedrawn cars. After 1904 came the subways, which began to shape new neighborhoods even before World War I.[19] Bridges were no less important to the expanding city. The Brooklyn Bridge, called at the time the "eighth wonder of the world," was completed in 1883, followed by the Manhattan (1903) and Williamsburg (1909) bridges. All these spans connected Manhattan to Brooklyn.

Between 1900 and 1910 the number of foreign-born Germans in the city declined from 332,000 to 278,000, and then the number of second generation German New Yorkers also began to fall. The *Staats-Zeitung* remained the nation's largest German-language daily, but the number of German publications was declining.[20] The movement out of Manhattan's *Kleindeutschland* did not mean the immediate disintegration of varied German institutional life. German gymnastic, musical, and shooting societies were still numerous and quite active at the turn of the century. Yet by 1910 the decline of German presence in the city was noticeable.

The Irish, poorer to begin with, were slower to move up from their poverty than the Germans. Most Irish remained working class on the eve of World War I, with many men holding laborers' jobs and some

■

young women still engaged in domestic employment. Rough and poor Irish neighborhoods continued to dot the city landscape, most notably Hell's Kitchen on Manhattan's West Side. It was here that the Tenderloin, home of gambling, drinking, prostitution, and rampant police corruption, had been a vice center for decades. Newspaper stories from 1881 described Hell's Kitchen, the area approximately from 57th to 34th Streets between Ninth and Twelfth Avenues, as a center of poverty and crime, with many residents living in squalid conditions. One room had "no carpet save one of filth [that] covered the floor. . . . Furniture, if fit to be called by that name, was none. A bundle of rags and straw in a corner sufficed for a bed." The occupants, generally of Irish descent, were described as "honest and industrious," whose principal fault "seems to be a love for the intoxicating cut."[21] Thirty years later little had changed. Efforts of reformers during the Progressive era brought a measure of relief to Hell's Kitchen, particularly through housing legislation, but it still remained a poor and unsafe neighborhood, "so notorious that vaudeville comedians used it as source of humor."[22]

Yet, as the years passed American-born Irish children were staying in school (both public and parochial) longer and finding better jobs upon leaving. A middle class—the "lace curtain Irish"—had emerged by the late 19th century, and its members were the backbone of the social and fraternal organizations associated with parish life. They held memberships in such national bodies as the Irish Catholic Benevolent Union and the Ancient Order of Hibernians, subscribed to at least one of the city's five Irish-American newspapers, and sent their children to one of the Catholic secondary schools.[23]

Among the few Irish New Yorkers who could be called wealthy were the noted lawyer W. Bourke Cockran, businessman Thomas Fortune Ryan, and art collector and attorney John Quinn.[24] Since Irish Catholics were unwelcome in the social institutions of the old Protestant upper class, they turned instead to the city's many Catholic and Irish organizations. The most prestigious of these were the Catholic Club and the Xavier Club, both of which served Catholics of all ethnic origins. The "less pretentious" St. Patrick's Club and the Gaelic Society existed exclusively for the Irish. The more affluent Irish often sent their daughters to the Academy of the Sacred Heart, designed for women "of the higher class," and their sons to St. Johns College (later

■

changed to Fordham College), St. Francis Xavier College, or Manhattan College. A few could even afford to summer with their families at Saratoga Springs.[25]

The Irish were also a bit slower than Germans to move up and out of Manhattan, but their mobility became quite marked after 1900. They relocated to better neighborhoods on both sides of Manhattan and crossed over into the Bronx, leaving behind the slums of the Sixth Ward.[26] Many of these uptown Irish had succeeded as entrepreneurs, especially as owners of saloons, while others became skilled workers. At the turn of the century the Central Federated Union, the local association of the American Federation of Labor (AFL), was dominated by Irish craftsmen.[27] Irish women also became active in the labor movement. Leonora O'Reilly helped establish the New York chapter of the Women's Trade Union League in 1904, and Annie Moriarty tried to organize the city's growing number of Irish women teachers.[28]

But it was always politics and the Roman Catholic Church that held the greatest attraction for Irish New Yorkers. They had moved into politics as foot soldiers of Tammany Hall before the Civil War. Subsequently, they dominated the Hall and much of New York City's municipal political life off and on for many years. The appeal of politics to the Irish was obvious, since a growing city provided both jobs and lucrative construction contracts. In 1888 it was estimated that control of city hall meant 12,000 jobs; the creation of Greater New York ten years later raised that figure to 60,000.[29] In the fire and police departments, the civil service, and the schools (where young Irish women became prominent), Irish New Yorkers claimed more than one third of the city's public jobs in 1900.[30] Connections to the political machine by the Irish were vital to obtaining jobs in a non-civil service era, but the English they spoke gave them an additional advantage over most immigrants. Mastery of English was a requisite for most municipal employment as well as for such private sector jobs as fare collectors on the city's subways, which were then privately owned. Many of these positions were blue collar and hardly provided middle class incomes, but they offered steady employment in an economy that experienced periodic recessions and depressions. Moreover, some jobs, especially in the police department, presented the possibility for graft, which was widespread at the turn of the century. For example, policemen regularly took bribes for permitting prostitution to flourish and saloons to operate illegally.

■

Historian Timothy J. Gilfoyle concluded, "While the police did not control every prostitute and madame in New York, the most lucrative operations were subject to police approval."[31]

New York police officers starting salary reached only $800 annually in 1901, but so lucrative was graft that one newspaper reported that it cost an assessment of $300 just to be a patrolman while a captain was worth $14,000. Thomas Byrnes, who became chief of the Detective Bureau in 1880 at a top salary of $5,000 annually, had an estate worth $350,000 and his wife one of nearly $300,000 when he retired.[32]

Of course, local politicians got their share of the boodle because they worked closely with the police to "regulate" prostitution.[33] Even more rewarding was inside knowledge of future city contracts. A few politicians acquired substantial fortunes through their connections to city hall. While reformers decried such practices as scandalous, Tammany boss George Washington Plunkitt put it more benignly with a suggestion for his epitaph: "George Washington Plunkitt—He seen his opportunities and he took 'em."[34]

There was another dimension to the Irish love of politics: Irish nationalism. The struggles of the people of Ireland for independence were not forgotten by those who left home. They founded organizations to foster the cause and sent money home to support activities against the British. On the eve of the First World War New Yorkers founded the Friends of Irish Freedom to support an independent Ireland. Important New York papers like Patrick Ford's the *Irish World* and John Devoy's *Gaelic American* were published to keep the dream alive. Irish leaders used their strength within the Democratic party to pressure local and national politicians to support their nationalist cause.[35]

Because there were more voters than jobs, Irish politicians offered other services beyond employment. Machine benefits begun in the mid-nineteenth century, including baskets of food at Christmas, fuel for cold winter days, help in finding housing, and picnics, singing and sport clubs for amusement, continued well into the twentieth. Big Tim Sullivan, leader of the Bowery district, was born in poverty to Irish immigrant parents and lived for years in some of the city's worst neighborhoods. The one-time saloon owner rose rapidly within the Tammany organization to become a master of urban politics. During the depression winter of 1894 he fed thousands of poor people Christmas dinners. He also gave away food and clothing, worked hard to see that

■

deserving voters got jobs, and still found time to run his burlesque and vaudeville house.[36]

But satisfying Irish voters was not enough, for the Irish made up only about one third of New York's electorate at the turn of the century. German New Yorkers, while not as intensely involved politically as the Irish, could also be effectively courted, particularly when anti-Tammany reform candidates, like Seth Low in 1899, included Sunday blue laws in their platforms or when fusion reform mayor John Mitchell made patriotism the issue in his 1917 re-election campaign and insinuated that German New Yorkers were potentially disloyal.[37]

Christmas baskets, fraud, jobs, and appeals to non-Irish voters could not always secure control of City Hall. Periodic reform movements, representing voter disgust at widespread graft, succeeded at times in capturing that main prize. However, despite setbacks, Tammany Hall and the Irish politicians who ran it remained the preeminent powers in New York City politics well into the fourth decade of the twentieth century.

After 1880 Irish New Yorkers continued their domination of the Roman Catholic Church. As Italian and Polish Catholics poured into the city, the Irish clergy criticized their particular practices of Catholicism and their folk traditions, but the church did expand its parishes, schools, and charities to serve them. Under Archbishop Michael Corrigan and later John Cardinal Farley, the Archdiocese initiated a major church-building campaign.[38]

While Irish men dominated the church, Irish women became nuns and served as teachers in the parochial schools and as nurses in the church's hospitals. Their labors made Catholic institutional life possible in New York City. The Catholic Sisters of Charity began their New York activities before the Civil War, and they expanded as the city grew. They tended the sick, administered hospitals, taught parochial school children, and staffed orphanages and other institutions serving the city's poor. Among the most notable of the city's Catholic hospitals was St Vincent's, which opened in response to the cholera epidemic of 1849. One of the organizers was Sister Mary Angela Hughes, sister of Bishop John Hughes. St.Vincent's cramped quarters quickly proved to be inadequate, and eventually the hospital moved to its present location in Greenwich Village.[39] Of course, German women were active too in organizing hospitals that served their community. One of the advan-

■

tages of ethnically based hospitals was that the sick received care from Sisters who spoke their language and knew their culture.[40]

As new Catholic immigrants flooded the city and as other Catholic New Yorkers moved northward up Manhattan and eastward into Brooklyn, the church struggled to finance its institutions. In time it raised more money for education, but many women taught for years in vastly overcrowded classrooms serving immigrant populations. Sister Monica Maria McInerney, for example, embarked upon her career in 1896 at St. Patrick's in lower Manhattan, which had opened more than a hundred years earlier. When McInerney began her long career (she would eventually become principal, in 1925), the school had 2,500 children, few of whom could speak English when they first entered. Classes contained more than 60 pupils.[41] The Archdiocese's first high school opened in 1894, staffed by members of the Sisters of Charity. That noteworthy order continued to play an important role in the Catholic elementary and secondary schools into the twentieth century.[42]

As immigration from Germany and Ireland slowed, the countries of southern and eastern Europe sent increasing millions across the Atlantic Ocean in search of a better life. Of these so-called "new immigrants"— Italians, Greeks, Czechs, Slavs, and Jews—some went to Canada and Latin America, but the vast majority came to the United States. Just as social and economic changes spurred emigrants to leave northern and western Europe between 1820 and 1880, those forces now spread eastward and southward. Commercial agriculture consolidated estates in the Austro-Hungarian Empire and forced thousands of peasants to leave. In Southern Italy and Sicily conditions had been bleak for generations, even before landlords began squeezing peasants off the land. To make matters worse, taxes were unbearable, population growth high, and prospects for alternative employment poor. World-wide competition for wheat and grapes after 1870 drove prices for these products down and tariff wars a few years later only added to the peasants' woes.[43] In both areas peasants drifted into the cities, but some eventually chose emigration to America. In addition, those European workers who labored in small handcraft industries, sometimes operating out of their homes, experienced growing competition from factory production. Everywhere rising population created additional pressures for emigration.[44]

■

Ethnic tensions in central and eastern Europe added to economic discontents, but no group experienced more discrimination than Russia's Jews. Already required, with few exceptions, to a live in a limited Pale of Settlement, the czar's May Laws of 1882 forced a half-million of his Jewish subjects to relocate from rural villages to cities and towns. Other decrees subjected Jews to long-term military service, banned them from certain professions, and severely restricted their access to universities. Slavic anti–Semitism reached a new high with the pogroms, government-sanctioned riots and bloodbaths against Jews that began in the early 1880s. As they watched their homes and business burned and fellow Jews murdered, many became convinced that emigration to America was their only salvation.[45]

For potential emigrants desire to come to America was often heightened by news of the bounties that awaited them. Railroads and steamship lines printed thousands of pamphlets in dozens of foreign languages explaining the wonders of the New World. And letters from those who had gone before urged their relatives and countrymen to join them. Mary Antin, a Russian Jewish immigrant, recalled in later years "America was in everybody's mouth . . . people who had relatives in the famous land went around reading their letters for the enlightenment of less fortunate folk. . . . All talked of it."[46] At times letters contained prepaid tickets, which made the voyage possible for many of Europe's poor.[47]

Eastern Europeans lived far from Bremen, Liverpool, Rotterdam, and other ports where ships sailed for America, but improved railroad systems eased the journeys of many. Some emigrants, eager to leave but too poor to afford train fare, made their way to the ports on foot or by horse or donkey-drawn carts. Improvements in oceangoing steamships cut the cost and the time required for the American journey to a matter of days. Steerage, in which most immigrants travelled on the big ocean liners, was hardly luxurious. Edward Steiner described his voyage in 1906:

> Crowds everywhere, ill smelling bunks, uninviting washrooms—this is steerage. The food, which is miserable, is dealt out of huge kettles into the dinner pails provided by the steamship company. . . . On many ships, even drinking water is grudgingly given, and on the steamship *Staatendam* . . . we had literally to steal water for the steerage from the second cabin.[48]

■

Yet passage on the steamships was a far cry from the unsafe conditions of sailing-ship days, and few perished enroute.[49]

The federal government had assumed total control of immigration during the 1880s, and in 1892 opened Ellis Island as a reception center for the newcomers. As passengers saw the Statue of Liberty and Ellis Island looming in front of them, they were exhilarated but at the same time feared being rejected. The average immigrant usually remained at Ellis Island for only a few hours, however, before embarking on a journey to a new life. Unscrupulous agents still waited to exploit innocent newcomers, but efficient immigrant aid societies were now available to offer assistance. After passing inspection at Ellis Island, the immigrants boarded ferry boats for a short trip to New Jersey or Manhattan. Most went on, seeking friends and families ready to receive them in other cities, but hundreds of thousands remained in New York City.

As has been pointed out, the "New Immigration" largely consisted of people from southern and eastern Europe. Of these the Jews and Italians arrived in such great numbers and played so major a role in the city that a separate chapter will be devoted to them. However, it is important to recognize that, in this great tidal wave of immigration, all the nations and places of Europe were represented. The 1911 Commission on Immigration found in one New York school district, which contained 20,000 of the city's over one half million pupils, that three quarters of the students were foreign born. It enumerated the following groups:[50]

| | |
|---|---|
| Bohemian and Moravian | Italian, North and South |
| Canadian | Lithuanian |
| Danish | Magyar |
| Dutch | Norwegian |
| English | Polish |
| Finnish | Romanian |
| French | Russian |
| German | Slovak |
| Greek | Spanish |
| Hebrew, German | Spanish-American |
| Hebrew, Polish | Swedish |
| Hebrew, Romanian | Syrian |
| Hebrew, Russian | Welsh |
| Irish | |

■

Like the mid-century Irish and Germans, the latest immigrants lived in crowded quarters side by side with peoples who spoke different languages and possessed different cultures. The Dillingham Commission, established by Congress to investigate immigration, found one Manhattan block where second generation Americans of English, German, and Irish descent lived among foreign-born Canadians (other than French), English, Finnish, French, Germans, Hebrew, Irish, Southern Italians, Magyars, Scots, and Swedes.[51] This block's mixture was not terribly exceptional in heterogeneous New York, where neighborhoods were in constant fluctuation as newcomers replaced the older residents.[52]

But all was not diversity; some areas earned reputations for being the centers of a particular group. One observer described how the "Servo-Croatian colony in New York is situated along Eleventh Avenue from Thirty Fourth to Forty-eight Streets and on the adjacent cross streets between Tenth and Eleventh Avenues."[53] Another observer pointed out that although the city's Hungarian population was comparatively small, Magyars lived in "three distinct quarters," the largest being on the Lower East Side of Manhattan.[54] Czechs were associated with Manhattan's East River blocks from 65th to 78th streets. While noting that a variety of groups lived in these blocks, one commentator said, "it is the Cech [sic] who gives this quarter of the city an atmosphere all its own."[55]

Immigrants who had arrived in small numbers before 1880 swelled their migration after that date. The first Greeks, who arrived as refugees from the turmoil of their War for Independence in the 1820s, were followed after 1880 by considerable numbers from the rural provinces.[56] Because these immigrants came from territories of the Ottoman Empire and other regions outside of Greece as well as from Greece itself, the actual size of the ethnic Greek community in New York City cannot be determined. Their number probably reached 20,000 or so by the time of World War I, scattered across several New York neighborhoods; no one district emerged as a strictly Greek enclave.[57]

Poles joined their countrymen in the Williamsburg-Greenpoint section of Brooklyn. The first Polish Catholic church was St. Stanislaus, but as the community grew and spread out, more churches as well as fraternal orders, parish schools, and a Polish National Home were created.[58] Though the Catholic church and religious observance were of utmost importance in the lives of these immigrants, they also eventual-

■

ly celebrated their ethnic holidays, Constitution Day (May 3rd) and Pulaski Day (October 11th), as major social events.

New immigrants worked in a variety of trades, but frequently clustered into selected occupations. New York Czechs (Bohemians), for example, labored as metal workers and in the garment trades, but were especially known for manufacturing pearl buttons and making cigars. One Czech journalist estimated that 95 percent of first Czech immigrants, including many women, found jobs in the tobacco industry.[59] In their homeland women had traditionally worked in cigar factories, while the men engaged in agriculture and in crafts. In America, necessity drove many husbands to take up their wives' trade. One worker noted, "Women could make better cigars than men, and it was therefore necessary that the wives help their husbands."[60]

As recent immigrants, these Bohemians never made the "high end" cigars and rarely ran their own shops. As a result their wages were lower than German cigar makers. Historian Dorothee Schneider noted the consequences: "Because of the extreme poverty of most Bohemian cigar-making families during the 1870s and 1880s, children, if they were old enough (six years or older), almost always had to help their parents." However, she informs us that children left this trade as soon as they could find better opportunities.[61]

The Greek community largely consisted of unskilled males usually from rural areas, but once in New York Greeks worked in several occupations. Labor bosses for a time funneled young boys into jobs as bootblacks, while their elders became peddlers, fur workers, cigarette manufacturers, and operators of confectioneries and restaurants. The worst conditions were those encountered by the bootblacks who labored long hours for little pay.[62] A study of Servo-Croats revealed that 70 percent of the men worked as common laborers in freight handling.[63]

The several ethnic groups published newspapers which flourished alongside the *Staats-Zeitung* and the *Gaelic American*. The city's foreign-language press was truly amazing; no other city had as many and so great a variety.[64] For Greeks, the *Atlantis* of Solon Vlasto became a national as well as New York newspaper. *Nowy Swiat* was the most successful but by no means the only Polish paper. For Russians there was *Russkoe Slovo* and for Norwegians *Nordisk Tidende*. New York's first Czech paper, *Lucerna*, was written by hand and lasted only one issue, but others quickly appeared, among them the *New Yorske* and *Delnicke*

*Listy*.[65] Within immigrant groups newspapers were published for religious, radical, labor, and fraternal readers. Czech social democrats, for example, could buy *Obrana* (Defense), while the parish of the Church of the Lady of Perpetual Help published a religious monthly, *Radost* (Joy).[66]

Following the German and Irish models, southern and eastern Europeans organized churches, fraternal associations, and clubs. Holy Trinity, formed in 1891, was the city's first church for Greeks, and New York ultimately became the center of America's Greek Orthodox Church.[67] The focal point of Greek male social life was the coffeehouse, which one historian described as having air "choked with clouds of smoke rising from cigarettes, pipes, and cigars." He noted that through the "haze one could see the dim figures of card players or hear the stentorian voices of would-be statesmen discussing every subject under the sun."[68] Some intensely patriotic Greeks returned to their homeland to fight in the Balkan Wars of 1912–1913, while others returned after earning and saving a few dollars.[69] The first Serbs and Croats lacked churches and political clubs, so their social and cultural activities centered around fraternal benefit societies.[70]

New York's Arab community, largely Syrian-Lebanese, also dates from the era of the "new immigrants." By 1900 half the Syrians in America resided in New York City. The first Arabs did not arrive in the city until the 1870s, but that population grew to several thousand by 1920, mostly located on the Lower West Side of Manhattan.[71] One commentator put it, "The Manhattan district is the dumping ground upon which most of the new arrivals are cast."[72] Others lived in Brooklyn, eventually the center of the city's Arab community, although they still commuted to work in Manhattan.[73] New York's Syrian population was overwhelmingly Christian and large enough to support several churches, newspapers, and ethnic organizations, such as the Syrian Ladies Aid Society, which helped new immigrants. Male immigrants made their living by peddling, factory work, and running small businesses, while the women who worked were concentrated in factories manufacturing negligees, kimonos, lace, and embroidery. Syrian craftsmen were noted for rugs and tapestries.[74]

Unlike some other immigrants who arrived before 1880, the Chinese did not increase their numbers substantially. American racism dictated the future of the city's Chinese residents as the Chinese exclusion movement, especially active in California and the West during the 1870s, gained strength. In 1870, Congress restricted naturalization to blacks and whites, and the courts later held that Asians were not white. Finally, in 1882 Congressional legislation banned most Chinese immigration.[75]

Immigration restriction made it virtually impossible for Chinese, including the wives of immigrants already here, to come to New York, and Chinatown, as it developed after 1880, was a bachelor society where men outnumbered women by a ratio of better than six to one. It was run by the six companies of the Chinese Consolidated Benevolent Association, dominated by the merchant elite. Life in the early twentieth century for males, many with wives back in China, revolved around laundries, restaurants, and small shops. The men resided in small, crowded apartments in which they, nonetheless, led a lonely existence. Some Chinatown residents turned to gambling and patronizing prostitutes, practices which angered white New Yorkers and convinced them that the Chinese were a degraded race. At the same time, Chinatown developed as a tourist center after 1900, an exotic place for visitors to gawk.[76]

While the period after 1880 is noted primarily for the massive influx of immigrants from southern and eastern Europe, those years were also ones of rapid growth of the city's Scandinavian population, which soared by 50 percent between 1900 and 1920.[77] The center of New York's Scandinavians and Finns was along Brooklyn's waterfront. By 1910 "Finn Town," in Brooklyn already had 1,000 residents, and around 1916 another wave of Finnish migrants arrived. This working class group was "infused with a socialist-labor ideology" and rapidly organized cooperatives for housing and saving.[78]

Sailors formed the basis of New York's Norwegian community. In the 1880s many jumped ship while in Brooklyn or Manhattan for jobs on better paying American vessels. Joined by migration from Norway, their numbers increased rapidly after 1880, although, since they were mostly male, they tended toward a somewhat transient existence. They waited for jobs aboard incoming ships or worked at crafts, such as carpentry, related to their maritime background.[79] Yet as leaders emerged and the numbers of women grew, Norwegian institutional life took root. The community had, as historian David Mauk notes, "gone on land." In 1891, Emil Nielsen began publication of *Nordisk Tidende*,

■

which continues to be published today.[80] Brooklyn's Little *Norge* boasted churches, stores, lodging houses, a hospital, temperance groups, and the Norwegian-American Seamen's Association. Women, who rarely worked outside the home, formed the backbone of this institutional life. In addition to the community observances of Christmas and Easter, during the 1890s the May 17th celebration of Lief Erikson Day was instituted. *Nordisk Tidende* reported in 1892 that at least 2,500 people honored the Norse sailor. Transient seamen were still numerous, but by the 1890s the permanently settled men and women formed the essential core of Norwegian New York.[81]

Among other newcomers to New York in the late nineteenth and early twentieth centuries were southern blacks. Some had begun to arrive following the Civil War, but more than 80,000 left the South between 1870 and 1890, and 107,796 followed in the 1890s. Nearly 100,000 came north during the first decade of the twentieth century. These migrants were escaping an intensified southern racism as well as a deteriorating economic situation and hoped to improve their lot in the North. New York City became one of the main termini for this migration, facilitated by frequent train service from Maryland, Virginia, and the Carolinas. New York and Brooklyn combined had fewer than 20,000 blacks in 1860, but the figure reached 33,888 in 1890 and 60,666 ten years later. By 1910 the five-borough city claimed over 90,000 black residents.[82]

Of the 3,552 foreign-born blacks residing in New York in 1900, most had immigrated from the West Indies. This small group then constituted the largest such settlement in the United States. Most had arrived during the previous decade, prompted by improved transportation, exaggerated stories of New York City's bounties, and poor economic conditions in the Caribbean. Harlem's emergence as the "capital" of black America, beginning around 1910, increased the lure of New York as West Indian laborers and domestics joined with skilled workers and professionals in seeking a better life.[83]

West Indians retained considerable ethnic identity as their churches and organizations differentiated them from native-born African Americans. They avoided intermarriage with American blacks, who in turn considered them haughty and aloof. But like the American blacks, West Indians faced racial discrimination, which limited their housing and employment opportunities.[84]

■

Whatever their origins, New York blacks confronted a virulent racism in the late nineteenth and early twentieth centuries. As the *New York Times* said in 1889, blacks in most cases were "hedged in by prejudice" in the "meanest tenement districts" and in the worst housing.[85] They remained scattered throughout most of Manhattan's and Brooklyn's wards, though some individual blocks or buildings became exclusively black. San Juan Hill in the west sixties became the largest black community in Manhattan, but a sizeable contingent lived just south of the Hill in the unsavory Tenderloin district alongside the Irish.[86] Adam Clayton Powell, Sr., who had a church in the Tenderloin and who later headed the large Abyssinian Baptist Church in Harlem, recalled that on occasion he ministered to "pimps, prostitutes, keepers of dives and gambling dens." He added that some prostitutes solicited "men as they left our service."[87] Yet even in this unsavory neighborhood, blacks paid higher rents than whites for similar quarters, usually two dollars more per month.[88]

New York State's civil rights laws were not rigorously enforced in the late nineteenth century. Court decisions as well as political hedging further confused the issue. Judicial interpretations of the New York 1873 Civil Rights Act apparently sanctioned all-black schools, and the state legislature did not explicitly ban them when it reenacted the Common School Act in 1894. Finally, in 1900 the state outlawed segregated schools. Black children subsequently attended schools in their local neighborhoods, and black teachers even taught white pupils on occasion. However, as residential segregation increased over time, neighborhood schools also became increasingly segregated and overcrowded.[89]

Civil rights laws did not cover religion, and white churches continued to practice segregation. A few black Christians did attend predominately white congregations, but most realized they were not welcome there, and ultimately they migrated to the black churches. When a new YMCA opened on West 53rd Street in the Tenderloin District, it was assumed to be for blacks only.[90]

Job discrimination in the early twentieth century was rampant. Blacks found themselves blocked from training as skilled workers, not wanted in trade unions, and rebuffed when they applied for construction or other skilled laboring jobs. Similar problems faced them when they applied to work in sales or for such white collar employment as clerks, bookkeepers, and typists. Not many had moved into these occu-

■

pations by 1910.[91] One exception, however, was the federal and city governments through which in 1900 more than 400 blacks found employment as clerks. Social worker Mary Ovington reported 176 African Americans employed in the city's post offices, but noted, "The clerkship, that to a white man is only a stepping-stone, to a Negro is a highly coveted position."[92] Manhattan had no black police or firemen as late as 1910, and overall blacks were underrepresented in municipal employment. In 1911, when the city appointed Samuel J. Battle as the first black policeman, people were taken on guided tours to see the "strange phenomenon." Battle remembered children taunting him, "There goes the nigger cop."[93]

Studies completed in 1911 and 1912 by a black sociologist and white social worker revealed only modest changes in the occupational status of the city's blacks since the 1850s. Most blacks worked as domestic servants and unskilled laborers.[94] Black women, more apt to work outside the home than white women, were confined to domestic labor. About one third of married black women worked for wages, some 90 percent as domestic or personal servants. Many others worked at home by taking in lodgers, a practice more common among blacks than whites and necessitated by high rents blacks paid for apartments and the low wages they earned from menial jobs.[95] Opportunities varied little for the unmarried black woman. A small black elite of professionals and businessmen had expanded somewhat since the Civil War, which led sociologist George Haynes to conclude in 1912 that the group's future was promising. But most black businesses lacked capital and confined themselves to serving a black community with little purchasing power.[96] Numerically, the most successful of black businesses, such as barbershops, were outgrowths of personal and domestic service and required only small amounts of capital. They existed to serve a strictly black clientele. Blacks were totally excluded from the city's banking, large manufacturing, retail, and financial institutions, unless they worked as janitors or maids.

The growth of the black population and the segregated nature of New York society did create a demand for growing numbers of black teachers, lawyers, doctors, ministers, and other professionals. Because African Americans achieved a modest success on the stage, vaudeville performers and musicians found some opportunities open.[97] Black composers Bert Williams, George Walker, Bob Cole, and J. Rosamund

■

Johnson wrote a number of popular songs and musicals that received praise from both whites and blacks.[98] However, attention to this emerging business, professional, and entertainment elite should not obscure the fact that blacks were underrepresented in the professions, that black business enterprises had limited futures, and that these black performers at times had to play stage roles degrading to their race. Indeed, as far as earnings and recognition by the larger white society was concerned, to belong to the black elite one could be a skilled worker or a waiter in an expensive and exclusive hotel or restaurant as well as be a professional or entrepreneur.

No event illustrated black New Yorkers' second class status more clearly than the riot of August 1900. The trouble began on a hot night in the Tenderloin on West 41st Street, when a black man, Arthur Harris, killed a white police officer. Harris's girlfriend, May Enoch, had been waiting for him when she was approached by a plain-clothes policeman and charged with "soliciting." Unaware that the white man addressing Ms. Enoch was a policeman, Harris believed that his girlfriend was being harassed, and he intervened. The two men started to fight, and in the scuffle Harris stabbed the officer, who died the next day. Not only had a white officer died at the hands of a black man, but also the victim was the son-in-law to be of the local acting police captain. The racially tense area was poised to explode.[99]

Rumors of violence abounded, and several days later another fight between a black and a white set off a full scale riot. For two days the white residents of the neighborhood ranged the streets, beating blacks who crossed their path. Nor were blacks riding the street cars safe. Recalled one observer, "Every car passing up or down Eighth Avenue . . . was stopped by the crowd and every negro [sic] on board dragged out. . . . The police made little or no attempt to arrest any assailants."[100]

Not satisfied with permitting violence, the police joined the assaults on blacks, both on the streets and in the jails. Most of those arrested were blacks, including some who had purchased revolvers.[101] African-American community leaders were outraged and demanded that white rioters and policemen be brought to justice. A group of prominent blacks organized the Citizen's Protective League, which gathered victims' statements of their experiences at the hands of the predominately Irish New York police.[102] Because many prominent whites were also shocked at the violence, and particularly the role of the police, hopes were high that

■

some form of disciplinary action would result. However, the Grand Jury refused to indict a single officer, and eight cases brought to court against individual policemen were dismissed. The police department set up its own investigating board, whose rules restricted the right of lawyers to cross examine members of the force. The board concluded, "there is nothing in the evidence taken by your committee which will justify preferment of charges against any officer."[103]

Little chance existed that the city government controlled by Tammany Hall's Democrats would move against the police department. Departmental corruption and Tammany went hand in hand, and blacks had no influence whatsoever in Democratic party politics.[104] Clearly racial hatreds ran deep, but blacks, constituting less than two percent of the city's population, could find few politicians willing to offer their support. While some white newspapers criticized police brutality and some sympathetic white citizens tried to bring offending officers to justice, they could do little other than urge police reform or suggest that black voters cast their ballots for Republicans. In the end no substantive changes occurred in the lives of most black New Yorkers. When another riot erupted on San Juan Hill in 1905, the results were the same. Nor did conditions improve after another migration of blacks entered the city during World War I.[105]

Post-1880 newcomers furnished much of the labor for the city's manufacturing, shipping, and construction, and they created a new ethnic diversity. But in this dazzling pluralism, as has been noted, special attention must be paid to the two largest groups settling in New York City. The Italians and the Jews would force changes in New York as had the Irish and Germans before them. Their role in the panorama of the immigrant city will be assessed in the next chapter.

■

# 5

*Jews*
*and*
*Italians*
*in Greater*
*New York*
*City,*
*1880 to*
*World War I*

## i

New York City had been offering refuge and economic opportunity for Jews since Dutch colonial times, first to Sephardic Jews of Spanish and Portuguese origin, later to Ashkenazim primarily from western and central Europe. What the city's Jews could not have foreseen in 1880 was the massive influx of their co-religionists from eastern Europe, which would in a few decades radically alter the size, shape, and character of Jewish New York. Between 1881 and 1914 two million Jews left Europe for the United States, 75 percent from lands of the Russian Empire, the rest primarily from Austrian-ruled Galicia and from Hungary and Romania. Nearly three quarters of these immigrants established residency in New York City. By 1910 Jews from Russia constituted the city's largest immigrant group. The *Jewish Communal Register* of 1917–18 required more than 1,500 pages to catalog the organizations and institutions established by and serving the city's approximately 1.4 million Jews.[1]

The nature and character of those who made up the great Jewish migration cannot easily be described in broad, general terms. Who came and when they came had much to do with economic, political, and even spiritual conditions. During the early years of the migration the bulk of emigres were *shtetl* (small town) dwellers, least prepared of all for urban life and labor, but they amounted to only approximately 170,000 of the two million who were to emigrate prior to World War I. Most of the others hesitated to leave in the 1880s and early 1890s. Quite the contrary, those with industrial skills saw opportunity in the towns of the Pale; others placed their hopes in movements like the Bund (Jewish branch of the Social Democratic Party) and Zionism; still others sought escape and salvation by abandoning their Jewishness and identifying with Russian culture and Russian radical politics.[2] Those for whom religion was of central importance also rejected emigration. They viewed America as a land where spiritual values had no place: "The New World stands on three things: money and money and again money. All the people of this country worship the Golden Calf."[3]

The leading rabbis and their followers never did join the mass migration, but as persecution intensified and economic conditions worsened, Jews representing every other walk of life became part of the flow. By the turn of the century well over half of the eastern European Jews arriving in New York came from urban centers and could be categorized as skilled or semiskilled workers.[4] Official immigration figures for the period 1899–1914 reveal that 40 percent of all Jewish arrivals had been employed in the clothing industry. Among other trades represented in sizeable numbers were building and furnishing workers, machine and metal workers, and food industry workers.[5] Irving Howe points out that some of the arrivals may well have declared occupations which they did not possess in order to get through Ellis Island and many of those who were listed under the category "skilled laborers" were likely to have been "small craftsmen and artisans without industrial experience." But Howe also acknowledges that "the statistics do indicate that the Jews coming to the United States had a considerably better

■

preparation for urban life than did most of the other immigrants from eastern and southern Europe."[6]

Particularly after 1905, intense oppression by the czarist government swept a goodly number of well-educated, politically active and cultured Jews into the immigrant stream: Bundists; radicals of all stripes; Zionists; Yiddish poets, authors and dramatists as well as those Russophiles who had sought acceptance through assimilation. The immigrants of the immediate pre-war years mirrored the changes that had occurred within the Pale. Compared with their *shtetl* forerunners they were more urban-industrial in experience and outlook, less likely to be faithful to orthodox religion, and more likely to have received some secular education.[7]

Forty-three percent of the Jewish immigrants were female; 25 percent were children. For other nationalities the percentages were 30.5 females and 12.3 children. The rate of returnees among non-Jewish immigrants was in the vicinity of 30 percent; among Jews from 1905 to 1920, it never rose above 8 percent.[8]

As Jewish immigrants swarmed into the city, occupying the streets and tenements that had been the domain of the Irish and Germans, Yiddish became the dominant language in a 20 square block area from the Bowery to the East River and from Market Street to 14th Street. However, within this district of Jewish settlers and in the Yiddish they spoke could be found variety aplenty. Historian Moses Rischin detailed the district's cultural geography:

> Hungarians were settled in the northern portion above Houston Street, along the numbered streets between Avenue B and the East River, once indisputably *Kleindeutschland*. Galicians lived to the south, between Houston and Broome, east of Attorney, Ridge, Pitt, Willett, and the cross streets. To the west lay the most congested Rumanian quarter . . . on Chrystie, Forsyth, Eldridge, and Allen streets, flanked by Houston Street to the north and Grand Street to the south, with the Bowery gridironed by the overhead elevated to the west. . . . [F]rom Grand Street reaching south to Monroe, was the preserve of the Russians— those from Russia, Poland, Lithuania, Byelorussia, and the Ukraine— the most numerous of the Jewries of Eastern Europe.[9]

To add a particularly exotic note, after 1907 a community of Levantine Jews settled among the Romanians between Allen and Chrystie streets.

■

These approximately 10,000 refugees from upheavals within the Turkish empire with their distinctive customs, religious practices, and languages were an island in a sea of east European Jews. The majority conversed in Ladino (Judeo-Spanish), but there were also some one thousand Arabic-speaking Syrian Jews and a slightly smaller contingent whose first language was Greek.[10]

Of course, while the various sub-ethnic groups tended to dominate specific neighborhoods, no part of the Lower East Side was the exclusive domain of any one. Also, several commercial streets drew residents from throughout the district; for example, Canal Street became the place to shop for clothing and to purchase religious articles, and one could find almost any item imaginable for sale in the pushcarts that jammed Hester and Orchard streets.[11]

As the Jewish population of New York City grew, the Lower East Side became by far the most congested district in the five boroughs.[12] The area's Tenth Ward, embracing about one half a square mile of Manhattan, was by the turn of the century reputed to be more densely populated than the worst districts of Bombay.[13] By 1900 the Jewish population had risen to 330,000, and the Irish and Germans had virtually abandoned the area.[14]

The Lower East Side was never the only area of Jewish residence in New York City. Though a most impressive 75 percent of the Jews lived there in 1875, the percentage dropped to 50 in a little more than ten years and fell to 28 by 1915. Yet in terms of absolute numbers the population continued to rise to a peak of 542,061 reached in 1910.[15]

New bridges and subways opened Brooklyn up to mass Jewish migration into Williamsburg, Brownsville, New Lots, East New York, Rego Park, and even Coney Island. Jewish neighborhoods also arose in Manhattan's Washington Heights and Harlem and in East and South Bronx. The rapidity and scope of the rise in Jewish population in several of these areas were remarkable. For example, Brownsville's 4,000 Jews in 1890 rose to 60,000 in 1904 and to 230,000 by 1915.[16] In 1904 the Yiddish *Forverts* (*Jewish Daily Forward*) described Harlem as "a Jewish city ... as busy and congested as our East Side, with the same absence of light and air."[17] As the *Forverts* comment suggests, not all of the Jewish neighborhoods beyond the Lower East Side offered significantly improved living. Slum conditions prevailed in areas such as Williamsburg, the east Bronx, and in the tenements of Harlem which lined the

■

streets between Fifth and Lenox avenues.[18] Furthermore, despite the proliferation of new Jewish neighborhoods, as one historian put it, "the Lower East Side maintained its position as the center of gravity, the focus of intellectual, cultural, and political life of American Jewry well into the twentieth century."[19]

Faced with a rising anti-Semitism in the late nineteenth century, German-Jewish community leaders feared that the eastern European Jews would fan this prejudice. They and the German-Jewish newspapers voiced their concerns with terms like "uncouth Asiatics" and "superstitious vestiges of antiquity," and warned that "only disgrace and a lowering of the opinion in which American Israelites are held . . . can result from the continued residence among us . . . of these wretches."[20]

Despite such sentiments, the German-Jewish community was by no means insensitive to the suffering endured by Jews of the Pale. What the uptown Jews wished for most dearly was to see the victims of pogroms resettled in western Europe.[21] However, western European Jewish community leaders would have none of that. They directed their philanthropy in large measure toward getting emigrants to ports of embarkation to America. Ultimately New York's German Jews had to acknowledge that they would have to share the city with thousands upon thousands of their east European brethren. Something would have to be done about the "uncouth," "jargon-speaking," "superstitious," Eastern Jews, and the prosperous, "civilized" uptowners concluded that it would have to be done in the city and in large measure by them. It was not the poverty and overcrowded conditions of the Lower East Side that posed the great problem but the customs, manners, and practices of the residents. These people would have to be Americanized, which in effect meant they would have to become as much like the uptown German Jews as possible. With seemingly boundless energy the leaders of the German-Jewish community set out to accomplish this goal through the establishment of associations and agencies, the largest of which was the Educational Alliance, designed to provide both vocational and citizenship training.

The immigrant Jews resented the patronizing attitude of those who founded and ran the Alliance, and they resented the hostility toward all things Yiddish so pronounced in some German-dominated organizations. Nevertheless, there was much that attracted the Lower Eastsiders to the five-story Alliance building on East Broadway and Jefferson

Street. And the Alliance directors, while upset by the stiff-necked resistance to aspects of their Americanization programs, learned to be less heavy handed in their approach so that, by the turn of the century, they had become more responsive to the interests of their constituents, even to the point of offering classes in Yiddish language and culture.[22]

The result was enthusiastic participation in numerous programs. From 9 A.M. to 10 P.M. the Alliance conducted classes in literature, history, philosophy, art, music, vocational subjects, and more. English-language classes, offered throughout the day and evening, were popular among all ages. In addition the library, numerous clubs, a gymnasium, lecture series, a day care center, and other facilities and programs drew approximately 37,000 people each week.[23]

Where the German Jews perceived potentially embarrassing problems among the new immigrants, they countered with organized remedies. They established the Hebrew Orphan Asylum, the Clara de Hirsch Home for Working Girls, and the Jewish Big Brothers and Sisters designed to keep the young from straying off the straight and narrow. The Jewish Prisoners Aid Society and the Lakeview Home for Jewish Unwed Mothers directed their efforts at those already in trouble, and the National Desertion Bureau addressed the serious problem of Jewish husbands who out of poverty and despair had abandoned their families.[24]

Poverty, despair, and dislocation ever breed crime, and the Jewish Lower East Side was no exception. While violent crimes were uncommon, other forms of illegal activity, among them arson, gambling, fencing stolen goods, picking pockets, and juvenile hooliganism, victimized the neighborhoods and attracted wide attention. Most disturbing of all was the  prostitution that ran rampant on Allen, Chrystie, and Forsyth streets.[25] In 1909 an article in the muckraking *Mc Clure's Magazine* referred to the Lower East Side as "the world's brothel," and the Dillingham Commission reported that three quarters of the more than 2,000 prostitutes brought before the New York City Magistrate's Court between November 1908 and March 1909 were Jewish.[26]

A number of books and articles had called attention to crime among east European Jewish immigrants. However, it was an anti-Semitic piece in the September 1908 issue of the *North American Review* by New York City's police commissioner Theodore Bingham that galvanized the Jewish community, particularly the uptown German branch, to action. Bingham had not only exaggerated the extent and variety of

■

crimes committed by immigrant Jews and Italians, but also argued that Jews had a particular "propensity" for crime. Under pressure Bingham apologized and retracted some of his more outlandish claims, including the charge that Jews, who made up 25 percent of the city's population, constituted 50 percent of the criminal element.[27]

Still the stir caused by the Bingham incident, the reality of criminal activity, and a sense that the Jewish immigrants were generally unruly convinced German-Jewish leaders of the need to take action to bring a semblance of order and unity in the community. Led by Rabbi Judah Magnes they created the New York City Kehillah, an umbrella confederation of Jewish organizations. Launched in 1908, some 200 organizations participated in the activities of its several bureaus charged with addressing issues ranging from improving Jewish education to supervising the preparation of Kosher food products to harmonizing worker-employer relations to dealing with the issue that provided the initial incentive for founding the organization, crime.[28]

The crime problem was the province of the Kehillah's Bureau of Social Morals, which acted as a sort of detective agency, gathering information about criminals and turning its findings over to the district attorney. The Bureau did some good work, but a measure of prosperity and improved living conditions ultimately mitigated the problem. By the outset of World War I criminality had ceased to be a major issue within the Jewish community or to attract much attention from the outside, but the Kehillah itself barely lasted out the war and officially disbanded in 1925. The Kehillah never did succeed in unifying the community. Socialists and labor unions refused to enroll, and many Orthodox Jews mistrusted the organization's secular thrust and its Reform Jewish leader.[29]

For all the attention to the differences between the "civilized" and assimilated Germans and the refugees from the Pale, both groups shared hundreds of years of a common religious and cultural heritage. The Jews of eastern Europe no less than those of the west had a long tradition of communal organization and philanthropic activity, and they lost no time in instituting them in New York. Quite understandably the earlier arrivals sought out familiar faces from their native *shtetlach*. Around these reunions of old country townspeople (*landslayt*) emerged the *landsmanshaft* organizations. The *landsmanshaft* provided its members sociability and a sense of cultural continuity. Perhaps most important, it

■

offered a variety of social services that to a considerable degree relieved them from dependency upon outside charities, among them life insurance, sickness and death benefits, aid in finding a job or housing and, of no small import, burial plots. While these were male organizations, several had women's auxiliaries. Early in the new century some loose, nationality-based federations of *landsmanshaftn* (*farbands*) were formed: a Galician in 1904, a Polish in 1908, a Romanian in 1909.[30] Some of the larger *landsmanshaftn* eventually established vocational or business subgroups.[31]

Probably most eastern European Jewish immigrants at one time or another belonged to a *landsmanshaft*. But there were other sources of aid and comfort in the community. In emergencies family and neighbors often provided assistance. Synagogues, trade unions, and fraternal organizations like the Independent Order B'rith Abraham (1887), the Workmen's Circle (1900), and the Jewish National Workers' Alliance (1912) engaged in benevolent-society activities.[32] As the community grew, so did the number of benevolent organizations; increasingly they were formed along national lines, and some even transcended nationality to embrace all immigrant Jews. With greater resources upon which to draw, they launched projects far more ambitious than those of the *landsmanshaftn*.

One of the most significant of the organizations, the Hebrew Immigrant Aid Society (HIAS), actually grew out of concerns of one of the *landsmanshaftn* for the need to provide burial facilities for immigrant Jews who died on Ellis Island.[33] Other major undertakings included the Hebrew Free Loan Society and several hospitals, among them Beth Israel, Lebanon, Beth David, the Hungarian People's Hospital, Har Moriah (sponsored by Galicians and Bukovians), and the Jewish Maternity Hospital (founded by a group of Lower East Side physicians).[34] As one scholar put it, "no ethnic group quite as thoroughly enmeshed itself in consociational activities as did immigrant Jews from Eastern Europe."[35]

The urban experiences and cultural traditions with which the eastern European Jews arrived had prepared them far better than most immigrants of their day to take advantage of the opportunities of New York City's world of commerce and manufacturing. By 1900 approximately one-third of the Jewish immigrants were engaged in some form of commercial enterprise, ranging from owners of retail shops to pushcart vendors to door-to-door peddlers.[36] Going from one tenement to

■

the next selling notions or hardware or whatever a housewife might buy was no easy task. Multi-storied stairways had to be climbed to reach potential customers, many of whom "refused to open the door, shouting they didn't need anything. Some did buy a couple of cents worth of goods, but with the air of giving alms, as though to pity a poor immigrant."[37] But for a poor man it was a start, a means of accumulating capital. Abraham, who had been a butcher in Europe, "became a peddler on the advice of his landslayt. . . . He still has hopes of becoming a butcher again. America is young."[38]

The swelling numbers of potential customers pushing into Jewish immigrant neighborhoods did indeed offer opportunity to work and save one's way up the retail ladder from peddler to pushcart operator to storekeeper. An overwhelming majority of the 25,000 pushcart entrepreneurs in the city in 1900 were Jews.[39] As for storekeeping, within the Tenth Ward alone in 1899 were 140 groceries, 131 butcher shops, 36 bakeries, 14 butter and egg stores, 62 candy stores, 21 fruit stands, 10 delicatessens, to mention but a sampling of the 631 food mongers doing business in the area. Religious and cultural demands as well as numbers drove New York City's ghetto commerce. For example, in 1910 five factories specialized in the manufacture of Passover matzos. The Jewish penchant for soda water resulted in the growth of firms producing the product from two in 1880 to more than one hundred in 1907.[40]

For those arriving in the city prior to 1905, the best available opportunity to earn a livelihood lay in the direction of the economy's most rapid expansion, in manufacturing—specifically in the garment industry, which by 1890 had grown to some 10,000 firms employing 236,000 workers.[41] By the end of the century Jews constituted three-quarters of the labor force in this industry; six of every ten Jewish workers were engaged in the production of clothing.[42]

Jewish dominance was no coincidence. Possibly as many as 10 percent of the eastern European Jewish immigrants were skilled tailors, and many more of the semi-skilled and unskilled had some experience in European garment factories. Learning to press a garment or to run a sewing machine was neither a difficult nor lengthy task. That 80 percent of the garment factories were located below 14th Street and thus within walking distance of most Lower East Side tenements was of some significance as was the fact that during the 1880s some 90 percent of the businesses were owned by German Jews.[43] Though, as we

■

have noted, a shared Judaism was no guarantee of harmony between German and eastern European, not to mention between employer and employee, workers took some comfort in knowing that in those shops anti-Semitism would not appear and that religious needs would likely be respected.[44] When during the 1890s German-Jewish proprietors began to abandon the garment industry for other branches of commerce and Russian Jews took their places, workers and employers were even able to converse in a common Yiddish language.[45]

The tenement sweatshops began to decline as a result of legal restrictions, starting with the 1892 Tenement House Act. Increased mechanization of production also contributed to moving more of the work into factory lofts. Between 1900 and 1915 the number of workers employed in licensed tenement shops dropped from 21,000 to 5,700.[46] Those who labored in the factories of the primary manufacturers were only slightly better off than the sweatshop laborers. They generally worked a sixty hour week and, according to an 1885 report of the New York State Bureau of Labor Statistics, "the very best workers" were getting ten dollars a week. Top weekly pay for women in the industry that year was six dollars.[47] And part of those salaries had to go toward paying for needles, thread, knives, and, up to 1907, for most workers even their own sewing machines. During the height of the season hours were increased to sixty-five and even seventy a week and so was the pace of production under the piece work or, as it was called, the "task system."[48] Particularly hard times came with seasonal layoffs and, even worse, with economic depressions like that in 1893, when "[by] September it was estimated that 32,000 of the city's 100,000 unemployed were clothing workers."[49]

Garment workers, hardly content with their lot, protested when conditions became unbearable, and resorted at times to strikes when their objections went unheeded. Jewish socialists, with the financial assistance of German unions, established an umbrella labor organization in 1888, the United Hebrew Trades, which published the weekly *Arbeiter Zeitung*. Workers attempted to organize Yiddish-speaking locals of garment workers, bakers, waiters, bookbinders, upholsterers, carpenters, and architectural iron workers, but a true, mass-supported Jewish labor movement did not arise until the second decade of the twentieth century.[50] Striking cloakmakers might accept union leadership, assistance, and even membership, but once the strike ended and until the next cri-

■

sis, the flow of dues all but ceased. So many of these early immigrants, with their *shtetl* backgrounds and loyalties, their previous experiences in crafts and commerce, were not yet attuned to the idea of working-class identity and organization.

The socialists who sponsored the early unions, though Jews themselves, tended to be hostile to Jewish religion and culture, which they believed hindered the promotion of universalistic ideals. Such sentiments certainly were not conducive for enlisting members among the newly proletarianized immigrants. However, the union cause would be better served after 1905. The failure of the Russian revolution that year resulted in the emigration of large numbers of Bundists, who not only proved to be more able organizers than the earlier socialists but also, as Irving Howe noted, were "'more Jewish' Jewish radicals" [sic].[51] Among them were men who would gain fame as union leaders in New York and nationwide: Sidney Hillman, David Dubinsky, and Jacob Potofsky. While by no means religious, these leaders saw themselves as belonging to the Jewish community and freely drew from religious traditions and historical experiences in their call for unified action to achieve social justice—a secular messianic age—through union and socialist activity. Their speeches, sprinkled with centuries-old Jewish concepts of *tzedakah* (charity) and *tikun olam* (repair the world), drew positive responses from Lower East Side audiences. By offering mutual aid benefits through the unions and the socialist-oriented Workmen's Circle lodges, they succeeded in weakening the bonds that tied the immigrants to their *landsmanshaftn*, heretofore the chief competitor for the Jewish workingman's loyalty.[52]

The years between 1909 and 1914 witnessed the spectacular growth of union membership and power within the Jewish dominated needle trades. From this surge of strikes and union organizing emerged the International Ladies' Garment Workers' Union and the Amalgamated Clothing Workers' Union.[53] Twenty thousand workers, mostly young women of the shirtwaist shops, initiated the most dramatic strike, a walkout begun on November 22, 1909. Never before had there been a massive strike of women in the United States. The justice of their cause and the courage and commitment of the young strikers won broad public sympathy and support from the well-bred, college educated reformers of the Women's Trade Union League as well as from members of German Jewish establishment led by Rabbi Stephen Wise. But

■

of all those involved none were more impressive than such youthful worker-orators as Rose Schneiderman and Clara Lemlich. It was Lemlich who on November 22 spurred to action a mass meeting of union members and their supporters. Leaping to her feet, she cried out in Yiddish, "I am a working girl, one of those striking against intolerable conditions. I am tired of listening to speakers who talk in generalities. What we are here for is to decide whether or not to strike. I offer a resolution that a general strike be declared—now."[54]

It was sad irony that many of the women who walked the picket lines in 1909–1910 were involved in an event that aroused even greater sympathy from beyond the ghetto and elicited even greater support for trade unionism from within. That was the aforementioned Triangle Shirtwaist fire of 1911, which took the lives of 146 workers, mostly young Jewish women.[55] The tragedy of Triangle and the small and large triumphs of strikes over a five year period culminated by 1914 in an immigrant Jewish community in which union membership was of central importance. That year the United Hebrew Trades represented more than one hundred constituent unions with a membership exceeding 250,000 workers.[56]

For Jewish immigrant workers, the socialists who so effectively organized and led unions were much admired; the socialism that spoke out for social justice and brotherhood, and often employed traditional Jewish concepts and Biblical references in doing so, was widely applauded. Jewish working people enthusiastically joined the socialist-sponsored Workmen's Circle, enjoying its social and cultural activities as well as its excellent program of life and medical insurance. But, while nearly one-third of the members of the Socialist party in Manhattan and the Bronx in 1908 were Jewish, the vast majority of Jewish unionists and Workmen's Circle members were not enrolled in the party.[57] There is a good deal of truth in Selma Berrol's assertion that "as a group the eastern European Jews were capitalist to the core, willing to endure self-exploitation and privation to amass the reserve that would enable them to become bosses and landlords themselves."[58] Furthermore, in pre-World War I New York City immigrant Jews did not gravitate by experience to ballot-box, party politics. Working-class politics was the arena of the Irish. In 1912, the Assembly district with the lowest percentage of registered voters was the predominantly eastern European Jewish Eighth.[59]

■

When Lower Eastsiders did go to the polls, they tended to support the candidate and party whose positions at the time were in close proximity to their own. On the national level, until the candidacy of Woodrow Wilson, they generally followed their German brethren in casting their votes for the party of Lincoln. The Republicans' progressive wing in particular had proven responsive to Jewish concerns regarding immigration policy and was vocally critical of Russia's anti-Semitic policies. At the local level two political strains competed for the East Side vote. On one hand stood Tammany, expertly playing the ethnic card. In 1900 the Hall's Henry Goldfogle won election to the first of several terms in Congress. The next year Tammany maneuvered Jacob Cantor into the Manhattan borough presidency, to be followed by a string of Lower East Side Jews to hold that office.[60] On the other hand was a considerable segment of the population for whom corrupt Tammany was an anathema and who voted for candidates—regardless of party—who offered clean government, legislation to improve living and working conditions, strong opposition to immigration restriction, and criticism of czarist Russia. Back in 1886 they had supported Henry George's candidacy for mayor; in 1901 they helped elect Fusionist Party's Seth Low mayor; Theodore Roosevelt's progressivism and defense of Russian Jewry gained considerable Lower East Side support for Jewish Republicans running for state and local offices. William Randolph Hearst, a non-Tammany Democrat, considered an advocate of Jewish interests here and abroad, carried the Lower East Side in unsuccessful bids for mayor in 1905 and for governor in 1906. In the 1912 three-way race for governor the Lower East Side gave the majority of its votes to Progressive party candidate Oscar Straus. He was irresistible: a Jew; a Democrat who served as Secretary of Commerce and Labor in Roosevelt's Republican administration; and in 1905, following the second Kishinev pogrom, chairman of the National Committee for the Relief of Sufferers by Russian Massacres.[61]

The real beginning of Lower Easter Side politics, a politics truly of the area, came in 1906 with Morris Hillquit's candidacy for a seat in Congress, running on the Socialist ticket in the Ninth Congressional district. An immigrant Bundist from Riga, Hillquit brought to the campaign the same message socialist union leaders were espousing in the shops, one of brotherhood, of material improvement, and of protest against corruption and inequality. He ran and lost five times. Despite

■

their enthusiasm, his supporters were unable to overcome Tammany's vote-buying and the cooperative efforts by local Democrats, Republicans, and Hearst's Independent League to ensure his defeat. But another Socialist party candidate, running from the Lower East Side's Twelfth District, won a seat in 1914 on his third attempt. Meyer London, Ukrainian-born labor lawyer, received broad community support in this campaign, including that of the Orthodox religious community and the Zionists, both traditionally hostile to the Socialist party.[62] Perhaps this backing was due to a growing realization that socialism was, as Moses Rischin characterized it, "Judaism secularized."[63] More likely, as Rischin also suggests, the voters showed their appreciation for a much-admired labor lawyer and his platform, with less attention to his affiliation with a party which "In an era of reform, prosperity, and a new internationalism" had "lost much of its distinctiveness and merged into the urban progressive stream."[64]

At the time of London's 1914 election, membership in the Socialist party among Lower East Side Jews had fallen to a handful. In like fashion, the Zionist cause had minimal success during the pre-war years. Many considered it a movement of dreamers, too far removed from the realities of the American ghetto. That the American Zionist movement was fragmented and actively opposed on ideological grounds by leaders of both Orthodox and Reform streams of Judaism as well as by the socialists didn't help matters. When the first World Zionist Congress assembled in Basel, Switzerland, in 1897, the American Jewish community of one million sent only a single delegate.[65]

The limited attraction of both socialism and Zionism was undoubtedly related to the immigrants' view of their new country. If the United States was not quite the promised land, it was at least the land of promise. Such an outlook also contributed to the failure of the messianic Judaism of the *shtetl* to travel well across the ocean. Indeed, the impact of urban life on the centrality of religion among Jews during this period was evident in eastern Europe as well, as the core of residence moved away from rural centers. In cities and towns, secular "isms," secular education, and the day-to-day struggle for survival substantially weakened Orthodox piety. On the Lower East Side in 1913, 60 percent of the retail shops and pushcarts were doing business on Saturdays, the Jewish sabbath, as were most of the garment factories. And Friday nights and Saturday afternoons were favorite times for attending the Yiddish theater.[66]

■

Jewish culture was too firmly rooted in religious ideals and practices to permit a complete break by more than a few. A minority of New York's East European Jews remained truly orthodox, but most others held to some forms of religious identity, such as joining a synagogue, attending High Holy Day services, observing Passover or conforming to dietary laws. Journalist Harry Golden's father found no inconsistency between his adherence to socialism and his regular attendance at synagogue: "These people are my brethren; they are the people among whom I was raised, and I love them. Dadja Silverberg goes to Shul [synagogue] to speak with God. I go to shul to speak with Dadja."[67]

The synagogue as a place of sociability as well as prayer was by no means unique to the one attended by the elder Golden. From the mid-1880s to World War I immigrants established hundreds of *landsmanshaft* congregations in New York City bearing the names of the towns or regions of their members' origin and often offering services similar to the ones provided by the *landsmanshaft* societies.[68] Despite the multitude of synagogues, the future of religious observance did not look promising in the Jewish immigrant community at the turn of the century. In addition to the secular outlook of the majority, trained rabbis were in short supply, and religious education was in a dismal state, the result of inadequate facilities, poor teaching, and, in many cases, parental indifference. In 1914, when nearly all of the 275,000 Jewish children between the ages of six and fourteen were attending public school, fewer than a quarter of them were receiving religious instruction.[69]

Lack of adequate religious training was not the only barrier between immigrant youth and the faith of their fathers. Religion as practiced in the *landsmanshaft* synagogues appeared foreign to many of them, dominated by Yiddish-speaking elders and lacking in the decorum they associated with American houses of worship. Reform Judaism was too "uptown" German, too far removed from familiar traditions to win more than a few East Side converts, but when Reform rabbi Stephen S. Wise spoke in Clinton Hall in 1911, many young people in attendance were impressed with the "eloquence and sophistication" of his English-language sermons.[70] In 1887 the city's Orthodox leaders attempted to bring some semblance of order and prestige to their community. That year Rabbi Jacob Joseph of Vilna accepted an invitation offered by an association of East Side synagogues to assume the title of Chief Rabbi. But the attempt to duplicate in New York City the

■

authority such a title bore in the Pale proved fruitless. Lack of unity within the religious community, jealousy, and resentment by many of its leaders, along with simple indifference by the masses, made his job impossible.[71]

The downward spiral of religion in the eastern european Jewish community would eventually be halted, but not by imposing European models of authority or by mass defections to Reform Judaism. Rather, it would in large measure result from significant adaptations in traditional Judaism initiated in New York City and leading to what historian Jeffrey S. Gurock termed "the emergence of the Americanized synagogue."[72] Though its impact would not be felt to any extent prior to World War I, efforts to significantly revitalize Orthodox Judaism culminated in 1912 with the formation of the Young Israel movement. Young Israel synagogues would come to offer decorous services led by broadly educated rabbis able to deliver sermons in English and to converse on matters secular as well as religious. In 1913 the organization of the United Synagogue of America by theologians based in New York's Jewish Theological Seminary marked the formal beginning of a third stream of Judaism in America, the Conservative movement. In their efforts to maintain the essentials of tradition while recognizing and adapting to change, in seeking to achieve "a synthesis of the old and the new, the rational and the spiritual" the Conservative synagogues ultimately attracted many of the children and grandchildren of the immigrant generation.[73]

Young Jewish immigrants were less attracted to religious observance than their elders for reasons stemming from without as well as within the synagogue. There were simply so many other seemingly more exciting, vibrant and, in their minds, more relevant distractions all around them. The schools offered them knowledge, which was highly valued in Jewish culture, and even before emigration most eastern European Jews had subscribed to the idea of secular education as a vehicle for attaining economic success and social status. Progressive reformers and German Jews believed the city's schools provided the very best hope for Americanizing immigrant children, a process involving the elimination of perceived cultural traits as well as introducing new values. As superintendent of schools William H. Maxwell put it, the school, "is the melting pot which converts the children of the immigrants . . . into sturdy, independent American citizens."[74] Children

■

would be taught English, proper manners and hygiene, and receive a solid grounding in the essentials of democracy. Improving economic and social conditions was viewed at best as a possible "by-product of their efforts to achieve a productive citizenry."[75]

In their passion to succeed school authorities could be overbearing and sometimes stumble badly. In the schools of district superintendent Julia Richmond, a German Jew, speaking Yiddish resulted in demerits, and even a trace of accent could bring down the wrath of a teacher. A young Jewish woman recalled an English teacher's response to her reading of a passage from Shakespeare: "I must have had an accent, because she said, 'You people come here and don't want to learn English!' And she really made me feel like dirt."[76] Perhaps the most notorious incident of heavyhandedness occurred when teachers at PS 2 on Henry Street attempted to have students' adenoids removed. It was commonly believed that enlarged adenoids inhibited learning. "When the mothers of the fifty intended victims heard of this, they descended on the school screaming 'pogrom! pogrom!' and the plans for surgery were hastily dropped."[77] Countering such incidents were examples of sensitive, dedicated teachers like the one remembered by her former Lower East Side student as "an absolutely beautiful person. She changed the course of my life. She gave us everything she had and more. . . . And I was introduced to everything that was cultural and good in the United States."[78]

No immigrant group matched the Jews in enthusiasm for schooling. Jewish children were less likely to fail, less likely to be tardy, and more likely to stay in school longer. Jewish parents valued education for more than its cultural contributions. They knew that schooling could lead to jobs. Even their daughters, whose participation in traditional religious schooling had been historically limited at best, were not discouraged from attending public school. Learning to read and write could be a step toward becoming a bookkeeper or typist. Vocational courses in the needle trades were also popular among Jewish girls.[79]

Support for schooling was very much related to the middle class aspirations of the Jewish immigrants. They strongly desired that their children enter the professions or become manufacturing or retail entrepreneurs; many wished their children to attend high school and the City College of New York (CCNY). But during the years of mass immigration, reality stood in the way of educational attainment for all but a few. For one thing, facilities were limited. In 1914 Bronx and Manhattan combined had only five high schools, and though by 1910 80 percent of CCNY's graduates were Jews, mostly of eastern European origin, the total class consisted of but 112 students.[80] But even if more facilities were available, necessity required children to leave school for jobs at an early age. Tradition still dictated that boys stay in school longer than girls, and in large families younger children were often granted more years of schooling than their older siblings. However, very few Jewish students in immigrant neighborhoods remained in school beyond the eighth grade.[81]

The belief that education provided the ladder of success for immigrant Jewish children has attained mythical proportions. But, it *is* largely myth. The numbers of doctors, lawyers, dentists, and pharmacists produced by the community did increase, approaching 200 in the first three cases and slightly over 100 in the last by 1907. But the relatively rapid mobility of immigrant Jews and their children was attained largely through the crafts and commerce, endeavors that did not require diplomas.[82] The desire to learn, however, was no myth. Forced to leave day school for work, the night became prime education time for thousands. Figures for 1906 reveal that the majority of the roughly 100,000 enrolled in the Board of Education's evening elementary, high school, and Americanization classes were Jewish immigrants, and that 40 percent of the students were women.[83] Probably two thirds of those enrolled were there to learn English.

For those who aspired to higher levels of learning, a variety of institutions offered classes and lectures on all matter of subjects drawn from the fine and practical arts, humanities, social sciences, Biblical and classical literature, and contemporary politics. For example, among the lecture topics offered at New York State's "Peoples University" were "The Times of the Roman Emperors," "How to Breathe," "Pictures from Hindu Life," and "Practical Electricity." Lecture series in Yiddish offered by the Board of Education drew 75,000 people a year by 1915. The sponsors of evening enlightenment were as numerous as the topics: the Educational Alliance, the Peoples Institute at Cooper Union, the Workmen's Circle, the William Morris Club, the unions, the Zionists, and the socialists, to mention but a sampling.[84] And enthusiasm for libraries was no less. A *New York Evening Post* reporter commented in 1903; "The Jewish child has more than an eagerness for mental food: it is an intel-

■

lectual mania. He wants to learn everything in the library and every-thing the libraries know. He is interested not only in knowledge that will be of practical benefit, but in knowledge for its own sake."[85]

For information and opinion mixed with light entertainment, read-ily available and capable of access in the privacy of a tenement apart-ment, nothing could match the Yiddish newspapers. Between 1885 and 1914 twenty Yiddish dailies had been established, representing every shade of belief and opinion within the immigrant community: from orthodox to secular; from conservative to socialist to anarchist. Most of them lasted a short time, including the *Yidisher Velt*, established by uptown Jews in 1904 as part of their campaign to Americanize the new immigrants. That paper died after two years; William Randolph Hearst's *Yidisher Amerikaner*, launched in 1904 to win support for the publisher among Jewish voters, lasted only a few weeks. By the turn of the cen-tury six dailies competed for readers. Though they bitterly attacked one another on ideological grounds, they were alike in many ways. Their style was sensationalist in the manner of the yellow journals of Hearst and Pulitzer. In addition to local, national, and international news, their pages included advice and encouragement in adjusting to the Ameri-can urban environment. Furthermore, readers were treated to Yiddish translations of classics of western literature as well as to poems, stories, and political tracts by contemporary Yiddish writers.[86]

During the mid 1890s the leading daily was the culturally tradition-alist, religiously orthodox *Yidisher Tageblatt*, but with the introduction of the *Forverts* (*Jewish Daily Forward*) on April 22, 1897, its prominence was challenged. Within a decade of its founding the *Foverts* had become the largest Yiddish newspaper in the world. By 1912 its ten-story plant on lower Broadway was producing a paper reaching 140,000 readers.[87]

As much as any business success can be attributed to one individual, the success of the *Foverts* was due to its brilliant editor, Abraham Cahan. Under his direction the paper espoused a Lower East Side brand of socialism, promoting the cause of organized labor and taking stands on bread and butter issues. Increasingly sensitive to the beliefs as well as the material needs of his readers, Cahan turned away from socialism's tra-ditional vocal hostility toward religion. The socialism of the *Foverts* was never that of narrow, partisan politics or ideology, but rather, in Cahan's words, that of "justice, humanity, fraternity—in brief, honest common sense and horse sense."[88]

■

With such an approach, Cahan and the *Forverts* played major roles in winning converts to unionism, support for strikers, and votes for Hillquit and London. As committed as he was to the humane ideals of socialism and to the pragmatic goals of trade unionism, Cahan was no less determined to lead his readers into full participation in American life. He spoke out on behalf of public schooling and particularly supported education for girls and women.[89] He explained to his readers the intricacies of baseball, and urged parents to allow their sons to "play baseball and become excellent at the game." On no account must they "raise the children to grow up foreign in their own birthplace."[90]

Under Cahan's direction the Yiddish of the *Forverts* was attuned to the Yiddish of the streets, increasingly adding English words while at the same time stripping away German influences. His most successful vehicle for communicating, for teaching, for helping was the "Bintel Brief" ("Bundle of Letters"), a column introduced in 1906. Through it readers wrote for advice and assistance on a whole range of problems pertaining to living and surviving in the new land. Needless to say, the column had many readers.[91] Abraham Cahan and the *Forverts* were teacher and textbook to thousands of Jewish immigrants.

While newspapers, night classes, and lectures provided educational outlets for the masses, the numerous coffee shops and cafes served as gathering spots for the Lower East Side's Yiddish intellectuals. Many of these eateries had their own special clientele representing a particular political philosophy or cultural specialty. The arguments varied, but the atmospheres tended to be uniform: smoke from Russian cigarettes and an aroma of hot tea and lemon emanating from glass tumblers.[92]

Authors, poets, literary critics—they employed their talents in the service of the immigrant masses and to advance Yiddish culture. Many, like the "sweatshop poets" Morris Winchevsky, David Edelstadt, Morris Rosenfeld, and Yosef Bovshover, had themselves experienced factory labor. Their works mirrored and protested against life in the shops. To the Jewish men and women who attended their lectures and read their pieces in the *Forverts*, they were heroes.[93] Not until 1907, with the arrival from Russia of a group of writers and poets who promoted an "art for art's sake" outlook, was the proletariat position in Yiddish literature challenged.[94]

Street games and street gangs abounded on the Jewish Lower East Side as they did in Italian and Irish neighborhoods. While thousands

■

found sociability, entertainment, and enlightenment at the settlement houses and lecture halls, others—young and old alike—spent their leisure hours hanging out in the candy stores that proliferated in the neighborhood. Dancing was a rage among young adults. In 1907 thirty-one dance halls dotted a ninety-block area between Houston and Grand streets, east of Broadway.[95] A year earlier the movie theater appeared on the Lower East Side and quickly became popular. In 1908 the *Forverts* reported, "There are now about a hundred movie houses in New York, many of them in the Jewish quarter. Hundreds of people wait in line."[96]

Of all the vehicles of Jewish immigrant culture none could match the popularity of the Yiddish theater. The first Yiddish play produced in New York appeared in 1882; by 1918 twenty Yiddish theaters were attracting an audience of two million people to one thousand performances.[97] Initially the theaters offered broad comedies, highly romantic musicals, melodramas on Biblical and historical themes, and "greenhorn" plays dealing, sometimes seriously and sometimes comically, with immigrant experiences. These theaters also produced corrupt Yiddish versions of European dramas.[98] Popular with the masses, the productions were dismissed as *shund* (trash) romances by the Yiddish intellectuals, who called for serious theater. Their fondest hopes came to fruition beginning in 1891, with the arrival from Russia of a talented playwright, Jacob Gordin, and the establishment soon afterward by actor-director Jacob Adler of the Independent Yiddish Artists Company. Adler declared that he would offer "only beautiful musical operas and dramas giving truthful and serious portrayals of life" and would reject "all that is crude, unclean, immoral."[99]

The first collaboration of actor-director Adler and playwright Gordin, *Siberia*, became an instant success. Gordin's *Jewish King Lear* followed three months later and was a sensation. The Yiddish art theater had arrived. Gordin wrote more than seventy plays, championing the cause of "realism" in the Yiddish theater and earning for himself the title "the Yiddish Ibsen," and he inspired a whole generation of Yiddish dramatists, among them Sholem Asch, Peretz Hirschbein, Leon Kobrin, and David Pinski.[100]

The art theater never totally defeated *shund*. Each had its periods of popularity, and each had to compete with such other diversions as Yiddish vaudeville and the movies. But the Yiddish theater, whether seri-

■

ous or frivolous, was unique in its ability to provide its audience an evening's escape from poverty and drudgery while at the same time holding up a mirror to their own lives. The patrons of those theaters were unrestrained in their response to the action on the stage—laughing, crying, at times shouting out advice or cheering heroes and hissing villains. The subject matter of the plays was rarely far removed from what they daily experienced or witnessed, for example generational conflict, balancing ethnic identity with loyalty to the new nation, dealing with opposing pulls of secular and religious life and of materialism and spiritual values.[101] The Yiddish theater, like New York's Yiddish community, began in eastern Europe but really was of the American ghetto, particularly of the Lower East Side, that way-station on the road to full participation in American life.[102]

## ii

The flourishing Jewish culture of New York City should not cause one to overlook the city's second largest immigrant group arriving in those years—the Italians. Italians also came for a better life, but they differed from the Jews in substantial ways. As we noted, many Jews arrived with skills, and a good number were literate. The newcomers from Italy were usually *contadino*, Sicilian and South Italian peasants or laborers, most of whom were illiterate. Italians more closely resembled the Irish of the "old immigration" in their lack of urban-oriented skills upon arrival. While they had not undergone a famine such as Ireland's Great Hunger of the 1840s, Italian newcomers, nonetheless, left a land of much suffering and poverty. It should come as no surprise then that they, like the Irish before them, encountered many difficulties in adjusting to life and getting by in New York City. Poverty, low-paid unskilled laborers jobs, inadequate housing, and prejudice were shared by both groups. At the same time, Italians arrived at a later period in the city's history, and they carried with them their own cultural baggage, thus making their experiences in New York somewhat different.

In 1850 Italian New Yorkers numbered 853 in the city's official count. The pace of emigration picked up after that, and grew rapidly from 1880 to 1914. Unlike Jews, who came largely as families, and the Irish immigration, in which women were in the majority for many years, Italian newcomers were at first mostly young men who often emigrated with the intention of making enough money in America

■

with which to return home and purchase land. In contrast to Jews, who rarely returned to Russia or Poland, the return rate among Southern Italians was more than 50 percent in some years. Those who intended to establish permanent homes in America usually found lodging as boarders and saved as much as they could to bring their kin over. Many married men returned to Italy in order to bring back their wives and children to America. Bachelors often returned home to find spouses and then remigrated. Thus, the early pattern of migration of men ultimately gave way to a family immigration that was so important to Italian life in New York City.

These migrant streams of men, women, and children swelled the Italian population of the city. By 1900 New York City counted nearly 250,000 Italians, and numbers continued to grow during the years of peak immigration between 1900 and 1914. Immigration slumped during World War I, but resumed again when hostilities ended. By 1920, the 391,000 foreign-born Italians almost equalled the number of foreign-born Irish and Germans combined. With their children, Italian Americans numbered over 800,000 in 1920, second only to the Jews among the city's ethnic groups.[103]

In the late nineteenth century the Little Italy of lower Manhattan's Fourteenth Ward rapidly became the city's most famous Italian colony, but it was by no means the only center of Italian population. Even before 1900 Italians were settling uptown. Northern Italians from Genoa, Piedmont, and Tuscany located in Greenwich Village as early as 1890.[104] After 1900 southern Italian immigrants sought housing in Greenwich Village and began to move to other parts of Manhattan and to cross rivers to settle in Brooklyn and the Bronx. By 1913 Brooklyn claimed 235,000 Italians to Manhattan's 310,000.[105] One author estimated that in 1913 New York's five boroughs had more than 25 individual Italian districts, ranging in size from 2,000 to 100,000. In addition, other smaller groups of Italians were scattered throughout the city.[106]

Building projects like the construction of reservoirs, bridges, and especially subways after 1900 were factors influencing the pattern of Italian settlement.[107] Just as Irish men had done before them, Italian males provided manual labor required for a growing city, and they preferred to live near their places of work, for example along the subway routes in the Bronx, Brooklyn, and even Queens. Historian George

■

Pozzetta pointed out, "Indeed, settlement patterns of Italians were often exclusively determined by local employment opportunities."[108]

Upper Manhattan's "Italian Harlem," above 96th Street on the east side, is a case in point. The first Italians to live there were workers brought in by an Irish-American contractor as strikebreakers to build the First Avenue trolley tracks. These laborers lived in a shanty town along 106th Street.[109] Others followed, and Italian Harlem claimed 4,000 residents by 1880. It reached its peak as an Italian neighborhood by the 1920s. Initially, Italians shared the neighborhood with Irish and Jews, but the latter gradually moved out as the Italians moved in.[110]

In the Bronx a small colony of Calabrians, Campanians, and Sicilians developed when Italian workers built streets and railways in that borough and helped construct the Croton Reservoir in neighboring Westchester County. The workers were followed by more prosperous Italians who left lower Manhattan to invest in Bronx real estate. As was often the case elsewhere, they moved into frame houses vacated by the Irish.[111] The first settlement in Brooklyn was located at Hamilton Ferry. Other Italian laborers followed and found homes near the waterfront where they gained employment.

The *padroni*, as labor contractors, also had a hand in determining settlement. They took a share of the newcomer's wages for their services in finding jobs and housing, but some also wrote letters home for the illiterate immigrants and helped them find their way during the early days of settlement. *Padroni* were looked down upon by native-born Americans who disapproved of their promotion of contract labor, which appeared to many scarcely different from slavery. Such activities were outlawed by the federal government in the 1880s and later by New York State. Despite the laws, the *padroni* continued their activities for a while. After 1900 they became less important in the Italian migration process and by 1910 were virtually out of the immigrant trade.[112]

As important as jobs were in determining residence among Italians, type of employment was by no means the only factor. Indeed, many who thought of themselves first as Genoese, Calabrian, Neapolitan, or Sicilian rather than as Italian preferred to live among persons from their own regions and villages. Some had traveled on prepaid tickets provided by their relatives or neighbors, who were on hand to greet them at Castle Garden and later Ellis Island. The *New York Times* estimated that each Italian was met by five others. The paper reported in 1897 that

■

when the *SS Trojan Senator* arrived, the 1,100 Italians on board were welcomed at the dock by over 5,000 friends and relatives.[113] Other immigrants came on their own but with knowledge of where friends and family had located in New York City. Hence, districts existed that were predominantly of folk from particular villages, towns, and regions in Italy. For example, historian Donna Gabaccia has traced the pattern of Sicilian (and especially the village of Sambuca) immigration to Elizabeth Street in Manhattan, a finding supported by the state census of 1905 and the Dillingham Commission.[114] A federal government report in 1908 noted the clustering of Italian immigrants:

> For instance, in the Mulberry Bend district are to be found Neapolitans and Calabrians mostly; in Baxter street, near the Five Points is a colony of Genoese; in Elizabeth street, between Houston and Spring, a colony of Sicilians. The quarter west of Broadway in the Eighth and Fifteenth wards is made up mainly of North Italians who have been longer in New York and are rather more prosperous than the others, although some Neapolitans have come into Sullivan and Thompson streets to work in the flower and feather trades. In "Little Italy," One hundred and tenth to One hundred and fifteenth streets, South Italians predominate. In Sixty-ninth street, near the Hudson River, is to be found a small group of Tyrolese and Austrian Italians.[115]

No matter where the immigrants settled, their housing was often overcrowded and unhealthy. Arriving with few, if any, economic resources, possessing little marketable skill, and not knowing English, Italian immigrants could not earn enough money to afford decent quarters. They took over the unwanted tenements abandoned by Irish, Germans, and others who were improving their lot. Italian residences were described in 1884: "These houses are old and long ago worn out. They are packed with tenants, rotten with age and decay, and so constructed to have made them very undesirable for dwelling purposes in their earliest infancy."[116] Yet even new housing was of poor quality. One scholar reminds us of East Harlem, "Housing stock in Italian Harlem was deteriorating from the moment it was built. Unlike West Harlem, which was constructed with the care lavished on luxury neighborhoods, East Harlem was always a working-class community and the immigrants inhabited substandard buildings from the first days of the community."[117]

■

Danish-born journalist and reformer Jacob Riis more than any other observer brought the city's slum conditions to public view. In *How the Other Half Lives*, published in 1889, Riis painted a grim picture of neighborhoods such as Mulberry Bend. Riis noted of that neighborhood, "Under the pressure of the Italian influx the standard of breathing space required for an adult by the health offices has been cut down from six to four hundred cubic feet."[118] Housing built prior to the enactment of the Tenement Act of 1901 contained too few rooms for too many family members. Immigrants and their families sometimes found themselves living in dark and damp cellars. Not a few, including children, literally lived on the streets. To make ends meet, families took in boarders or lodgers. Sometimes they were relatives, but they nonetheless took up space and aggravated the already overcrowded dwellings.

In addition to their cramped quarters, buildings were foul smelling and unhealthy.[119] To add to the misery of their residents, these neighborhoods had more than their share of crime. Robert Orsi noted that "Italian Harlem was plagued by crime and juvenile delinquency."[120] Sensational press reporting soon imposed upon Italians in general an unwarranted reputation as criminals. Especially prominent were the charges that Sicilian immigration brought with it members of the Mafia and that Sicilian criminals resorted to written threats—"Black Hand" letters—demanding money in return for protection of businesses. Black Hand threats and violence were certainly common in the city's Italian districts, but little evidence existed of a supposed, large-scale Mafia migration to the United States. Nevertheless, charges about the Mafia prompted the New York City police in 1904 to establish a separate Italian division to investigate crime and extortion threats in Italian neighborhoods and possible ties to criminals in Sicily.[121] When Lieutenant Joseph Petrosino of the Italian detective squad was murdered in Palermo in 1909 while investigating possible Mafia connections to New York City, public opinion was inflamed and "tremors of terror" traveled though Little Italy communities.[122] Images of dangerous and violent Mafia and Black Hand criminals also helped feed the anti-immigrant sentiment that resulted in the restrictions imposed by Congress during the 1920s.

Yet Italians also had their defenders who insisted with reason that they were no more apt to be criminals than other immigrants or native-born

■

Americans and that the vast majority of Italian immigrants struggled to make a living at physically demanding, low paying jobs. Kate Claghorn in her 1908 *Report* for the U.S. Industrial Commission wrote, "All classes [of Italians] are highly industrious, thrifty, and saving. They are strict in keeping to their agreements; always pay their rent, doctor's bills and lawyers fees. They are considered very desirable tenants."[123] Moreover, Black Hand activities ceased around the time of World War I.[124]

Among the most fortunate immigrants were those who found employment on the municipal payroll; the sanitation department claimed the greatest number, although the police department employed a few in its special Italian division. That the vast majority of Italians became common laborers is hardly surprising. Jobs demanding muscle power were plentiful in the expanding city and attractive to unskilled immigrants from rural Italy.[125] However, as important as common labor was to Italian males, they found jobs in other occupations as well. The colorful organ grinder was noted by many observers as were rag pickers, those who rummaged "the garbage cans, gleaning paper, rags, bones, [and] broken glass."[126] They also became barbers—providing half of New York's supply—shoemakers, masons, waiters, teamsters, and bartenders. Historian Thomas Kessner notes that musicians were about the only Italians categorized as professionals in the 1880 census. A few Italian immigrants opened small shops, while others attained the position of *padrone*. But the most noticeable entrepreneurs were the street merchants, the peddlers who sold their wares on New York City's streets. Kessner found a few who began as peddlers and acquired dozens of pushcarts and control of vending stands.[127]

Increasingly Italians gained entry into the city's rapidly expanding garment business. Some shop owners turned to them to counter the union organizing efforts of Jewish needle trade workers. Initial employment as longshoremen was also achieved in many cases as strikebreakers. In 1880, just when Italians began to arrive in large numbers, practically all of Manhattan's longshoremen were Irish. When a strike led by the Knights of Labor temporarily crippled the shipping industry, employers looked to Italian laborers for relief. Once begun, their employment on the docks, which were riddled with corruption and payoffs, increased rapidly. One scholar noted that bosses loved Italians because of their "eagerness . . . for the work, their willingness to submit to deductions from the wages, leaving a neat little

■

commission to be divided between foreman, saloon keepers, and native bosses."[128]

Because some Italian workers were used as strikebreakers, they earned reputations as scabs. Most had no contact with trade unions before emigrating to America, and for those who intended only to stay in America for a few years before returning home, unions appeared to offer few benefits. Thus, employers were quick to use Italian immigrants to break strikes or as a source of potential replacement workers with which to threaten employees contemplating union organization.[129]

Few Italian women emigrated to New York City by themselves. Mostly they came as wives, daughters, or sisters and lived within kinship networks. Rarely did the census takers find unmarried Italian women living alone.[130] Once here, women, if single, were expected to marry, raise the children, care for the home, and in general not participate in the larger society as paid workers. While most did conform to the greater part of this formula, the reality about work was quite different from cultural expectations. Because so many males held low-paid, unskilled construction jobs, which often meant layoffs during slack and seasonal times, and because Italian immigrant families were large, these women lived in households that desperately needed extra income. Various governmental and private studies revealed that Italian immigrant family incomes were among the lowest in the city, often below the "essentials of a normal standard of living in New York City."[131]

The rapidly expanding New York economy at the turn of the century provided numerous jobs for women workers. The garment industry was a particularly rich source of employment, and many Italian daughters found places in the mushrooming shops of the city; in 1905 some 85 percent of young, single Italian women were working in garment and garment-related jobs.[132] Even married women were to be found in the sweatshops and clothing factories, but once children came, continued employment was difficult. Yet money could be made within the home by doing finishing "homework" on garments and by taking in paying boarders. The Dillingham Commission reported that nearly one fourth of South Italian families took in boarders.[133] The artificial flower and feather industry, mostly home based, was dominated by Italian women in early twentieth century New York City.[134] Some women began homework as young children. One mother, in whose household two daughters age three and four and a grandmother worked, reported, "We all must work if we want to earn anything."[135] Of course young girls were socialized at an early age to clean house, cook, and help care for younger children, but their wages were needed too.

While the working conditions of Italian men were hardly ideal, with their long hours and dangerous tasks, women's work was no less arduous. As noted in our discussion of immigrant Jews in the garment factories, the small shops that also claimed so many Italian women workers were unsanitary, unsafe, dirty, poorly lighted places that paid their laborers low wages.[136]

In time many within the Italian immigrant community were able to improve their lot. The upward path of occupational mobility was not easily traversed, but many laborers did abandon the pick and shovel for more skilled jobs by the time of World War I. This was particularly true of the children of the immigrants, who were more likely to speak English, to be familiar with American mores, and to have received some education in the city's public schools. Some even managed to find white collar work.[137] Members of the second generation might have achieved even better jobs if they had been permitted to stay in school longer and acquire additional skills. Unlike Jewish parents, Italian mothers and fathers generally were distrustful of the city's public schools, which they saw as, among other things, competitors for control of their children. South Italians, Miriam Cohen tells us, "came from a society in which, given the social, demographic, and political conditions, schooling had little place." She notes further that "if Italian families invested in advanced schooling for their offspring at all, they were more likely to invest in the boys than the girls."[138] Family life was extremely important to these immigrants. They had arrived in America from a society with strong family structures in which outsiders were viewed with distrust. As strangers in a new world, many continued to view nonfamilial institutions like public schools with suspicion.

Moreover, economic factors loomed large. Their low family incomes prompted many to withdraw their children and send them into the workforce at an early age, even before the permissible school leaving age of fourteen.[139] Young girls made artificial flowers or finished garments in their tenements, and young boys sold newspapers on the streets until they were old and strong enough to find jobs requiring prolonged and hard physical labor. "In short, economic and demographic conditions encouraged Italian parents to view their children as wage-earners, rather than as students."[140]

New York unions and labor struggles were on the rise during the first two decades of the twentieth century and, despite an early association with strikebreaking, many Italian workers found themselves drawn into union activity. As we noted, Jews formed the backbone of the emerging garment unions, the International Ladies' Garment Workers' Union and the Amalgamated Clothing Workers of America, but Italian men and women were involved too. The great clothing industry walkout of 1909 found Italian workingpeople divided. Most opposed the strike; some resisted union pleas for solidarity and took jobs as scabs. Yet newspapers like *Corriere della Sera* backed the strikers, and Salvaroe Ninfo, the chief organizer among Italians, said that more than 1,000 Italian workers had joined the strike.[141] Subsequent strikes in the garment trades, including an important and successful one in 1913, won increasing Italian support.[142]

Unskilled construction workers were rarely touched by union organization, but among skilled Italians, unions of bricklayers and hodcarriers and the like were more successful in their recruitment efforts. Those Italians replacing Irish at the docks were initially slow to organize or join unions.[143]

While the bulk of New York's Italian-American men and women still held laboring jobs, by the outset of World War I a middle class had emerged. The city's Little Italys contained bankers, real estate promoters, newspaper editors and publishers, white collar workers, shop owners, importers, owners of large barber shops that employed other Italian haircutters, and a few professionals, among them musicians, lawyers, and doctors.[144] They acquired property and moved to districts with better housing. A house with yard was high on the wish list of upwardly mobile Italians. One immigrant, Guiseppe Tuoti, began selling real estate in lower Manhattan's Little Italy in 1887. He branched out into New Jersey, Brooklyn's Coney Island, and Staten Island. In 1906 he was honored by the Italian government for his success, and by the 1920s "million dollar transfers of property" were reportedly daily occurrences for Tuoti.[145] As we noted in previous chapters, the city's Irish Americans had moved quickly into politics and began to dominate municipal affairs in the early 1880s, just at the outset of the massive Italian immigration. During the last decades of the nineteenth century, despite their

■

growing numbers, the Italians were virtually ignored by Tammany Hall. They were unfamiliar with electoral politics, and because so many came with the intention of returning to Italy, they had a very low naturalization rate. Rocco Corresca, an Italian bootblack, recalled in 1902 of his contact with the Irish-run Democrats, "There are some good Irishmen, but many of them insult Italians. They call us Dagoes. So I will be a Republican."[146]

After 1900, however, Tammany showed greater interest and began competing with the Republicans in forming political clubs in Italian districts. Even then few from those communities ran for office, and only a handful were elected; most Italian officeholders gained their positions by appointment. Fiorello La Guardia, the most successful Italian American politician to emerge in New York City just before World War I, faced an uphill battle to win a seat in Congress. In 1914, seeking election in a solidly Tammany district, he ran as a Republican and lost. Yet in the next contest, by marshalling Italian and anti-Tammany voters, he narrowly won election to the House of Representatives, the first Italian American to do so. Substantial success at the polls for Italian Americans, however, would have to await a later day.[147]

Some Italians, who found both the Republicans and Democrats unresponsive to the problems of poverty and working class life, joined the Socialist party, even though in New York City it was dominated by Jews. A few had experience with both socialism and anarchism in Sicily and took the lead in forming Italian-American socialist clubs such as Brooklyn's Club Avanti. The most well known Italian radical was Carlo Tresca, who founded and edited the anarchist newspaper *Il Martello* and who attempted to organize Italians for political action until his assassination in 1943. Radicals published another newspaper, *Il Proletario*, the official organ of the Italian Socialist Federation. Socialists drew their Italian members from among shoemakers, garment workers, and even barbers; but at their peak they attracted few from this immigrant community, whose members largely remained outside political circles in the years prior to World War I.[148]

Settlement houses, which had success serving the Jewish community, were hardly more attractive than political parties among Italians. Settlement house workers were seen as outsiders, competing for control of the family. But if political parties, radical groups, and settlements made only slight headway in the city's Italian neighborhoods, their own eth-

■

nic associations were more successful. Though not as wide-ranging or influential as were the Jewish associations, the Italian organizations, nonetheless, served their constituencies well. Some, in typical immigrant fashion, aimed at helping newcomers adjust to their new environment and protecting them from unscrupulous persons who preyed upon the innocent. Most notable was the Society for the Protection of Italian Immigrants, formed in 1901. As did other ethnic groups, Italians also organized mutual aid societies to provide death benefits, sickness insurance, funds for emergencies, as well as to serve as social centers. Dozens of these societies appeared in New York's Little Italys. Mostly with small memberships, they were usually organized around men from particular villages in Italy. Many locals finally banded together to form the Sons of Italy, a national organization which became influential within the Italian communities of New York City.[149]

The professional elite within the immigrant community became members of the *promineti*, "a loose confraternity of successful wealthy (by immigrant standards) Italians."[150] Northern Italians also had their *promineti*-like associations, which made certain to remain apart and aloof from their southern countrymen.

In true immigrant fashion, Italians published newspapers in their own language, both of the radical stripe noted above as well as those appealing to a more general audience. Dozens appeared after 1880, and many failed. The most prominent newspaper to emerge was *Il Progresso*. It began with a small budget and a staff of three, but by 1915 had a circulation of 82,000.[151]

Italian immigrants came from a country where practically everyone was at least nominally Catholic. But as we have noted, the church in New York City was Irish-run, and it "differed greatly from the institution that they left behind, although it carried the same name."[152] An Italian priest had been appointed to serve northern Italians as early as 1859, but his efforts were not successful nor was the church prepared for the great influx after 1880.[153] To meet the needs of these newly arrived Catholics, Italian priests were appointed to serve in "annexes" of parishes, usually a basement room provided for services.[154] This accommodation permitted an Irish-run parish to offer its Italian members a separate service.

The Irish hierarchy was critical of Italian parishioners, whom they thought were lax in observance, anti-clerical, and ignorant of doctrine.

To the Irish clergy, Italian peasant beliefs about the evil eye and the power of magic were little more than paganism. The Irish believed that Italian priests were poorly trained and represented the "dregs of Italy."[155] One Irish priest wrote:

> The Italians are not a sensitive people like our own. When they are told that they are about the worst Catholics that ever came to this country, they don't resent it, or deny it. If they were a little more sensitive to such remarks they would improve faster. The Italians are callous as regards religion.[156]

Irish clergy could be similarly harsh in their views of other ethnic Catholics. Cardinal McCloskey refused a request from Polish Catholics for their own church, remarking that "what they needed was not their own church but a pig shanty."[157]

Italian Catholics in turn were distrustful of the church they found in their new country. To begin with, they had viewed the church in Italy with some suspicion as a hierarchical organization unresponsive to their needs. The men, especially, scorned church-going as "women's work." The Irish-dominated church here seemed no better and ill suited to their concerns. Moreover, whereas Catholicism was the established religion in Italy and individual churches often the only social organization in a village, in America Catholicism was a minority religion, competing with other denominations and with other social organizations. As a result many immigrants, particularly the men, did not attend church at all and had little to do with it.[158] Richard Gambino, a sociologist who was raised in Brooklyn, recalled of his father, "Typical of males of contadino origins, my father had been an infrequent churchgoer, attending Mass only on major holidays like Christmas and on these traditional occasions when family loyalty made presence compulsory—weddings and funerals."[159]

It is understandable that Protestant groups believed that Italians represented a fertile field for evangelism. They sent missionaries into Italian neighborhoods and did manage some successful conversions.[160] Methodist, Baptist, and Presbyterian activities included summer camps for the children and other social programs. Yet in spite of these energetic efforts, not many Italians found a permanent home in the city's Protestant churches.[161] In the long run a modus vivendi was

■

gradually achieved between the Irish-run church and the Italian immigrants.

To solve the "Italian Problem," the hierarchy, beginning with Archbishop Michael A. Corrigan and followed by John Cardinal Farley, neither of whom displayed the anti-Italian prejudices common to the Irish, requested more Italian priests and expanded parish activities in Italian neighborhoods. To counter Protestant missions and settlement houses, Catholic charities were established to serve Italian immigrants.[162] By 1911 the city had fifty Italian Catholic churches served by more than eighty Italian priests. Church leaders also encouraged Italian parishes to build parochial schools. While the new parishes enjoyed some limited success in this endeavor, Italians, poor to begin with, were not especially keen on raising funds to pay for Catholic schools when the public ones were free. Besides, the parochial schools were inevitably staffed with Irish nuns who appeared indifferent to Italian pupils.[163] Early efforts to recruit Italian girls as nuns were not successful.[164]

Some parishes like Our Lady of Pompei, located in Greenwich Village, became very important to Italian immigrants. Founded in 1892, Pompei was headed by Father Antonio Demo from 1898 until the Great Depression. Father Demo, who was born in Italy and was fluent in Italian, served as an important link between his immigrant parishioners and secular American institutions. Members of his flock came to him for help in locating jobs, dealing with immigration authorities, coping with the judicial and prison systems, and finding financial assistance. One woman even wrote him for a character reference for a potential husband.[165] Father Demo also worked with Protestant groups and agencies like the Charity Organization and Mary Kingsbury Simkhovitch's Greenwich House, one of the city's most prominent settlement houses.[166]

Central to Italian parishes were the *festa*, elaborate religious celebrations, each associated with a particular saint. The churches themselves and various fraternal orders raised money for these festivals, which sometimes lasted several days. Their processions, headed by a statue of the saint, drew thousands who gathered to honor the festival's namesake but also to socialize, eat food, listen to music, and enjoy the fireworks. The most famous *festa* were the one held at the Church of Our Lady of Mt. Carmel, the feast of Saint Rocco, and those of San Gennaro and St. Anthony of Padua.[167]

■

The gradual upward mobility of some Italian immigrants and their children, their growing accommodation with the Roman Catholic Church, the emergence of a second generation, and the beginnings of political activity all pointed in the direction of acculturation. But like the massive number of Jews who arrived at the same time, Italian New Yorkers remained a tightly knit community on the eve of World War I. Indeed, many were just beginning to abandon the primacy of their provincial identity and to see themselves as Italians, let alone as Italian Americans or as just new Americans. The outbreak of World War I in Europe and the drastic decline in immigration after the restriction acts were passed in the 1920s stimulated the Americanization process for European immigrants and their children. But even then the transition was gradual. Many retained strong ethnic attachments for years.

■

## Ethnic
## New Yorkers
## from the
## Great War
## to the
## Great
## Depression

In New York City's immigrant neighborhoods World War I was both a cause for anxiety and a generator of pressure for assimilation. The city's German Americans did not want the United States to align itself against their native land, but neither they nor other opponents of war could halt the drift toward involvement on the side of the Allied Powers. Before America entered the conflict, New York's Germans had called upon the government to be even-handed in its treatment of combatant nations. Some raised money for war relief in Germany. A ten day New York bazaar sold 56,000 tickets and raised considerable funds for that purpose.[1] A few German Americans, such as New York's George Sylvester Viereck, a poet and publisher of *The American Week-*

*ly*, continued defending Germany even after the American declaration of war. His cause was considerably injured when the United States government demonstrated that he was on the Kaiser's payroll. The Poetry Society of America then dropped a discredited Viereck from its membership.[2]

Following America's declaration of war in April 1917, the majority of German-American New Yorkers not only repudiated Viereck's views, but were actually strident in their support of the Allied cause. The *Staats-Zeitung* insisted that German Americans were loyal citizens and blamed "the German military party" for the debacle.[3] One association of New York German societies offered its shooting range to the War Department, yet even loyal Germans found themselves under suspicion.[4] Given their traditions of achievements in science, higher education, art, literature, and music, Germans had generally been highly esteemed in the country, but in 1917 many Americans focused on other aspects of German culture such as militarism and imperialism. Once war came, politicians like Theodore Roosevelt insisted that the nation could not tolerate disloyalty and that hyphenated Americans must commit themselves to the American cause without reservation. The most extreme statement from a New Yorker came from the Rev. Newell Dwight Hillis of the Plymouth Congregational Church in Brooklyn, who announced from the pulpit his belief "that Germans were genetically defective," and advocated sterilization of millions of German-American men.[5]

Such strident voices stirred the public and helped create an atmosphere of intolerance. The intense emotions with which many Americans supported the conflict on the home front prompted them to view German Americans as potentially disloyal citizens who might aid the enemy. During the wartime hysteria old German-American New York institutions changed their names. The German Hospital and Dispensary became Lenox Hill Hospital, and the German Polyclinic became Stuyvesant Polyclinic.[6] The Germania Life Insurance Company insisted that it was an American company, loyal to the United States; it was the first insurance company to purchase Liberty Bonds. When that gesture proved inadequate, the managers changed the Germania's name to the Guardian Life Insurance Company and began to withdraw from European operations.[7] German-speaking churches switched to the English language or became bilingual; schools stopped teaching German, and the German language press experienced a sharp decline in readers. Even the Metropolitan Opera Company echoed the spirit of hysterical patriotism and refused to perform the works of German composers like Richard Wagner.[8]

While New York's German Americans experienced the emotionalism of the war more deeply than others, members of other ethnic groups also found their lives disrupted; some even returned to Europe to fight for their native lands. Jewish New Yorkers, however, were understandably not eager to be allied with czarist Russia, whose persecution they had fled. Thus, the Yiddish socialist *Forverts* opposed American involvement until the overthrow of the czarist regime. As the *Forverts* put it at that moment, "it is no longer a capitalistic war. Neither is it imperialistic or nationalistic. It is a war for humanity."[9] But for some socialist purists neither the Allies's cause nor that of the Central Powers was just. In the election for mayor in the fall of 1917 Mayor John Mitchell played the patriot and denounced Socialist candidate Morris Hillquit as a virtual traitor for his criticism of the war.[10]

While most radical New Yorkers eventually supported the war effort, a few strongly opposed both America's involvement and its later participation in the Allied intervention against the Bolsheviks in Russia. A handful of Jewish anarchists living in East Harlem printed circulars denouncing this intervention; in August 1918 the government arrested, then tried and convicted them for violations of the Sedition Act. Ultimately, they were deported to Russia along with other victims of the Palmer Raids of 1919.[11]

At the war's outset the city's Irish Americans had little reason to support the British, especially when Great Britain suppressed Dublin's Easter Rebellion of 1916. Shortly after the Easter uprising, a gathering of 3,000 New York Irish hailed the rebellion and thanked Germany for supporting the cause of the Irish freedom.[12] For the "professional" Irish, those who championed the cause of Irish independence above all else, neither the eventual Allied victory nor the Treaty of Versailles, which ignored Irish freedom, were deemed worthy of praise. John Devoy's *Gaelic American*, Judge Daniel F. Cohalan, and the *Irish World* all severely attacked America's pro-British foreign policy. Nevertheless, the bulk of the city's Irish supported the American war effort as did Irish leadership of the Catholic church.[13] They were, after all, Americans of Irish descent and no longer living in Ireland. The "fighting 69th" regi-

■

ment, recruited mainly from the city's West Side Irish, won great praise for its military action against Germany.

The war in Europe also disrupted the normal flow of immigration to America, which was so vital for reinforcing ethnic life. In 1914 more than 1.2 million newcomers arrived on American shores, but during the next three years the combined total was under one million. In 1918, while the United States was at war, only 110,330 persons arrived. After hostilities ended, immigration began again. In 1921 800,000 people, many of whom settled in New York City, were admitted. Then Congress passed new and severely restrictive laws that affected European immigration. After previously barring Asians and passing several stopgap anti-immigrant measures, Congress enacted the National Origins Act of 1924, imposing quotas designed to limit immigration from southern and eastern Europe. The bulk of the 150,000 annual visas were reserved for northern and western European nations such as Great Britain, Ireland, and Germany. Most New York Congressmen, including Emanuel Celler and Fiorello La Guardia, strongly opposed this legislation.[14]

During the 1920s, before the law became effective, about 600,000 new immigrants settled in New York. However, the National Origins system drastically reduced the flow. Since it established a quota of less than 6,000 for Italy, about 300 for Greece, and a few thousand for Russia and Poland, the major sources of immigration for New York City for the previous thirty years suddenly were virtually shut off.

Among Germans, already reeling under World War I's hysteria, few new immigrants arrived to buttress German-American life. The heyday of *Kleindeutschland* and of German culture in New York had passed before 1910, and during the 1920s the Yorkville section of Manhattan and German districts in Brooklyn and Queens lost much of their German flavor. Readership of *Staats-Zeitung* (which merged with another German language newspaper, the *Herold*) declined as did the population of German neighborhoods and the number of their organizations and German-speaking churches.[15] A Works Progress Administration (WPA) survey of *Kleindeutschland* in 1936 reported, "While most of the old landmarks of German activities in New York during the last Century have disappeared in the course of years, enough of them are left to give a fairly good picture of their former extent."[16]

Other immigrant and ethnic groups began to follow the path of *Kleindeutschland*'s residents after 1910 as they moved from their immi-

■

grant ghettoes to newer developing neighborhoods. The movement of people from lower Manhattan to other boroughs was made possible by the ever-expanding city subway system. From the time Mayor George McClellan threw the switch on the first subway in October 1904, until 1940, the city built more than 800 miles of underground track. Over 200 miles of rapid transit were built between 1914 and 1921 alone, helping to stimulate postwar urban decentralization.[17] In spite of the decline in immigration, the city had a plentiful supply of construction workers and real estate entrepreneurs on hand to create housing for its citizens in newer neighborhoods. One historian has noted that the prosperity of the 1920s produced 658,789 new one- and two-family houses and apartments, "a volume of new housing which has never again been equaled, quantitatively or qualitatively."[18] About one third of the new buildings were one- or two-family units, but most were multifamily dwellings. New laws enabled buildings with self-operated elevators to replace the old walk-up tenement, and a surge of construction in the outer boroughs produced tens of thousands of four and especially six story apartment buildings.[19]

Queens and Bronx farmlands gave way to garden apartments as mass transportation made getting to work anywhere in the city much easier. As new apartments and transit routes were constructed, amenities like schools, sewers, stores, and libraries followed. The administration of John Hylan (1918–1925) proved willing to embark on major public improvements so vital for neighborhood expansion. The construction of dozens of new public schools relieved overcrowding in the city's classrooms. Many of these newer facilities were built in the outer boroughs.

Private entrepreneurs also constructed stores, recreational amenities, and hotels. When the baseball New York Giants refused to permit the Yankees to play in their park because the latter drew larger crowds, owner Jacob Ruppert built Yankee Stadium directly across the Harlem River, in the south Bronx. Opening day of the 1923 season drew a large crowd and many celebrities to the stadium, including baseball commissioner Judge Kenesaw Mountain Landis and New York's Governor Alfred E. Smith. Babe Ruth completed the festivities by hitting the first of his many home runs at the ball park, soon dubbed the "House that Ruth Built." That same year, only a few blocks away, the luxurious Concourse Plaza Hotel had its grand opening, during which the governor told an avid audience that the "Bronx is a great city. . . . After seeing this new structure, I am convinced that anything will go in the Bronx."[20]

Smith's Bronx prophecy bore fruit, as the borough's population nearly doubled from 1920 to 1940. Queens went from 469,000 to 1,297,129; and some of its neighborhoods like Jackson Heights more than tripled. Brooklyn's rate of growth, which had been substantial before 1920 was considerably less between World War I and World War II, but that borough's population nonetheless increased. Coney Island, for example, exploded from a quiet Brooklyn resort of 33,000 in 1910 to 280,000 residents by 1930. Manhattan's population reached its peak about the time of World War I and then began to decline; Brooklyn replaced it as the most populous of Greater New York City's boroughs after 1920.[21]

New York's developing neighborhoods after World War I, like the old immigrant "ghettos," usually contained mixtures of people: Irish, Italians, Greeks, Poles, Jews, Germans, and Czechs among others. Yet many districts maintained a distinctly ethnic character. For example, a researcher in 1920 reported that Jews and Italians made up the largest numbers in East Harlem and were culturally dominant.[22] Neighborhoods were constantly in flux, with older settlers moving on to more prosperous sections as the new arrivals from abroad or Manhattan moved in.

While both German and Irish emigration to America had declined after 1900, a surge in the 1920s helped revitalize old Irish neighborhoods. More than 40 percent of America's Irish immigrants settled in New York City during the 1920s, and like the great nineteenth century migration, these newcomers were usually young people in search of a better life.[23]

Overall, however, the larger Irish community was increasingly on the move to more desirable neighborhoods. Middle class Irish had begun to leave Manhattan's slum districts and migrate across the Harlem and East rivers into Brooklyn and the West Bronx before the turn of the century. Alexander Avenue in the Bronx became known as the "Irish Fifth Avenue," because so many Irish doctors lived there.[24] During the early years of the twentieth century some Irish neighborhoods in the outer boroughs were established by laborers employed by the railroad lines or as bridge builders who settled where they worked. Both work-

■

ing and middle class Irish developed the Inwood section of northern Manhattan, Woodlawn in the Bronx, and Woodside in Queens as ethnic enclaves.[25]

Marion Casey has traced the movement of Irish workers into Mott Haven and other sections of the Bronx once they discovered that they could afford the new apartments. As she put it, the "most striking conclusions about the Bronx Irish community in the period 1920–1930 is its relative youth, and the shift to working-class apartment dwellers from the middle-class home owners typical of the [borough's] nineteenth-century Irish."[26] Frank Hanrahan was typical of these movers. He was born in 1915 to Irish parents in a cold water tenement on 101st Street in Manhattan, an overwhelmingly Irish neighborhood. A few years later the family relocated to West 147th Street, another mostly Irish neighborhood. In 1921 his family moved to the Bronx from upper Manhattan because the "father's credit rating was good as a result of his obtaining a job with New York City. Frank's father had entered the city fire department in 1917." The move was also possible because the IRT subway "opened what had been an area of large estates and summer retreats to the common man. . . . Wherever a subway was built, people followed." After World War II Hanrahan moved again, as did so many white New Yorkers, to Queens. In time blacks and Hispanics would replace the Irish Hanrahans in the Bronx.[27]

During the 1920s the exodus to the Bronx was reinforced by new Irish immigrants who settled there initially rather than in Manhattan. For example, immigrant William O'Dwyer, later district attorney of Brooklyn and mayor of New York from 1946 to 1951, went directly from the boat by subway to an Irish saloon in the Bronx, where he made arrangements to find a room and job. His first subway ride was "smooth as silk." His contact told him, "There are several Irish men who have been successful in the grocery business. I talked to a manager of one of them. If you mind your business and work hard, there is no reason why you should not succeed."[28]

Many Irish found housing in the older neighborhoods like Mott Haven, but for the more affluent, new apartments in University Heights and Fordham were readily available. Only 5 percent of New York's Irish-born population lived the Bronx in 1900, but by 1920 the figure was 9 percent, and by end of the Great Depression it was 24 percent.[29]

■

Historian Deborah Dash Moore has chronicled the life style changes of New York Jews during this era. At the turn of the century the majority of the city's eastern European Jews lived in the Lower East Side and in other crowded tenement districts. With jobs and education, they began to move, and in the twenties alone 160,000 abandoned their old neighborhoods. In the mid-1920s statisticians announced the "startling fact" that Brooklyn had about as many Jews as Manhattan and the Bronx together and that the trend was toward Brooklyn and the Bronx and away from Manhattan.[30]

These upwardly mobile Jews were following the paths of Germans and Irish before them. The Bronx's Grand Concourse, lined with new apartments, was a destination so attractive that it drew Jews not only from the Lower East Side but also from Harlem and from Brooklyn's Williamsburg and Brownsville. Indeed, Brownsville, before World War I considered to be a slightly better neighborhood than the Lower East Side, began to lose whatever attraction it had. Its population peaked in the mid-1920s as residents began to seek better housing. The exodus slowed during the Great Depression but rose rapidly after World War II.[31]

Boro Park in Brooklyn was also typical of neighborhood growth. Rows upon rows of modest semi-attached single family homes and multi-family apartments were built during the 1920s. Novelist Michael Gold told of his visit to the "suburb" of Boro Park: "Real estate signs were stuck everywhere. In the midst of some rusty cans and muck would be a sign, 'Why Pay Rent? Build your House in God's Country.' "[32] While Jews had moved to Boro Park before World I, their numbers greatly increased during the postwar years; by 1930 they accounted for half of the neighborhood.[33]

The persistence of anti–Semitic restrictions closed some neighborhoods to Jews, among them Fieldston and Riverside in the Bronx and Brooklyn's Park Slope and Brooklyn Heights.[34] But Jewish builders and real estate entrepreneurs filled the residential gap by providing housing and the networks that coordinated Jewish relocation. Changes in taxes and the easy availability of loans completed the requirements for the 1920s expansion. "The tax abatements, strong demands for new housing, amortizing mortgages, available real estate, reasonable construction costs and timetables ignited a tremendous building boom in New York City."[35]

∎

While the growth of outer boroughs was spectacular after World War I, some upwardly mobile, second-generation New Yorkers sought better housing in Manhattan. An attractive neighborhood for rising Jews was the Upper West Side along Central Park West, Riverside Drive, and West End Avenue.[36] That section had originally been developed with the expansion of the horse-drawn omnibus, but after the 1870s the steam-powered elevated trains arrived and infrastructural improvements led to rapid development. Among the first inhabitants were Irish and German Catholics who rented dumbbell flats along the El of Columbus Avenue, but apartment houses, including the legendary "Dakota," on Central Park West and 72d Street, rapidly followed. While the Depression of the 1890s set back construction, a second boom beginning after 1901 saw the erection of many large apartment structures on West End Avenue. Some Jews moved there before World War I, but the big surge came during the 1920s. As Harlem became increasingly black, thousands of Jewish families fled to Brooklyn or the Bronx; but many, usually the most affluent, also found Manhattan's West Side congenial.[37]

Successful eastern European Jews followed the German Jews to the West Side. Some of the newcomers owned elegant brownstones, but most lived in the recently constructed large apartment buildings. New Jewish organizations and congregations appeared alongside those that relocated from Harlem. After the Great Depression and until the 1950s the West Side remained predominantly an established and affluent Jewish neighborhood. Even in the 1990s, by which time a new, more diverse upper West Side had emerged, an important Jewish community remained.

New York City's Italian inhabitants also began to move from congested slums in the early twentieth century. Yet Italians were not as upwardly mobile as Jews or as financially successful as the Irish. The first Italians to settle in upper Manhattan in the 1870s were construction workers seeking housing away from the congested Mulberry Bend. By the end of the century East Harlem contained an established Italian community, which grew substantially during the 1920s and 1930s as Jews and Irish left for greener pastures. Although less crowded than Mulberry Bend, East Harlem was still a working class community with dirty and congested streets and inadequate housing.[38] Brooklyn increasingly became attractive for Italian workers, and by 1930 it

■

claimed nearly half of the city's Italian stock.[39] Many dockworkers located along the waterfront in close proximity to their jobs.[40]

While European migration to New York City declined following the outbreak of World War I, that of southern blacks continued to increase. During the "Great Migration" (1910 to 1920) about one half million headed to northern cities, including New York. In 1910 the five-borough city claimed more than 90,000 black residents. By 1920 the total was 152,407; in 1930 it reached 327,706, about 4.7 percent of the city's total population.[41]

In 1900 Manhattan's San Juan Hill and Tenderloin districts contained sizeable black populations, and individual blocks and tenements in the city were exclusively black, but no racial ghetto existed in either Manhattan or Brooklyn. Within two decades this situation had changed.

At the turn of the century, Harlem was practically an all-white residential community with a rural quality. Annexed to the city in 1873, Harlem had experienced a building boom tied to improved transportation. Many German and Jewish middle and upper middle class families sought its "genteel" quality.[42] Harlem's fringes contained some Italians in the east and a handful of Irish and black families. A number of the blacks worked as domestics in the homes of the affluent white residents, but few expected their numbers to increase.[43]

A Harlem building boom in the first years of the new century suddenly collapsed in 1904–1905, leaving many houses vacant and builders and landlords eager to find tenants. When the Lenox Avenue Subway Line was completed, connecting Harlem to lower Manhattan, the stage was set for Harlem's metamorphosis. A black realtor, Philip Payton, Jr., organized the Afro-American Realty Company to serve blacks interested in renting or buying in Harlem. Many blacks, jammed into overcrowded housing in San Juan Hill and other run down neighborhoods, welcomed the opportunity to move.[44] Unlike second-generation whites, black New Yorkers could not obtain housing in the rapidly expanding boroughs, even if they had the money.

Whites continued to move to Harlem between 1910 and 1920, but many became anxious at the black influx into "their" neighborhood. John Taylor, founder of the Harlem Property Owners' Improvement Corporation, shouted, "Drive them [the blacks] out, and send them to the slums where they belong."[45] However, landlords failed to prevent whites from moving out, and rather than face ruin with vacant

■

buildings, they rented to black newcomers. By 1914 50,000 blacks called Harlem home, and they were quickly served by black churches and YMCAs.[46] White flight was apparent during the interwar years, but some white-owned businesses remained along with white property owners who rented to blacks. Both proved to be sources of future difficulties.

As Harlem held two thirds of black New York's 300,000 residents in 1930, it became a must on the itineraries of foreign visitors. Black writer James Weldon Johnson romanticized Harlem by calling it "the recognized Negro capital" of the world, and he described the extraordinary black renaissance of the 1920s that centered there.[47] During that decade a group of Harlem's writers, musicians, actors, artists, and journalists produced an astounding artistic output stressing racial consciousness and a unique black culture. Harlem's nightclubs attracted whites eager to hear the nation's most famous black jazz bands and blues singers.[48]

The African-American cultural and business elite bought homes along 139th Street, called "Strivers' Row," whose buildings had been designed by the noted architect Stanford White. A few blocks away was Sugar Hill, which had the reputation of being the center of Harlem's cafe society.[49]

One of the most popular black nationalists of the period was Marcus Garvey, founder of the Universal Negro Improvement Association. A native of Jamaica, Garvey had lived in Harlem since 1916. His message of racial pride, freedom for African colonies, and black economic development found a ready audience among many poor and working class black New Yorkers. Although Garvey's economic schemes failed and he was eventually convicted of mail fraud and deported, he left his mark on black consciousness. Later black leaders echoed his emphasis on black pride and the need for African Americans to build and control their own institutions.[50]

Across the East River, Brooklyn contained New York City's second largest black population. As in Manhattan, Brooklyn's blacks had lived mostly in scattered neighborhoods until 1900. Yet by 1930 the outline of another black ghetto had emerged. Like Harlem, the Bedford-Stuyvesant section had been a middle class white neighborhood of "mansions" which housed a "cultured and church-going population," one of the "most attractive home sections of the entire borough."[51] As

■

rapid transit routes bypassed the area and as the large homes (more suitable for an era when cheap immigrant servant help was readily available) became obsolete, Bedford-Stuyvesant became fertile ground for a black influx.[52] Indeed, whites sold or rented houses to blacks, and black congregations purchased white churches.[53] A few white groups like the Gates Avenue Association tried to stem the black influx, but to no avail.

Brooklyn's emerging ghetto never shared the glamour of the Harlem Renaissance, but both neighborhoods experienced the slow process that makes a slum. The housing stock of both sections contained solid and large homes, but because of high prices it became necessary for families to double up or take in boarders to make ends meet. Historian Gilbert Osofsky concluded that Harlemites paid $8 monthly more per three room apartment than did New York whites, and the National Urban League found in 1927 that the typical New York white family paid $6.67 per month per room while Harlem blacks were charged $9.50. And landlords rarely exhibited much interest in the maintenance of ghetto buildings.[54]

Along with expanding transportation networks and new housing construction. the movement of European immigrants and their children to better neighborhoods was made possible by rising incomes. By the time of World War I, most Germans had moved into skilled laboring positions or middle class occupations.[55] And the Irish were not far behind. Politics had given the Irish jobs on the city payroll, especially as policemen and firemen. For Irish women, school teaching had beckoned. In 1910 three quarters of the public school pupils were foreign born, but the majority of teachers had been born in New York City. Among these pedagogues the Irish predominated, constituting some 20 percent of the total.[56] As Deborah Dash Moore informs us, immigrants before World War I learned from "teachers named Jones, O'Reilly, Smith and Kennedy." Irish women still entered public school teaching in the 1920s, but Jewish women were rapidly overtaking them.[57]

Many Irish employed in the private sector held working class jobs. For example, Irish made up the lion's share of the employees in the private transit system of the 1930s, so that the Interborough Rapid Transit was sometimes referred to as the Irish Rapid Transit.[58] Because many transit positions required dealing with the public, command of English gave them an advantage in getting jobs as guards, conductors, and motormen. Though second-or-third-generation Germans usually held

■

a majority of the skilled craft positions on the lines, Irish men also could be found in skilled jobs as well as in a few managerial and supervisory positions.[59] The Irish domination of transit jobs was hardly surprising because prior to 1940 these were obtained through "political connections"; Tammany clubs undoubtedly took care of their own.[60]

As in the nineteenth century a few Irish women working in the private sector found jobs as domestic servants, but this low paid occupation was increasingly being taken over by African Americans. Irish accents could also be heard in the Schrafft's and Stouffer's restaurant chains where many Irish women found jobs. Still other Irish women went into nursing, a field they ultimately dominated. In addition, they found white collar jobs in the phone company, so much so, that one woman recalled that those positions seemed "part of the Catholic Church."[61]

New York's Irish and the Tammany Hall machine they dominated reached the peak of their power in politics during this era. Mayor John Purroy Mitchell, elected on a reform ticket in 1913, promptly alienated a number of interest groups, and consequently suffered defeat in 1917.[62] The reign of John Hylan for eight years (1918–1925) was followed by that of Jimmy Walker for nearly six (1927–1932); both were Tammany stalwarts. In 1926, at the beginning of Walker's administration, the Board of Estimate, the city's main governing body, consisted of six Irish Catholics, a German, and a Jew. Nor did it hurt that Al Smith, another Irish Tammany man from the streets of New York City, was governor of the state.[63]

Changes in naturalization procedures after 1900 made it more difficult to obtain citizenship, but Jews and Italians were still voting in growing numbers in the 1920s. In Brooklyn, as the Jewish and Italian population increased and as the immigrants naturalized and their children came of age, Irish politicians saw power beginning to slip from their hands. In 1919, Hyman Schorenstein became the first Democratic Jewish district leader in Brownsville. And in that borough's Crown Heights section, Irwin Steingut became a Democratic party leader in the early 1930s.[64]

Yet Italian and Jewish attempts at either significantly influencing or controlling city hall or the Democratic party were frustrated. Jews and Italians did not fare too well in the Walker administration when it came to appointments. Jews, with one quarter of the city's population, won

■

only 9 percent of Walker's cabinet appointments, while Italians, with 17 percent of the population, received only 1 percent.[65] Fiorello La Guardia, a liberal Republican, represented predominately Italian East Harlem in Congress when he made his first race for mayor. In 1929 he suffered a crushing defeat at the hands of "Beau James," Jimmy Walker, the candidate of Tammany Hall.

Although they did not move to the top of urban politics, of all immigrant groups New York's Jews made the most rapid economic progress. Most German Jews of the "Old Immigration" had attained middle class status or higher before World War I. Some of the eastern European Jews, who began their New World careers in the city's fast growing garment industry, within a short time owned their own shops. Others, who had begun as peddlers, gradually opened more stable retail businesses and prospered modestly as did real estate entrepreneurs during the building boom of the 1920s. The stage and entertainment industry offered another avenue for "making it" in New York City. The ethnic Yiddish theater reached its zenith about the time of World War I when 20 theaters were in operation. But it was vaudeville and the movies that launched the careers of such Jewish Eastsiders as George Burns, Al Jolson, the Marx Brothers, and Eddie Cantor. As movies, the radio, and finally the depression ended vaudeville, many of the performers moved to Hollywood to seek wider fame.[66]

Athletics opened doors for a few young men. Before World War I practically no immigrants became professional baseball players, but during the interwar years a handful of Jews and Italians played in the big leagues. Jewish and Italian youths of New York City lacked access to facilities necessary to develop baseball skills. Comedian George Burns recalled that: "Our playground was the middle of Rivington Street. We played games that needed very little equipment. . . . When we played baseball we used a broom handle and a rubber ball. A manhole cover was home plate, a fire hydrant was first base, second base was a lamp post, and Mr. Gitletz, who used to bring a kitchen chair down to sit and watch us play, was third base. One time I slid into Mr. Gitletz; he caught the ball and tagged me out."[67] Among Jewish second generation boys another barrier existed, opposition from parents. Eddie Cantor recalled of his youth, "To the pious people of the ghetto a baseball player was king of loafers." And Irving Howe remembered his father's opposition to his playing baseball was so intense that his

■

"mother would sneak out my baseball gear and put it in the candy store downstairs."[68]

However, not all Jewish parents objected to their sons' ball playing. Some enjoyed sports themselves, while others realized that their children might achieve American-style success through sports. Of the few Jewish athletes who would emerge from the city streets and make the major leagues, the most famous was Hank Greenberg, who played for Detroit in the 1930s and 1940s. Here was a son of the Bronx who was idolized by millions.[69]

Among the most famous Italian big leaguers who learned the basics of the game in Little Italys during the 1920s were the Brooklyn Dodgers' Ernie Lombardi and, of course, the great Joe DiMaggio of the New York Yankees. Although DiMaggio came from California, New York Italians quickly claimed him as one of their own.

Men now in their sixties and seventies who lived in the Italian enclaves remember the pride they felt that one of their own became the great "DiMage." In the evenings they would walk to the newsstands beneath the elevated lines in Brooklyn or the Bronx to buy the night edition of the *Daily News* or *Daily Mirror* to see how "DiMage" or Mancuso or Cuccinello had done that day. And the next weekend they imitated DiMaggio's open stance at the plate or Lazzeri's catlike play at second during the sandlot games.[70]

For Jewish youngsters it was basketball even more than baseball that they loved. Although few could make a living playing professional basketball before World War II, New York's Jewish youth played in recreational centers, boys clubs, YMHAs, public schools, and colleges, especially the City College of New York. The latter produced a national championship during the 1949–1950 season with a predominately Jewish team.[71]

While Italian and Jewish boys played baseball, basketball, and street games, it was through boxing that they achieved their greatest fame and fortune. Like poor Irish immigrants before them, Jewish and Italian youth facing hostile neighborhood toughs quickly learned to defend themselves. For the best, the next move was from the street to the ring. Professional victories and paychecks brought prestige and even parental acceptance for Jewish boxers. As one historian noted, "They were regarded as race heroes who defended the honor of the Jewish people and proved to the world that the Jewish man had athletic ability and

■

was not meek and cowardly but rugged, brave and courageous."[72] In the 1920s Irish, Italians, and Jews topped the boxing championship lists; but during the 1930s, Italians were first and Jews second in producing winners. One observer recalled, "During the '20s and '30s, New York became a figurative ethnic battleground between the Irish and Jews over the exploits of three fighters: McLarnin, Leonard, and Ross."[73]

Using the city's public schools and colleges, Jews began to pursue professional careers. Jewish graduates of Hunter College and the City College of New York, especially women, made their appearance as teachers as early as 1910, and, as noted, after World War I they rapidly moved into positions as public school faculty.[74] Others who received professional educations opened offices as physicians, dentists, and lawyers. However, the growing number of applications from Jews during the 1920s prompted both Columbia and New York universities to restrict Jewish enrollment.[75] Jewish educational quotas were part of a growing anti-Semitism of post–World War I America, and New York City was not exempt from this ugly trend. The immigration restriction acts of the 1920s, for example, were partly motivated by a desire to curtail Jewish immigration.

More important than the professions for Jewish mobility was business. While most Jews remained employees, a growing number were owners and operators of small establishments. By 1937, reports Henry Feingold, Jews owned two-thirds of the city's 34,000 factories and 104,000 wholesale and retail enterprises.[76]

Except for "mom" and "pop" businesses  most Jewish-run enterprises were managed by men. However, within them young Jewish women found employment. While larger white Protestant-dominated firms refused to hire Jews (or other new ethnics for that matter) before World War II, Jewish-run businesses needed clerks to keep their books, manage their records, act as secretaries, and wait on customers. Here was an opportunity for Jewish women, who, in increasing numbers were earning high school diplomas required for such jobs. As early as 1914 one commentator compared Italian and Jewish women, "It is interesting to note that the Jewish girl is to be found in office work and stenography while the Italian girl is found in factories."[77] Around the time of World War I, the same observer summarized data about Jewish girls age 14 to 16: 5 percent were working in factories, 10 percent in office work, and 75 percent still in public and trade schools.

■

Those still pursuing their educations represented the highest percentage of any ethnic group.[78]

Jewish women also found jobs in the city's department stores. By 1932 they reportedly represented about half of their employees. One journal commented that department stores had to hire many gentile young women to fill in during the Jewish holidays.[79]

For many first-generation Jews opportunities for upward mobility were limited. They remained toilers in the garment trade and other working class occupations. Irving Howe recalled about his boyhood in the 1920s that the streets of the East Bronx were "crammed with Jewish immigrants from Eastern Europe, almost all of them poor. We lived in narrow five-story tenements, wall flush against wall, and with slate-colored stoops rising sharply in front." If they were not as bad as tenements on the Lower East Side or Brownsville, "they were bad enough." The modern apartments for the middle class were in the "West Bronx."[80]

As a group, the upward mobility of Italians was less rapid than it was for Jews. We have seen that Italian men and women began work at the bottom, making flowers, taking in boarders, building subways, unloading ships, sewing garments, and doing day labor. Although many improved their lot, New York's Italians remained a predominately working-class population. A 1916 survey of Italian-born men revealed that half were laborers; by 1931 in another survey laborers constituted only 31 percent but still represented the largest single group.[81] Some of the better jobs were on the docks, but dockworkers faced a harsh world of corrupt labor practices.

Italian women in the labor force were also working class. Around World War I, while 43 percent of Italian girls age 14 to 16 were still in school, 40 percent worked in factories and only 1 percent found jobs as white collar workers. By age 18 most had dropped out of school and gone to work in manufacturing.[82]

After World War I more Italians stayed in school longer, and a growing number of both men and women found white collar employment.[83] Yet the situation did not change significantly until the end of the 1930s. Compared to some other groups, progress was slow. Vito Marcantonio, Congressman from East Harlem in the 1930s and 1940s, grew up in that Italian neighborhood at a time when practically no child went beyond elementary school. East Harlem did not even have a high school before 1934. Because his father was a skilled worker and the family had relatives to help, Marcantonio became an exception that proved the rule; he and one other neighborhood youngster attended De Witt Clinton High School, four miles away. When he returned home at night, other youths taunted him with the nickname "The Professor." His companion dropped out of high school after one year.[84]

Italians did run a number of small businesses. The WPA survey of New York's Italians during the 1930s found 10,000 grocery stores, 673 drug stores, and 757 restaurants owned and operated by Italians. Like the Irish, Italians were also prominent in the building trades and real estate.[85] Of city agencies, Italians dominated the sanitation department.[86]

Of course some immigrants and their American-born offspring engaged in illegal activities to make money. As we have seen, crime often flourished amid the poverty of immigrant neighborhoods. For some Irish connected to the city's politics and Tammany Hall, graft and bribery were common and periodically aroused the public. The enactment of national Prohibition opened the door for ethnic bootleggers. One such entrepreneur later bragged "we had a bigger company than Henry Ford . . . and we had lawyers by the carload, and they was on call twenty-four hours at day."[87] Most immigrants did not consider drinking of alcohol a crime or a sign of moral laxity. Jewish gangsters like Waxy Gordon and Dopey Benny were two of the many city bootleggers providing thirsty New Yorkers with their booze. Benny also branched out into labor racketeering, and became involved with the garment unions. His thugs became adept at shooting scabs for a reported $60 cost and wrecking nonunion shops for up to $500.[88]

From Brownsville emerged Murder Inc., a combination of mostly Jewish but some Italian criminals who specialized in the killing of rival gang members.[89] The most notorious Jewish criminal, however, was not a member of Murder Inc. The gambler Arnold Rothstein, best known as the alleged fixer of the thrown 1919 World Series, bankrolled a number of illegal activities; one wag called him the "Morgan of the underworld, its banker and master of economic strategy."[90] He was a member of cafe society, living in a plush west side neighborhood of Manhattan. When he was murdered in 1928, the New York police were unable, or unwilling critics said, to solve the crime. How closely Rothstein was connected to Tammany Hall and New York political leaders was never revealed, but his murder served to provoke cries about city corruption.[91]

■

Italian mobsters also flourished during Prohibition. According to historian Mark Haller, New York City bootlegging was dominated by Jews, Italians, and to lesser extent Irish and Poles.[92] As did Jewish criminals, Italians became involved in labor racketeering, especially along the Brooklyn waterfront, which had turned from being heavily Irish to Italian after 1910.[93] Like Murder Inc., these gangsters engaged in a variety of criminal activities and were known to kill criminal rivals and others who would not do their bidding.[94] In return for favors, Italian criminals also worked with Tammany leaders to win elections.[95]

The prosperity of the twenties had little impact on African Americans, Puerto Ricans (a relatively new group), and Asians. Blacks remained by and large poor.[96] Study after study found low black family incomes, racial discrimination in employment, inadequate health standards, and poor schooling.[97] Even when blacks obtained jobs generally reserved for whites, they often were paid less. Black women were mostly domestics and black males unskilled workers, although of the latter a few had found factory jobs opening during the war when the demand for labor was high. The small black middle class, as before, was limited to serving the ghetto population as teachers, small shop owners, preachers, doctors, and lawyers. Black doctors were virtually barred from public hospitals, and in 1919 Harlem blacks ran only 20 percent of the businesses in their neighborhood.[98] J. Raymond Jones, a prominent black political leader, recalled that African Americans prized a red cap's job in Pennsylvania Station. "For anyone unfamiliar with the economic history of Black people, it will come as a surprise that in the Jazz Age, a Red Cap's job was a very good one in any northern city. In fact, a Red Cap was ranked with a Pullman porter, who was just a shade beneath the professionals such as medical doctors, and such." The job of red cap, he concluded, provided security and a "good income."[99] In short, opportunities were limited and economic conditions were indeed bad in Harlem. As journalist George Schuyler said, "The reason why the Depression did not have the impact on the Negroes that it had on the whites was that the Negroes had been in the Depression all the time."[100]

The appearance and expansion of an all-black community in Harlem (and later Bedford-Stuyvesant) offered the potential for a greater political role. For many years after the Civil War blacks remained faithful to the Republican party but received few rewards for their loyalty. Whereas in earlier days the scattered black population had little hope of influencing white politicians (let alone electing black officials), now the concentrated black community was capable of putting a black in office.

In 1913 Harlem's blacks, frustrated with both political parties, organized the independent United Civic League to pressure white politicians and eventually elect black office holders. In 1917 the League succeeded when Edward Johnson became the first black elected to New York State's Assembly.[101] In the 1920s several other blacks won election. In addition black Harlemites took over the Republican party in that district. This victory proved to be pyrrhic, as blacks began moving into the Democratic party during the 1920s, and Tammany only reluctantly gave black Harlemites much say in party affairs.[102]

African Americans also tried to use their votes to influence white politicians to improve conditions in Harlem. John Hylan, mayor from 1918 to 1925, was the first New York chief executive to hold conferences with blacks. He responded with political appointments, although blacks remained underrepresented on the public payroll. As in the past, the jobs granted blacks were low level. As late as 1930 the city employed only five black firemen and ninety blacks in the city's 17,700 man police force.[103]

Mayor Hylan was also responsible for a few governmental improvements in Harlem, but the most vexing municipal racial problem, that of segregation and discrimination at Harlem Hospital, was not resolved satisfactorily. In the early 1920s this hospital served a predominately African-American clientele, yet its medical staff remained nearly all-white. Nor could black nurses and doctors find employment in the city's other hospitals. In 1925 Mayor Hylan agreed to appoint several black doctors to the Harlem staff and promised that "visiting" black physicians would be given preference as interns at the next examination, a change that did not fully satisfy black demands. Under Mayor Jimmy Walker in 1929, the city moved to bring Harlem Hospital under closer supervision as part of the newly established Department of Hospitals and to expand black medical participation at that facility.[104] Little progress was made in achieving the latter goal until after Walker's departure from City Hall, but, to his credit, the flamboyant mayor did increase the number of blacks on the city payroll to a high of 2,275.[105]

■

In Brooklyn some political appointments of African Americans had been made in the late nineteenth century, and a black Republican, Fred Moore, had once been nominated for the New York State Assembly, a seat he had no chance of winning.[106] But Bedford-Stuyvesant developed as a black community more slowly than did Harlem; consequently, Brooklyn blacks lacked a geographic base to influence politics. Both parties in Brooklyn gave blacks a few patronage jobs, but little else. Brooklyn blacks had to wait until the 1940s for a greater say in that borough's political life; black politics in Kings County remained the "politics of invisibility."[107]

Like blacks, Puerto Ricans, who after 1917 as American citizens had the right of unrestricted migration to the United States, did not find much opportunity for advancement in New York City. They became a ghettoized population laboring largely in unskilled jobs. Only a few Puerto Ricans had settled in the city in the late nineteenth century, but it was there that political exiles had formed the first Puerto Rican organizations dedicated to the overthrown of Spanish rule.[108] Puerto Rican migration increased when the United States annexed the island after defeating Spain in the Spanish-America War. A Puerto Rican *barrio* emerged in East Harlem, which had listed its first Puerto Ricans as early as 1890; the 1920 census counted 7,364 persons of Puerto Rican birth in the city. During the 1920s thousands of other islanders left for New York, and in 1930 the New York Health Department reported nearly 45,000 Puerto Ricans in the city. Migration slowed during the Great Depression, and it practically stopped during World War II.[109]

Among the first Puerto Rican migrants were cigar makers, most of whom were literate and attracted to left wing politics. During World War I many Puerto Ricans found employment in the Brooklyn Navy Yard and filtered into the nearby Fort Greene area of the borough. Migration of the 1920s was primarily of skilled or semiskilled urban workers who took the often run down apartments of Jews and later Italians who were leaving East Harlem for newer housing. Many worked outside of the neighborhood, but East Harlem's *El Barrio* soon contained a number of Puerto Rican theaters, fraternal orders, political clubs, and churches. Holy Agony, the first Roman Catholic Church catering to them, opened there in 1930.[110] Although the total number of Puerto Ricans was relatively small at the outset of the Great Depression, the foundations for the large post-World War II migration had been laid.

■

New York's Asian population remained largely insulated from the city's other ethnic groups and scarcely felt the prosperity of the 1920s. Chinatown had been shaped by the racist immigration restriction acts, and only a few merchants could bring their wives or "paper sons," to America. Chinatown remained a lonely and isolated bachelor society, with six men for every woman. After 1900 the area did attract tourists, whose guides told lurid tales of "opium dens," prostitutes and tong murders by "hatchet men." Chinatown, dominated by the Chinese Consolidated Benevolent Association, did have tong wars, prostitution, gambling, and gang fighting, but their impact was overdramatized and the violence generally ended by the 1930s.[111]

Because of the immigration laws, the city's Chinese population numbered only 12,000 in 1940, although a WPA survey insisted its true size was several times the official figure.[112] About half of the Chinese lived and worked in Chinatown with the others scattered throughout the city. The latter mostly ran the ubiquitous Chinese hand laundries, estimated to number from 7,000 to 8,000 by 1930. The hand laundry was one of the few occupations open to Chinese settlers, but it required long, lonely hours for its workers to eke out a living. Most Chinese males in New York were not involved in tong wars but in a struggle to make a living running shops, restaurants, and hand laundries.[113]

Other Asians were present in minuscule numbers. Japanese immigration was unrestricted until the Gentlemen's Agreement of 1907 and the Nationa Origins Act of 1924, which contained a provision totally barring further Asian immigration. But most Japanese immigrants had settled in the West or in Hawaii, and New York claimed only a few thousand, mostly males, on the eve of the Great Depression. In the 1890s the Japanese New Yorkers had generally settled in Brooklyn near the Navy Yard, where they found employment as kitchen workers, stewards, mess-boys, or cooks in the yard or on battleships. A number of Manhattan's Japanese were also in food service, but a few others worked for the Japanese government or businesses or ran their own independent small enterprises. Among the latter were operators of amusement concessions at Brooklyn's Coney Island. On the whole these jobs did not pay high wages, and the Japanese community thus lived a marginal existence. Although the city contained no Japan Town, it did support several Japanese churches, and many Japanese workers congregated in boarding houses.[114]

■

Korea, as a possession of Japan, was also affected by the immigration restrictions imposed on the latter. The WPA study found about 200 Koreans in the city during the 1930s, most of whom were domestic or restaurant workers.[115] A small number of Filipinos and Asian Indians had also settled in New York, either in Manhattan or Brooklyn. Indian immigrants formed a Pan Aryan Association and an Indo-American Association, both of which focused on ending British rule in the homeland.[116] Filipinos apparently worked as sailors or as nonskilled laborers and lived by the docks of South Brooklyn.[117] The WPA study even located a colony of Indonesians in Brooklyn, commenting that other Brooklynites did not "even know of their existence."[118] Like many other Asians they worked at domestic service jobs, washing dishes in restaurants or employed as "pin boys" in local bowling alleys.[119]

The social mobility of European immigrants and their children and their movement into more upscale neighborhoods undoubtedly weakened the cohesiveness of the city's ethnic communities. Many of the immigrants themselves became citizens during the periodic "Americanization" drives, and growing numbers participated in the city politics. The second and third generations began to take on American customs and to speak only English. The WPA guide believed that

> whatever may separate the Italian-American from the rest of his fellow citizens disappears in the third generation. There are now growing up in New York's schools alone 300 thousand "Italian" children, most of them the offspring of second-generation Italian-Americans. To them the country of their grandparents will be a distant, almost unreal memory. . . . They will no longer be bi-lingual like their parents or their more advanced grandparents, and they will disappear in that countless mass of native Americans whose origin it is as difficult to establish as it is to trace the streams whose waters have flowed into the ocean.[120]

Yet the old neighborhoods, while losing population, still held onto many and received some new immigrants during the 1920s. The Lower East Side continued to house a large Jewish population and many Jewish institutions. The Yiddish *Forverts* was published there; fraternal and mutual benefit societies catered to their members' needs, and the immigrant theater, shops, synagogues, and restaurants served their clientele. Irving Howe's East Bronx "was still a self-contained little world," in which "Yiddish was spoken everywhere. The English of the young, if

■

unmarred by accent, had its own intonation, the stumbling melody of immigrant speech. . . . At the corner newsstands . . . the *Forward*, sold about as well as the *News* and *Mirror*, the two-cent tabloids with crime stories, pictures, gossip."[121]

Studies of New York's Jewish population during the interwar years describe a changing but persistent Jewish culture. The city's Orthodox represented only a minority of its Jews, but the 1920s and 1930s marked the "heyday of New York's Orthodox," according to Jenna Joselit.[122] As the more prosperous Orthodox Jews left the Lower East Side after 1900 and settled in middle class neighborhoods, they established Orthodox centers in the Upper West Side of Manhattan, in Boro Park and Williamsburg in Brooklyn, and in the Bronx, which combined ancient ritual with modern middle class trappings. Synagogues grew larger and more elaborate as did the *mikvahs*, the ritual baths. Before World War I the forty *mikvahs* on the Lower East Side had been condemned by city officials as a "menace" to health. Most were nothing more than "rusty tanks located in the basements of immigrant Jewish neighborhoods." But the modern Orthodox built model *mikvahs* that combined sanitation with ritual.[123]

English-language sermons became standard after World War I, and English prayers often supplemented Hebrew in Orthodox as well as in Conservative and Reform synagogues. Since organizational life was built around men's and women's clubs, rabbis encouraged women to participate more actively in the life of the community as well as to make a proper Orthodox home. Finally, Orthodox communities began to emphasize Jewish day schools and afternoon Hebrew schools. The day school, or yeshiva, "bore little resemblance to its predecessor" since it emphasized secular as much as religious education.[124]

All of these aspects of modern orthodoxy sought an accommodation with secular, middle class American culture. After World War II that accommodation would come under attack, this time from the refugees of the 1930s and survivors of the Holocaust who tended to be hostile toward modernity. Indeed, one European rabbi would declare in 1956 that there were three dangers to the development of a "pure and enduring orthodoxy." They were Reform Judaism, Conservative Judaism, and the modern Orthodox.[125]

In a second study, Deborah Dash Moore notes that the Bronx's Grand Concourse "did not forget its Jewishness in the pursuit of middle-class security."[126] Intense synagogue building among all the major branches of Judaism occurred during the 1920s, along with expansion of other Jewish organizations, such as the Jewish community centers and YMHAs. But the new synagogue centers became the main expression of the second generation. They contained athletic facilities and schools as well as sanctuaries for prayer. Jewish philanthropy, which had been the preserve of the wealthy German Jews, was reconstructed after the war into a modern communal-wide endeavor.[127]

The Italians of Mulberry Bend, Greenwich Village, and East Harlem also maintained a strong ethnic culture. Robert Orsi has described the *festa* of the Madonna of 115th Street in Italian East Harlem during these years as an intense expression of popular religion, a *festa* that was a "sacred theater of a community like Italian Harlem." After weeks of preparation, each July 16th the *festa* began in front of the Church of Our Lady of Mount Carmel. Thousands jammed the streets of this already overcrowded neighborhood to find security and meaning in the immigrant drama.[128]

Often Italian-American dramas were played out on the stage. During the interwar years dozens of Italian theater groups performed before thousands of their countrymen. One of the most famous was the Gennaro Gardenia Company, which lasted for more than forty years. These troupes offered Italian actors roles not available in the mainline Broadway theaters. Vincent Sardi, of the family that founded the famous Sardi's Restaurant in 1921, recalled that when he played a street urchin in a Broadway show in 1925, he was billed as the "Little Wop."[129]

In the years following World War I the Catholic church, though still dominated by Irish clergy under Patrick Cardinal Hayes, had some success in recruiting Italian women as nuns and employing them as teachers in Italian parish schools. It also recruited more Italian priests both from Italy and New York and built a number churches and schools in Italian neighborhoods.[130]

A surge of Irish immigration in the 1920s, numbering about 17,000, helped to invigorate the New York Irish community. Newcomers with musical talent had no trouble finding jobs in flourishing Irish bars, restaurants, and clubs. The development of radio gave them opportunities to perform before even larger Irish-American audiences. Irish sports were also popular; in 1928 the Gaelic Athletic Association began to build a stadium in the Bronx for Irish football and hurling.[131]

■

Among smaller groups ethnic culture also remained strong. The Norwegians of Brooklyn, originally part of a seamen's community, had declined in numbers, but during the 1920s a substantial Norwegian immigration provided reinforcements. Most Brooklyn Norwegians remained employed in the shipping and building trades. The tie to maritime industry held the community together as did Lutheran churches and *Nordisk Tidende* (Norse News), the leading Norwegian newspaper on the East Coast.[132] The Finns, who had followed Norwegians to Brooklyn and congregated in the Sunset Park section, also published a newspaper, *New York Utiset* (New York News). The small Finnish community maintained several women's organizations, a Finnish Aid Society, and several co-ops.[133]

The immigration restriction acts of the 1920s drastically cut southern and eastern European immigration, yet the WPA's *New York Panorama* of 1938 located many thriving neighborhoods of southern and eastern European background. It found about 80,000 Ukrainians, including 5,000 exiles from the Communist revolution in the Soviet Union who had settled in upper Manhattan in the early 1920s.[134]

New York City also contained the nation's largest number of Greeks, who lived in three different Manhattan neighborhoods. The city's Greeks operated a day school and supported several Greek Orthodox churches. Greeks, like Jews and Italians, maintained theatrical troupes and a variety of fraternal organizations.[135]

Among the other eastern Europeans were Romanians, Hungarians, Czechoslovaks, Slavs from Yugoslavia, Estonians, Lithuanians, and Letts. These groups supported restaurants, churches, day schools, bookstores, importing shops, and newspapers. Some newspapers like the Hungarian *Amerikai Magyar Nepszava* were published daily, while others appeared weekly. The Elore Hungarian Players provided a taste of Budapest theater in New York City.[136]

The continuity of strong ethnic neighborhoods and organizational life made the era appear one of contrasts. On the one hand greater opportunity for European immigrants gave them the chance to leave their ghettos and become ethnic Americans rather than immigrants. On the other hand, they did not feel totally American or wish to totally cut free from their roots, even if their children often did. The children especially looked forward to continued prosperity and a chance to achieve the American dream. After all, they lived in the town of Jimmy

■

Walker, who rose from the streets to dominate city hall. His world was, in biographer Tom Kessner's words, "the sparkling mecca of the polished rich."[137] It was the glittering world of the 1920s, with its high spending, titillating night life and wild speculation. Walker, the writer of the popular song "Will You Love Me In September as You Do in May?," was a stylish dresser with a show girl mistress, who in the eyes of many symbolized the times. That world died with the Great Depression. When the crash came in 1929, Walker quickly seemed sadly in over his head, unable to cope or reassure New Yorkers faced with a deteriorating economy.

*A Time
of Trial:
New Yorkers
During
the Great
Depression
and World
War II*

The Great Depression had a significant impact upon immigration and upon ethnic and non-white New Yorkers. With so many people out of work during the early 1930s, few Europeans looked to America as the land of golden opportunity. After 1935 the spread of fascism made many Europeans desperate to seek a haven despite economic conditions in the city, but America's restrictive immigration policies were tightly enforced. As a result only approximately 100,000 immigrants settled in New York during the 1930s. Nor did many Puerto Ricans journey to the depression-ridden city. American blacks continued to migrate north but only because conditions for them were so appalling in the rural South. Caribbean immigration virtually stopped during the

1930s, and some West Indian New Yorkers returned to their home islands.

Among the Jews and other victims of Nazi persecution who succeeded in gaining entry visas to the United States were distinguished artists, musicians, scholars, and intellectuals. The New School for Social Research, originally founded as a university for adult education, responded by creating "a university for exiles." Under the leadership of Alvin Johnson, the New School hired dozens of refugee scholars, chiefly Germans, and helped find places for others.[1] Most of these immigrant intellectuals did not associate with New York's ethnic communities, but some Jews among them did. Of the German-Jewish refugees who did escape to America from 1938 to 1940, several thousand settled in the Washington Heights area of upper Manhattan where they maintained a distinct community of exiles into the 1960s. Mostly middle or upper class, in the professional, business, or white collar occupations, their adjustment to New York was not easy, and some professionals had to change careers to survive. They published their own newspaper, *Aufbau*, and organized several German-Jewish social and cultural groups. In contrast to the nineteenth century German-Jewish immigrants, many of these newcomers were Orthodox.[2]

Henry Kissinger, future secretary of state, was one of those German-Jewish refugees. His father found little demand in depression New York for his occupation as a teacher. After sporadic work for two years, he got "a low-paying job as a bookkeeper at a factory owned by friends from Germany." Fortunately, Kissinger's mother was able to gain employment and help support the family.[3] Like other Orthodox German families, the Kissingers belonged to Congregation K'hal Adath Jeshurun, whose rabbi had headed the yeshiva in Frankfurt.[4]

The Great Depression battered nearly all New Yorkers, especially in the early years. Lines of unemployed men and women patiently waited for handouts at soup kitchens, while nearby stood apple sellers. In Central and Riverside parks and vacant city lots the unemployed and homeless lived in pockets of shacks called "Hoovervilles." One historian reported that on a single day in January 1931, 85,000 people "waited for free meals at eighty-one locations in front of churches, the Salvation Army, and other charitable institutions."[5] In 1930 the Municipal Lodging House in the city provided more than 400,000 lodgings and one million meals for homeless men and women, and the next year

■

both figures doubled.[6] About one fourth of New York's workers were unemployed by 1933.

The economic collapse affected some workers more than others. Manufacturing and mechanical industries were especially devastated. By 1934 more than one third of workers in those occupations were on relief. The building industry was also hard hit. The construction of offices, homes, and apartments was curtailed, and the middle class dreams of many New Yorkers were put on hold. Despite depression-era projects connecting the city and the suburbs (the George Washington Bridge in 1931, the Lincoln Tunnel in 1937), the rate of suburban growth declined from the pace of the 1920s. The completion of the Triborough Bridge in 1936 and the Queens-Midtown Tunnel in 1940 augured increased development of the outer boroughs, but many Manhattan residents simply could not afford to move, and here too the rate of growth declined.

Unskilled laborers in manufacturing and construction, mainly Italians, Poles, and to a lesser extent Irish, Germans, and Jews, suffered more than all but blacks. In lower Manhattan's Little Italy, 16.5 percent of the families had no adult wage earner in 1930. Two years later the figure was 47.6 percent.[7] Uptown, Robert Orsi noted, "The residents of Italian Harlem did not need outside researchers and statisticians to inform them about the plight of their community. They could see Italian Harlem crumbling around them; they inhabited its primitive housing and walked its dangerous streets." He quoted one social worker as saying, "Evictions were going on right and left. Landlords not being able to collect their rent were putting people on the streets."[8]

New York's Jewish industrial workers experienced similar difficulties. The Federation of Jewish Philanthropies concluded after a study conducted in 1930 that "the normal absorption of Jews within the American economic structure is now practically impossible."[9] Alfred Kazin, who grew up in Brownsville during the 1930s, recalled, "From the early 'thirties on, my father [a painter] could never be sure in advance of a week's work.... It puzzled me greatly when I came to read in books that Jews are a shrewd people particularly given to commerce and banking, for all the Jews I knew had managed to be an exception to the rule." He concluded, "I grew up with the belief that the natural condition of a Jew was to be a propertyless worker like my painter father and my dressmaker mother and my dressmaker uncles and

■

cousins in Brownsville—workers, kin to all the workers of the world, dependent entirely on the work of their hand. All happiness in our house was measured by the length of a job."[10]

Deteriorating social and economic conditions in the city's black ghettos took a further tumble during the Great Depression. Exact figures do not exist for unemployment and income in the 1920s for precise comparisons, but black New Yorkers suffered more than whites during the 1930s. Median black income in Harlem fell 44 percent between 1929 and 1933; and in the bottom years of the depression more than 40 percent of blacks were out of work, nearly twice the proportion of whites.[11]

The city's economy remained about as closed to blacks as it had been for the three previous decades. Construction crews hired only a few blacks, and those employed on the subways served as porters, not as higher paid motorman. Department stores and other large employers of white collar workers generally refused to hire black workers. Some— but by no means all—of Harlem's larger stores made token gestures by taking on a few black clerks in the 1920s. In 1934 L. M. Blumstein, owner of a large department store on 125th Street, noted that he gave a donation to the National Urban League and had hired a few blacks as porters, maids, and elevator operators in the previous five years. Blumstein admitted that 75 percent of his customers were black, but he did not see the need to employ black sales clerks.[12]

Among the most demeaning jobs open to black New Yorkers were the "slave markets," found on certain blocks of the Bronx, where unemployed black women congregated on street corners, carrying signs advertising themselves as available for house work. Housewives went from woman to woman, "shopping" for the lowest priced workers. A state committee reported it was "not surprising that householders find it very easy to secure day-work help for 15 and 20 cents an hour."[13]

Given the deplorable depression conditions, it is easily understood why more than 40 percent of black families in 1933 were on relief. Public support funds were woefully inadequate, paying only $2.39 per week in 1932, and many individuals who were out of work were unable to receive any help at all.[14] Inevitably housing and health conditions for blacks deteriorated further during the 1930s, while rents remained higher in Harlem than elsewhere. Modest slum clearance and public housing projects inaugurated under the New Deal late in

■

the 1930s had minimal impact upon either Harlem or Bedford-Stuyvesant.[15]

Rising relief rolls were a sign of hard times, but they alone do not tell the extent of suffering. New York Chinese experienced an estimated unemployment rate of 30 percent in the early depression as dropping incomes adversely affected their hand laundries and restaurants, the mainstays of the city's Chinese population. Scholar Peter Kwong noted that the Federal Emergency Relief Administration reported only 1.2 percent of the Chinese population was on relief compared to 23.9 of blacks and 9.2 of whites. "Many Chinese held to traditional concepts of pride and would not lose face by admitting they needed help," he tells us. To make ends meet they turned to job sharing and aid from their tongs and loan associations.[16]

Until World War II ended the depression, one's status as a white collar worker or city employee did not render one exempt from economic woes.[17] One white collar worker reportedly told persons handing out food in a soup kitchen, "I wouldn't do this, but if I eat here it makes what little there is at home last longer for my wife while I am walking the streets."[18] Yet white collar workers on the whole did get by better than blue collar ones, which meant that Jewish New Yorkers "because of their overall while-collar occupational profiles . . . fared better during the Depression than many other groups."[19] Among Italians who were white collar workers conditions were also better than among the less skilled; a depression era survey in Italian East Harlem revealed that the overwhelming majority of parents thought that office work was the most desirable employment for their children.[20]

Facing limited job prospects for their children and realizing that white collar work offered a likely path to economic stability and mobility, many New Yorkers kept their children in school for more years. The number of students attending high school increased 45 percent between 1930 and 1935.[21] While Italians and others increasingly stayed in school longer, Jews continued to lead in seeking educational opportunities. High school enrollment became the norm for both Jewish men and women. Although the Jewish men were more apt to attend college than Jewish women, Jewish women were more likely to avail themselves of higher education than females from other ethnic groups. In 1934 Jewish women represented more than one half of female students attending New York's public colleges.[22]

■

Besides keeping their children in school, families coped in other ways. Young couples postponed marriages, or if they did tie the knot, they moved in with their parents until they could earn enough to afford their own housing. Couples also had fewer children during the Great Depression.[23]

Unemployed New Yorkers, blue and white collar, turned to traditional sources of aid; and Protestant, Roman Catholic, and Jewish religious agencies and charities all expanded their activities in response to the emergency. Jewish philanthropies reported a 40 percent increase in requests for assistance in the first six months of 1931 alone. Contributions were up in the early years of the depression, but Jewish charities still could not keep up with the demand. The rapid synagogue-building of the 1920s came to an abrupt halt, and many congregations struggled to maintain services for their members. Yeshiva University nearly closed, and some old-age homes, nurseries, and orphanages actually shut their doors.[24]

During the 1920s Archbishop Patrick Cardinal Hayes coordinated Catholic welfare efforts through Catholic Charities, whose annual parish appeals soon grossed one million dollars. In the 1930s, however, Catholic Charities soon found itself unable to meet all requests for aid. By the time Francis Cardinal Spellman assumed the leadership of the Diocese of New York in 1939, it had a $28 million debt.[25]

Harlem's churches also reached out to the unemployed residents. They had traditionally helped the poor, and with poverty on the rise they expanded their efforts.[26] The largest and most prestigious church, Adam Clayton Powell, Sr.'s Abyssinian Baptist, provided food, clothing, coal, and kerosene to those in need. A cooperative effort of Harlem churches, led by the Rev. Shelton Hale Bishop of St. Philips Protestant Episcopal Church, also gave away food, clothing, and carfare and searched for jobs for the unemployed.[27]

The most colorful figure in depression Harlem was George Baker, known as Father Divine. Claiming to be God, he attracted many followers, both white and black, and raised funds to run fifteen "heavens" in Harlem, which served daily banquets for all visitors. Whether or not all participants really believed Father Divine was God is not known, but allegedly 3,000 persons a day willingly accepted his meals.[28]

Welfare associations like the Charity Organization Society, the Children's Aid Society, the Urban League, and the New York Association for

■

Improving the Condition of the Poor all expanded their efforts to meet depression needs. In the end, however, private charities were overwhelmed by the magnitude of the crisis. New Yorkers, as did Americans elsewhere, turned to government, first to municipal and state agencies and eventually to Washington. By 1934 between 70 and 90 percent of Jews on relief received aid from public funds rather than from Jewish welfare agencies.[29]

In attempting to respond to demands for financial assistance, New York City's government was overwhelmed. The city could not balance its budget without curtailing municipal services and laying off employees. A desperate Mayor Jimmy Walker dismissed several thousand school teachers in 1930–1931, and more city cutbacks followed.[30] Social workers reported that they "saw much more distress last winter [1930–1931] than they had ever seen before."[31] Even though municipal funds were increasingly limited, New Yorkers nonetheless recognized that government continued to represent a source of possible employment. Sociologist Roger Waldinger noted:

> In 1933, under Tammany, 6,327 individuals applied for government jobs; six years later, 250,000 job seekers knocked at the municipal service's door. Openings in just one city agency, the newly competitive welfare department, attracted 100,000 testakers in 1939. The search for upward mobility through civil service also accelerated, as applications for promotional exams climbed from 6,270 in 1935 to 26,847 in 1939.[32]

Yet it was not relief or jobs alone that caused New Yorkers to focus on the municipal government. In the face of economic hardship, the all too traditional graft and poor quality of municipal services became more glaring and, for many, unacceptable. As stories surfaced and rumors circulated about corruption in city government, including the office of the mayor, Governor Franklin Roosevelt appointed a commission headed by Judge Samuel Seabury to investigate. Seabury's investigations in 1930 revealed payoffs to the police, clerks, and bondsmen. Then the commission turned to magistrates and labor racketeering. Among a growing list of public officials taking graft, the investigators uncovered the county registrar of Brooklyn, the Hon. James A. McQuade, who had managed to accumulate more than $500,000 in five years on an annual salary of $12,000. He claimed he had friends who loaned him

■

large sums. When asked if he could remember who loaned him hundreds of thousands of dollars, he replied, "Oh Judge, offhand I could not."[33] As the trail of corruption pointed to City Hall, Jimmy Walker was faced with possible prosecution. His charm no longer adequate to the task, Walker resigned in 1932 and sailed off to Europe with his new wife.[34]

The stage was set for Fiorello La Guardia, considered by many to have been New York's most outstanding mayor. When Walker quit, Joseph V. McKee, an Irish Tammany man and President of the Board of Aldermen, became acting mayor until the election of 1933. In that year's campaign, drawing upon discontented voters, La Guardia ran as a Republican-fusion candidate supported by good government clubs. The "Little Flower," as La Guardia was called, won by only a plurality of the votes.[35] However, in winning reelection in 1937 and 1941, La Guardia accomplished an extraordinary feat for a fusion reform candidate.

The feisty mayor was perfect for New York's polyglot population. His father was an Italian Protestant and his mother Jewish; he was Episcopalian. The mayor had learned about nation's immigrant heritage while working in Budapest with emigrants who wanted to come to America, by serving as an interpreter at Ellis Island, and later by representing East Harlem in Congress. He spoke Yiddish, Italian, German, Croatian and two other foreign languages that he used when campaigning. Once, when charged with being anti-Semitic, he issued a challenge to his accuser to debate the campaign's issues; the debate was to be "ENTIRELY IN THE YIDDISH LANGUAGE."[36] The new mayor could not, and did not, appease all groups. In 1933 Italians overwhelming supported him. Jews also favored La Guardia, though not as strongly as Italians. Jews became increasingly more supportive of the mayor as he raised the number of city positions available through civil service, appointed a number of Jews and Italians to high municipal jobs, and when he chose as running mates for the president of the board of alderman and comptroller a Jew and Irishman respectively.[37] Jewish voters generally also approved of the social programs of the La Guardia years and applauded his attacks upon Nazism (he was more cautious in criticizing Mussolini). La Guardia also did well among New York's growing number of black voters. Aligned with Tammany, as many Irish were, La Guardia's standing among that ethnic group was rather low during his twelve years in office.[38]

■

Many of La Guardia's supporters were drawn to him because of his crusade against political corruption and gambling.[39] Moreover, he was a highly visible mayor. He could be seen rushing to fires and heard on the city's radio stations on Sunday mornings reading the funny papers during a newspaper strike. "I felt," said the mayor, "that the children should not be deprived of them due to a squabble among the adults."[40] He believed New York City should have its own airport instead of using Newark's. To dramatize the point in 1934, he refused to disembark from his flight when the plane landed in Newark. The mayor noted that the ticket said "New York," and Newark was not New York. Eventually, with the aid of the federal government, the city built La Guardia Airport, which opened in 1939.[41]

As Jews and to a lesser extent Italians gained politically during the Great Depression, black political leaders also sought more influence. They won control of the Democratic party in Harlem and elected a few more blacks to city and state offices. In 1941 the voters sent Adam Clayton Powell, Jr., to the city council, the first time that a black man had been elected from an area larger than a single district.[42] The hiring of more black police and firemen and the increased number of blacks holding municipal jobs represented progress, but African Americans remained underrepresented in governmental employment, a mere 1.7 percent of the total in 1940. In that year they made up about six percent of the city's population.[43]

Blacks in the depression decade employed a new protest technique. Several organizations banded together in 1934 to boycott stores that would not hire black clerks. The coalition included ministers such as Adam Clayton Powell, Jr., the colorful nationalist and anti-Semite Sufi Abdul Hamid, black and white communists, and working-class blacks. Faced with internal division and a court injunction banning picketing, the coalition eventually fell apart after achieving modest success when Blumstein's department store agreed to hire black women as salespersons.[44] Blacks also continued protesting against conditions at Harlem Hospital and won gains, including the appointment of more black medical and administrative personnel.[45]

With municipal funds inadequate to meet the costs of battling the depression, federal and state monies were necessary and forthcoming. Mayor La Guardia turned to Robert Moses, the "master builder" or "power broker" to employ them in a vast series of city projects. Moses,

■

as park commissioner, quickly utilized Civil Works Administration funds to hire 68,000 men to refurbish city parks and beaches.[46] Later, using Works Project Administration (WPA) money, Moses also built roads, parkways, and other city projects, the largest of which was La Guardia Airport. WPA-sponsored projects also supported a number of New York City artists, musicians, teachers, and white collar workers.

Prior to 1935 the depression had curtailed construction, but with New Deal funds available, New York City had an opportunity to again erect public housing. The municipal government had already initiated a modest housing project, when the possibility of federal aid loomed. Utilizing federal funds, 17,000 family units were completed, a step forward but hardly adequate to meet the city's housing needs.[47] Also insufficient were the few new public facilities—parks, swimming pools, and playgrounds—constructed in black neighborhoods under Robert Moses's leadership. As Robert Caro noted, "Robert Moses built 255 playgrounds in New York City during the 1930s. He built one playground in Harlem."[48]

As exciting as La Guardia's tenure was and as helpful as governmental programs were, for some New Yorkers more fundamental changes were required. Labor organizers sought to revive the city's unions from their sluggishness of the 1920s. The Amalgamated Clothing Workers' Union, centered in New York, had experienced a drop in rolls from 177,000 in 1920 to only 7,000 dues payers in 1932.[49] On the eve of the New Deal the ILGWU had lost 60 percent of its 100,000 members in 12 years and suspended publication of its paper. The elevator did not "run at the union headquarters because there was no money to pay the electric bill."[50] With a climate of opinion supportive of organized labor in both Albany and Washington, unions like the Amalgamated and the ILGWU experienced a new militancy and made substantial gains during the New Deal years. By 1934 the ILGWU claimed a membership of more than 200,000, the largest in its history, and it looked to political action to win further benefits.[51]

Struggling municipal unions, like that of the badly divided teachers, faced a city short of funds. In response to the depression the Board of Education hired low paid substitutes and cut salaries and other services. Federal funds eventually led to new classroom construction and an expansion of educational programs, but the teachers' union would have to wait until after World War II for official recognition.[52]

■

The experience of the predominantly Irish transit workers was somewhat different. Prior to the 1930s workers on the city's subways and busses were so poorly organized and paid that if alternative employment became available, transit men would leave the system. With the coming of the depression, alternative employment dried up and wage cuts set the stage for considerable union sentiment. Spearheaded by Irish-born Mike Quill, a core of immigrants who had fought for the Irish Republican cause, and communist activists, the transit employees established the Transport Workers Union (TWU) in the early 1930s. The union's first success was in organizing workers on the Interboro Rapid Transit line (IRT). The strong Irish connection was noted when the transit workers celebrated their victory in Madison Square Garden. TWU members marched into the Garden while the band played "The Wearing of the Green."[53] The first TWU contracts signed in 1937 brought important benefits to its members.[54] After the city consolidated the subway lines and assumed their direction, the TWU generally maintained its bargaining position in spite of La Guardia's opposition to the closed shop and to the right of municipal workers to strike.[55]

Even the city's Chinese laundrymen felt compelled to organize during the depression. Conditions were bad enough when technological changes in the laundry business threatened to further weaken the livelihood of these workers. Then the large scale laundries persuaded the Board of Aldermen to pass a laundry ordinance establishing a $25 yearly registration fee and requiring laundries run by one person to post a $1,000 bond upon applying for a license. Both of these measures imposed hardships on Chinese laundrymen. Because Chinatown's most powerful organization, the Chinese Consolidated Benevolent Association, offered virtually no assistance, the laundrymen organized the Chinese Hand Laundrymen Alliance, hired a lawyer, and pressured the Board of Aldermen to substantially reduce the registration fee and bond price.[56]

The ferment of the Great Depression in New York City also generated a renewed radicalism. Although the Communist party (CP) never claimed more than a few thousand members in the city, it had many sympathizers and influenced both the trade unions and the newly formed American Labor Party (ALP). Mike Quill, for example, was closely associated with the CP for many years, as were some Jews, in

■

particular some teachers, social workers, and white collar employees.[57] Italians tended to be more conservative than Jews, but radical Italian American politicians Vito Marcantonio and Peter Vincent Cacchione attracted a good number of that community's voters during the depths of the depression. Communists also made a special effort to win over African Americans, but although many blacks praised the integrationist positions of the party, few joined it.

Not content with New Deal policies, radicals came together in 1936 to form the American Labor Party. The party's base consisted of members of the Amalgamated Clothing Workers' Union of Sidney Hillman and the ILGWU of David Dubinsky, communists, and union leaders like Mike Quill and International Longshoremen's Union president Joseph P. Ryan.[58] The ALP, gaining most of its support from among left-leaning Jewish voters, provided a ballot spot for those who wanted to vote for Franklin Roosevelt but not be associated with the Democratic party and its New York bosses Ed Flynn and James Farley. It also provided a ballot place for the independent Mayor La Guardia, who won nearly 500,000 votes on its line in his 1937 reelection campaign.[59]

The ALP, however, was a party hopelessly divided between the far left with its sizeable communist component and the anti-communists. The leader of the far left was Congressman Vito Marcantonio, La Guardia's successor in Congress from East Harlem.[60] As communists appeared to be increasingly gaining control of the ALP, the party split, and the rupture led to the formation in 1944 of a new, more moderate political organization, the Liberal Party. The ALP would disappear in the 1950s, when Cold War anti-communism dominated American politics. The communists reached the peak of their electoral success in the 1940s with the election for the first and only time of two party members to the City Council, African-American Benjamin Davis and Peter Cacchione.

Many residents of ethnic neighborhoods increasingly gave their allegiance to and received support from political parties, unions, and radical causes, as their traditional immigrant institutions proved fiscally incapable of meeting the economic crisis—one indication of movement away from ethnicity and toward acculturation. There were others. Ethnic neighborhood theaters found themselves competing with Hollywood made films and English radio programs. For example, though the city's Yiddish-speakers still patronized Yiddish films during the

1930s (some of which were produced in New York), and new Yiddish dramatic troupes continued to appear, the appeal of these endeavors to English-speaking second and third generation Jews was limited at best. One historian pointed out that most of these Yiddish cultural outlets "had lost their audience by the advent of World War II."[61] The same was true for the Yiddish press, which had reached its peak about the time of World War I. Newspapers like the *Forverts*, the *Tageblatt*, and the *Tag* had many subscribers, but their numbers were declining as readers turned increasingly to the English-language newspapers.[62]

Yet ethnicity and ethnic identity did not by any means disappear. It must be remembered that unions and political parties made direct ethnic appeals and built bases of support in ethnic neighborhoods. Also the economic despair and keen competition for jobs after 1929 called attention to racial and ethnic differences and fostered intergroup tensions. A study by the American Jewish Congress in 1938 claimed that anti-Jewish specifications in help-wanted ads were at an all time high. Medical and law schools also tightened their restrictions further against Jewish applicants.[63] The percentage of Jews in Columbia University's College of Physicians and Surgeons fell from 46.94 in 1920 to 6.45 in 1940.[64] Yet some Catholics complained that anti-Catholicism and not anti-Semitism was the greater problem in New York City. Ronald Bayor reports that the often anti-Semitic *Brooklyn Tablet*, the official paper of the diocese of Brooklyn, declared that Jews were overrepresented in the professions and had nothing to complain about.[65]

Jewish women, in addition to anti-Semitism, encountered sexual bias when they attempted to become doctors or lawyers. Quotas and other restrictions were common against women in those years. Moreover, Jewish parents, like nearly all immigrant parents, were more apt to support their sons' career aspirations than their daughters.' Hence, many Jewish women chose to become teachers, a profession that required fewer years of formal education. As noted, Jewish women had begun to enter the teaching ranks as early as World War I. Those were mostly German Jews, but in the 1920s and 1930s the daughters of eastern European immigrants entered the profession in growing numbers. For them and their parents teaching had a relatively high status compared to other feminized professions like nursing, which was considered menial and "the bastion of Irish-American women, who controlled entrance into both nursing schools and hospitals." Most young women

■

received their training at Hunter College (limited to women), the City College of New York, and Brooklyn College, founded in 1930.[66]

To many Irish New Yorkers, the increase of Jewish women in the teaching ranks and Mayor La Guardia's extension of the civil service to a growing number of municipal jobs seemed to represent a loss of opportunity. Appointment of Jews and Italians to non-civil service jobs in city agencies and the election of others to municipal offices appeared to be further signs of declining Irish influence in governing New York City.[67]

Events overseas also aggravated conflict among New York's ethnic groups. The rise of Nazism in Germany and the triumph of Mussolini's Italian fascism triggered strong responses among many of the city's Jews, Italians, and Germans. Nazism even came to America. A few local Nazi units had been organized in the 1920s, but the major pro-Nazi group of the depression years was Fritz Kuhn's German-American Bund. Numbering only a few thousand members, many of whom were recent German immigrants, and centered in Manhattan's Yorkville, the Bund made strenuous efforts to win the support of the German-American New Yorkers.[68] It had little success in that endeavor, yet with its Nazi-style uniforms and salutes, the Bund was a frightening, ugly organization. It supported Hitler, verbally attacked Jews in America, assailed a Jewish boycott of German goods, and held political rallies complete with Nazi banners and music. In 1939 it conducted a massive rally at Madison Square Garden, during which an audience of 20,000 heard speeches in praise of Hitler. When a reporter on the scene laughed at their carryings on, she was beaten.[69]

As the war came closer, the Bund was generally discredited and subjected to investigation by the federal government. Moreover, German Americans increasingly attacked the Bund and Hitler's Germany, and some reached out to improve German-Jewish relations in the city. In 1933 a self-proclaimed leader of Nazism, Heinz Spanknobel, tried to order Victor Ridder, one of the publishers of *Staats-Zeitung und Herold*, to support the Nazi cause, but Ridder threw him out of his office, and the paper became increasingly anti-Hitler.[70] Yorkville was also the center of anti-Nazi organizations like the German Workers Club and the German Central Book Store which "was stocked with books banned by Hitler." The anti-Nazi newspaper, the *Deutsches Volksecho*, also had many readers in Yorkville.[71] Once war was declared, the government prosecuted Bund leaders, and the organization dissolved.[72]

■

While not necessarily endorsing fascism, many of the city's Italian Americans admired Mussolini's accomplishments. As one said, "Whatever you fellows may think of Mussolini, you've got to admit one thing. He has done more to get respect for the Italian people than anybody else. The Italians get a lot more respect now than when I started going to school. And you can thank Mussolini for that."[73]

Among Mussolini's more prominent supporters was Generoso Pope, editor of the city's major Italian-language newspaper, *Il Progresso*. Pope was connected to Tammany and had contacts in Washington, D.C. Until 1940 his newspaper was friendly to the Italian leader as were other Italian language newspapers and organizations like the Sons of Italy. However, after America entered the war, these newspapers and organizations strongly supported the Allied cause.[74]

The rise of anti-Semitism in Italy, which accompanied the growing ties between that nation and Nazi Germany, had no significant impact on relations between the city's Italian and Jewish communities.[75] However, conflict did erupt between Italian New Yorkers and African Americans. Many Italian Americans defended Mussolini's invasion of Ethiopia, while black leaders supported Ethiopia's pleas to the League of Nations for assistance and condemned Italy for its aggression. After Italy attacked Ethiopia, black religious leaders helped organize the "Committee for Ethiopia," which was chaired by the Rev. Adam Clayton Powell, Jr., of the Harlem's Abyssinian Baptist Church.[76]

When African-American boxer Joe Louis, who was idolized in Harlem, fought a heavyweight title bout against the Italian Primo Carnera in July 1935, Mayor La Guardia posted 1,500 policemen, the "largest detachment ever assigned to a prize fight," to keep the peace. While the crowd was not unruly that night, street fighting between Italian and black New Yorkers occurred throughout the summer. In Harlem, blacks on one occasion smashed the widows of Italian stores, and the number of Italian owned bars in the area declined. A few black nationalists urged that Italian-owned stores in Harlem be boycotted.[77]

Another contributor to the climate of racial and ethnic tension was Father Charles E. Coughlin, the Detroit radio priest. Originally Coughlin had been supportive of Roosevelt and the New Deal, but in the late 1930s he began to attack FDR and his policies, praise Nazism, and characterize Jews as dangerous radicals or as plutocrats who had too much power in the United States. His journal *Social Justice* and his

■

Christian Front organization held some appeal to Catholics, particularly among the Irish. Moreover, in Coughlin's view of the Spanish Civil War Francisco Franco was the protector of the Catholic church, so Jews, many of whom strongly supported the republic, earned his wrath.[78]

Coughlin's vehement attacks on Jews aggravated Irish-Jewish tensions and stirred up anti-Semitism. Nor were relations helped by the failure of the Catholic church in New York to condemn the radio priest or the Christian Front.[79] Christian Front activities in the city led to several street brawls in the Bronx and upper Manhattan. In those neighborhoods the organization encouraged gangs of youth to break the windows of Jewish merchants and to beat up Jewish children. Jewish leaders accused the heavily Irish police force of doing little or nothing to stop anti-Semitic violence. One Jewish newspaper proclaimed, "We are tired of approaching a police captain, hat in hand, saying 'Please Captain McCarthy (or O'Brien).... My boy was hit because he is a Jew. Will you send a cop?' And we are damned sick and tired of watching the sickly Hitler-like grin and hearing the usual answer: 'Ah, the boys are just playing.' "[80] Incidents continued into the 1940s, even after the Bund and Christian Front had been disbanded.

That ethnic groups took a strong interest in events overseas was hardly unusual, since immigrants frequently remained close followers of affairs in their homelands. Although the Great Depression concentrated most people's attention on domestic economic issues, the coming of war in Europe was hardly to be ignored. As Hitler's armies overran Poland in September 1939, New York's Polish community joined the growing chorus of those opposing the spread of fascism. On October 15, 1939, an estimated 100,000 Polish Americans marched up Fifth Avenue in their third annual General Pulaski Day Parade. Beyond celebrating their Polish heritage, the parade marchers also grimly protested against the Nazi and Russian conquest of Poland.[81] Other ethnic groups reacted in similar fashion as Hitler's armies engulfed their homelands. Members of New York's small Chinese community were no less concerned about Japan's war against China.[82]

The most violent racial outburst of the 1930s took place in Harlem in 1935. The trouble began on March 19, 1935, when a black youth was caught trying to steal a knife from the E. H. Kress and Company on 125th Street. When the police arrived, the manager decided not to press charges, but rumors quickly spread that the youngster had been beaten and killed, and when the police attempted to break up a street protest rally, crowds gathered and began smashing store windows and looting shops.[83] A commission established by Mayor La Guardia concluded,

> The explosion on March 19 would never have been set off by the tri-fling incident described above had not existing economic and social forces created a state of emotional tension which sought release upon the slightest provocation. As long as the economic and social forces which were responsible for that condition to operate [continue], a state of tension will exist in Harlem and recurrent outbursts may occur.[84]

Some authorities blamed the communists, who were very active in Harlem in the 1930s, for inflaming the crowd, but the mayor's commission rejected this idea.[85] Instead, after holding hearings and investigating the riot and Harlem, the commissioners specifically cited poor housing, health, and public facilities, as well as unemployment, inadequate relief, rundown schools, and Harlem's antagonism toward the police as the underlying causes of the riot.[86] So dismal was the picture the commission painted that Mayor La Guardia did not release the final report.

The commission made recommendations to improve social and economic conditions in Harlem. The city instituted a few improvements, and the mayor promised better social services for the community, including more places in public housing. Increased numbers of black nurses and doctors won positions at Harlem Hospital, and La Guardia appointed a few blacks to municipal offices. But little actually changed in the lives and status of the majority of black New Yorkers.[87]

The depression finally came to an end with the entrance of the United States into World War II. The Federal Bureau of Investigation rounded up and interned a few German and Italian aliens, but the city did not experience persecution of an ethnic group such as occurred with the West Coast Japanese Americans. Ethnic groups like the Poles and Czechs also wanted their nations liberated from Nazism; hence, they enthusiastically supported the war effort.[88] Jews, of course, had special reason to support a war against Nazi Germany, and they too participated in the various civilian war drives with enthusiasm. Jewish students at the City College of New York complained that they were not asked to do enough to support the war effort.[89] As the horrors of the

■

Holocaust became known, Jewish leaders called for efforts to assist their coreligionists in escaping European death camps. Several rallies were held at Madison Square Garden, but these had little impact upon federal government policies.[90]

For German-American and Italian-American New Yorkers the conflict appeared in a somewhat different light. The United States was, after all, at war with their homelands. Yet both of these groups also vigorously backed America's war goals. Italian newspapers that had supported Mussolini and Italian organizations that had praised him reversed policy after Pearl Harbor, denounced the dictator and fascism, and called for all out support of the American military. The *New York Times* reported, "The American flag was hung up and pictures of Mussolini were taken from store windows or turned to the wall in Little Italy on the lower East Side and Harlem."[91] The first Columbus Day Rally held after American entry into the war featured professions of Italian-American loyalty to the United States and wild cheers for President Franklin Roosevelt. That demonstration of patriotism, held at Columbus Circle in Manhattan, was sponsored by Generoso Pope, publisher of *Il Progresso*, who only two years before had been an ardent supporter of Mussolini.[92]

The city's most dedicated German Bundist friends of Hitler found themselves being prosecuted for sedition by the federal government, and several of the organization's leaders were imprisoned. But by 1941 Bund followers were few even in Yorkville, the center of German-American New York. When *New York Times* reporters visited that district right after Germany's declaration of war against the United States, they found that the great majority of its citizens appeared to be loyal and outspoken opponents of Hitler and Nazism. German language signs were "taken down from some Yorkville theaters and beer halls, and German movies were discontinued," noted the *New York Times*.[93] During the nation's first scrap-metal drive, Yorkville, a neighborhood of Czechs and Hungarians as well as Germans, participated eagerly. After collecting piles of metal, Yorkville youth hung effigies of Hitler above their heaps of scrap.[94]

New York City benefitted economically from the war. Because nearly 900,000 New Yorkers had entered the armed forces, workers were needed to fill jobs in a number of war-related businesses. The city's garment factories produced clothing for the armed forces, and ship build-

■

ing and dock work boomed. The Brooklyn navy yard employed an all time high of 75,000 persons during the war, and hundreds of thousands of soldiers and countless tons of military hardware sailed for the European theater of war from New York harbor.[95]

All racial and ethnic groups benefitted from the expanding wartime economy. Even blacks, backed by a Presidential order banning discrimination and similar New York State action, found new opportunities. Black women won places as nurses at municipal hospitals, while black workers were hired by the city's bus and subway systems. Some unions that had traditionally barred black members changed their policies. These gains did not come without a struggle. In 1941 black groups organized a boycott against two privately owned transit firms, The Fifth Avenue Bus Company and the New York Omnibus Company, in order to protest their discriminatory hiring policies and their refusal to employ blacks as drivers. A hesitant TWU finally worked with black organizations to effect changes.[96] Additional pressure applied by the newly created Citywide Citizens' Committee, an interracial group, against the New York Telephone ultimately led to the hiring of six African-American operators in 1944; two years later, some 200 were employed by the phone company. Historian Cheryl Greenberg tells us that prior to this breakthrough there were only 230 black operators in the entire nation. Other protests led to changes in city and private welfare agencies' discriminatory policies.[97]

Gimbel's Department Store " 'broke with tradition' when it hired 750 Negroes during the war."[98] A few other retail stores, large and small, began to employ blacks as stock and sales persons. But not all followed suit. A study a year after the war revealed that only about one half of these enterprises employed African Americans in sales.[99]

Blacks in New York City, as elsewhere, experienced the economic recovery at a slower rate than did whites. The Fair Employment Practices Committee, established to fight job discrimination, lacked teeth; and New York City's black citizens continued to face widespread discrimination and segregation. Indeed, the WPA rolls became increasingly black, because so many African Americans could still not obtain other jobs.[100]

Housing was in demand by all groups, and the shortage prompted the imposition of rent control. Yet here again blacks were the most deprived. Poor housing, inflation, low incomes, and tensions between

■

black New Yorkers and white police led to frustration that in 1943 exploded into yet another Harlem riot. An incident during a hot August weekend involving two white policemen and several blacks triggered rumors that a black soldier had been shot. The resultant riot left five blacks dead and many others injured. Little city action followed.[101]

Even Mayor La Guardia, popular among black voters for his criticism of those firms that would not employ African Americans, in effect accepted public racial segregation when he allowed the Navy, which in that era was very much a segregated institution, to train white but not black women in a municipal college and a high school. In addition, on the eve of the 1943 riot, the mayor agreed to permit the Metropolitan Life Insurance Company—not known to by sympathetic to black concerns—to build Stuyvesant Town, a large Manhattan housing project, which would be available to whites only.[102] Metropolitan Life, although it had thousands of policy holders in Harlem, had "refused to hire one black agent in or out of that community."[103] The company had already constructed the all-white Parkchester housing project in the Bronx, but that had been on vacant land. Stuyvesant Town required the city's acquiring and clearing some existing housing and some tax concessions, thus making it a quasi-public project. Pressured by civil rights advocates to open Stuyvesant Town to blacks, Metropolitan dug in its heels and refused. The company had the active aid of the powerful Robert Moses who insisted that charges of racial discrimination were irrelevant because the project was a "private development." But winning the mayor's approval was another matter.[104] La Guardia wanted to improve the city's housing stock, and the project was an attractive way of doing that. At the same time, he could not ignore the fact that the development was quasi public, and he certainly had no wish to appear to condone racial discrimination. In the end, however, the mayor agreed to the contract, expressing the hope that the courts would address the issue and open the housing to all.

The triumph of discrimination at Stuyvesant triggered the movement for city enactment of a fair housing law. Pushed by Republican Councilmen Stanley Isaacs, Democrat Adam Clayton Powell, Jr., and Communist Benjamin Davis, the City Council eventually passed such a bill. The 1944 act did not cover Stuyvesant Town retroactively, as had been originally suggested, but only future housing projects. Thus New Yorkers put off until after World War II any serious effort to confront

■

the city's prevailing racism, not only in housing but in most other areas of life as well.[105] As ever black New Yorkers remained at the bottom of the city's social and economic life.

Tens of thousand of New Yorkers joyfully poured into the streets upon hearing of Japan's surrender on August 14, 1945. People were eager to celebrate the war's conclusion and anticipated the end of rationing, Broadway's dimmed lights, and the acute housing shortage. For them victory meant the speedy return of servicemen and women and a chance to live in a peaceful world. Yet New Yorkers, like other Americans, could not be certain of what lay ahead in either the nation or the world. Pessimists feared a postwar economic slump and a continuation of the racial and ethnic conflict that had marked the 1930s.

■

*A*
*Better*
*Time:*
*New*
*York*
*City,*
*1945–1970*

**F**ears of a renewal of economic woes, expressed by some at the end of World War II, proved groundless. With the resumption of peace there followed a quarter of a century of improved living for most New Yorkers. A pent-up demand for housing kindled a boom in construction. The Great Depression and especially the war had curtailed new housing starts, and many potential home owners had accumulated savings during the high employment war years. New York City's many other assets also contributed to prosperity. For almost three decades after the beginning of World War II, its natural harbor continued to be a boon. As before the war, the city remained America's leading financial and banking center, and it maintained a solid base in manufacturing, with one million New Yorkers employed in that sector.

Economic growth from 1945 to 1970 made for "a better time" for those ethnic New Yorkers, particularly Jews and Italians, who found new opportunities in the private sector of the city's economy, in politics, and on the public payroll. So attractive was the New York during those years that immigrants from Europe, the Caribbean, and even Asia looked to New York for new opportunities. Entry into the United States was made possible by modifications in the immigration laws. Puerto Ricans, who as American citizens were exempt from restrictions, also poured into the city. New York's black residents too encountered better economic opportunities as well as more tolerance after the war. But racism was by no means eradicated by 1970, and the progress and acceptance of African Americans in the city was considerably less than that experienced by the descendants of European immigrants.

It took more than economic growth for racial and ethnic groups to experience "a better time." The fierce anti-Semitism that restricted Jewish enrollment in universities and professional schools came under attack during the 1940s as the United States struggled to defeat the racism of Nazi Germany. In 1945 ethnic organizations prodded the legislature to pass the nation's first state law, the Ives–Quinn Law, banning racial and religious bias in employment. The act established the State Commission Against Discrimination (SCAD), a watchdog agency to oversee the enforcement of its provisions. Neither the Ives–Quinn Law nor the chronically underfunded SCAD guaranteed an end to bigotry, but they nonetheless represented a growing public commitment to tolerance.[1] The city also acted, establishing a City Commission on Human Rights (CCHR) to deal with a wide number of discriminatory issues in housing, employment, public accommodations, and education. The CCHR initially focused on incidents of religious prejudice, but after the 1960s racial matters received more attention.[2]

The American Jewish Congress joined with other organizations to pressure the state and city to outlaw discrimination by nonsectarian colleges and universities.[3] After an investigation by the New York City Council revealed widespread bias and that "during the last decade conditions have grown rapidly worse," Mayor William O'Dwyer announced that public funds would be withheld from institutions of higher education that continued to discriminate.[4] The Council backed the mayor's

■

plan to withhold tax exemptions from nonsectarian institutions that employed racial or religious criteria in admitting students.[5] Institutions like Columbia and New York universities, including their professional schools, subsequently dropped their Jewish student quotas and began to hire Jewish faculty.[6] The end result was a growing number of Jewish dentists, physicians, academics, and lawyers.

Educational institutions were not the only organizations to gradually abandon discriminatory practices. A widely publicized 1967 Anti-Defamation League study of thirty-eight large New York City companies in a variety of industries revealed that Jews were underrepresented in upper management, a finding confirmed by the Federal Equal Opportunity Employment Commission.[7] But, in fact, Protestant-dominated banks, investments companies, corporations, and law firms were beginning to alter hiring practices during the 1960s. Edwin Miller, a Jew who became a high official in the Manufacturers Hanover Trust Company, joined the bank in 1962. Boris Berkovitch, also Jewish and later vice chairman at Morgan Guaranty Trust, likewise began his upward path in banking during the 1960s.[8] A few Jews made fortunes as real estate promoters during the postwar boom years. Harry Uris was prominent in city real estate development between 1945 and 1970 as was Julius Tishman, who was allegedly responsible for 13 percent of the city's new office buildings in those years. The Tisch brothers, Lawrence and Preston, also did extremely well in New York real estate and expanded their operations beyond the city by purchasing the Loews Corporation. Other prominent promoters were Samuel LeFrak and William Zeckendorf.[9]

Of course not all Jews could be classified as middle class or elite professionals by the 1970s. A 1972 study prepared for the Federation of Jewish Philanthropies of New York noted a number of impoverished Jews, usually elderly people who had been bypassed by the postwar prosperity.[10] More reflective of the changing status of New York's Jews, the report noted, "The number of Jewish workers in New York City employed in industrial, factory, and low white collar work has declined sharply during the past two decades." Union officials told investigators that in the past Jewish parents used to send "us their children and ask us to give them jobs. Now they no longer come."[11]

As for Italians, who traditionally lagged behind Jews in their utilization of education as a route to economic success and mobility, begin-

■

ning in the early 1970s they too began to avail themselves of the city's colleges and universities. Scholar Richard Gambino noted that in 1957, when he attended Queens College, a branch of the City University of New York, he was but one of a handful of Italian-American students. By 1972, after the open admissions policy of the City University went into effect, 34,000 of the system's 169,000 matriculated undergraduate students were Italian Americans. At Fordham University, a private Catholic university once heavily Irish, a significant proportion of the students were of Italian background by the mid-1970s.[12]

New York's Irish also found new economic opportunities in the city, even as their influence in City Hall politics was declining. New York had an Irish middle class in the nineteenth century and an Irish elite by 1900, but a mid-1970s survey financed by the federal Office of Economic Opportunity of three predominately Irish-American communities in the city revealed a wide spread of income, occupation, and education among families, with some elderly couples living on very modest means.[13] Yet as a group the Irish were clearly on the way up. After World War II most abandoned working-class jobs like those as transit workers to incoming blacks and Hispanics.[14] At the top of the Irish elite stood prominent families like the McDonnells, the Murrays, and the Cuddihys. The Fifth Avenue apartment of James Francis McDonnell, owner of a prosperous brokerage house, was at one time the largest in the city.[15]

Ethnic whites who remained working class, especially those members of the city's older Polish, Italian, and to a lesser degree Irish communities, labored in construction projects, in the declining manufacturing sector, or in new service jobs. While jobs in areas such as the garment industry and fast food chains did not offer particularly high wages, other blue collar occupations paid very well. The city's periodic building booms after 1945, for example, brought substantial salaries to the mostly white, union construction workers. Unfortunately for these workers, construction employment was generally cyclical.[16]

Descendants of turn-of-the-century immigrants continued to gain power in municipal politics following World War II. That is not to say that the Irish were completely vanquished in that arena. Even though La Guardia's mayoralty had diminished their strength, in 1945 all Democratic county chairmanships were held by Irish Americans, the most powerful being Edward Flynn, boss of the Bronx. Upon his death in 1953, Congressman Charles Buckley became kingpin of that borough. Voters elected Irish-born William O'Dwyer mayor in 1945 and reelected him in 1949. But O'Dwyer was the last Irish mayor of New York. Robert Wagner, who served three terms (1954–1965) stands as a transitional figure. Half Irish and half German and the son of an influential and popular United States Senator of the same name, Wagner initially depended on the support of the regular Democratic party leadership led by Carmine DeSapio of Manhattan and the Bronx's Charles Buckley. Wagner, after two terms of cohabitation with the machine, in an amazing reversal repudiated the regulars and joined with the reform Democrats who had been gaining strength since the late 1950s. Carmine DeSapio, boss of Tammany, said of Wagner, "We are faced with the spectacle of a candidate who seeks reelection on a platform of cleaning up the mess which he himself has created."[17] To the charge that he was running against himself, the mayor retorted privately, "I could find no better opponent."[18] While winning a third term and repudiating the old guard, Wagner gained support from liberal Jews and blacks. His victory ushered in a new kind of city politics.

Wagner's successor John V. Lindsay (1966–1973), white and Protestant, was a most unlikely mayor for New York's polyglot population. A Republican, Lindsay had attended elite private schools, had earned degrees from Yale University, and "the best he could do for immigrant roots was a grandfather from the Isle of Wight, off the coast of southern England." He could hardly be considered an ethnic New Yorker; yet running as a reformer, with strong backing by liberal whites and blacks and aided by divisions among the Democrats, he twice won election as mayor.[19]

It was Italian and Jewish politicians who gained most at the expense of declining Irish-American power and influence. Fiorello La Guardia, the first Italian American elected mayor, had run on ethnically balanced tickets. Copying that model, in 1945 the Democrats for the first time nominated an Italian American and a Jew for city wide offices. They ran many more after that.[20] The second Italian-American mayor was Vincent Impellitteri, who served from 1950 to 1953, after William O'Dwyer resigned to become ambassador to Mexico. Mayor Impellitteri, who proved to be colorless and none too competent, was easily defeated by Robert Wagner in the Democratic primary in 1953, only doing well in heavily Italian Staten Island. Then, choosing to run as an independent,

■

he lost by a large margin in the general election.[21] The first Italian-American leader of Tammany Hall was Carmine DeSapio, who achieved that position in 1949. Other Italian Americans ran and held office in growing numbers on the City Council and in the borough governments. They were active but less successful in mayoral campaigns. In 1973 the city elected its first Jewish mayor, Abe Beame (1974–1977), who had the misfortune to hold that office during the New York fiscal crisis in 1975.[22]

If by 1970 the Irish lost their hold on city hall, they still kept several congressional seats and continued their domination of the Roman Catholic Church in New York City. The Catholic church, long a victim of religious prejudice, received growing respect and acceptance after 1900. Under Patrick Cardinal Hayes, the "Cardinal of Charity," the archdiocese was known for giving relief during the bleak days of the Great Depression.

Hayes's successor, Francis Cardinal Spellman, archbishop of the Diocese of New York from 1939 until his death in 1967, modified the church's agenda. Spellman, the grandson of Irish immigrants, downplayed his Irishness but not his politics or church building. Contributions from the increasingly prosperous Catholic community of New York permitted him to build schools and hospitals and to fund numerous charities. Spellman also cultivated politicians and important business leaders. His conservative views on morals, birth control, and church-state relations were stated often and aggressively, and he vigorously endorsed Senator Joseph McCarthy's anti-communist campaign. His backing of the unpopular Vietnam War diminished his influence.[23] As Daniel Moynihan and Nathan Glazer put it, his reign "went on too long by half."[24] Nonetheless, when he died, attendance at his funeral was mandatory for many civic and political leaders, including President Lyndon Johnson. Spellman was followed by another Irish-American priest, New York native Terence J. Cooke, a more modest man. Like so many New York Irish he was born on Manhattan's West Side and raised in the Bronx.[25] Under Cooke the church was less involved in politics and controversy.

Just as Jews and Italians increasingly won elective offices, they also entered municipal jobs in greater numbers as the public payroll expanded in mid-century New York. The city's employees numbered about 100,000 at the end of World War II, but grew to 200,706 by 1961

■

and 294,555 in 1975, on the eve of the city's fiscal crisis.[26] After World War II several Italians and Jews were appointed commissioners of various city agencies.[27] Jews were heavily represented among the city's public school teachers, amounting to about 60 percent of the instructional staff. Many other professionally trained Jews entered social work, as the city expanded its social services. Italians had dominated the sanitation department for decades, and after 1945 they too found other municipal employment opportunities as teachers, police officers, and clerks.

City jobs became attractive to ethnic New Yorkers in part because of the effectiveness of municipal employees' organizations. Unions for fire, police, and sanitation personnel dated from the 1890s, though they initially were labelled benevolent associations. By the 1930s some employees dared to call their organizations unions, and the transit workers secured important contractual gains after 1937. The main thrust for the teachers and other city unions came after World War II.[28]

During the Wagner years, the mayor's office made it clear that it was supportive of municipal unions. In 1958 Mayor Wagner issued an executive order permitting city employees to organize and engage in collective bargaining.[29] The mayor also worked closely with labor leaders, who represented an important voting bloc. One scholar noted, "While Wagner could not always provide generous contracts to labor, he always took pains to give the union hierarchy a feeling of importance. No city initiative in labor policy was ever undertaken without first clearing it with organized labor."[30] Wagner's executive order was given state backing when the legislature passed the New York City Collective Bargaining Law of 1967. One of the key city unions to benefit from these developments was District 37 of the American Federation of State, County, and Municipal Employees (AFSCME) under the leadership of Victor Gotbaum and Lillian Roberts. AFSCME represented traditionally low paid clerical and hospital workers, at first mostly Italian but later largely black and Hispanic. Teachers, social workers, and others also organized to win significant salary, health, and pension benefits from the city between 1958 and 1970.[31] The Irish stronghold remained in the police and fire departments, whose benevolent societies likewise flourished during the Wagner years.

If City Hall proved unresponsive to labor's demands, the unions resorted to strikes. The militant and colorful Mike Quill often threatened to shut down the city's transport system. The most famous Quill-led walkout was a city wide affair that greeted Mayor John Lindsay when he assumed office on New Year's Day 1966. Working-class Quill had no use for Lindsay, who he said was "strictly silk stocking and Yale. This nut even goes in for exercise. We don't like him." The city managed to have Quill jailed, but the Irish leader boasted of telling the judge to "drop dead in his black robes." In the end, after a twelve day walkout crippled the city, the TWU won major concessions.[32]

With enhanced incomes and with growing toleration easing access to housing, New York's white ethnics enjoyed improved living conditions in newer neighborhoods. Housing had almost always been a problem for New Yorkers, but during the war shortages became acute. After 1945, aided by various state, city, and federal programs, the city experienced a building boom for private homes, rental apartments, and business offices. Of necessity, much of the new housing went up in the outer boroughs of the Bronx, Staten Island, and Queens, areas accessible to Manhattan because of the tunnels, bridges, and the subway system built prior to World War II. Large areas of these boroughs remained underdeveloped when the housing expansion of the 1920s slowed during the Great Depression and virtually stopped during the war. They were now ripe for building.

The development of Canarsie in Brooklyn illustrates the growth of postwar white ethnic communities. Located along Jamaica Bay, Canarsie was inhabited by a few thousand Dutch, Irish, Germans, Scots, and British when Italians and Jewish garment workers began moving there in the 1920s. Large parts of the area still remained undeveloped marshland at the outset of World War II, yet by the 1950s developers gave the community a "new sleek look."[33] Two builders, Harry and Sidney Waxman, constructed private residences on more than two hundred acres of Canarsie land, which attracted primarily Jewish and Italian homeowners. Canarsie's population rose from 3,000 or so in the 1920s to 30,000 in 1950, and 80,000 in 1970.[34] Many of the new residents came from Brooklyn's Brownsville, fleeing a black influx. Brownsville's Jewish population declined from 175,000 in the 1930s to only 5,000, mostly elderly, in the 1960s. The last synagogue there closed in 1972.[35] Brooklyn was not alone in witnessing shifts in the Jewish population. The Bronx's Grand Concourse was developed in the 1920s and became a Jewish center with large apartments, synagogues, and a variety of cul-

■

tural institutions. But the area was almost totally abandoned by Jews after the 1950s as blacks and Hispanics moved in. Jews moved northward to Riverdale and other neighborhoods on the periphery of the borough. In the north Bronx Co-op City was constructed to house 80,000 persons, and Jews constituted its largest ethnic group for years.[36]

Italians lived in several areas of the city, but they too demonstrated similar mobility in housing patterns. In 1970 some Italians still resided in lower Manhattan's "Little Italy," just north of Chinatown, but many more lived in Brooklyn's Canarsie, Red Hook, Bensonhurst, and Cobble Hill neighborhoods. New York's least populated borough, Staten Island, became particularly known for attracting Italian residents. The ethnic community there boomed after 1964, with the construction of the appropriately named Verrazano Bridge, which connected the island with Brooklyn.[37]

The 1980 census revealed that Italians were the largest foreign-born group in the city. "The Italians are in first place," declared a knowledgeable city demographer, "because alone among the older immigrants groups they tend to stay in the city. They pass the house on from one generation to another."[38] One could even find a very few Italian-American neighborhoods that had changed little from the days of their initial immigrant settlement. The Belmont section of the Bronx, near Fordham University, was originally settled by Calabrians who helped build the city's Croton Reservoir in Westchester County. At the end of the 1980s it still contained an Italian component. One Italian who grew up there noted, "I go to the same butcher that waited on my grandmother."[39]

Right after the war the main concentration of a still-large Irish population was centered in the Bronx, but by the 1970s Queens had become the most Irish borough. Half of the city's declining Irish population lived there or in nearby Brooklyn. The Woodside section of Queens is one of the last neighborhoods to retain a distinctly Irish flavor. First- and-second-generation Irish New Yorkers in those neighborhoods were outspoken in criticizing Great Britain when troubles began again in Northern Ireland in 1969, and IRA backers published a newspaper in support of the unification of Ireland.[40]

As striking as the movement of whites to new city neighborhoods was, even more impressive was the scope of their migration to the mushrooming suburbs. Commuter rails, highways, tunnels, and bridges

■

enabled New Yorkers to move to nearby Long Island, Westchester County, and New Jersey and still commute to work in the city. Some connections had been built before the war, but the volume of traffic greatly increased after 1945 and strained their capacities. Indeed, a needed second deck was added to the George Washington Bridge in the 1950s. Many of the new traffic arteries were the work of city planner Robert Moses.[41]

Mass transportation and the auto culture provide only part of the explanation for the suburbanization of the Greater New York area. Higher incomes during the good years from 1945 to 1970, governmental subsidies of mortgages, the desire to leave deteriorating neighborhoods, white flight from blacks, and the constant search by Americans for greener pastures all played roles. Moreover, businesses, jolted by high taxes and high rents in New York City, often sought relief in the suburbs. As offices and stores opened in the suburbs, workers found it desirable to live nearer their places of work.

The 1940s had witnessed a net migration out of the city; only a high natural population increase kept the city's population growing. During the next decade the movement to the suburbs became "a flood," and the city actually lost population. This exodus continued in the 1960s, although the city once more gained population in that decade because of a large in-migration of blacks and immigrants.[42] A loss of jobs beginning in the late 1960s and a major fiscal crisis in the mid-1970s added fuel to the white exodus.

How extensive was the post war white flight? The net outflow of whites exceeded 400,000 in the 1940s, 1.2 million in the 1950s, and another 500,000 in the 1960s. Who moved? Members of nearly all white ethnic groups. In 1970 Jews still represented the largest European group, accounting for about a third of the city's declining white population with Italians a close second. The Bureau of the Census does not record religious affiliation, but a study by the Federation of Jewish Philanthropies of New York put the city's Jewish population at 2,114,000, in 1957, its highest total ever. By 1981 the estimate had fallen to just over one million, and the number probably has decreased further since then.[43] Irish, German, and Italian New Yorkers were also on the move, and their city populations diminished after 1945.

The loss of so many middle class taxpayers began to strain city finances, but perhaps more serious was the flight of jobs from 1945 to

■

1970, an exodus that became even more marked in the years that followed. Brooklyn, which lost more people than the other boroughs, was especially hard hit. For example, the Brooklyn Navy Yard, founded in 1801 when the frigate *Fulton* was built there, employed more than 70,000 workers during World War II, but afterward its economic and military importance rapidly declined. Finally in 1966 it closed.[44] In a parallel decline, the Brooklyn Army Terminal also radically cut its staff. Businesses dependent upon the Army Terminal and the Navy Yard suffered. The borough's beer industry also fell upon hard times. In 1940 Brooklyn could boast of having 132 breweries, an all time high. That number soon fell drastically, and by the end of the 1950s only four remained. In 1976 the last Brooklyn brewery shut its doors.[45] In 1973 one columnist suggested a desperate way to keep the last two open. New Yorkers should "demand that every saloon have both New York beers on tap. And they can drink [New York's] Rheingold and Schaefer, and forget they ever heard of Bud, Schlitz, Pabst, or any of the other foreign beers."[46]

Even sadder for Brooklynites was the 1955 closing of its newspaper, *the Brooklyn Eagle*, and the move of the baseball Brooklyn Dodgers to Los Angeles two years later. The *Eagle* had been especially important for reporting borough news and events for generations, but it could no longer meet its payroll. Perhaps no institution personified Brooklyn in the twentieth century as did the Dodgers. A struggling team during the 1930s, "the Bums," became a consistent winner after 1940. Frequently atop the National League race, the Dodgers were unable to defeat their Bronx rivals, the American League Yankees, until 1955, when they became World Series champs. Emotional Brooklyn supporters jammed the tiny Ebbets Field to cheer their club, but the front office decided to leave for the more lucrative promises of California. One fan summarized the team's move, "Boy, it sure is quiet since the Dodgers left."[47]

The loss of employment was by no means confined to Brooklyn. Manufacturing plants, in particular those in the garment industry, began an exodus that increased in speed after 1970. While New York remained an important port, other cities like Baltimore challenged its supremacy as did facilities in nearby New Jersey. Moreover, technological changes along the waterfront reduced employment among dockworkers. One scholar, Louis Winnick, described a portion of Brooklyn's once thriving docks in the 1980s: "At Sunset Park's last hiring hall on

■

60th Street, a thousand longshoremen 'badge in' each day, but there are no jobs. The gesture is pure theater, acting out a script hammered out years ago in an extraordinary agreement between the dock unions and maritime employers, in which the union accepted labor-saving container ships in exchange for a guaranteed life time income for their workers."[48] The continued hemorrhaging of jobs and population would loom even larger after 1970 as the city struggled to deliver a growing number of municipal services.

The postwar decline of New York's white population, both in actual numbers and as a proportion of the total population, would have been even greater but for the white migration from abroad and from other parts of the nation. After the war more liberal immigration laws made possible a new influx of Europeans, chiefly from southern and eastern Europe, more than one million of whom settled in New York from 1946 to 1970.[49] They entered a city quite different from that experienced by prior generations of immigrants, for modern New York was vastly more hospitable to its postwar newcomers. It offered a number of governmental programs to aid in their settlement.

Included among the new immigrants were Jewish survivors of the Holocaust, refugees from the early days of the Cold War, Italians, Greeks, Irish, Chinese, and people from the Caribbean. Some early refugee programs called for dispersal of the refugees, but many immigrants, especially Jews, desired to remain in New York City. About one quarter of the persons arriving under the Displaced Persons acts of 1948 and 1950 did stay, as did a similar number of other refugees entering in the 1950s.[50]

Of the 85,000 Jews settling in the city, many were members of ultra orthodox Hasidic sects from eastern Europe, who settled in sections of Brooklyn. A large contingent of Satmar Hasidim found homes in Williamsburg near the Navy Yard, where Orthodox had lived since 1920.[51] The city's largest Hasidic community, the Lubavitch, took root in the Crown Heights section of Brooklyn, replacing other Orthodox Jews who moved to Boro Park. Opposed to birth control on religious grounds, the Hasidic community grew rapidly with average family sizes of seven to eight.[52] While New York's community of unaffiliated, Conservative, and Reform Jews declined, the Hasidim vastly increased, although no exact figures of the size of the community exist. Experts estimated it was about 70,000 in 1989, large

■

enough to be courted along with other Orthodox Jews by candidates running for mayor.[53]

The intensely religious Hasidim organized their lives around a highly structured system of Judaic practices. Both Satmar and Lubavitch Jews published weekly Yiddish newspapers which kept their people informed on issues of concern to the community. These religious communities had little contact with outsiders, observed the Sabbath strictly, used the Jewish calendar, segregated the sexes in many social and religious activities, taught their children Yiddish, and arranged marriages for them. Their rabbis scorned television, which they considered an evil, modern amusement.[54]

Italians and Greeks wishing to come to the United States benefitted from special immigration laws and an immigration act passed in 1965, which among other provisions eliminated discriminatory national origins restrictions. During the peak years, 1965 to 1975, about 6,000 Italians and 3,000 Greeks annually settled in New York City.[55] By the early 1970s the backlog of visa applicants had eased, and that, combined with improved economic conditions at home, lessened the pressures for emigration to America.[56] By the late 1980s the immigration authorities recorded only about 3,000 Italians entering the United States annually and a similar number of Greeks. Of these about one quarter indicated they intended to live in New York City.[57]

Italian immigrants seeking economic opportunities settled mostly in Queens, Brooklyn, and Staten Island, where they could count on hearing Italian spoken and where family, friends, churches, and ethnic organizations helped them find housing and jobs.[58] Such was the case of Francesco Pecse who migrated to the United States during the 1950s because he believed his sons would have more opportunity here. The Pecse family went to Red Hook in Brooklyn, a predominately Italian neighborhood. One son became a lawyer and New York State assemblyman who specialized in helping other Italian immigrants.[59] The single largest Italian-American area in the city was in the Bensonhurst section of Brooklyn. One forty-five-year old Italian resident of that neighborhood commented, "My parents' generation moved out, and another wave of Italian immigrants bought their houses."[60]

Unlike the turn-of-the-century Italian migrants, who were mostly uneducated male rural workers and peasants, the new arrivals were predominately artisans, semi-skilled workers, or professionals. They usual-

■

ly came as families, originated in urban centers, and had experience with city living. More than a few had worked in industrial cities of Europe outside of Italy, but the majority had gained their work experience entirely in the growing industrialized urban areas of their own country. Although they were not highly educated, in contrast with their predecessors they were literate and on the whole had an easier time adjusting to life in America.[61]

In New York City the men found jobs in construction, barber shops, restaurants, and factories, while the women most often worked in the garment industries or became hairdressers.[62] Locating in Italian-American neighborhoods, they helped to reinforce Italian institutions and strengthened to some degree Italian-American ethnicity. But their numbers were not large, and immigration from Italy declined in the 1980s, while earlier immigrants and their children and grandchildren moved in increasing numbers to the suburbs.

The city's Greek community grew markedly during the prime years of postwar European immigration, from 1960 to the early 1970s.[63] Community leaders in the heavily-Greek Astoria section of Queens insisted that the census undercounted their cohort, in part because Greeks arrived not only from Greece but also from Turkey, Cyprus, and Egypt and were counted as nationals from those countries. One community leader claimed that New York's Greek community by 1990 numbered 350,000, counting both the foreign born and the descendants of earlier Greek immigrants, but others have cited lower figures.[64]

As with the Italians, recent Greek immigrants differed from their turn-of-century predecessors. They too emigrated most often as families rather than as single males and arrived equipped with higher levels of education and skills. Also, as with the Italian newcomers, there were a few highly educated professionals among them. Yet, like so many immigrants without English language proficiency, the majority initially took what jobs they could find, frequently in factories, in construction, as pushcart vendors, or in entry-level service occupations.[65] Employment opportunities did exist in traditional Greek-American business fields, and some found positions in the fur business, where Greeks had a presence for several generations both as workers and shop owners. However, such employment was declining by the 1970s as competition from Asian producers forced American firms out of business.[66] The most conspicuous new Greek business ventures were as

■

owners of coffee shops and of "un-Greek" pizza parlors. Hellenic businessmen purchased dozens of Manhattan's coffee shops and hired Greek immigrants to work in them. In 1980 *Newsweek* reported: "Greeks have all but taken over the coffee shops, conquering the quick lunch business under their ubiquitous symbol: the drink container with a picture of a discus thrower."[67] Community social life revolved around coffee houses, restaurants, and churches like St. Demetrios Greek Orthodox Church in Astoria. Strong community assistance groups, particularly the Hellenic American Neighborhood Action Committee (HANAC), were established in the early 1970s. The growing community supported several Greek-language daily newspapers, a number of other publications, as well as several TV and radio programs.[68] Some Greek community leaders took a keen interest in the conflict between Turkey and Greece over Cyprus and lobbied Congress in support of the Greek cause.

Ireland, which had a favored quota under the national origins formula, began to send newcomers to New York after the lean immigration years of the Great Depression and World War II. Several thousand arrived annually during the 1950s and early 1960s, but then the numbers dropped. The Irish economy picked up in the 1960s, and by the 1980s fewer than 1,000 annually were emigrating to the United States.[69] Those Irish who did come were on the whole better educated than their predecessors. They settled in the new Irish neighborhoods in Queens or Brooklyn where they followed the traditional immigrant search for a better life.[70]

From the Caribbean came Haitians and Dominicans and from South America came Colombians. Among the Haitians were upper and middle class political exiles who were fleeing the dreaded and oppressive American-supported Duvalier regime that assumed power in 1957. But politics alone does not explain this immigration. Haiti was the most economically destitute nation in the Caribbean, and the exodus included thousands escaping poverty. Those who could not comply with American immigration restrictions often entered illegally or as visitors who stayed on after their visas expired.[71]

Dominicans were also driven by economic forces, and like many Haitians, if they could not obtain an immigrant visa, they came as visitors and stayed on illegally. Many found jobs in the garment industry, while others worked as janitors in offices, as dishwashers and busboys in restaurants, and as service workers in hospitals. Their principal location in New York was the upper west side of Manhattan, an area that would receive many more of their countrymen after 1970.[72]

Small numbers of Asians, benefitting from modifications in the formerly exclusionary Asian immigration policies, also arrived between 1945 to 1970, but their numbers substantially increased only after the 1965 immigration act went into effect. Discrimination against Chinese had decreased after the outbreak of World War II, one consequence of which was that in 1943 Congress repealed the Chinese Exclusion Act and granted China a small quota. Subsequently Congress passed the War Brides Act, which permitted several thousand Chinese women to enter. Anthropologist Bernard Wong tells us, "Older informants remember this period as the first time they saw young Chinese women and children living in the community."[73] This movement was the forerunner of a large scale Chinese immigration to New York City after 1970.

Puerto Ricans were numerically the largest Hispanic group to migrate to New York City between 1945 and 1970, when following World War II the flow of these islanders renewed. They traveled largely by plane, inaugurating the first massive air migration in history. Attempts in the 1950s to improve the Puerto Rican economy, such as "Operation Bootstrap," had only limited success, and many islanders looked to New York City as a place to seek better living conditions. The major period of Puerto Rican migration to New York City lasted from the mid-1940s to the mid-1960s, when 30,000 to 50,000 persons annually came to the city.[74] East Harlem was the main area of Puerto Rican settlement in Manhattan, as long-time Italian residents moved to other sections of the city or to the suburbs. A second major neighborhood for these newcomers emerged in the South Bronx, while other substantial Puerto Rican barrios also arose in Brooklyn. By 1970, the migration slowed, and many of New York's Puerto Ricans returned home.

Institutions such as the Migration Division of the Department of Labor of Puerto Rico helped Puerto Ricans adjust to life New York. Leaders responsible for the creation of this agency argued that the city's social agencies and schools were inadequate to accommodate the new migrants and that a special office was required. The Migration Division did succeed in placing thousands of Puerto Ricans in jobs and helped others prepare for civil service examinations. The agency's staff also

■

worked with New York bureaucrats in aiding Puerto Ricans to adjust and explained to school leaders the importance of teaching English to Puerto Rican children. During the 1960s the federal government played a more active role in such activity, pouring funds into new urban-oriented organizations and creating anti-poverty agencies. Consequently, several of the Division staff left to serve in these new initiatives, and in the 1970s the Division disbanded.[75]

Groups like the Puerto Rican Forum, the Puerto Rican Family Institute (the only grassroots Puerto Rican family agency in the city), and the Puerto Rican Legal Defense and Education Fund sought in one way or another to improve the life of New York's Puerto Ricans. So did ASPIRA, an important organization founded in 1961 to promote higher education for these New Yorkers.[76] Puerto Rican Studies programs developed after 1970 on several campuses of the City University, with particularly active ones at Hunter College and at The City College of New York.

No less important in attracting other Puerto Ricans to the mainland and in helping them cope with their new environment was the Puerto Rican family. Family networks were key in the migration process; they provided funds for travel and help in finding housing and jobs. Gradually the character of New York's Puerto Rican families changed, with a growing number of second- and third-generation members marrying non-Puerto Ricans and an increasing number of families being headed by women.[77]

The Roman Catholic Church also played a significant role in the Puerto Rican community. Most Puerto Ricans retained the Catholicism of their homeland after settlement in New York. Yet the largely Irish-dominated Catholic church was slow in responding to the needs of the new arrivals. Puerto Ricans were expected to become members of integrated English-speaking parishes, but many of the first migrants did not speak English well. In the 1950s the church inaugurated new policies aimed at teaching the clergy Spanish and Puerto Rican culture and encouraging them to hold services in Spanish.[78] Some priests became involved in attempts to promote stability in the barrios.

During the peak migration years some scholars viewed the Puerto Ricans as simply the latest migrant group to come to New York. While they were American citizens, the argument ran, they spoke a foreign language and hailed from a different culture, thus resembling previous waves of New York immigrants. In the end it was assumed they would pursue the same ladder of upward mobility in a traditional path of "ethnic succession."[79]

In the early years of their New York experience, these latest newcomers did indeed seem to be doing just that. They entered with low levels of education, and many were rural workers with limited English-language skills. They settled largely in the barrios of East Harlem or the South Bronx, where housing was crowded and in poor repair. They took jobs in the city's garment industry or in unskilled occupations. As the children attended the public schools, they learned English, achieved higher levels of education than their parents, found better jobs, and in some cases moved away from Puerto Rican neighborhoods and married non-Puerto Ricans. Puerto Ricans usually spoke Spanish at home, but their children rapidly became bilingual.[80]

In city politics, initial signs indicated that perhaps Puerto Ricans would exercise considerable influence. Some activity was evident before 1941, but with the rapid growth of the Puerto Rican population after the war, the potential for influence increased.[81] After 1945 a number of Puerto Ricans were elected to public office. Herman Badillo served as Borough President of Manhattan in the 1960s, following a term in Congress. He was replaced in Congress by Robert Garcia.[82]

The influx of blacks into New York continued during the postwar decades. In 1940 the city's blacks, numbering about 450,000, accounted for about 6 percent of the population. By 1970 they numbered 1,668,115, constituting a larger proportion (about 20 percent) of the city's residents than at any time since the middle of the eighteenth century.[83] Of course, natural population growth as well as small immigration from the Caribbean contributed to this increase, but most significant was the migration from the South.[84] For black New Yorkers 1945–1970 was also "a better time," but much less so than for whites. All black New Yorkers faced the common problem: racism. They lived in a city and nation with a long history of racial bias and segregation, but just as anti-Semitism decreased after 1945 so did racial discrimination. In no area was the improved status of blacks more apparent than in politics and municipal employment. Building on the early precedent of Adam Clayton Powell, Jr., the city's first black congressman, blacks were successful in electing black candidates for city, state, and federal offices.[85] The key element in this success was the increasing number of

■

black voters. Before 1960, the highest municipal elective office won by a black New Yorker was the borough presidency of Manhattan. In 1953 Hulan Jack, an assemblyman and Democratic district leader, achieved this victory.[86] Within the Democratic party itself, J. Raymond Jones moved slowly up the ladder and won a reputation as an astute politician. After holding various party and municipal positions, he served as Manhattan's Democratic county leader from 1964 to 1967 and became one of that borough's most powerful political figures.[87]

In Brooklyn, African Americans won several local elections before sending one of their own to Congress. Racial gerrymandering prevented the election of a black to represent Brooklyn in the House of Representatives until 1968, but then black Assemblywoman Shirley Chisholm won a seat in Congress. After enactment of the 1970 Voting Rights Act and under federal pressure, New York redrew Brooklyn's congressional boundaries so that two districts had black majorities. In the 1976 election, two African Americans were sent to Congress from the borough.[88] A similar situation prevailed in the Bronx, where the Irish boss, Edward J. Flynn, realized that the population was changing and that he needed to grant blacks some recognition.[89]

Among the blacks increasingly turning to urban politics were a number of West Indians. During the 1920s black nationalist Marcus Garvey, a Jamaican, had demonstrated how to mobilize the city's blacks, although he did not venture into organized politics. Within the Democratic party, West Indians began to make their mark during the 1930s. In 1935 Barbadian-born Herbert Bruce became the first black to serve on the Tammany executive committee, and by 1953 four of five Democratic district leaders from Harlem and the only black one in Brooklyn were West Indians. J. Raymond Jones was born in the Virgin Islands; Hulan Jack was born in British Guiana and raised on St. Lucia. Other prominent West Indian political stars were Percy Sutton and Congresswoman Shirley Chisholm.[90] By the 1970s the influence of this generation was coming to end, and when Representative Chisholm retired in 1982, the last of the old guard of West Indian political leaders passed from the scene.

The growing political clout of African Americans reaped dividends in municipal employment. Far underrepresented on the city payroll in 1940, blacks had reversed this by 1970. Political pressure, a growing commitment to equal opportunity in public employment, and affirma-

■

tive action programs after the 1960s opened up opportunities. The employment pattern of blacks varied from agency to agency and from rank to rank. They were prominent in agencies devoted to health and welfare but underrepresented in the police and fire departments. They were underrepresented in the top managerial positions of city agencies. Even as late as 1988 a mayor's commission reported that "there are *no* black senior managers in almost half of the city's agencies."[91]

Progress did not always come easily. In the police department, long a bastion of Irish domination, court fights were required to change both qualifying examinations and hiring practices to increase the number of black officers. The Patrolman's Benevolent Association (PBA), the white controlled police union, opposed these pressures.[92] The PBA also fought against the establishment of a civilian review board, which most black New Yorkers favored, to hear charges regarding suspected police misconduct. As late as 1987 no black sat on the PBA's executive board, and there were only four blacks among the association's 360 delegates.[93] Consequently, black officers—as had many other ethnic groups—formed their own organization, the Association of Guardians. In the Police Department there existed separate black, Puerto Rican, Jewish, Irish, Polish, German, Catholic, and Protestant societies.[94] African Americans also had organizations within the fire and sanitation departments.[95] Only the PBA, it should be pointed out, had the bargaining power and status of a union.

While the municipal government was the largest single employer in New York, and while state, municipal, and federal governments employed about one third of working native-born blacks in the 1970s, the private sector provided the vast majority of jobs for African Americans as discriminatory hiring practices ebbed somewhat. Some New York blacks founded their own businesses, and a few did very well, even in the world of high finance. Most black enterprises, however, were small, family-run operations with low sales and profits. While increasing after World War II, these businesses employed only a small proportion of black New Yorkers.[96] In 1968 blacks owned a scant majority of the businesses in Harlem.[97]

In the world of entertainment—particularly in sports, music, and theater—African Americans made many inroads after World War II. Blacks had occasionally appeared before white New York audiences prior to World War II. In 1912, for example, an all-black musical group

■

had appeared at Carnegie Hall, and during the twenties and thirties all-black variety shows were popular on Broadway.[98] A few blacks, notably the famed actor Paul Robeson, appeared on stage before 1940, but too often in limited and stereotypical roles.[99] Robeson also gained fame as a singer and made his first appearance at Carnegie Hall in 1929.[100] But by no means were all New York theaters and concert halls receptive to blacks. Marian Anderson, the noted black singer who had sung at Carnegie Hall as early as 1928, was not offered a contract at the New York's Metropolitan Opera until 1955, after her voice was past its prime.[101] Gradually, however, other African Americans began to appear in prominent roles at the Met.

Nowhere was the segregation of black professionals more noticeable at the close of World War II than in baseball, the so-called national pastime. Black baseball players did play in the New York Giant's Polo Grounds and in Yankee Stadium before 1945, but only with all-black teams which rented the stadiums for their games. Indeed, in the 1940s the Yankees earned more than $100,000 annually from renting their Bronx stadium and other fields in their farm system to blacks. In 1946 the major league owners cited this added income as one reason not to desegregate.[102] With pressure mounting on baseball brought on by the passage of the New York's Ives-Quinn Law on discrimination in employment as well as by the more positive racial attitudes stemming from the war, Branch Rickey, owner of the Brooklyn Dodgers, hired Jackie Robinson to break the color line. In 1947, after a year in the Dodgers' farm club in Montreal, Robinson became the first African American to play in the big leagues. While blacks and most whites throughout the league cheered for Robinson, he was not warmly received by all the players. Dixie Walker, a popular Dodger, rallied other players to block Robinson from playing. The protest collapsed, however, and Walker requested a trade to another club. Rickey subsequently hired other black athletes as did the New York Giants beginning in 1949. The Yankees dragged their feet and did not field black players until the end of the 1953 season, when they placed two on their roster.[103]

Shortly after baseball began to desegregate, professional football and the newly formed National Basketball Association (NBA) hired black players.[104] By 1970 black athletes were fixtures on all New York City's professional teams (except hockey). But they were noticeably scarce in the front offices and in the coaching ranks. Neither the Yankees nor the

■

Brooklyn Dodgers nor the New York baseball Giants (while the latter two were located in New York) ever employed a black manager.

Few African-American New Yorkers were highly paid athletes, or professionals, or owners of businesses. For the working and middle classes, opportunities opened very slowly after World War II.[105] SCAD investigations in the 1940s and 1950s revealed that many New York hotels, manufacturers, and other business refused to hire blacks and that employment agencies continued to fill positions for "whites only."[106] In the 1960s the United States Equal Employment Commission reported either total absence or token representation of blacks in banking, insurance, advertising, and communications (including publishing, radio, newspapers, and television). On the city's major newspapers, for example, blacks accounted for fewer than one percent of white collar employees.[107] Employment opportunities were hardly better in the construction industry, where the Italian and Irish-run unions restricted entry into their membership. Two reports by the City Commission on Human Rights in the 1960s revealed great ethnic imbalance in the building trades and little sign of improvement.[108]

Like other black Americans, those in New York organized on behalf of civil rights during the turbulent 1960s. Directed by the National Association for the Advancement of Colored People, the Congress of Racial Equality, and ad hoc groups, activists picketed a number of construction sites and businesses, protesting against racial discrimination in hiring. Black ministers like Adam Clayton Powell and the Rev. Milton Galamison of Brooklyn were especially important in the civil rights struggle. Established black churches had always played a key role in addressing their congregants' social and economic concerns as well as their spiritual ones, and they continued to be influential during the civil rights era.[109] These efforts won the support of some politicians who insisted that public building projects, including a number of schools and the heavily picketed Downstate Medical Center in Brooklyn, employ companies and unions with records of fair hiring practices.[110]

Not all blacks agreed with the emphasis mainline civil rights advocates placed on achieving integration. Some urged that blacks build their own institutions within their community instead of attempting to desegregate white ones. The Black Muslims, the most important religious group urging separation, worked among the black poor, often dealing effectively with drug problems and employment issues.

■

Although the Nation of Islam, as the group was formally named, did not have an especially large following, it had an eloquent spokesman in Malcolm X. Before he was assassinated in 1965, he touched many black New Yorkers with his pleas for racial uplift.[111]

Civil rights advocates achieved only limited success in reversing discriminatory union hiring practices. Progress in black employment in the construction field was just beginning by 1970s, and was often resisted by unions in court actions.[112] In the public sector, among municipal transport workers, as late as 1938 only a few blacks were employed as porters and none as motormen.[113] By the mid-1960s black workers made up one half of all nonsupervisory positions in the industry, though the old Irish guard of the Transport Workers Union had effectively resisted black gains for years.[114] Other unions proved more accommodating to blacks as union members and even leaders. Membership in the American Federation of State, County, and Municipal Employees (AFSCME) was dominated by white males until the 1950s, when the union began major organizational drives among the city's low paid (usually black female) employees in the schools, hospitals, and government offices. With the support of leaders of District Council 37, Victor Gotbaum and Lillian Roberts, a black woman, the power base of DC 37 shifted from white males to black women by the 1970s, and the concerns of its minority group members began to be seriously addressed.[115]

Most service employees in private hospitals were also recruited from minority groups. Hospital Workers Union 1199, headed by older Jewish radicals, successfully organized most of these workers after New York state passed a law in 1963 guaranteeing them the right to union representation. Black unionists also began to take over leadership in 1199 as the older leaders retired.[116]

Like whites, blacks tended to move from traditional neighborhoods; often away from Harlem, the pre-war center of black New York. But there the similarity ended, because blacks generally found housing available only in racially segregated areas or in neighborhoods becoming all black because of white flight. The black settlement in Brooklyn's Bedford Stuyvesant, well on its way to becoming a racial ghetto by 1940, expanded rapidly to contiguous Crown Heights and Brownsville. Historian Harold Connolly wrote of the rapid flight of whites, "The speed of some of these neighborhood reversals could be blinding. In less

■

than ten years much of East New York was transformed from a comfortable, predominately white, lower-middle-class community into an impoverished, overwhelmingly black and Puerto Rican area."[117]

For the city's black and Puerto Rican poor segregated housing frequently meant run down, dilapidated accommodations in high crime areas, where many landlords abandoned their buildings rather than maintain them. As a result apartments fell into city hands because of tax delinquency, and the municipal government found itself in the position of becoming a slum landlord. Beginning in the 1960s thousands of buildings were simply abandoned, and once unoccupied, they were vandalized and fell victim to arson. City blocks in the South Bronx, Harlem, and Bedford Stuyvesant looked as if they had experienced wartime air raids.[118] Some buildings, technically abandoned, nonetheless housed squatters or became drug centers.[119]

During the New Deal years, the federal government had embarked upon a modest public housing program. After the war, the state and city, with federal backing, built housing for low income as well for middle class families. By 1990 the federal government had subsidized the construction of about 175,000 low rent units, which housed approximately 600,000 New Yorkers. Of the nation's public housing projects, New York's had a reputation of being among the best. As a result, there was always a long waiting list for the their apartments. The city's low income residences certainly provided improved housing for many poor citizens, but they sometimes became centers of crime, and frequently lacked adequate maintenance. Also, they were often segregated because of racial steering.[120]

Sadly, in some instances the postwar urban renewal programs aimed at slum clearance meant less rather than more housing for the poor. In constructing projects like the Lincoln Center for the Performing Arts and highways and bridges, builders tore down tenements and destroyed many small businesses as well without always providing new accommodations for the former occupants. Critics tagged urban renewal "Negro removal." In addition, corruption plagued slum clearance in New York City. Charges of scandal and of ignoring the poor became so frequent while Robert Moses ran urban renewal in the city that he was removed as director of the Mayor's Slum Clearance Committee.[121] After 1960, when reformers and city officials proposed scattering low income housing for the poor among middle-class neighborhoods

■

instead of building more large scale public housing projects, they encountered stiff opposition. Such was the case with a plan to place 7,500 units for low income families in Corona, an Italian community, and in Forest Hills, a predominately Jewish neighborhood, both in Queens. Forest Hills residents resisted the proposal and blamed Mayor John Lindsay for supporting it. "Don't Let Adolph Lindsay Destroy Forest Hills" became one of their slogans. Mario Cuomo, future governor of New York, finally arranged a compromise, but the incident ended practically all talk of more scattered low income housing.[122] Instead, many poor families began to receive rent subsidies.

Federal, state, and local housing programs failed to keep up with demand, and their inadequate funds were cut during the Reagan years. The City's Commission on the Year 2000 estimated in 1988 that the city was short 231,000 apartments and that, given the lack of construction, the figure would rise to 371,805 by the year 2000. To make ends meet, some poor families even doubled up, which often led to severe crowding. In sum, adequate housing for the poor remained an illusive goal in the decades following World War II.[123]

Even middle-class black New Yorkers who had found improved employment opportunities faced racial discrimination in renting and buying homes and apartments. In some interracial, middle-class neighborhoods, like the Laurelton section of Queens, community efforts maintained a mixed population for a number of years.[124] But these were exceptions rather than the rule. Researchers found little change in housing segregation in the decades after World War II. Douglas H. White, Commissioner of the New York State Division of Human Rights, concluded in 1989, "Housing is amazingly closed in the city.... I think its's striking the degree to which we have segregation."[125] Not until 1968 did the federal government enact a fair housing law, ten years after New York City had passed its Sharkey-Brown-Isaacs Act. Yet the federal law was difficult to enforce, while the agency to enforce the local law, the New York Commission on Human Rights, was understaffed and underfunded. Thus, neither the city nor the federal government successfully halted discriminatory practices in the housing market.[126]

Some black New Yorkers had long looked to schooling as the road to a better future for their children, and the issue of educational opportunities for minorities did receive more consideration after 1945. The city's special high schools—such as Hunter College High School,

Bronx Science, and Stuyvesant—were among the nation's finest and accepted only the top academic students. These elite institutions took pride in having rigorous curricula, with most of their graduates going on to prestigious universities and some winning national academic prizes. Yet they accommodated only a small fraction of the city's high school students and an even smaller percentage of minority pupils. New York also ran a number of experimental educational programs, a few of which resulted in lowered dropout rates and improved reading and math scores.[127] But here too the percentage of the whole was small.

Most New York youngsters attended the city's regular public schools, which were rapidly being abandoned by whites. After World War II the system was beset by social and economic problems—drugs, dilapidated old buildings, vandalism, high dropout rates, low test scores, violence, and de facto racial segregation. Civil rights advocates had long urged desegregation of the city's public schools and had organized demonstrations to force the Board of Education to act.[128] But because of white flight from the city and its public schools, the goal became increasingly illusive. A 1964 report by State Commissioner of Education James Allen, Jr. praised the goal of racial integration but noted that blacks and Hispanics accounted for three quarters of the school population.[129] In the city's private independent and parochial schools whites were in the majority, though many black and some Hispanic parents, seeking quality education, enrolled their children in them as well.[130]

As the goal of racially integrated public schools became impossible to achieve and as New York City's educational system seemed to be deteriorating, reformers suggested decentralizing control of the schools in order to give parents more input into the education of their children. In 1967 the city adopted a plan for decentralization suggested by a panel headed by McGeorge Bundy of the Ford Foundation.[131] It provided for elected district school boards that would have considerable administrative control over the city's elementary schools. The central school board would retain direct supervision of the high schools.

One immediate result of decentralization was the outbreak of a serious conflict between black leaders in the Ocean Hill-Brownsville District and Albert Shanker's United Federation of Teachers (UFT). In an emotional atmosphere replete with charges of anti-Semitism by the teachers and of racism by the local community leaders, the UFT won reinstatement of teachers who had been fired by the district's

■

school board. This beginning did not bode well for decentralization.[132]

For those who had earned a high school diploma, the city offered the chance for a college education. Few blacks attended private college and universities or even the tuition-free branches of the City University of New York (CUNY) prior to the 1960s. In 1960 minority students accounted for only five percent of the matriculants in the city's municipal colleges, the same percentage as in 1950.[133] Rising standards for admission and a shortage of space further limited the black presence at the city's colleges. A few special programs to boost black enrollment achieved little. A columnist for the *Amsterdam News* wrote in 1964, "The campus of the College of the City of New York (CCNY) is rapidly becoming as lily-white as the campus of Ole Miss University was the day after James Meredith graduated."[134]

Building on the civil rights momentum of the 1960s, black and Puerto Rican college students staged protests and demonstrations in the spring of 1969 at various CUNY schools. They closed CCNY and pressured the Board of Higher Education to agree that beginning in fall 1970 all of New York City's high school graduates would be granted a place in one of CUNY's branches.[135] This "open admissions" policy offered real hope for the city's minority students.

The presence of a substantial black middle class supporting an expanding black culture enabled New York City to remain a center of African-American literary and artistic creativity. No American city was as accepting of black performers. Alvin Ailey arrived in New York during the 1950s, became a noted black dancer on Broadway, and in 1958 formed the Alvin Ailey Dance Company. At first Ailey used only black dancers, but he began to add whites to his troupe in 1963. Ailey's inspired use of jazz and Afro-Caribbean dance as well as other modern idioms and classical ballet soon won him international recognition.[136] Arthur Mitchell joined the New York City Ballet in 1955, became a leading dancer within a few years, and then starred on Broadway. In 1969 he founded the acclaimed Dance Theater of Harlem. The Negro Ensemble Company, a theatrical group, received praise from mixed audiences, and Lorraine Hansbury's play, *A Raisin in the Sun*, won acclaim on Broadway in the 1960s. Harlem's Schomburg Library, the nation's largest collection of materials on black history, attracted many scholars and viewers when it ran special exhibits on black culture and history.

■

In contrast to these cultural achievements was the harsh reality that thousands of black New Yorkers lived in poverty and attended deteriorating schools. Moreover, racial bitterness made violence ever ready to explode, as it did in 1964 when a riot occurred pitting Harlemites against white police.[137] Upon taking office, Mayor John Lindsay expressed determination to do something about the plight of black New Yorkers. During the summer of 1967, when several cities—among them Newark, New Jersey—experienced racial rioting, Lindsay walked the streets of black neighborhoods and kept the peace.[138] Some called it his finest hour. In addition, he supported Lyndon Johnson's War on Poverty programs to aid the urban poor and urged the creation of a civilian review board to hear complaints about police mistreatment of blacks. The mayor also established a variety of special programs aimed at helping black neighborhoods.[139]

Mayor Lindsay won considerable praise from African Americans for these efforts, though some black leaders complained that he promised more than he was able to deliver.[140] Lindsay's programs suffered from a white backlash in the late 1960s when voters defeated his civilian review board proposal by a two to one margin. The measure did especially poorly in white working class neighborhoods.[141] Moreover, as noted, proposals for scattered public housing also encountered fierce opposition and had to be scrapped.

Given the city's economic growth; the enactment of laws banning racial, religious, and ethnic discrimination; affirmative action programs; the more enlightened political discourse of the 1960s; and the opening of new opportunities for Jews, Italians, other white ethnics, blacks, and Puerto Ricans, one would have to conclude that on balance the period from 1945 to 1970 indeed represented "a better time" for most New Yorkers. But neither poverty nor racial and ethnic conflict were by any means eradicated by 1970. Moreover, with signs of a deteriorating city economy emerging and the repudiation of President's Johnson's War on Poverty by his successor Richard Nixon, the future appeared uncertain.

■

*Truly
a Global
City:
New York,
1970
to the
Present*

## i

**E**ven as its economy slumped in the 1970s, New York City received yet another wave of newcomers, and ever since immigration has once again been reshaping the city. Six years after the enactment of the immigration restrictions of 1924, 34 percent of the city's residents were foreign born, but the figure decreased until 1970, when it stood at only 18 percent. The new post-1970 arrivals pushed the percentage up again; the city gained about 800,000 immigrants during the 1970s and nearly a million during the 1980s. A liberal immigration law enacted in 1990 helped make it possible for 120,000 newcomers to settle in the city even during the economically depressed year of 1992, and raised the likelihood that New York City would be receiving more than 100,000 immigrants annually during the 1990s.[1] These figures refer to legal immigrants; it was impossible to determine the precise number of illegal or undocumented aliens in the city, but in 1993 the Department of City Planning estimated their number to be about 400,000.[2] If they were added to officially counted immigrants (28.2 percent of the city's population in 1990), it would reveal that close to one in three New Yorkers was foreign born in the mid-1990s.

Whereas prior to 1970 the vast majority of the city's immigrants hailed from Europe, subsequent arrivals mostly came from the Caribbean, South and East Asia, and the Middle East. Whites continued to leave the city, while at the same time the population mix became more globally diverse than ever before in its history. In 1940 persons of European origin accounted for almost 95 percent of the residents. By 1990 they made up less than half that figure. That year the half-million Asians constituted about 7 percent of the city's population, while Hispanics accounted for about one quarter and blacks slightly more. Of the city's blacks, more than 500,000 hailed from the Caribbean.[3]

The signs of this diversity were everywhere. Nearly half of the city's 80 foreign-language and ethnic newspapers (of which 22 were dailies) had been established between 1970 and 1990.[4] The city boasted Filipino, Korean, and Spanish newspapers and nine dailies alone in Chinese by 1990, many sold by Asian Indian news vendors.[5] After buying their newspapers, New Yorkers could purchase fresh fruit and vegetables from the Korean greengrocers who operated 90 percent of the city's produce stores.[6]

As had their predecessors, the new immigrants came seeking economic opportunity or political freedom. Thanks to modern communications and contacts with countrymen living in New York, information about America and the city was plentiful, and air travel cut the journey to only a few hours. If the latest New Yorkers could learn of the experience of those who had arrived earlier in the century, they might well be heartened. For the descendants of European immigrants continued to find opportunities for social mobility in New York and in the process assimilated into the larger institutional life of the city. If the new immigrants looked at black New Yorkers, however, they would have observed a different pattern. In spite of the gains by African Americans, racism had by no means been eradicated by the 1990s.

■

The largest numbers of post-1970 immigrants came from the Caribbean. After the 1960s, Puerto Rican migrants declined, but the figures for other Caribbean newcomers increased. Whereas in the 1950s about 90 percent of the city's Hispanics were Puerto Ricans, by 1990 only about 50 percent were.[7] As the mayor's first *Annual Report on Hispanic Concerns* explained in 1986, "The City's Hispanic community is very diverse and is, in actuality, several different communities."[8] The single largest nationality to arrive was Dominican. By 1990 Dominicans had surpassed Italians to become first in population among the city's foreign-born. Dominicans and their American-born children numbered over 300,000 in that year, and their numerical growth showed no signs of abating.[9] Their exact population was unknown because many lived in the city without proper immigration papers. Some had overstayed visitor's visas, while others had entered with fraudulent papers or had arrived via Puerto Rico, passing as Puerto Rican natives.[10]

Dominicans settled mainly in Washington Heights in upper Manhattan or in Queens. Women predominated in this immigrant stream, as they did in most others coming to the city during this period. Most Dominican women at one time or other found jobs in the city's service sector and even in the declining garment industry. Many of their households had at least two workers, which pushed their family incomes above those of Puerto Ricans, though Dominicans were still clearly a working-class immigrant group.[11] In common with the general Hispanic population of the city, they had lower than average educational achievement levels and higher than average poverty rates.[12]

Dominican males sometimes accumulated enough capital to open garment factories, an economic enterprise dominated at the time by Chinese entrepreneurs.[13] Other Dominican men could be found among the many Hispanics who labored as construction workers, largely in the non-union rehabilitation business.[14] Dominicans also appeared to be taking over the city's 8,000 bodegas, small grocery stores catering to the growing Hispanic population.[15] By 1990 they controlled more than 70 percent of Hispanic-run businesses, even though they constituted less than 40 percent of the city's Latinos.[16] Unfortunately, Washington Heights became a drug center in the 1980s. Resident dealers sold drugs to their neighbors, other New Yorkers, and commuters from New Jersey, who arrived via the nearby George Washington Bridge. As

■

elsewhere, drug dealers fought among themselves for control of the trade, and in the process some innocent bystanders were injured and killed. One alarmed resident testified, "We hear gunshots all the time. And we all know a stray bullet has no conscience."[17] Conflicts with the police inevitably arose, and in 1992, after a patrolman shot and killed a man he claimed was dealing, a riot ensued.[18]

As had blacks and immigrants before them, some young Dominicans males sought a way out of poverty through sports. Baseball was popular in the Dominican Republic, hence, as a reporter for the *New York Times* wrote, it was "nearly a religion" in an "impoverished Washington Heights."[19] With supportive adult coaching and hours and hours of practice, baseball offered a way to a college scholarship or the major leagues for the fortunate few. It had been that way for Hall of Famer Rod Carew, a Panamanian from the same neighborhood, who signed a big league contract in the 1960s.[20] Dominicans hoped that their neighbor Manny Ramirez, who signed with the Cleveland Indians, would become a future star. He played his first big league games against the New York Yankees in 1993.[21]

In the 1980s a small but growing Mexican community appeared. Numbering 20,000 in 1980, it had tripled ten years later. Following the pattern of other ethnic groups, Mexicans opened restaurants, organized soccer and baseball teams, ran social clubs, and celebrated a national holiday—Mexican Independence Day.[22] Some entered illegally and became street vendors of flowers, much to the chagrin of flower shop owners. In Queens twenty florists went to the police to get these street vendors removed for selling without a license. They "kill us," complained one florist, and he insisted that they "would put small flower shops out of business."[23]

Small groups of Hispanics from other Caribbean nations also settled in New York. One of these new communities consisted of Cubans who left their homeland in the years following the 1959 victory of Fidel Castro and communism. They came in several waves, the most notorious being 10,000 who arrived as part of the Mariel Boat Lift in 1980. The violence in Central America—in El Salvador, Guatemala, and Nicaragua—beginning in the 1970s sent tens of thousands of refugees fleeing north to the United States. If they were unable to enter as regular immigrants or refugees, they chose to enter illegally and take their chances here rather than returning to their strife-torn homelands.[24]

Some national communities in the city were so small that they only came to public attention when a crisis struck. When a fire in the Bronx Happy Land Night Club claimed eighty-seven lives in early 1990, New York's Hondurans mourned deeply. The club had been a center of that community's little known social life, and many of the dead were Hondurans.[25]

The new migration from the non-Hispanic islands of the Caribbean added to the city's black population. West Indian immigration, which had dropped drastically in the 1930s and remained low in the 1940s and 1950s, picked up again when Congress liberalized the immigration laws. Newcomers came from Jamaica, Trinidad and Tobago, St. Vincent and Grenada, Barbados, and every other island in the Caribbean as well as from Panama and Guyana. Jamaicans and Guyanese constituted the two largest English-speaking groups; one half of the nation's Jamaicans were located in New York City, and nearly 100,000 Guyanese emigrated there after 1965.[26] Some West Indian immigrants were the descendants of East Asian Indians who had been brought there as contract workers long ago. Haitian immigrants added Creole and, to a lesser extent, French to the multiplicity of languages heard on the city's streets. Brooklyn drew nearly half of the Caribbean blacks to homes in Bedford-Stuyvesant, Flatbush, and Crown Heights, while the more prosperous settled in Queens.[27] Brooklyn neighborhoods took on a Caribbean flavor as restaurants and stores advertised Jamaican pastries, codfish cakes, peas, rice, and spicy jerk chicken. West Indian accents and music became common, and travel agencies and other stores displayed flags and other symbols of Caribbean nations.[28]

Earlier generations of black immigrants had earned a reputation for opening successful businesses, for political participation, for home ownership, and for organizing self-help credit associations. A resurgence of West Indian politics might have been sparked by the election in the early 1990s of Una Clark to the City Council and Nick Perry to the New York State Assembly. Both were Jamaicans.[29]

The new West Indians seemed to be continuing the entrepreneurial spirit of earlier generations. One city official noted in 1988 that New York City had six to eight thousand Caribbean businesses with Brooklyn claiming more than any other borough. "Ten years ago," he said "there would have been half as many."[30] Some West Indians rapidly found special niches of opportunity in the city's economy. For example, they oper-

■

ated most of New York City's 20,000 car service vehicles as well as jitney buses, which were "known to accept subway tokens as payment."[31]

In spite of their reputation for entrepreneurship, however, West Indians were in fact not statistically more involved in business ownership than other ethnic groups, and they lagged behind Asians. Most found jobs in the new service economy of the city. West Indian women, who outnumbered men in the migration process, often worked as nurses and nurse's aids and, more than any other New York group except perhaps for "New Irish" women, as domestics. About one tenth of West Indian women worked as domestics, often as live-in help. The actual figure may have been higher than that because, like many of the "New Irish," some worked illegally, without proper immigration papers.[32]

West Indian family incomes, though less than whites, were higher than those of most Hispanics and native-born black New Yorkers, primarily because in many West Indian families both husbands and wives were in the workforce. In 1980, 74 percent of recent immigrant West Indian men and 66 percent of the women were employed, figures higher than for native-born blacks and for many immigrants. Few West Indian families received public assistance.[33]

West Indians brought with them a host of associations. Group activity organized around politics, occupations, sports, and the culture of the islands. Although the city had several African-American newspapers, the circulation of *Carib News*, founded by island immigrants in the 1980s, climbed to over 60,000 within a few years.[34] The annual Labor Day Carnival, held since 1969 along Brooklyn's Eastern Parkway, was a significant expression of West Indian ethnic identity, featuring elaborate costumes, music (such as Jamaican Reggae), and parades. It drew an estimated 800,000 spectators and participants by the late 1980s. Even black Caribbeans who had no tradition of Carnival and American blacks from all over the United States attended and participated with great enthusiasm. Carnival became a political event as well, with politicians jockeying for invitations and space from which to address the crowd. Largely ignored at first by the city's press, by the late 1980s Carnival's attendance surpassed that of other ethnic parades and celebrations, including the Puerto Rican Day Parade, founded in 1958, and even the venerable St. Patrick's Day Parade.[35]

Like English-speaking West Indians, Haitians were unprepared for the racism they encountered in their search for housing and jobs. Some

Haitians located in upper Manhattan and Queens, but most lived in Brooklyn. Discrimination was not their only problem. Because many were poor and lacked English language and occupational skills, they experienced trouble finding employment; consequently, most labored in the relatively low-paying service jobs of the city. Haitian family incomes were probably below those of other non-Hispanic Caribbean people. Those who were undocumented faced particularly difficult times in the job market.[36]

Because of their concern for conditions in their homeland, New York Haitians often focused their attention on politics there rather than on New York issues. With the overthrow of the Duvalier government in 1986, a few Haitians returned home, but most remained in the United States. After the democratic government that replaced the Duvaliers fell to a coup in 1991, a new exodus began.[37]

In addition to political associations concerned with events in their homeland, Haitians also established organizations to address matters pertaining to city life. Many Haitians joined Catholic churches, even parishes that held services in Spanish or English rather than Creole or French. In at least one Brooklyn church Haitians divided over whether to use French or Haitian Creole in the service.[38] In another Catholic parish Haitians breathed new life into a dying festival. After one hundred years the festival of Our Lady of Mount Carmel Church, held annually along 115th Street in East Harlem, was losing its Italian flavor. By the late 1980s only 1,000 Italians still lived in the neighborhood where 85,000 had resided sixty years before. Then immigrant Haitians heard of the festival, and those who had worshipped the Madonna at Haiti's Ville de Bonheur joined the celebration in East Harlem. In recent years about half of those participating in a thriving festival were Haitian.[39]

The 1990 census indicated that Chinese constituted about half of the city's 512,000 Asians, and their numbers have continued to increase.[40] Up to the 1970s the majority of the Chinese had come via Taiwan or Hong Kong, both swarming with refugees since the 1949 communist victory in China. But many post-1980 newcomers hailed from a number of regions within China as well as from other Southeast Asian lands and spoke different Chinese dialects.[41] In 1981 the United States had given the People's Republic of China a separate quota, and consequently the number immigrants coming directly from the mainland increased substantially.[42]

The arrival of so many new immigrants placed great pressure on Chinatown's housing. Speculators from Hong Kong, with funds to invest and uneasy about the approach of that colony's transfer from British to Chinese control scheduled for 1997, purchased buildings in Chinatown, north in Little Italy, and east on the Lower East Side. Even the resultant expansion of Manhattan's Chinatown did not provide enough housing for the new immigrants, and as prices soared many sought homes in the city's other boroughs.[43]

Queens's Flushing district, through which the number 7 subway line runs, rapidly emerged as the city's second major area of Chinese concentration, composed mainly of people of Taiwanese origin. Because many Koreans and Asian Indians also lived in the district, the number 7 became known as the "Orient Express." When the city expanded the line's facilities, it printed notices in English, Spanish, Korean, and Chinese to inform residents of the changes.[44]

In the 1980s, another Chinese settlement, primarily of Hong Kong people, emerged in the Sunset Park–Bay Ridge district of Brooklyn. It occupied an area once known as Little Scandinavia, whose Norwegian former residents had since moved to Staten Island or the suburbs.[45] Because Sunset Park was home to a variety of New Yorkers who had moved there in the 1980s, it was unlikely that a Chinatown on the order of Manhattan's would develop, but it was, nonetheless, an important and growing Chinese community.[46]

Many of the new Chinese immigrants lived outside ethnic enclaves, scattered throughout the city and in nearby suburbs. Unlike the earlier arriving Chinese, these were not proprietors of hand laundries, a business that was disappearing in the face of competition from laundromats and home machines. Rather, they constituted what Peter Kwong has called "the uptown" Chinese, highly educated professionals employed by universities, corporations, and research and medical centers. "Uptown" Chinese professionals had often studied English in Taiwan and then come to America to complete their educations, especially in the sciences. From 1965 to 1985 some 150,000 Taiwanese students came to the United States, most of whom remained as immigrants by finding jobs upon completing their graduate studies. In contrast, Kwong points out, the immigrant residents of Chinatown tended to be working-class with lower levels of education and limited English language skills.[47]

■

While the city's "uptown" Chinese earned livings in ways not available to pre-1945 Chinese, many other newcomers became small-business entrepreneurs. Chinatown remained a tourist attraction, and its 400 restaurants catered to thousands of outside visitors as well as to its Chinese population. Chinese eateries appeared in many other neighborhoods of New York City. The growing popularity of Chinese food gave them a sizeable clientele as did their low prices and New Yorkers' traditional love of "eating out." Costs of running restaurants were kept low because of the abundance of cheap, nonunion Chinese male laborers, including immigrants who were smuggled into the United States without proper papers.[48] With limited English and few employment options, many sought jobs as cooks, waiters, and kitchen helpers. Some even hoped eventually to open their own restaurants, a dream realized by a few who managed to run establishments as family enterprises.[49]

Chinese immigration occurred during a period of decline in New York's garment industry, the employer of so many turn-of-the-century European immigrants. Yet the industry still offered opportunities for small enterprises that could adjust quickly to meet the demands of rapid changes in fashion. Chinese entrepreneurs moved to take up this challenge. Immigrant capital provided start-up funds for Chinatown's small garment shops, and Chinese women immigrants provided the (largely low cost) labor.[50]

Anxious to help support their families and not yet fluent in English, these women, especially if they were here illegally, had few alternatives. They sometimes brought their preschool children to the shops during the working day in violation of labor laws. Moreover, slightly older children were reported to be employed in the shops in further disregard of those laws. Factory safety laws were also regularly ignored, leading a state inspector to remark about one shop, "I've never seen a worse fire exit."[51] Occasionally friendship and kin networks of employment provided for a paternalistic relationship between boss and worker, but such ties were limited. Many garment factories re-created the earlier immigrant sweatshops. In response to these conditions, the International Ladies' Garment Workers' Union managed to organize most of Chinatown's shops and more than 20,000 women workers during the 1980s. For the women unionization brought higher wages, safer conditions, and health insurance benefits.[52]

■

Some Chinese garment workers hoped to save enough money to open their own shops. A number of men did succeed in starting needle-trade factories, but by the late 1980s rising costs of labor, spiraling prices for building space, and foreign competition made this ethnic enterprise a risky venture. Indeed, many Chinatown shops appeared to be in financial difficulties in the early 1990s.[53]

Workers in low paying jobs in restaurants and in the needle trades on the one hand and higher paid, well educated professionals on the other made the city's new Chinese a people of contrasts. Some commentators pointed to the economic success of the "uptown" Chinese and the growing number of Chinese students in the city's elite colleges and universities and called New York's Chinese a "model minority" of high achieving people. Chinese New Yorkers along with other Asians did come to the fore in the 1980s as winners of academic honors and prestigious awards, including the annual Westinghouse Science Scholarships. Young Chinese students did make up a disproportionate share of students in the city's academically selective high schools and in its colleges and universities.[54] But, because younger recent settlers of Chinatown were often without adequate English language skills, many had difficulties in school.[55] Furthermore, observers noted that the proportion of Chinese living at or below the national poverty line exceeded the city average. According to the 1980 census, 71 percent of the adults in Chinatown never finished high school, and over half could not speak English well. Many were products of the earlier bachelor societies, who had been barred from decent jobs by racial discrimination; now, in their old age, they were living on meager funds.[56] Ten years later the census revealed that one quarter of all families in Chinatown lived on incomes below the poverty line.[57]

Not the least among problems encountered by Chinese newcomers was crime. Chinatown in the 1920s had been racked by tong wars, violent struggles for control among gangs, but by the 1930s these conflicts had largely ended. For the next thirty years Chinatown earned a reputation for its low crime rates. However, the arrival of new immigration after 1970 featured gangs who for a price protected gambling houses and drug dealers and who extorted money from merchants, theaters, nightclubs, and massage parlors. The gangs, composed largely of teenaged males, quickly won reputations for fearlessness and violence. Ethnic Chinese from Vietnam were alleged to be the most dangerous and feared of Chinatown's gang members, especially the group known as "Born to Kill." Remarked one police official, they "have no associations, no ties to adults, so they have no sense of shame and no qualms about using violence."[58] New York Police officials also suggested that Chinese immigrants were dominating the heroin trade, moving into other organized criminal activity, and expanding their interests into Queens and Brooklyn. In this they followed the example of earlier immigrants.[59] Not coincidentally, similar charges were made about Colombians, Dominicans, Soviets, and Jamaicans.

The vast majority of the city's Chinese had no connections to the emerging street gangs, but rather in traditional immigrant fashion struggled to make a living for themselves and their children. A growing number of Chinese turned to the courts and governmental agencies for assistance. The Chinese Consolidated Benevolent Association, long the dominant political force in Chinatown, consequently lost some of its influence and hold on Chinatown's residents. After 1960 Chinatown received some poverty funds, which further encouraged residents to turn to politics and political action. Groups like the newly formed Chinatown Planning Council ran a variety of programs to assist new immigrants.[60]

The demise of the national origins quota system in 1965 also made it possible for substantial numbers of Koreans, Filipinos, and Indians to immigrate to the New York City area. Many Koreans, who settled in various city neighborhoods but mostly in Queens, worked as medical professionals. They played a crucial role in helping to fill intern and resident vacancies in municipal hospitals and in providing care in neighborhoods inhabited by poor blacks and Hispanics.[61] Korean greengroceries made up one third of the estimated 15,000 Korean enterprises in New York. Other Koreans turned their hands to a variety of small businesses, including dry cleaners, liquor stores, and nail salons.[62]

The initial greengrocers did not require large start-up funds. They purchased stores from older Italians and Jews throughout the city, even in ghetto areas inhabited by blacks and Hispanics. Operators of these stores were often college graduates, whose opportunities were limited by a lack of English language skills or by the prejudiced employment practices of some American firms. Like so many immigrants of the past generations, they turned to small businesses requiring little initial capital and worked long hours, assisted by a ready supply of family work-

■

ers. Several business surveys in the late 1980s indicated that greengrocers labored an average of sixty-six hours per week.[63]

Koreans published several newspapers and organized business and mutual benefit associations. They conducted weekend schools specializing in the Korean language and the study of Korean culture.[64] As other immigrant groups traditionally did, they ran a variety of social programs. Perhaps their most important cultural institutions were many Protestant churches, which claimed more than half the city's Koreans as members. Although a majority of South Koreans are Buddhists, a disproportionate number of Korean immigrants in America are Christians, especially Methodists and Presbyterians. Replacing declining white English-speaking Protestant congregations, they turned a number of these churches into thriving institutions.[65] In 1990, the Catholic Archdiocese of New York established its first Korean parish—St. John Nam—in the Bronx. Within a year it was serving 400 Korean families.[66]

As did the Koreans, Filipinos and Indians found homes throughout the city, though the multiethnic Flushing area of Queens was particularly popular. Many Indians and Filipinos were medical professionals—physicians, nurses, and technicians—but there were sufficient numbers of nonprofessionals available to establish more traditional immigrant businesses. Filipinos opened stores specializing in ethnic food on Manhattan's West Side, adjacent to non-Filipino shops, and Asian Indian restaurants proliferated throughout the city during the 1980s.[67]

But Asian Indians and Filipinos found their cultural ties mostly outside their scattered areas of residence.[68] What kept them cohesive were their proliferating professional groups and social and religious organizations. For example, the first Hindu Temple, founded in 1977, had seven full time priests by 1991.[69] While Indians claimed that Sikhs and Hindus shared a sense of Indian identity, in fact Sikhs established their own community groups, such as the Sikh Cultural Society, and annually held their own Sikh Day Parade (in April) instead of participating in the India Day Parade (in August).[70] Many Filipinos joined Catholic churches in New York, became members of Filipino professional associations, or affiliated with the Filipino Community Center of New York, which held annual festivals in Queens. Others enlisted in the Ninoy Aquino Movement to support democracy in their homeland.[71]

Of the Asians arriving after 1965, no group was as well educated as the Indians.[72] Indian nationals filled a niche in the American economy

■

as native born Americans increasingly tended to avoid careers in science.[73] The first Indians to emigrate were usually men, but they soon sent for their families. In later years, as more arrived, their overall skill and educational level tended to be lower (the same was true of Filipinos). Moreover, although disproportionately classified as professionals, not all of them were able to meet the professional standards of this country. Still others simply were not highly educated; they turned to business or working class jobs.

The most visible Indian enterprise was that of the Kapoor brothers, who emigrated from New Delhi in the mid-1970s. They started their business empire by buying several newsstands and then rapidly acquiring many more, especially in subways and at bus and railroad stations. Until their 1987 conviction on income tax evasion charges, they had built a $20 million a year empire with the help of their mostly Indian and Pakistani immigrant employees.[74] Nevertheless, Indians continued to run many of the city's newsstands, while others purchased and operated gas stations. Parmjit Singh worked for three years as a busboy and cook before opening his first station. "It's very hard work but it's easy to run—to order gas, to clean, to keep the books." By 1900 he and his partner owned thirteen stations.[75]

Among other South and East Asian immigrants to settle in the city after 1970 were a small number of refugees from Burma fleeing that nation's dictatorship. A few Bangladeshi arrived after 1980, but their numbers substantially increased after 6,500 of them won visas in an immigrant lottery held by the United States late in the decade. The winners subsequently brought in their families and formed networks to support a growing immigration stream. Bangladeshi found jobs in construction, as cab drivers, and as delicatessen and restaurant workers.[76] In addition, several thousand Thais arrived, and some opened restaurants that became quite popular in the 1980s. In response to immigrant pleas, a Buddhist monk arrived from Thailand in 1974 to serve a temple in the Bronx.[77] Pakistanis also increased their numbers during the 1980s, as did the Japanese.

Approximately 20,000 Vietnamese, Laotian, and Cambodian refugees from the war in Indochina settled in New York City. Among the Vietnamese were ethnic Chinese who found homes in Chinatown.[78] Voluntary organizations reported that these people were making a rapid if difficult adjustment to New York City. Skills used in Indochina

■

often could not be employed in the city, thus these newcomers, in typical fashion, took what unskilled jobs were available.[79] For the many Cambodians and Laotians who had been farmers, the adjustment to urban life was particularly difficult. The language barrier was formidable for many (especially wives who remained at home), although schoolchildren picked up English rapidly. The most notable success story of the early 1980s was that of Chi Luu, an ethnic Chinese from Vietnam. One of the "boat people," he lived in a refugee camp for five months before coming to the United States. Within five years of his arrival he had learned English, completed high school, and graduated as valedictorian of his class at the City College of New York.[80]

Among the problems encountered by Asians were outbreaks of anti-Asian violence. In July 1988 an attack by a group of Hispanics on Pakistanis worshipping at a Queens Mosque prompted an investigation by the police department's Bias Investigation Unit.[81] Operating greengroceries in largely black neighborhoods brought Koreans into conflict with the black customers. In 1988, quarrels over claims of shoplifting and counter claims of harassment of customers led to black-led boycotts of greengrocers in Harlem and Brooklyn. Black political leaders managed to settle these disputes, but new conflicts emerged in 1990.[82] Blacks again boycotted several Korean-owned stores in Flatbush, insisting that the Korean storekeepers insulted and abused them. The Koreans denied these charges.[83] When Mayor David Dinkins tried to mediate the dispute, which had erupted into violence, a demonstrator shouted, "Nothing can stop us! We ain't going to listen to Uncle Tom Dinkins."[84] A Brooklyn jury eventually acquitted a Korean manager charged with assault, and calm gradually returned to Flatbush. However, a month later still another boycott began in Queens.[85] The ramifications of that dispute were particularly ugly, including attempted robbery and the burning of a Korean store to the ground.[86]

Post-1970 liberal immigration policies encouraged a considerable number of Middle Easterners to emigrate to the United States. They had economic motives for doing so, but the constant turmoil in that region also fed their desire to escape. Wars between Israel and her Arab neighbors and the civil war in Lebanon left many homeless. The Islamic revolution in Iran in 1979 sent thousands of Christian, Jewish, and Bahai Iranians to America, and many students from Iran who were in the United States at the time of the uprising elected to stay here.[87] The

■

Soviet invasion of Afghanistan in 1979 also triggered a movement of refugees to the United States. By 1992 Afghans owned over 200 stores in New York, including fast-food chicken restaurants as well as those specializing in Afghan cooking.[88] The center of Arab settlement in New York City was Brooklyn's Atlantic Avenue section with its many restaurants, bakeries, and Arab-run shops.[89]

This new Arab immigration differed from that of the early twentieth century. Those coming before World War II were usually Christians, but although some Maronite Catholics and Antiochian Orthodox Church members also arrived, most of the newcomers were Muslims.[90] Growing numbers of Muslim New Yorkers attended the seventy old and newly established mosques which existed in 1993 and participated in the annual spring observation of Ramadan.[91] Such occasions brought Arabs together with Muslims from Afghanistan, Egypt, Pakistan, and Bangladesh as well as with African Americans of that persuasion.[92] In April 1991, the newest and largest Mosque in New York opened on West 96th Street in Manhattan, with space for 1,000 worshippers.[93] Muslims had also established ten schools in the city to provide religious and secular education for their children.[94]

The new Muslims felt secure enough in their status to even demand a change in the city's parking rules. Every New Yorker knows that parking is banned on alternate sides of many roadways for a few hours each day so that the city can clean its streets. These rules do not apply on Sundays or on many national holidays such as Thanksgiving and the Fourth of July. The city also suspends the cleanups on twenty-two Jewish and Christian holidays. In early 1992 Muslim leaders claimed that there were at least 700,000 adherents of Islam in the city and urged the City Council to approve a measure that would add two days of parking rule suspensions during their annual observance of Ramadan. The city administration, while praising the city's "mosaic" of many peoples and cultures, worried about the effect more suspensions would have on the city's efforts to keep the streets clean. A spokesman for Mayor David Dinkins said, "There are not enough days of the year to observe all of the holidays of the ethnic and religious groups in the gorgeous mosaic." On the other hand, a council member remarked, "It's pretty hard to say to a major religious group in the city that the other religions got theirs first, and it's too late for you."[95] Ultimately, the City Council finally agreed to the Muslims' request.[96]

■

Of course not all Middle Easterners were Muslims, Christians, or Bahais. Prominent among this immigrant stream were Israeli Jews. Official figures indicated that only a thousand or so Israelis annually settled in New York after 1970.[97] But scholars and New York Israelis claim that the numbers were considerably larger because so many came as visitors, found jobs, and simply stayed as illegal immigrants when their visas expired. Whatever their precise number, most settled among other Jews in Queens and Brooklyn. Israeli cab drivers became common in the 1980s. A fairly well educated group, many worked in professions or ran their own small businesses, such as the El Al Moving Company in Manhattan. Israelis published their own newspaper and tended to socialize with one another, thus keeping somewhat apart from the city's larger Jewish community.[98]

As was the case from 1945 to 1970, the largest group of post 1970 South America immigrants were Colombians, whose primary community was initially in Jackson Heights, Queens.[99] The Catholic Archdiocese of New York estimated that 200,000 Colombians lived in the city by the late 1980s, a number larger than the official census and immigration figures.[100] Whatever their exact population, the Colombians were numerous enough to develop an active community in the city. In addition to their growing presence in the affairs of the city's Roman Catholic Church, Colombians supported two weekly newspapers and established a Colombian Civic Center in Elmhurst, Queens. An umbrella group, the Federation of Colombian Organizations, organized in the late 1980s, encouraged Colombians to participate in politics and to counter what many believed were "unfair media portrayals of Colombians as drug criminals."[101]

Adding to the city's global mix were Africans. Small but growing numbers of Egyptians, Ethiopians, South Africans, Nigerians, and Senegalese settled in New York after 1970. Among the Nigerians were medical professionals and other well educated persons. Ethiopian immigrants included refugees from a Marxist regime and a civil war, and a few South Africans, white and black, came because of political unrest and violence in their homeland. The city's Ghanaian community was large enough to elect their own king of the Ashanti people in the United States.[102] Collectively, these Africans amounted to only a few thousand persons by the 1990s, but they and their newly formed organizations did add to the growing diversity of black New York and pointed

■

to a potential source of future immigration.[103] For the most part the African immigrants went unnoticed until the 1980s when Senegalese street vendors, many of whom lacked proper immigration papers, became a visible presence. Selling street goods ranging from umbrellas on rainy days to socks, toys, books, and watches, they generated a controversy when police cited them for peddling without proper licenses. A Manhattan judge charged the Police Department with racial bias for selectively enforcing laws against the Senegalese and dismissed the charges.[104]

While people from the Third World dominated the immigrant flow, some Europeans continued to seek a new beginning in America. The largest number of post-1970 European refugees settling in New York City were Soviet Jews who came first in the 1970s and again beginning in 1988, after a period in which the Soviet government refused to let many emigrate. Following the 1989 Soviet liberalization thousands of Soviet citizens, mostly Jews but also a number of Armenians, rushed to migrate to the United States. New York immigration agencies reported a "deluge" of new refugees.[105] By far the largest Soviet community was established in the Brighton Beach section of Brooklyn, the home of prior waves of Jewish immigrants.[106] The newcomers formed their own organizations, published a newspaper, and opened stores, restaurants, and night clubs with a distinctive Russian flavor.[107] Commenting on the abundance of food in Brighton Beach's social clubs, one emigre said, "These clubs are a Russian's version of paradise. Russians suffered from a lack of food for years and so the notion of dieting is alien to our culture. Every calorie is prized, even if it is all fat."[108]

The Soviets generally came in family units and often possessed professional skills. Unlike the Jewish immigrants from Russia at the turn of the century, most of whom were raised in a religious tradition, these newcomers, after years of Communist anti-religious policies, had little knowledge of Judaism. Like all immigrants faced with a new language to learn, they worked at entry level employment until they mastered English and the mores of their new land. Not untypically, Rafail Fishman, a violin teacher who emigrated from the Ukraine in 1989, found a job as an appliance repairman, even though he "had never seen a microwave or a dishwasher and dryer in the Soviet Union. . . . It was very difficult to find a job, with no friends here, little English and no experience except as a music teacher."[109] Soviet Jews were aided by

■

federal refugee programs, which had not been available for most earlier European refugees, and by Jewish agencies. Among the latter there was a strong desire to teach the Russians about their religion and to absorb them into the larger American Jewish community. Because of this assistance, most made a fairly rapid adjustment.[110]

Among the new European immigrants were a few Czechs who arrived after the Soviet Union and the Warsaw Pact nations crushed their uprising in 1968.[111] In the 1980s Poles escaped to America following the temporary collapse of the Solidarity movement. Nearly 8,000 arrived between 1982 and 1989. Even after the collapse of communism in Poland, immigrants from that country continued to settle in New York City. When a lottery was held in 1991 for visas under the provisions of the 1990 immigration act, Poles won more than 12,000 slots, second only to the Irish. As might be expected, many of these winners picked New York City for their new homes; over 4,000 did so in 1992.[112]

Irish nationals discovered that the 1965 immigration act ending preferential quotas for northern Europeans made it difficult for them to get an American visa. Annual legal Irish immigration to New York was only a few hundred in the early 1980s, but many came as visitors and stayed illegally. Congress eventually legalized many of these newcomers and made it possible for Ireland to increase emigration to the United States.[113] Unlike previous waves of Irish immigrants and like so many other recent European arrivals, these latest newcomers were well educated. The "New Irish" settled in older Irish-American neighborhoods such as Woodside in Queens or Woodlawn in the Bronx. "You go into a diner and it doesn't take 10 seconds before you hear the brogue, which you wouldn't have heard around here 10 years ago except occasionally," remarked one of Woodside's old Irish.[114] Irish bars reported Gaelic revivals as did the New York Gaelic Athletic Association football league, which held games in a sixty-three-year old stadium in Van Cortlandt Park in the Bronx.[115] Unlike the historical pattern of Irish immigration in which women formed the majority, scattered surveys indicated the "New Irish" were typically males who relied on the city's Irish community to find work mainly in the construction industry. In these jobs they sometimes received wages "off the books" in cash. "New Irish" women often worked in childcare; the *Irish Echo* carried dozens of ads for the placement of nannies.[116]

■

## ii

While new immigrants poured into the city, persons of European ancestry pursued their upward mobility both politically and occupationally, enabling them to move to the suburbs or to more upscale neighborhoods in the city. About one million whites left New York City between 1970 and 1990. Those Jews and Italians who still lived in the city continued their pattern of ethnic succession in replacing the Irish in political leadership. At the end of the 1980s, the Bronx, once an Irish bastion of political strength, had only two Irish-American elected officials, Assemblyman John C. Dearie and Civil Court Judge Douglas E. McKeon.[117] Even the office of Police Commissioner ceased to be an exclusively Irish stronghold when Mayor Ed Koch appointed Benjamin Ward, a black, to lead the department. When David Dinkins's commissioner, Lee Brown, who was also black, resigned in 1992, the mayor appointed an Irish policeman, Raymond Kelly, to the post, but he immediately announced that special efforts would be made to recruit more black police officers.[118]

In 1973 Abe Beame became the first Jew to be elected mayor of New York City. In 1977 Ed Koch became the second Jewish mayor when he won election to the first of three terms. Koch, who had begun his career as a Reform Democrat in Greenwich Village, put together a winning coalition of white ethnic voters, Hispanics, and blacks. His popularity grew initially, and he triumphed by wider margins in his second and third campaigns. Political scandals in his third administration and deteriorating relations with the black and Hispanic communities led to defeat in his 1989 bid for an unprecedented fourth term. Italians also sought the mayor's office. Mario Cuomo made a strong run against Ed Koch in 1977, and Rudolph Giuliani barely lost to David Dinkins in 1989.[119] The 1993 election witnessed another Dinkins-Giuliani confrontation and another extremely close result. But this time Giuliani reversed his loss of 1989 and barely defeated the incumbent Dinkins.[120]

The continuing movement of New York's Jews into finance, real estate, and educational and cultural institutions was extraordinary. By the 1980s Jews were well represented in the top ranks of banking and legal firms formerly dominated almost exclusively by white Protestants.[121] Wealthy Jews won appointment to major philanthropic institutions and made significant donations to charitable and cultural caus-

■

es. Real estate millionaire Leonard Stern, for example, donated 20 million dollars to New York University's business school. In 1980 Michael Sovern became Columbia University's first Jewish president, succeeding the school's first Irish Catholic president, William J. McGill. One historian noted, "Had Sovern applied for admission to Columbia as an undergraduate prior to World War II, he might not have even been admitted."[122]

Italians lagged behind Jews in mobility, but they too began to obtain higher educations and pursue careers unavailable to their grandparents. In the 1980s, at the top level of two of New York's largest banks stood Anthony P. Terracciano, vice-chairman of Chase Manhattan Bank and Peter C. Palmieri, vice-chairman of the Irving Trust Company.[123] In 1974 the College of Staten Island's Edmond L. Volpe became the first Italian-American president of a City University (CUNY) college In 1991 New York University appointed its first Italian-American president, L. Jay Oliva.

The pattern was similar for the Irish. Paul O'Dwyer, a lawyer and one time President of the City Council, said in 1986, "Twenty years ago, if an Irishman had a daughter who was a stenographer he thought he was doing pretty good. Now, the young Irish-Americans want to get into the yuppie class. Some of my own grandchildren, even!"[124] The *New York Times* noted in 1986 that while fewer Irish names could be found in the police department, there are many Irish stockbrokers. "The police commissioner is no longer Robert J. McGuire, but the chairman of the New York Stock Exchange is John J. Phelan, Jr."[125]

Although the poverty rate for white New Yorkers was considerably less than that of Hispanics and blacks, sizeable pockets of white poverty continued to exist. The Community Service Society estimated that 23.1 percent of whites in the city lived below the poverty line in 1991, up from 12.9 percent in 1979. A goodly number of the city's white poor were older, while many others were women heads of households trying to rear children on low wages or welfare.[126]

In post-1970 New York few predominately white neighborhoods, old or new, were composed exclusively of one ethnic group. Rather, like Canarsie, for example, they had become mixtures of peoples from many lands. But while most white ethnics lived scattered about the city, they came together at times to shop in the old neighborhoods, to attend festivals, and to play amateur sports. Soccer enjoyed a boom during the

■

1980s, as many teams organized along nationality or linguistic lines to compete in the city's expanding Cosmopolitan Soccer League. Though founded by Germans in 1923, the league no longer had a single German team, but the Albanians fielded no less than five teams to battle clubs of Turkish, Italian, Irish, Ukrainian, Polish, Yugoslavian, and Croatian make-up.[127]

Often post-1970 New York neighborhoods contained only remnants of years gone by, ethnic stores and restaurants in rapidly changing areas. In a small section of East Harlem, once Manhattan's uptown Little Italy, "a shadow of the old neighborhood" survived. "Elders play cards and argue politics in a storefront social club." Some residents had lived there for generations, watching the influx of Puerto Ricans and other newcomers replace their own kind.[128] A reporter for the *New York Times* wrote in 1990 of a handful of elderly Jews who still came to the South Bronx's Intervale Jewish Center even though it was often impossible to gather the 10 men required for a *minyan* (prayer service). The center's leader remarked, "The ritual says there have to be 10 men, and I have no doubt at all there have to be 10. The idea is how you count those 10."[129] Of the flourishing 1930s Jewish refugee community of Washington Heights, by 1992 only a few, mostly older residents remained. German Jews had dwindled to only 6 percent of what had become a predominately Dominican community. One elderly resident remarked, "We always say when we go to the cemetery that there are more people we know there than here."[130]

The Ridgewood section of central Queens, settled by Germans around the turn of the century, was still home to many of the city's declining German-American population, including a few postwar immigrants. Berliner Jes Rau, who emigrated to United States in 1975, settled in Ridgewood and became editor of the city's oldest German language newspaper, *Staats-Zeitung und Herold*.[131] But Rau's Ridgewood was rapidly losing its exclusively German character. In addition to postwar German immigrants, Yugoslavs and Romanians arrived in the 1960s to work in the neighborhood's small knit shops, and more recently Hispanics and Chinese have located there.[132] By 1990, much of Little Italy was owned by or rented to Chinese settlers, and Chinese stores and signs stood next door to the dwindling Italian ones. The Chinese moved into the Lower East Side as well, replacing a declining Jewish population.

■

One could still buy foreign language newspapers published and read by descendants of European immigrants, but they became smaller with each passing year.[133] The Jewish newspaper *Forverts* celebrated its ninetieth year of publishing in 1987, but its circulation was down to 20,000 from 238,000 in 1917. The staff had dropped to four from a high of seventy. In 1974 its building was sold and became a Chinese cultural center. Today it is a predominately English language paper of Jewish affairs.[134]

The circulation of the century-old *Nordisk Tidende*, now carrying the *Norway Times* on its masthead, dropped to 5,000 weekly issues from 20,000 in the 1940s. Eighty percent of its copy was in English. Its editor, Tjoralv Ostvang, remarked, "The situation of the paper mirrors that of the Norwegian community. The population is steadily diminishing. I guess it will eventually assimilate and vanish, because many who still live here are older, their children have moved out of Brooklyn and there's no more Norwegian immigration."[135] Ostvang's observation about the impact of declining immigration was apt and could be applied to other groups as well. *Staats-Zeitung und Herold*, founded in 1834, had a circulation of only 18,000 by the mid-1980s and only 14,500 in 1991. It had ceased daily publication in the 1970s and by the 1980s had become strictly a weekly.[136] "You know," remarked the paper's associate publisher, "around 1900, there were 700 German-language newspapers in this country and now only 14 survive. And I'm afraid these too will die in a few years because the young generation assimilates fast and easily and there is no immigration."[137]

The decline of ethnic neighborhoods of the late nineteenth and early twentieth century European immigrants was one sign of growing acculturation in New York City. With less employment and neighborhood segregation, new European immigrants and the descendants of older immigrants mingled with one another under many new circumstances: political, social, and economic. Intermarriage across nationality and religious lines, virtually unheard of among first-generation immigrants, had become common by the 1980s.[138]

At the same time that the descendants of European immigrants moved upward and outward, the ethnic and religious prejudices that had restricted opportunity for their forbears all but disappeared. Who in the 1990s would say that Irish-American Catholics were a danger to the United States, that Jews and Italians were unworthy citizens, or that

■

Germans would not fight for the United States? New York City was not a center of pressure for immigration restriction, nor did the city's residents demonstrate much inclination to make English the official language as did citizens in a number of states, including California.

It is important not to overstate the extent of either the disappearance of old ethnic areas or of the waning of ethnic identity. The fact is that there still remain neighborhoods identified as being Polish, Greek, Scandinavian, Ukrainian, Jewish, Irish, or Italian. Greenpoint in Brooklyn was considered Polish, and *New York Magazine* in 1981 said that Polish-born Pope John Paul's picture "seems to grace every other store in the neighborhood."[139] A considerable number of Greeks lived in the Astoria section of Queens and Scandinavians in the Bay Ridge section of Brooklyn. The Norwegian settlement there, though declining, still supported two churches holding Norwegian-language services and hosted several Norwegian associations and civic groups.[140] In Manhattan's East Village, where so many immigrants had made their first homes in the new world, lived several thousand Ukrainian Americans whose community centered around St. George's Ukrainian Catholic Church. The Kobasniuk Travel Inc., in the heart of that neighborhood, advertised that it had been conducting tours to the Ukraine for twenty-five years.[141]

Furthermore, continuing immigration was a key factor in reinvigorating older ethnic groups and in maintaining New York's multiethnic character. In the 1970s the Greek community of Astoria, Queens consisted primarily of recent immigrants, and Polish Greenpoint maintained much of its identity because of new immigration.[142] Christopher Olechowski, who in 1952 arrived in the United States with his parents after spending time in a Siberian labor camp, observed, "If it hadn't been for the [post-1970] emigres, we would have lost much of our language and traditions." And another Polish American remarked in 1984, "We feel a new surge in Greenpoint's Polish identity, with new immigrants arriving and young people who moved out to Long Island coming back."[143] Unlike many other European language newspapers, the Polish *Daily News (Dowy Dziennik)* gained in circulation during the 1980s.[144] A daily Russian broadsheet, *Novoye Russkoye Slovo*, originally founded in 1910, also reported a surge in new readers as the new Soviets arrived. Its circulation tripled after 1968.[145]

Recent immigrants from Ireland also reinforced older Irish communities. Queens's Woodside, a center of Irish population since the 1920s,

■

was in danger of totally losing its Irish character as many new Asian and Latin Americans moved in and the more affluent Irish moved out. It was becoming like so many New York neighborhoods, a polyglot area. Yet enough Irish remained to make it attractive to the "New Irish." It was they who reinvigorated its traditional Irish flavor.

Irish New Yorkers continued to maintain many close knit neighborhoods and ethnic organizations. Irish musical events, sports, and social activities attested to a strong interest in Hibernian culture as did shops specializing in Irish imports. The St. Patrick's Day Parade was still a major city event, despite recent controversy over whether or not to include gay and lesbian marchers. In 1972 the new Irish Arts Center opened, and soon afterward the Irish Repertory Theater began producing plays.[146] The United Irish Counties Association's annual feis, founded in the 1930s, drew thousands to hear Irish music and participate in Irish sports. Moreover, for some first- and second-generation Irish Americans unrest in Northern Ireland remained a matter of keen interest. A few organized the controversial Northern Aid Committee, which some accused of aiding IRA militants in Northern Ireland.[147]

The Irish continued their domination of the Roman Catholic hierarchy in a church that was about one third Hispanic by 1990. When Terrence Cardinal Cooke died in 1984, he was succeeded by another conservative Irish-American priest, John J. O'Connor. O'Connor spoke forcefully against gay rights and abortion and even co-authored a book with Mayor Ed Koch, in which each author in a friendly way discussed controversial issues.[148]

Yet neither Cardinal O'Connor nor Bishop Thomas Daily, who became head of the Diocese of Brooklyn after retirement and death of Bishop Francis J. Mugavero in 1990, could arrest the declining political influence of New York Catholicism. Following the church's inability to halt a public school condom program in 1991, one religious leader concluded, "The church's influence has shrunk over the years. In the days of Cardinal [Francis] Spellman there's no doubt that if an issue arose which the Cardinal thought had potential impact on family life, he could pick up the phone and speak to leading political lights, and they would give careful thought to what he said."[149] The church's impact on the lives of New Yorkers was further eroded when, during the 1980s, financial difficulties forced the closing of a number of parochial schools.

■

By the 1990s it was clear that the city had several different Jewish communities. The latest Jewish immigrants, the Israelis and Soviets, maintained much of their own cultures. So too did members of the growing Hasidic communities and non-Hasidic Orthodox Jewish communities. Boro Park's Jews constituted the largest Orthodox community in the nation. Egon Mayer's 1979 study of that neighborhood noted that though *yeshivas, mikvas,* kosher butcher shops, and Orthodox synagogues are for most American Jews, including those in New York City, "part of the fading memories of an ancestral world," these institutions have "achieved a vitality in the Boro Park community that would have been unthinkable even for first-generation immigrants of the turn of the century."[150] Orthodox community expansion in Brooklyn, however, did not always occur peacefully. In the early 1990s relations between blacks and Hasids in Crown Heights deteriorated, and violence erupted at times.

New York is the center of a vast number of Jewish philanthropies, hospitals, and cultural institutions. Even many nonaffiliated, nonobservant Jews have defended the cause of Israel and donated generously to Jewish charities. A study of the New York area Jewish population in the early 1980s provided corroboration for both those who saw assimilation increasing and those who noted the persistence of a strong Jewish culture. In spite of rising intermarriage rates, many Jews remained religiously observant, gave their children a Jewish education, and participated in Jewish organizational life.[151]

Much the same pattern was evident among Italian New Yorkers. One scholar, commenting on their intermarriage rates, said that Italian Americans seemed to be slipping "into the twilight of ethnicity." While exogamous marriages did soar among younger Italians after 1970, and Italians increasingly associated with non-Italians, it was probably an exaggeration to see them sinking "into the twilight of ethnicity."[152] Italians had entered the city's political arena; many other Italians had joined the exodus to the suburbs while immigration from Italy dropped after 1970. Yet Italian ethnicity had by no means disappeared in the early 1990s.[153] Italian values, traditions, neighborhoods, and culture, though changing, still flourished in New York City.

It was in the working-class communities like Bensonhurst in Brooklyn, home to many postwar Italian immigrants, that Italian-American cultural continuity was most apparent. Like many New York neighborhoods, Bensonhurst had a mixed ethnic population, but it stood out as the city's largest Italian-American community. Notoriety came to the area after a widely publicized shooting of a black youth in 1990. Although residents witnessed the crime, they refused to testify against their fellow neighbors. With Italian youth having a higher school dropout rate than most other whites and with a shortage of high paying jobs for the uneducated, many in that community felt beleaguered.[154] Bensonhurst was, according to one reporter "close-knit, with strong cultural ties to the small rural towns of Southern Italy. Social life revolves around family, church, and neighborhood. Outsiders are often distrusted."[155]

It is important to note that despite differences among New Yorkers of European origin, the great divider in both the city and nation always has been race, and it continued to be so after 1970. Remarkable changes in race relations swept through New York society after World War II, but racism and racial consciousness remained ever present.

Because of this racism, prospects for mobility and assimilation were less promising for some new non-European immigrants and for Puerto Ricans and African Americans than for whites. Despite the emergence of a Puerto Rican middle class, gains in education, and increasing proficiency in English, the future for many Puerto Ricans did not look very rosy in the early 1990s. One expert put it, "The second generation is beginning to do better and once Puerto Ricans get up there they seem to do fairly well relative to other groups. But that's the trick—getting there."[156] Many Puerto Ricans arrived in New York at a time of decline in the city's manufacturing base and of the restructuring of its economy. Employment opportunities in light manufacturing, such as the garment industry, were bleak as thousands of these jobs had been leaving the city since 1970. Following cuts in the municipal payroll during the budget crisis of 1975, Puerto Ricans along with other minorities and women were victims of a "last hired first fired" policy. Puerto Ricans were under-represented in these positions to begin with.[157] When the city began to hire again in the 1980s, Puerto Ricans and other Hispanics benefitted, but they still lagged behind other groups, particularly in managerial positions.[158]

After 1970, while educational achievements of the second generation exceeded those of the first, the dropout rate among Puerto Ricans in the city's public schools remained alarmingly high. Some studies

■

placed it near 60 percent and declared that it had reached "epidemic proportions."[159] Under pressure from Puerto Rican organizations such as ASPIRA, the Board of Education established controversial bilingual educational and other remedial and cultural programs in an attempt to cut the number of school leavers. But the school system was beset by shortages of qualified teachers and funds, and many children eligible for these programs never received them.[160] In higher education, after Puerto Rican enrollment initially increased through the open admissions policy of CUNY, the city's fiscal crisis forced budget cuts and the imposition of tuition. The actual number of Puerto Rican students in CUNY dropped between 1975 and 1986.[161] In 1986 one third of CUNY's Puerto Rican teaching staff was located at bilingual Hostos Community College in the Bronx.[162]

During the years of the city's deteriorating economic situation and even during the upturn of the 1980s, many Puerto Ricans struggled to make ends meet.[163] The 1990 census reported that the median family income for Puerto Ricans was about half of that of the rest of New Yorkers and that many Puerto Ricans continued to live in poverty; Puerto Ricans were the city's poorest ethnic group. In the 1990s about half of Puerto Rican children lived in families headed by women, and the same proportion of Puerto Rican children lived in poverty. For those families depending on Aid to Dependent Children (ADC), inflation cut the real benefits after 1970.[164]

In addition, predictions of growing Puerto Rican political power failed to materialize. As American citizens Puerto Ricans could vote, but they had lower registration and voter participation rates than other ethnic groups. This did not bode well for influence at City Hall. During a period of 30 years only Herman Badillo and Robert Garcia had emerged from the community as significant political leaders. Hopes were raised when Puerto Rican educator Joseph Fernandez became chancellor of the public schools, but his controversial programs led to opposition and eventually his release in 1993. Puerto Ricans also cheered when Nydia M. Velazquez won election to Congress from a newly created heavily Hispanic district in 1992, but whether this indicated the beginning of increased political influence was yet to be determined.[165]

Like Puerto Ricans, blacks still suffered from alarming high rates of unemployment and poverty, but they did considerably better in the city's political arena. Voters elected more African Americans to office after 1970, and by the late 1980s six of the City Council 36 members were black as were about 20 to 30 percent of the city's State Assembly and Senate seats. African Americans held four of the city's 14 Congressional seats.[166] Finally, Manhattan's African-American borough president David Dinkins defeated Mayor Ed Koch in the September 1989 Democratic primary. In the November election he narrowly defeated Republican Rudolph Giuliani to become the city's 106th mayor. Dinkins won with 90 percent of the city's black vote, 65 percent of its Hispanic vote, and an estimated 27 percent of the white vote. Italians and Irish voted heavily for Giuliani. Dinkins did better among the traditionally Democratic Jewish electorate, but even there he received only about 40 percent of the ballots.[167]

In 1991, a court-ordered reorganization resulted in a new and enlarged City Council, which increased Hispanic and black representation from 25 to about 40 percent. Growing political clout by African Americans and some foreign-born blacks reaped dividends in municipal employment. The financial crunch of the mid-1970s had caused a disproportionate number of African-American layoffs; minority members represented about one third of the city's work force but 43 percent of the separations.[168] But in the 1980s new hirings brought many blacks into city jobs. By the end of the 1980s blacks made up a higher share of the city's payroll than they did of the city's population. In 1990, while blacks constituted one quarter of the city's population, they held more than one third of its municipal jobs.[169] In a pattern of ethnic succession New York's blacks, like the Irish and to a lesser extent Jews and Italians before them, benefitted significantly from municipal government employment opportunities.

The job pattern of blacks in city government continued to vary from agency to agency: prominent in areas devoted to health and welfare, underrepresented in the police and fire departments. In 1987, while accounting for one third of city employees, African Americans made up only about 11 percent of the police force. The same percentage of sergeants was black, but only 3.4 percent of the lieutenants and 1.9 percent of the captains. As noted, under Mayor Ed Koch for the first time a black, Benjamin Ward, was appointed commissioner of police, and black officers increased slightly in the 1990s under Mayor Dinkins's African-American commissioner, Lee Brown.[170] But in the Fire Department in 1990, blacks accounted for only 5 percent of the employees.[171]

■

Although black New Yorkers were moving up through the ranks of city agencies, they were not well represented in the managerial ranks, where, of course, both salaries and educational requirements were highest.[172] In the school system, 75 percent of the teachers were white as were 80 percent of the principals and assistant principals. Even in an area of school employment requiring little education, that of custodians, African Americans had less than 5 percent of the positions in 1994.[173] Not until 1988, when the Board of Education named Richard Green as Chancellor, did the city have a black school leader. Upon his death in 1990, Green was succeeded by Fernandez.

The municipal government has been the city's largest single employer, accounting for about one quarter of jobs held by native-born blacks in the 1980s. Many other African Americans worked for the state and federal governments and regional agencies like the Port Authority. Unlike whites, who found expanding opportunities in the private sector, blacks often recognized that their best chances for managerial positions lay within the ranks of government.[174] But the private sector always accounts for the vast majority of jobs, and there blacks achieved a few illustrious successes. Most notable of the nation's largest black enterprises were TLC Group, Inc., headed by Reginald Lewis until his untimely death in 1993, and the Carver Federal Savings and Loan Association, at one time the nation's third largest black-owned savings and loan institution. Yet a more accurate picture of the status of black management in the private sector is revealed in the fact that in 1990, whereas self-employed New Yorkers made up 6.7 percent of the city's workforce, only 3.4 percent of the city's African Americans were in this category.[175]

While the progress of black New Yorkers in post-1970 New York City was by no means spectacular, there was clearly some upward movement. In Queens, New York's most middle class borough, median income for black households slightly surpassed that of whites by 1990. Perhaps this was because Queens attracted black civil servants and many families with two wage earners. Income parity was not reached in the city's other boroughs, nor in any other American municipality, and in the city as a whole in 1990 white median income was $10,000 higher than that of blacks.[176]

Blacks, like Puerto Ricans, continued to face economic discrimination.[177] In addition, they also suffered from the loss of manufacturing jobs in the city. New York City's recovery following the fiscal crisis of

■

the late 1970s did not necessarily benefit them, for as the city's economy moved from manufacturing to high tech service industry, high-paying jobs went primarily to whites. Better positions in fast-growing sectors required education and skills, and minority group members with histories of leaving school early were at a distinct disadvantage. Black employment suffered severe setbacks during the crisis years, and unemployment remained high in the decades that followed, more than double the white rate.[178]

Official unemployment rates do not tell the full story, because they do not include the discouraged workers, those out of work who have stopped looking for jobs. Another indicator of the dismal employment picture is the labor force participation rate, which for blacks dropped substantially; according to this measure only 54.1 percent of the city's black adults held jobs in 1986, a rate lower than the national average. It had been 71.3 percent in 1970.[179] Clearly a large number of young black men and women not attending school were unemployed. Moreover, many new jobs in the city, such as dishwashers or clerks in fast food chains, lacked promising futures. Some paid wages not much above the poverty line.[180]

To make matters worse, employers discovered that even those job applicants who had graduated from New York's high schools were often lacking in the basic skills. In the 1980s four banks agreed to hire 250 graduates of the five high schools in the East New York section of Brooklyn, but they found that only 100 could pass an entry test geared to "the eighth-grade level."[181] City University of New York (CUNY) officials also complained about inadequate preparation of graduating high school students entering their community and senior colleges.[182] Clearly the hopes of black New Yorkers that education would offer their children a way out of poverty and entry into middle class status were not being fully realized by the 1990s. True, overall educational achievement levels for minorities did rise, and the number of college graduates among them increased. And true, the selective admission high schools and those in middle class areas graduated students bound for the nation's top colleges and universities and annually produced a disproportionate share of the prestigious national Westinghouse Science Talent Search winners.[183] Yet twenty years after the decentralization of the city's public schools, many of them continued to be centers of crisis. In 1976 the fiscal emergency forced the firing of teachers, the cutting of

■

programs, and the canceling of needed building repairs and new construction, leading many observers to declare that deterioration best characterized the general status of public education in the city. A study by the state in 1987 found that 41 percent of all schools and 64 percent of the high schools failed to meet minimum standards established by the city's Chancellor of Education.[184] And a new fiscal crunch in 1990 forced further cuts in the system. To make matters even worse, by 1990 some district school boards were engulfed in scandals involving misuse of school funds and charges that political power, not education, was the dominant concern of many school board members.[185] A scandal over asbestos inspection and removal in school buildings forced delay of the opening of the 1993–1994 academic year.[186]

Precise data were unavailable, but dropout rates at the outset of the 1990s were high in the public schools, upwards of 30 percent for blacks, most of whom lived in poverty neighborhoods. Some educators hoped that decentralized specialized high schools being established in the 1990s would result in a major improvement in the city's system, but that remained to be seen.[187]

In contrast to the above picture, the college scene has been more promising. After open admissions was instituted in 1970, black student enrollment increased rapidly. Within a decade the number of African Americans attending both private and public colleges in New York increased from 30,061 to 114,172. By the 1980s 37 percent of the students in CUNY's community colleges were black, with a somewhat smaller percentage attending the four year colleges.[188] As noted, the city was pressured into abandoning the free tuition policy during the 1975 fiscal crisis, and consequently some students were forced to drop out. But the costs of attending CUNY, even after additional tuition hikes in 1991, were among the lowest of any public university in the nation, and the state aid programs provided substantial help for the very poor.[189] As a result, a growing number of blacks earned college degrees after 1970, with many receiving training as social workers, computer experts, engineers, accountants, and teachers. Among the teachers were some who joined the CUNY faculty, while other black college graduates with advanced degrees found employment as administrators within the CUNY system.[190]

Given the initially deteriorating and then shifting New York economy, it is not surprising that poverty was on the rise for blacks as well as

Puerto Ricans after 1970. Poverty had declined among all New Yorkers, including blacks, right after World War II. But one quarter of African Americans were below the federal poverty line by 1969, and by 1988 the figure was 33.8 percent.[191] An increasing number of poor households were headed by women, often unwed, who lived on Aid to Dependent Children (ADC), low paying jobs, or irregular handouts from the fathers of their children. By the 1980s more than 40 percent of black families were headed by women, and two thirds of these were in poverty.[192]

For the black and Puerto Rican poor, living conditions have been bleak. For those on welfare, such as ADC, the inflation after 1970 eroded their benefits. Fiscal crises led to cuts in municipal services in such critical areas as health and education. Neighborhood social conditions have also deteriorated. Crime rates are high in the low income areas of the city, and drugs are common. Moreover, shootouts among drug dealers make these neighborhoods dangerous places in which to live. These neighborhoods already had high rates of heroin addiction before the crack epidemic broke out in the mid-1980s. Unlike heroin, which was largely used by men, crack use spread rapidly among women as well. The city spent millions of dollars to fight drugs, but with limited success.[193] If drugs and crime were not enough, AIDS, which first emerged within the male homosexual community, by the late 1980s appeared most threatening to IV drug users, which meant that a disproportional number of new cases were black and poor.

Even those middle-class black New Yorkers who found improved employment opportunities faced racial discrimination in renting and buying housing. Some interracial middle-class communities, like the Laurelton section of Queens, emerged, but in general researchers have found little change in housing segregation over the past two decades.[194]

Moreover, racial conflict continued to plague the city as whites and blacks contended over turf, education, housing, and jobs. Italian and black confrontations also erupted periodically into violence. They fought over school desegregation and housing in neighborhoods like Brooklyn's heavily Italian Canarsie. Residents in Canarsie resorted to violence to halt busing for school desegregation and vigilantism to keep blacks out of their turf. By a vote of nine to one that area resoundingly rejected the proposed civilian review board to investigate charges against the police.[195]

■

In December 1986 in the Howard Beach section of Brooklyn, a white area, a gang of whites chased three black males emerging from a pizza parlor onto an expressway where one of the blacks was killed by an oncoming auto.[196] The Howard Beach defendants had scarcely been convicted and sentenced when the city was rocked by another violent incident on August 24, 1989 in which a black youth was killed in the Brooklyn Italian neighborhood of Bensonhurst.[197] Blacks and Jews had also been pitted against one another over the 1968 decentralization of the schools and the appointment of teachers.[198] In addition, during the 1980s Mayor Ed Koch appeared to exacerbate tensions between Jews and blacks with his strongly stated personal comments regarding relations between the two groups. Even after his defeat, tension persisted; the Crown Heights section of Brooklyn was the scene of ugly confrontations between Hasidic Jews and blacks. That neighborhood experienced a full scale riot in the summer of 1991 and further tension in late 1992.[199] Thus, in the mid-1990s the global city like the globe itself yearns for peace but remains beset with conflict.

*Afterword*

New York City's ethnic and racial diversity is clearly visible to all who walk its streets. It has always been so. The city's history as home to a multicultural population began more than three hundred and fifty years ago. Unable to persuade enough of their own countrymen to come to New Netherland, the West India Company actively encouraged a number of non-Dutch to settle and somewhat begrudgingly accepted others. It was a policy of toleration of foreigners dictated by the need for labor to build a town and colony; it was a policy welcomed by those who sought to begin their lives anew, to escape poverty or persecution or both. This condition of complementary needs, though not always in perfect balance, has continued to exist down through the years, as New Amsterdam's hundreds became New York's millions, as predominantly western Europeans immigrants gave way to eastern Europeans and in recent decades to those arriving from Asia, the Caribbean, and Central America. Throughout the city's history most of the new settlers have been immigrants: Irish, Jews, Chinese, Italians, Poles, West Indians, and Dominicans, to name but a few. Many others, however, have been American citizens, most notably southern African Americans and Puerto Ricans.

It is well to remember that these millions of people had much in common. They came to find better opportunities; they frequently faced hostility, and they underwent difficult adjustments in their new urban environment. Consequently, almost all sought out their compatriots and created institutions to help them cope with the city. Starting at the bottom of the economic pile, each first generation of immigrants inevitably found life exceedingly hard. However, of no small importance were the differences that marked one group off from another. European Protestants generally have had an easier time adjusting, especially those who arrived with some combination of knowledge of the English language, education, and vocational skills that could be utilized with profit in the city's economy. Thus, Walloons, Scotch Irish, Scandinavians, French Huguenots, English, Welsh, and Dutch were able to acculturate quickly and eventually to assimilate into the larger white New York culture. Even Germans, considered somewhat clannish, found it possible to join the mainstream of New York society after a generation or two. Remarkably, the anti-German sentiment brought on by World War I, which encouraged their desire to assimilate, did not stand in their way. As a result of this assimilating process and lacking significant numbers of new arrivals from their mother countries, visible evidence of many "Old Immigrant" cultures are difficult to find today: a few establishments remaining in Yorkville to remind us of the vibrant German community it once housed, a small Norwegian settlement still hanging on in Brooklyn.

For Catholics and Jews the situation has been somewhat different. The Irish were welcomed by some for their labor but despised and ill treated by many for their poverty and Catholicism. Over time, however, Irish Americans improved their economic condition, gained political power, and eventually won the acceptance that led the *New York Times* to remark in 1988, "So many Irish-Americans have succeeded in various fields that their prominence no longer is noteworthy."[1]

■

Jews encountered anti-Semitism from the time they first set foot in Dutch New Amsterdam. Yet, they too prospered: the Sephardim, the German Jews, and finally the descendants of eastern European Jews. Their political, economic, cultural, and social progress has been remarkable. So much so that anti-Semitism no longer seems to be a significant factor in the life choices of New York City's Jewish population. While the city's Italians, often scorned for their poverty, Catholicism, and way of life, have been slower than Jews to prosper, they nonetheless have experienced nearly full acceptance in New York's institutional life.

Prosperity and the waning of ethnic and religious prejudice were major factors in the decline of many of the old immigrant neighborhoods. But acculturation—participation in the life of the larger community—did not necessarily require total assimilation. Toleration also brought the opportunity to choose the extent of one's allegiance to ethnicity. And the range of choice is wide, from remaining almost completely apart from others as Hasidic Jews do to complete abandonment of one's ethnic ties. Probably most descendants of immigrants have chosen a path somewhere between those two extremes. The growing acceptance of ethnicity as a life style ingredient has become noticeable in recent decades and, coupled with fresh immigration from such countries as Poland, China, Italy, and Greece, has served to reinforce cultural ties and institutions that once seemed in danger of disappearing.[2] Furthermore, during the last fifty years there has been an influx of immigrants whose nationalities had barely been represented in the city prior to World War II. They have established whole new neighborhoods in which the immigrant drama is again being played out. Whether these newcomers will evolve the way that past groups have remains to be seen.

Today's immigrants enter a city more ready than ever to assist them. The municipal government runs special programs to help them adjust to urban life. Since World War II federal, state, and local laws have been passed banning racial and ethnic discrimination in a wide area of public life. Spokespersons like former Mayor David Dinkins have often praised the city's "gorgeous mosaic." But acceptance of others has had its limits. For example, a 1993 poll conducted by the Empire Foundation and Lehrman Institute found that a majority of city residents believed that too many immigrants were arriving and that these newcomers made the city a worse place to live.[3]

■

Many of the most recently arrived immigrants and migrants have been people of color, and such people have long been victims of the most intense prejudice in the city and in the nation. The earliest Asians, the Chinese, found their lives restricted by bigotry for decades. African Americans came first as slaves and when slavery ended endured generations of racial discrimination in nearly all phases of city life. Racism has declined since 1940, but not nearly to the extent that intolerance toward national and religious minorities has.

What future lies ahead for the residents of an increasingly pluralistic New York City? For native born, white citizens as well as for many immigrants, the business, financial, and cultural capitol of the nation continues to hold out promise of success. For blacks and Puerto Ricans, who are and have been for decades the poorest of city's poor, prospects do not appear nearly so bright. And their poverty and lack of opportunity in the end endangers the futures of all the city's people. Discontent has ignited recent incidents of racial and ethnic conflict, and many residents have expressed a lack of confidence that a climate of multicultural harmony can be created. Yet, as we have noted, New York has been from the earliest times a multiethnic, multiracial city. It has experienced periods of tension and conflict among the several groups, ultimately resolved them and, sometimes stumbling and tripping, has gone on to greatness. Those who truly love this great city believe that its future should and can be no less than its past.

■

*Notes*

## Chapter 1. Multiethnic from the Beginning

1. George J. Lankevich and Howard B. Furer, *A Brief History of New York City* (Port Washington, N.Y., 1984), pp. 2–3.

2. Ibid., pp. 3–4.

3. Ibid., p. 4.

4. Oliver A. Rink, *Holland on the Hudson: An Economic and Social History of Dutch New York* (Ithaca and London, 1986), pp. 3 and 36–37.

5. Ibid., pp. 155–56; also in Oliver A. Rink, "The People of New Netherland: Notes on Non-English Immigration to New York in the Seventeenth Century," *New York History* (Hereafter *NYH*) 62 (Jan. 1981): 28.

6. Alice P. Kenney, *Stubborn for Liberty: The Dutch in New York* (Syracuse, 1975), p. 19.

7. Quoted in Rink, "The People of New Netherland," p. 9.

8. Ibid., p. 10.

9. Quoted in David Steven Cohen, "How Dutch Were the Dutch of New Netherland?" *NYH* 62 (Jan. 1981): 54–55.

10. Rink, *Holland on the Hudson*, p. 80.

11. Ibid., pp. 81–84; Rink, "The People of New Netherland," p. 13; Kenney, *Stubborn for Liberty*, pp. 20 and 22.

12. Lankevich and Furer, *A Brief History*, p. 6.

13. Rink, *Holland on the Hudson*, p. 87.

14. Quoted in Kenney, *Stubborn for Liberty*, p. 32.

15. Jon Butler, *The Huguenots in America: A Refugee People in New World Society* (Cambridge, 1983), p. 44.

16. Ibid., pp. 44–45.

17. Quoted in Kenney, *Stubborn for Liberty*, pp. 38 and 121.

18. Quoted in Thomas J. Archdeacon, *New York City, 1664–1710: Conquest and Change* (Ithaca and London, 1976), p. 32.

19. Cohen, "How Dutch Were the Dutch," pp. 43, 51, 55, and 57.

20. Quoted in Rink, *Holland on the Hudson*, p. 231.

21. Quoted in ibid.

22. Ibid., pp. 231–33.

23. The Treaty of Hartford in 1650, established a boundary line between British and Dutch Long Island running from Oyster Bay eastward to the ocean.

24. Quoted in Kenney, *Stubborn for Liberty*, p. 122; Rink, *Holland on the Hudson*, pp. 235–37; and Lankevich and Furer, *A Brief History*, p. 20.

25. Jacob Rader Marcus, *Early American Jewry: The Jews of New York, New England and Canada, 1649–1794*, Vol. 1 (Philadelphia, 1951), p. 14; Philip Sandler, "Earliest Jewish Settlers in New York," *NYH* 36 (Jan. 1955): 40.

26. Marcus, *Early American Jewry*, pp. 20–21; Sandler, "Earliest Jewish Settlers," pp. 40–41.

27. Marcus, *Early American Jewry*, pp. 21–22; Sandler, "Earliest Jewish Settlers," pp. 39 and 41.

28. Sandler, "Earliest Jewish Settlers," pp. 39–40.

29. Quoted in ibid., p. 40.

30. Quoted in Morris U. Schappes ed., *A Documentary History of the Jews in the United States, 1654–1875* (New York, 1950), pp. 1–2.

31. Quoted in Sandler, "Earliest Jewish Settlers," p. 42.

32. Quoted in Schappes, *A Documentary History of the Jews*, pp. 2–4.

33. Quoted in ibid., pp. 4–5.

34. Quoted in ibid., pp. 8–9.

35. Quoted in Sandler, "Earliest Jewish Settlers," p. 48.

36. Quoted in ibid., p. 49.

37. Kenney, *Stubborn for Liberty*, pp. 27–28.

38. Thomas Archdeacon, "Anglo-Dutch New York, 1676," in Milton Klein ed., *New York: The Centennial Years, 1676–1976* (Port Washington, N.Y., 1976), p. 26.

39. Quoted in Rink, *Holland on the Hudson*, p. 214.

■

40. Rink, "The People of New Netherland," p. 30; Bayrd Still, *Mirror for Gotham: New York As Seen by Contemporaries from Dutch Days to the Present* (New York, 1956), pp. 7 and 10.

41. Rink, *Holland on the Hudson*, p. 210.

42. Rink, "The People of New Netherland," pp. 39–40.

43. Quoted in ibid., p. 41.

44. Ibid., pp. 38 and 41.

45. Cohen, "How Dutch Were the Dutch," p. 47.

46. Ibid., p. 48.

47. Still, *Mirror for Gotham*, p. 7.

48. Ibid., p. 8.

49. Ibid., pp. 32–34; Rink, *Holland on the Hudson*, pp. 163–64; and Joyce Diane Goodfriend, *Before the Melting Pot: Society and Culture in Colonial New York City, 1664–1730* (Princeton, 1992), p. 10.

50. Joyce D. Goodfriend, "Burghers and Blacks: The Evolution of a Slave Society at New Amsterdam," *NYH* 58 (Apr. 1978): 126–28; Edgar J. McManus, *A History of Negro Slavery in New York* (Syracuse, 1966), pp. 2–4.

51. Goodfriend, "Burghers and Blacks," pp. 131–33.

52. Ibid., p. 142.

53. Quoted in McManus, *A History of Negro Slavery*, p. 50.

54. Thelma Foote, "Crossroads or Settlement?" in Richard Beard and Leslie Cohen Berlowitz eds., *Greenwich Village: Culture and Counterculture* (New Brunswick, 1993), p. 121.

55. Thomas Davis, "Slavery in Colonial New York City," PhD diss., Columbia University, 1974, pp. 48–55.

56. Roi Ottley and William J. Weatherby eds., *The Negro in New York: An Informal Social History* (New York, 1967), p. 12. A few of the town's free blacks may have entered the colony as freemen.

57. Foote, "Crossroads or Settlement?" p. 122.

58. Ibid.

59. Goodfriend, "Burghers and Blacks," pp. 138–41. McManus takes the view that slavery was a relatively humane and loose institution under the Dutch. See McManus, *A History of Negro Slavery*, pp. 15–20.

60. Goodfriend, *Before the Melting Pot*, p. 16. Goodfriend's data analysis of population figures indicates that as many as 76% of the white population of New Amsterdam by 1664 may have been Dutch.

61. Ibid., p. 17.

62. Norval White, *New York: A Physical History* (New York, 1987), p. 20. The *Heere Gracht*, or Gentlemen's canal, was filled in 1676 to form Broad Street.

63. Morton Wagman, "Liberty in New Amsterdam: A Sailor's Life in Early New York," *NYH* 64 (Apr. 1983): 109.

64. Lankevich and Furer, *A Brief History*, pp. 24–25.

65. David William Voorhees, " 'In Behalf of the true Protestant Religion': the Glorious Revolution in New York," PhD diss., New York University, 1988, p. 13.

■

66. Archdeacon, *New York City, 1664–1710*, pp. 97–98; Lankevich and Furer, *A Brief History*, p. 25.

67. Firth Haring Fabend, "Becoming American: A Dutch Family in the Middle Colonies, 1660–1800," PhD diss., New York University, 1988, pp. 14 and 16.

68. Goodfriend, *Before the Melting Pot*, p. 24.

69. Archdeacon, *New York City, 1664–1710*, pp. 98–99.

70. Archdeacon, "Anglo-Dutch New York, 1676," pp. 100–101.

71. Ibid., pp. 90 and 112.

72. Quoted in Archdeacon, *New York City, 1664–1710*, pp. 101–2.

73. Goodfriend, *Before the Melting Pot*, pp. 84–92.

74. Ibid., pp. 56–57. The city's first Presbyterian church was completed in 1716.

75. Quoted in Robert E. Cray, Jr., *Paupers and Poor Relief in New York City and its Rural Environs, 1700–1830* (Philadelphia, 1988), p. 20.

76. Ibid.

77. Archdeacon, *New York City, 1664–1710*, pp. 53–54; Goodfriend, *Before the Melting Pot*, pp. 69–75. From 1678 to 1694 New York City had a government-granted monopoly on the grinding and packing of all flour exported from the province.

78. Dudley served for only seven months before being replaced by Andros in December, 1686.

79. Archdeacon, *New York City, 1664–1710*, pp. 104, 114, and 115.

80. Quoted in the Rev. J. R. Bayley, *A Brief Sketch of the Early History of the Catholic Church on the Island of New York* (New York, 1870, reprinted, 1973), p. 33.

81. Among these were Nicholas Bayard, Frederick Philipse, and Stephen Van Cortland of New York City. Voorhees, " ' In Behalf of the true Protestant Religion,' " pp. 299–300.

82. Ibid., p. 315.

83. Goodfriend, *Before the Melting Pot*, p. 85.

84. Kenney, *Stubborn for Liberty*, pp. 124–25.

85. Archdeacon, *New York City, 1664–1710*, p. 142.

86. Quoted in Goodfriend, *Before the Melting Pot*, p. 188.

87. Kenney, *Stubborn for Liberty*, p. 125.

88. Bruce M. Wilkenfeld, "New York City Neighborhoods, 1730" *NYH* 57 (Apr. 1976): 180.

89. Ibid. p. 177.

90. Visitors' quotes and observations in Still, *Mirror for Gotham*, pp. 16 and 22.

91. Bruce M. Wilkenfeld, "Revolutionary New York, 1776," in Klein ed., *New York: The Centennial Years*, p. 63.

92. Archdeacon, "Anglo-Dutch New York, 1676," p. 31.

93. Quoted in Still, *Mirror for Gotham*, p. 21.

94. Quoted in Archdeacon, *New York City, 1664–1710*, p. 33.

95. Quoted in Still, *Mirror for Gotham*, p. 21.

96. Butler, *The Huguenots in America*, pp. 7 and 57–58.

97. Ibid., pp. 146–147.

■

98. Quoted in Goodfriend, *Before the Melting Pot*, p. 90.

99. Butler, *The Huguenots in America*, p. 146.

100. Ibid., pp. 147–153; Goodfriend, *Before the Melting Pot*, pp. 77–78. Popular election of municipal officers was provided for in the municipal charter of 1686, the Dongan Charter.

101. Butler, *The Huguenots in America*, p. 156.

102. Ibid., pp. 158–59 and 187.

103. Ibid., pp. 159–61, 169–73, and 189–98.

104. Archdeacon, *New York City, 1664–1710*, pp. 45–46. The estimated Jewish population of the city stood at 100 in 1695, 300 in 1750, and 350 in 1794. Hyman B. Grinstein, *The Rise of the Jewish Community of New York, 1654–1860* (Philadelphia, 1945), p. 469.

105. Grinstein, *Rise of the Jewish Community*, p. 22; Marcus, *Early American Jewry*, p. 82.

106. Marcus, *Early American Jewry*, pp. 35–42; Schappes, *A Documentary History of the Jews*, pp. 18, 19, and 26–30.

107. Quoted in Still, *Mirror for Gotham*, p. 22.

108. Quoted in Marcus, *Early American Jewry*, p. 48.

109. Quoted in Archdeacon, "Anglo-Dutch New York, 1676" p. 29; Schappes, *A Documentary History of the Jews*, pp. 18–19.

110. Marcus, *Early American Jewry*, pp. 48, 55, and 57; Grinstein, *The Rise of the Jewish Community*, p. 31.

111. Grinstein, *The Rise of the Jewish Community*, pp. 84, 228–29, 398, and 491; Marcus *Early American Jewry*, pp. 82–83.

112. Marcus, *Early American Jewry*. pp. 94–95.

113. Foote, "Crossroads or Settlement?" p. 123.

114. Harold X. Connolly, *A Ghetto Grows in Brooklyn* (New York, 1977), pp. 4–5.

115. McManus, *A History of Negro Slavery*, pp. 46–47.

116. Davis, "Slavery in Colonial New York City," pp. 73–83.

117. Ibid., pp. 152–55 and 174–76; McManus, *A History of Negro Slavery*, pp. 70–75.

118. McManus, *A History of Negro Slavery*, pp. 101–8.

119. An excellent account of the 1712 rebellion is Kenneth Scott, "The Slave Insurrection in New York in 1712," *New York Historical Quarterly* 45 (Jan. 1961): 43–74. Davis gives higher figures for those indicted, convicted, and executed. See Davis, "Slavery in Colonial New York City," pp. 101–6.

120. McManus, *A History of Negro Slavery*, pp. 124–25; Davis, "Slavery in Colonial New York City," pp. 109–14.

121. For different views, see Thomas J. Davis, *A Rumor of Revolt: The "Great Negro Plot" in Colonial New York* (New York, 1985); Irving Werstein, *The Plotters: The New York Conspiracy of 1741* (New York, 1967).

122. Davis, "Slavery in Colonial New York City," pp. 201–3.

123. Ibid., p. 205.

124. Edgar McManus, "Anti-Slavery Legislation in New York," *Journal of Negro History* 46 (Oct. 1961): 208–10; Arthur Zilversmit, *The First Emancipation: The Abolition of Slavery in the North* (Chicago, 1967), pp. 146–49.

125. Cray, *Paupers and Poor Relief*, p. 22; Archdeacon, *New York City, 1664–1710*, pp. 144–45.

126. Patricia U. Bonomi, *A Factious People: Politics and Society in Colonial New York* (New York, 1971), pp. 25–26.

127. Lankevich and Furer, *A Brief History*, pp. 40–45 and 66; Still, *Mirror for Gotham*, pp. 18–21, 27, 37, 40, 43, and 45; and Wilkenfeld, "Revolutionary New York, 1776," pp. 43–47, 52, 55–56, and 68.

128. Wilkenfeld, "Revolutionary New York, 1776," pp. 61–62, 67 Still, *Mirror for Gotham*, pp. 21–22.

129. Quoted in Wilkenfeld, "Revolutionary New York, 1776," p. 64.

130. Wilkenfeld, "Revolutionary New York, 1776," p. 62; Jay Dolan, *Immigrant Church: New York's Irish and German Catholics, 1815–1865* (South Bend, Ind., 1983), p. 11.

## Chapter 2. Dynamic Growth and Diversity

1. Ira Rosenwaike, *Population History of New York City* (Syracuse, 1972), p. 16.

2. Sidney Pomerantz, *New York An American City, 1783–1803: A Study of Urban Life* (Port Washington, N.Y., 1965, originally published 1938), pp. 203–5.

3. Ibid., pp. 204–5.

4. Frances Childs, *French Refugee Life in the United States, 1790–1800* (Baltimore, 1940), pp. 195–99; Jay P. Dolan, *The Immigrant Church: New York's Irish and German Catholics, 1815–1865* (South Bend, Ind., 1983), p. 9.

5. Pomerantz, *New York: An American City*, pp. 205–6.

6. Quoted in ibid., p. 206.

7. Ibid., pp. 200 and 203.

8. Quoted in ibid., p. 203.

9. Quoted in ibid., p. 203. See also James Morton Smith, *Freedom's Fetters: The Alien and Sedition Laws and American Civil Liberties* (Ithaca, 1956), p. 162.

10. Pomerantz, *New York: An American City*, pp. 204, 206, and 208.

11. Rosenwaike, *Population History*, p. 16; George J. Lankevich and Howard B. Furer, *A Brief History of New York City* (Port Washington, N.Y., 1984), pp. 65–66; and Robert Albion, *The Rise of New York Port, 1815–1860* (Boston, 1984; Originally New York, 1939), p. 8. The city's political prominence as the seat of state and national governments, however, had been lost to Albany (1797) and Philadelphia (1790).

12. Lankevich and Furer, *A Brief History*, p. 76; Albion, *New York Port*, p. 9. News of peace reached New York on Feb. 11, 1815.

13. Edward Robb Ellis, *The Epic of New York City: A Narrative History* (New York, 1990), pp. 216–17; Lankevich and Furer, *A Brief History*, pp. 76–77; Albion, *New York Port*, pp. 13, 14, and 85–94; and Robert Ernst, *Immigrant Life in New York City, 1825–1863* (New York, 1979, Original printing, New York, 1949), p. 14.

■

14. Ernst, *Immigrant Life*, pp. 17 and 18; Lankevich and Furer, *A Brief History*, p. 77; Albion, *New York Port*, pp. 63–64; and Edward Spann, *The New Metropolis: New York City, 1840–1857* (New York, 1981), p. 405.

15. Spann, *New Metropolis*, pp. 403–5.

16. Quoted in ibid., pp. 3–4.

17. Ibid., p. 6.

18. New York City's population, which stood at 96,373 in 1810, rose to 813,669 by 1860. The neighboring city of Brooklyn by that latter date had attained a population of 266,661. Rosenwaike, *Population History*, pp. 16, 36, and 51.

19. Albion, *New York Port*, pp. 235 and 241–42; Spann, *New Metropolis*, p. 7.

20. Quoted in Albion, *New York Port*, p. 242.

21. Ibid., pp. 236–39.

22. Rosenwaike, *Population History*, pp. 36 and 39. In 1860 Brooklyn's foreign born population constituted 39 percent of its total of 266,661 residents. Ibid., p. 63.

23. Quoted in Ernst, *Immigrant Life*, p. 24.

24. The Panics of 1819, 1837, and 1857 in the U.S. resulted in sharp declines in immigration. Albion, *New York Port*, p. 338.

25. Richard Stott, *Workers in the Metropolis: Class, Ethnicity, and Youth in Antebellum New York City* (Ithaca, 1990), pp. 72–75. The author suspects that the increasing demand for domestic help accounts for the increase in female immigration. As the leading industrial nation in Europe, England was the one country from which a considerable number of urban residents emigrated.

26. Ernst, *Immigrant Life*, pp. 7–10.

27. Wales, for example, experienced a nearly 50 percent increase during the first half of the century. Juliana F. Gilheany, "Subjects of History: English, Scottish, and Welsh Immigrants in New York City, 1820–1860," PhD diss., New York University, 1989, p. 32.

28. Stott, *Workers in the Metropolis*, p. 80.

29. Ibid., pp. 77–82.

30. Albion, *New York Port*, pp. 337 and 418.

31. Ibid., pp. 339–40 and 348.

32. Gilheany, "Subjects of History," pp. 50–58. Detailed descriptions of the numerous hazards of the voyage are found in Albion, *New York Port*, pp. 341–49.

33. Ernst, *Immigrant Life*, pp. 25–29; Albion, *New York Port*, pp. 348–49.

34. Albion, *New York Port*, pp. 350–52; Ernst, *Immigrant Life*, pp. 29–32; and Lankevich and Furer, *A Brief History*, pp. 90–91.

35. Spann, *The New Metropolis*, p. 24.

36. Ibid.

37. Dolan, *The Immigrant Church*, pp. 13–15; Carol Groneman Pernicone, "The 'Bloody Ould Sixth': A Social Analysis of a New York City Working-class Community in the Mid-Nineteenth Century," PhD diss., The University of Rochester, 1973, p. 33.

38. Pernicone, "The 'Bloody Ould Sixth,' " pp. 33–34.

■

39. Quoted in Dolan, *The Immigrant Church*, p. 34.

40. Gilheany, "Subjects of History," p. 153.

41. Stott, *Workers in the Metropolis*, p. 169.

42. Quoted in Dolan, *The Immigrant Church*, p. 34

43. Stott, *Workers in the Metropolis*, p. 172; Lankevich and Furer, *A Brief History*, p. 72.

44. Lankevich and Furer, *A Brief History*, p. 92.

45. Roy Lubove, *The Progressives and the Slums: Tenement House Reform in New York City* (Pittsburgh, 1962), pp. 5–6.

46. For women's missionary efforts and the response of the residents, see Carroll Smith Rosenberg, *Religion and the Rise of the American City: The New York City Mission Movement, 1812–1870* (Ithaca, 1971); Pernicone, "The 'Bloody Ould Sixth,' " pp. 182–96.

47. Quoted in Lubove, *The Progressives and the Slums*, p. 7.

48. Dolan, *The Immigrant Church*, p. 34; Bayard Still, *Mirror for Gotham: New York as Seen by Contemporaries from Dutch Days to the Present* (New York, 1956), p. 243. For a full description of housing reform see Lubove, *The Progressives and the Slum.*

49. Quoted in Miriam Z. Langsam, *Children West: A History of the Placing-Out System of the New York Children's Aid Society, 1853–1890* (Madison, 1964), p. 8.

50. Ibid., chapter 2.

51. Marilyn Irwin Holt, *The Orphan Trains* (Lincoln, 1992), pp. 106–13.

52. Spann, *The New Metropolis*, pp. 147–48.

53. Ellis, *New York City*, pp. 231–32.

54. Quoted in Still, *Mirror for Gotham*, p. 123.

55. Charles E. Rosenberg, *The Cholera Years: The United States in 1832, 1849, and 1866* (Chicago, 1962), p. 184.

56. Quoted in ibid., p. 62.

57. Ibid., p. 135.

58. Ernst, *Immigrant Life*, p. 54.

59. Lankevich and Furer, *A Brief History*, pp. 104–05 and 107; Ernst, *Immigrant Life*, pp. 51–52.

60. Rosenberg, *The Cholera Years*, pp. 184–85.

61. In her study of the Sixth Ward Carol Pernicone found that young Irish immigrants were an exception to the rule, generally preferring to board with Irish families rather than in boardinghouses. Pernicone, "The 'Bloody Ould Sixth,' " pp. 62 and 63.

62. *Ibid.*, p. 63, citing Thomas B. Gunn, *The Physiology of New York Boardinghouses* (New York 1857), pp. 111–12.

63. Stott, *Workers in the Metropolis*, p. 215. Stott provides an excellent description of the New York boardinghouse scene (pp. 214–16).

64. Pernicone, "The 'Bloody Ould Sixth,' " p. 63.

65. Quoted in Gilheany, "Subjects of History," pp. 178–79.

66. The Sixth Ward's economy included iron foundries, machine shops, tan-

■

neries, breweries, rope works, jewelers, type foundries, printing shops, slaughter-houses, and manufacturers of clothing, carriages, furniture, pianos, sewing machines, and silverware. Ibid.; Pernicone, "The "Bloody Ould Sixth,'" p. 49.

67. Pernicone, "The Bloody Ould Sixth,' " p. 36.

68. Ernst, *Immigrant Life*, p. 193.

69. The wards cited had the highest percentage of Irish and German immigrants in 1855. Ernst, *Immigrant Life*, p. 193; Stott, *Workers in the Metropolis*, pp. 204–5.

70. Ernst, *Immigrant Life*, p. 42; James Sigurd Lapham, "The German-Americans of New York City, 1860–1890, " PhD diss., Saint John's University, 1977, pp. 24, 25, and 67–68.

71. Rosenwaike, *Population History*, p. 42.

72. Gilheany, "Subjects of History," p. 183; Ernst, *Immigrant Life*, pp. 42–44. The Eighth Ward was bordered by the Hudson River on the west, Houston Street on the north, Broadway on the east, and Canal Street on the South.

73. Gilheany, "Subjects of History," pp. 111–15, 123–24, and 137–40.

74. Ibid., pp. 137–45.

75. Michael A. Gordon, *The Orange Riots: Irish Political Violence in New York City, 1870 and 1871* (Ithaca, 1993), pp. 22–23.

76. Ibid., p. 22.

77. Ibid., chapter 4.

78. Ibid., chapter 8.

79. Ernst, *Immigrant Life*, pp. 42–44.

80. Ibid., pp. 44–45.

81. Michael Contopoulos, "The Greek Community of New York City: Early Years to 1910," PhD diss., New York University, 1972, chapters 1–2.

82. Sister Adele Dabrowski, "A History and Survey of the Polish Community in Brooklyn," MA thesis, Fordham University, 1946, pp. 78–79 and 152.

83. Kate Claghorn, "The Foreign Immigrant in New York City," *Industrial Commission*, Vol. 15 (Washington, 1908), p. 472.

84. Quoted in ibid.

85. Josephine Hendin, "Italian Neighbors," in Richard Beard and Leslie Berlowitz, *Greenwich Village: Culture and Counterculture* (New York, 1993), p. 142.

86. Quoted in ibid.

87. Ibid., pp. 143–44.

88. Quoted in Claghorn, "The Foreign Immigrant in New York City," p. 472.

89. Jack Kuo Wei Tchen, "New York Chinese: The Nineteenth-Century Pre-Chinatown Settlement," *Chinese America: History and Perspectives* (San Francisco, 1990), pp. 16–63.

90. Jack Kuo Wei Tchen, "New York Before Chinatown: The Formation of an American Political Culture, 1784–1882," PhD diss.: New York University, 1992, pp. 168–76. For a popular account of early Chinatown, see Louis Beck, *New York's Chinatown: An Historical Presentation of Its People and Places* (New York, 1898).

91. Dolan, *The Immigrant Church*, pp. 22–23; Ernest A. McKay, *The Civil War and New York City* (Syracuse, 1990), pp. 75–76.

■

92. Rosenwaike, *Population History*, p. 42.

93. Shane White, *Somewhat More Independent: The End of Slavery in New York City, 1790–1810* (Athens, Ga., 1991), p. 54. Early efforts to achieve manumission are discussed in chapters 1 and 2.

94. Leo Hirsch, "The Negro and New York, 1783 to 1865," *Journal of Negro History* 16 (Oct. 1931): 391.

95. The movement for black suffrage is discussed in Phyllis Field, *The Politics of Race in New York: The Struggle for Black Suffrage in the Civil War Era* (Ithaca, 1982).

96. Quoted in ibid., p. 117.

97. Rhoda Freeman, "The Free Negro in New York City in the Era Before the Civil War," PhD diss., Columbia University, 1966, p. 274.

98. Ibid., p. 291.

99. Quoted in Hirsch, "The Negro and New York," p. 436.

100. Robert Ernest, "The Economic Status of New York City Negroes," *Negro History Bulletin* 12 (Mar. 1949): 132.

101. Ibid., pp. 139, 142, and 143; Hirsch, "The Negro and New York," p. 438; and Freeman, "The Free Negro," p. 285. Figures are not always precise.

102. George Walker, "The Afro-American in New York City, 1827–1860," PhD diss., Columbia University, 1975, p. 41.

103. Herman D. Bloch, *The Circle of Discrimination: A Economic and Social Study of the Black Man in New York* (New York, 1969), p. 28; Walker, "The Afro American," pp. 44–45.

104. Hirsch, "The Negro and New York," pp. 436–37; Albon P. Man, Jr., "Labor Competition and the New York Draft Riots of 1863," *Journal of Negro History* 36 (Oct. 1951): 376–77. Rhoda Freemen does not believe the Irish and blacks were in direct competition. Freemen, "The Free Negro," pp. 289–90.

105. Man, "Labor Competition," pp. 393–94; Leon Litwack, *North of Slavery: The Negro in the Free States, 1790–1860* (Chicago, 1961), p. 160.

106. Man, "Labor Competition," pp. 389–90.

107. Freeman, "The Free Negro," pp. 219–20.

108. Ibid., pp. 217–19.

109. Quoted in Gilbert Osofsky, "The Enduring Ghetto," *Journal of American History* 40 (Sept. 1968): 246.

110. Freeman, "The Free Negro," pp. 229–31; Walker, "The Afro American," pp. 13–16.

111. Freeman, "The Free Negro," pp. 102–5.

112. Ibid., pp. 106–12; Hirsch, "The Negro and New York," pp. 425–26.

113. Quoted in Hirsch, "The Negro and New York," pp. 424–25.

114. Freeman, "The Free Negro," pp. 376–409.

115. Quoted in Walker, "The Afro American," p. 153.

116. Ibid., pp. 149–55.

117. Freeman, "The Free Negro," pp. 320–46 and 356–72.

118. Robert Swan, Jr., "Did Brooklyn (N.Y.) Blacks Have Unusual Control over Their Schools: Period I: 1815–45?" *Afro Americans in New York Life and History* 7 (July 1983): 25–46.

■

119. Quoted in Osofsky, "Enduring Ghetto," p. 253.

120. Walker, "The Afro American," pp. 140–45.

121. Ibid., p. 158.

122. Seth Scheiner, *Negro Mecca: A History of the Negro in New York City, 1865–1920* (New York, 1965), p. 174; Gilbert Osofsky, *Harlem: The Making of a Ghetto, Negro New York, 1890–1930* (New York, 1968), p. 36.

## Chapter 3. Diversity in Action

1. Ira Rosenwaike, *Population History of New York City* (Syracuse, 1972), p. 21.

2. Quoted in Jay P. Dolan, *The Immigrant Church: New York's Irish and German Catholics, 1815-1865* (South Bend, Ind., 1983), p. 33.

3. Carol Groneman Pernicone, "The 'Bloody Ould Sixth': A Social Analysis of a New York City Working-Class Community in the Mid-Nineteenth Century," PhD diss., The University of Rochester, 1973, pp. 54–55.

4. Edward Spann, *The New Metropolis: New York City, 1840–1857* (New York, 1981), p. 27. The 1860 census revealed that there were a third more women than men among the Irish living in New York City.

5. Pernicone, "The 'Bloody Ould Sixth,'" pp. 71–72 and 163. The 1855 census of Irish male workers in the Sixth Ward reveals that almost 53% were unskilled laborers, 34% were skilled artisans and members of the building trades, and fewer than 145 were in other occupations, ranging from clericals, shopkeepers, and salesmen to professionals and factory owners. Ibid., pp. 100–101.

6. Ibid., p. 141, citing an 1853 investigation of the "Needlewomen of New York" by the *New York Tribune*.

7. Christine Stansell, *City of Women: Sex and Class in New York, 1789–1860* (New York, 1986), p. 156; David Katzman, *Seven Days a Week: Women and Domestic Service in Industrializing America* (New York, 1978), pp. 66–67.

8. Faye E. Dudden, *Serving Women: Household Service in Nineteenth-Century America* (Middletown, Ct.: 1983), p. 61.

9. Stansell, *City of Women*, pp. 156–65.

10. Quoted in ibid., p. 178.

11. Dolan, *The Immigrant Church*, p. 32; William Shannon, *The American Irish* (New York, 1963), p. 40.

12. Shannon, *American Irish*, p. 40.

13. George J. Lankevich and Howard B. Furer, *A Brief History of New York City* (Port Washington, N.Y., 1984), p. 95; Edward Robb Ellis, *The Epic of New York City: A Narrative History* (New York, 1990), pp. 231 and 233.

14. Lankevich and Furer, *A Brief History*, p. 94.

15. Iver Bernstein, *The New York City Draft Riots: Their Significance for American Society and Politics in the Age of the Civil War* (New York, 1990), pp. 5 and 119–20; Robert Ernst, *Immigrant Life in New York City, 1825–1863* (New York, 1979), p. 107.

16. While the Irish participants were likely driven primarily by hatred of England, class sentiments played a significant role in motivating most of the rioters.

■

For them Macready, England, and aristocracy were linked together as were Forest, America, and democracy. Ellis, *New York City*, pp. 260–65.

17. Ibid., pp. 277–81; Spann, *The New Metropolis*, pp. 392–94. The mayor finally disbanded the Municipals in the fall, after the state courts upheld the law creating the Metropolitans as the city's police force.

18. Spann, *The New Metropolis*, p. 504, n.37.

19. It has been estimated that 90 percent of the Irish Catholics were in the Democratic fold by 1844. See Dennis Clark, "East Side, West Side—New York," in Dennis Clark ed., *Hibernia America: The Irish and Regional Cultures* (Westport, Ct., 1986), p. 52.

20. Lankevich and Furer, *A Brief History*, pp. 142 and 146.

21. Shannon, *American Irish*, pp. 49–50; Anthony Gronowicz, "Labor's Decline within New York City's Democratic Party from 1844 to 1884," in William Pencak, Selma Berrol, and Randall M. Miller eds., *Immigration to New York* (Philadelphia, 1991), p. 9.

22. Richard Stott, *Workers in the Metropolis: Class, Etnicity, and Youth in Antebellum New York City* (Ithaca, 1990), p. 236.

23. Ernst, *Immigrant Life*, p. 165; Shannon, *American Irish*, pp. 15 and 52.

24. Lankevich and Furer, *A Brief History*, p. 99.

25. Stott, *Workers in the Metropolis*, p. 236; Shannon, *American Irish*, pp. 52–54.

26. Shannon, *American Irish*, p. 68.

27. Bernstein, *New York City Draft Riots*, pp. 228–33. For a detailed description of the riot as well as one the previous year see Stephen J. Sullivan, "The Orange and Green Riots (New York City: July 1870 & 1871)," *New York Irish History* 6 (1991–92): 4–12 and 46–59; Michael Gordon, *The Orange Riots: Irish Political Violence in New York City, 1870 and 1871* (Ithaca, 1993).

28. Shannon, *American Irish*, pp. 72–73.

29. Lawrence H. Fuchs, *The American Kaleidoscope: Race, Ethnicity, and the Civic Culture* (Hanover, N.H., 1990), p. 45.

30. Gronowicz, "Labor's Decline," p. 16.

31. Dolan, *The Immigrant Church*, pp. 12–15 and 22–23.

32. Ibid. p. 6.

33. Ellis, *New York City*, pp. 268 and 361; Dolan, *The Immigrant Church*, p. 165. For a biography of Archbishop Hughes see Richard Shaw, *Dagger John: The Unquiet Life and Times of Archbishop John Hughes* (New York, 1977).

34. Spann, *The New Metropolis*, p. 29.

35. The cornerstone of the new St Patrick's was laid in 1858; the completed church was dedicated on May 25, 1879. Ellis, *New York City*, pp. 217, 272–73, and 360.

36. Dolan, *The Immigrant Church*, pp. 54–58. Dolan reveals "that not more than 60 percent and closer to 40 percent of the people attended Sunday services in the 1860s." Ibid., p. 56.

37. Frederick M. Binder, *The Age of the Common School, 1830–1865* (New York, 1974), p. 64.

■

38. The school controversy is covered in ibid.; Joseph J. McCadden, "Governor Seward's Friendship with Bishop Hughes," *New York History* (hereafter *NYH*) 47 (Apr. 1966); and John W. Pratt, "Governor Seward and the New York City School Controversy, 1840–1842," *NYH* 42 (Oct., 1961).

39. Quoted in Pratt, "Governor Seward and the New York City School Controversy," pp. 361–62; Binder, *Common School*, p.66.

40. Dolan, *The Immigrant Church*, pp. 104–5.

41. Ibid., p. 108.

42. Ibid., p. 109; McCadden, "Governor Seward's Friendship With Bishop Hughes," p. 179.

43. Quoted in Robert Ernst, "Economic Nativism in New York City During the 1840's," *NYH* 29 (Apr. 1948): 173.

44. Douglas T. Miller, "Immigration and Social Stratification in Pre-Civil War New York," *NYH* 49 (Apr., 1968): 159 and 167.

45. Ibid., p. 162.

46. Spann, *The New Metropolis*, p. 41.

47. Quoted in Leonard R. Riforgiato, "Bishop John Timon, Archbishop John Hughes, and Irish Colonization: A Clash of Episcopal Views on the Future of the Irish and the Catholic Church in America," in Pencak, Berrol, and Miller, *Immigration to New York*, p. 33.

48. Ibid.

49. Quoted in Riforgiato, "Bishop John Timon, Archbishop John Hughes, and Irish Colonization," p. 43. Brownson's remarks were reported in the Know-Nothing organ the Buffalo *Commercial Advertiser*, whose editors provided the emphasis.

50. Leo Hershkowitz, "The Native American Democratic Association in New York City, 1835–1836," *New York Historical Quarterly* 46 (Jan. 1962): 41.; Ira M. Leonard, " The Rise and Fall of the American Republican Party in New York City, 1843–1845," *New York Historical Quarterly* 50 (Apr. 1966): 151; and Spann, *The New Metropolis*, p. 338.

51. McCadden, "Governor Seward's Friendship With Bishop Hughes," pp. 177–78; Hershkowitz, "The Native American Association in New York City," pp. 46 and 50. The Know Nothings in 1854 advocated barring all Catholics from public office; Spann, *The New Metropolis*, p. 338.

52. Leonard, "The Rise and Fall of the American Republican Party in New York City," pp. 155 and 192; McCadden, "Governor Seward's Friendship with Bishop Hughes," p. 179; and Shannon, *American Irish*, p. 71.

53. Ernest McKay, *The Civil War and New York City* (Syracuse, 1990), pp. 75–76.

54. Ibid., pp. 21–22. New York had a property requirement for blacks only of $250.

55. Quoted in ibid., p. 150.

56. Quoted in Dolan, *The Immigrant Church*, pp. 24–25.

57. Quoted in McKay, *The Civil War and New York City*, p. 196.

58. Ernst, *Immigrant Life*, p. 173.

59. Illustrations are reproduced in John Grafton, *New York in the Nineteenth Century* (New York, 1980, 2nd edition), p. 19.

60. Quoted in Shannon, *American Irish*, p. 58. It is interesting to note that, while the rioters depicted in *Harper's* illustrations are drawn with clearly Irish features and dress, there is nothing Irish about any of the policemen depicted.

61. James Sigurd Lapham, "The German Americans of New York City, 1860–1890," PhD. diss., St. John's University, 1977, p. 17; and Dolan, *The Immigrant Church*, p. 10. See also Dorothee Schneider, *Trade Unions and Community: The German Working Class in New York City, 1870–1900* (Urbana, 1994), pp. 1–22.

62. Dolan, *The Immigrant Church*, p. 35.

63. Stanley Nadel, "From the Barricades of Paris to the Sidewalks of New York: German Artisans and the European Roots of American Labor Radicalism," in Pencak, Berrol, and Miller, *Immigration to New York*, p. 33.

64. Schneider, *Trade Unions and Community*, pp. 22 and 24.

65. Lapham, "The German-Americans," pp. 19 and 44; Stanley Nadel, *Little Germany: Ethnicity, Religion, and Class in New York City, 1845–1880* (Urbana, 1990), p. 88.

66. Spann, *The New Metropolis*, pp. 25–26; Nadel, "From the Barricades," p. 71.

67. Nadel, *Little Germany*, pp. 1 and 29–32. The borders of *Kleindeutschland* were East 14th Street on the north, Third Avenue and the Bowery on the west, Division Street on the south, and the East River on the east. The district later gained fame as the heavily Jewish Lower East Side.

68. Ibid., p. 36, quoting Otto Lohr, "Das New York Deutschtum der Vergangenheit," in Otto Spengler, *Das Deutsche Element der Stadt New York* (New York, 1913), p. 12. See also Schneider, *Trade Unions and Community*, pp. 15–16.

69. Lapham, "The German-Americans," p. 2; Dolan, *The Immigrant Church*, p. 70.

70. In 1880, 80 percent of Bavarians were married to spouses born in Bavaria or adjacent states. By this time "Bavarians constituted a much smaller pool of possible marriage partners in *Kleindeutschland*." Nadel, *Little Germany*, p. 49. Nadel provides a detailed description of regional settlements within *Kleindeutschland*. Ibid., pp. 37–39.

71. Quoted in ibid., p. 93

72. Ibid., pp. 92–93; Dolan, *The Immigrant Church*, pp. 72–73.

73. Dolan, *The Immigrant Church*, pp. 90–91. Another divisive issue involved the hierarchy's strong pro-temperance position, which found little support in the German community. Ibid., pp. 128–29.

74. Nadel, *Little Germany*, p. 92; Lapham, "German-Americans," p. 55. By 1890 Manhattan housed 12 German parishes; in 1891 Brooklyn numbered 23 German parishes. Lapham, "German-Americans," pp. 49–50.

75. Lapham, "German-Americans," pp. 54–59.

76. Dolan, *The Immigrant Church*, pp. 73 and 80–81; Nadel, *Little Germany*, pp. 92–95.

■

77. Lapham, "German-Americans," pp. 69–71.

78. Ibid., pp. 120–28; Ernst, *Immigrant Life*, p. 139.

79. Ernst, *Immigrant Life*, pp. 85, 112, and 114.

80. Ibid., p. 109; Nadel, *Little Germany*, p. 97.

81. Nadel, *Little Germany*, pp. 95–96.

82. Ibid., 97–99; Ernst, *Immigrant Life*, p. 139.

83. Barry E. Supple, "A Business Elite: German-Jewish Financiers in Nineteenth-Century New York," *Business History Review* 31 (Summer 1957): 148, 148n. Estimated population figures indicate that from 1846 to 1860 German Jews constituted more than half the Jewish population of New York. In all probability this held true at least until 1880. Hyman B. Grinstein, *The Rise of the Jewish Community of New York* (Philadelphia, 1945), p. 469; Nadel, *Little Germany*, p. 100.

84. Supple, "A Business Elite," pp. 147–49, 148n.

85. Grinstein, *The Rise of the Jewish Community*, pp. 472–76; Nadel, *Little Germany*, p. 100; and Ernst, *Immigrant Life*, pp. 137–38.

86. Grinstein, *The Rise of the Jewish Community*, pp. 90 and 171; Nadel, *Little Germany*, p. 100.

87. Nadel, *Little Germany*, pp. 101–2.

88. Supple. "A Business Elite," p. 162.

89. Ernst, *Immigrant Life*, pp. 153–55; Nadel, *Little Germany*, p.154.

90. Ernst, *Immigrant Life*, pp. 153–55; Lapham, "German-Americans," pp. 25–27.

91. Stott, *Workers in the Metropolis*, pp. 219 and 221; Nadel, *Little Germany*, pp. 104–6.

92. Stott, *Workers in the Metropolis*, p. 228; Nadel, *Little Germany*, p. 106; and Lapham, "The German-Americans," p. 27.

93. Ernst, *Immigrant Life*, pp. 130–31; Nadel, *Little Germany*, pp. 120–21; and Schneider, *Trade Unions and Community*.

94. Nadel, *Little Germany*, pp. 107–8; Ernst, *Immigrant Life*, p. 131.

95. Nadel, *Little Germany*, pp. 66–67.

96. Ibid.

97. Ibid., pp. 81–82 and 83–86; Supple, "A Business Elite," p. 155.

98. Lapham, "The German-Americans," p. 34.

99. Ibid., 31–32; Ernst, *Immigrant Life*, pp. 108–11. For German union activity see Schneider, *Trade Unions and Community*.

100. Ernst, *Immigrant Life*, pp. 115–17; Lapham, "The German-Americans," pp. 37–38; and Nadel, *Little Germany*, pp. 124–25.

101. Ernst, *Immigrant Life*, pp. 118–21; Lapham, "The German-Americans," pp. 38–42; Nadel, *Little Germany*, pp. 128–30, 137, and 141; and Schneider, *Trade Unions and Community*, chapters 3 and 5. Weydemeyer founded *Stimme des Volkes* in Chicago in 1860, rose to the rank of brigadier general in the Union Army, and, following the war, edited *Die Neue Zeit* in Chicago.

102. Lapham, "The German-Americans," pp. 42–44; Ernst, *Immigrant Life*, p. 56.

■

103. Nadel, *Little Germany*, pp. 138–39. Organized in the spring of 1872, a central employers' association led by piano magnate William Steinway was able to turn back and ultimately defeat a massive eight-hour day movement dominated by German unionists. As many as 100,000 workers had participated in "eight-hour" strikes by the end of that summer. Ibid., pp. 143–47.

104. Lapham, "The German-Americans," pp. 134–52.

105. Quoted in ibid., p. 156.

106. Ibid., p. 157. Percentage based on the 1880 census.

107. Nadel, *Little Germany*, p. 135; Ernst, *Immigrant Life*, p. 167.

108. Nadel *Little Germany*, p. 136; Lapham, "The German-Americans," pp. 186 and 196–97; and Bernstein, *The New York City Draft Riots*, p. 222.

109. Nadel, *Little Germany*, p. 152; Lapham, "The German-Americans," pp. 227–29.

110. Nadel, *Little Germany*, p. 152; Lapham, "The German-Americans," pp. 231–33.

111. Lapham, "The German-Americans," pp. 185 and 189.

112. Nadel, *Little Germany*, p. 152.

113. Fuchs, *The American Kaleidoscope*, p. 22.

114. Lapham, "The German-Americans," pp. 167–73.

115. Ibid., p. 12; Nadel, *Little Germany*, pp. 155 and 159.

## Chapter 4. Old and New Immigrants in Greater New York City

1. David Hammack, *Power and Society: Greater New York at the Turn of the Century* (New York, 1982), chapter 7.

2. Ellis Island was temporarily closed after a fire but reopened in 1897.

3. Hammack, *Power and Society*, pp. 31–9.

4. Ibid., pp. 39–40. Piano, clock, and printing manufacturing did require large space, and the city was fortunate to keep these industries in Manhattan and Brooklyn.

5. Irving Howe, *The World of Our Fathers* (New York, 1976), pp. 80–84.

6. Gilbert Osofsky, *Harlem: The Making of a Ghetto* (New York, 1966), chapter 4. For the settlement houses, see Allen Davis, *Spearheads for Reform* (New York, 1967); Robert Bremner, *From the Depths* (New York, 1956), pp. 57–62.

7. See Roy Lubove, *The Progressives and the Slum: Tenement House Reform in New York City* (Pittsburgh, 1962).

8. For the controversy over movie censorship, see Lary May, *Screening Out the Past* (New York, 1980), chapter 3, and for the campaign to outlaw home work, see Eileen Boris, *Home to Work: Motherhood and the Politics of Industrial Homework in the United States* (New York, 1994).

9. Sister May Fabian Matthews, "The Role of the Public School in the Assimilation of the Italian Immigrant Child in New York City, 1900–1914," PhD diss., Fordham University, 1966, p. 144.

10. Selma Berrol, "Immigrants at School: New York City, 1898–1914," PhD diss., City University of New York, 1967, pp. 4–22; Diane Ravitch, *The Great School Wars, New York City, 1805–1973* (New York, 1974), chapters 11–14.

■

11. Hammack, *Power and Society*, chapter 9.

12. Berrol, "Immigrants at School," pp. 109–13; Mathews, "The Role of the Public School," pp. 141–47 and 155–80.

13. Bonnie Mitelman, "Rose Schneiderman and the Triangle Fire," *American History Illustrated* 167 (July 1981): 38–47.

14. Dorothee Schneider, *Trade Unions and Community: The German Working Class in New York City, 1870–1900* (Urbana, 1994), pp. 7–8.

15. Ira Rosenwaike, *Population History of New York City* (Syracuse, 1972), p. 68.

16. Hammack, *Power and Society*, pp. 66–69.

17. For the decline of Little Germany see Stanley Nadel, *Little Germany: Ethnicity, Religion, and Class in New York City, 1845–1880* (Urbana, 1990); Rosenwaike, *Population History*, pp. 83–85.

18. Thomas Henderson, *Tammany Hall and the New Immigrants* (New York, 1976), pp. 73–74.

19. For the subway's impact, see, Clifton Hood, *722 Miles: The Building of the Subways and How They Transformed New York* (New York, 1993).

20. Henderson, *Tammany and the New Immigrants*, p. 74.

21. Quoted in Richard O'Connor, *Hell's Kitchen* (New York, 1958), p. 65.

22. Ibid., p. 182.

23. Kerby Miller, *Emigrants and Exiles* (New York, 1985), pp. 495, 506, and 533; Jay Dolan, *Immigrant Church: New York's Irish and German Catholics, 1815–1865* (South Bend, 1983), pp. 111–13.

24. Henderson, *Tammany and the New Immigrants*, p. 72.

25. Hammack, *Power and Society*, p. 69.

26. Henderson, *Tammany and the New Immigrants*, pp. 74–79; Kate Claghorn, "The Foreign Immigrant in New York City," *Industrial Commission*, Vol. 15 (Washington, 1908), p. 471.

27. Henderson, *Tammany and the New Immigrants*, p. 83.

28. Janet Nolan, *Ourselves Alone: Women's Emigration from Ireland, 1885–1920* (Lexington, Ky.: 1989), pp. 84–85.

29. Chris McNickle, *To Be Mayor of New York* (New York, 1993), p. 9.

30. Steven Erie, *Rainbow's End: Irish-Americans and the Dilemmas of Urban Machine Politics, 1840–1985* (Berkeley, 1988), pp. 88–90.

31. Timothy J. Gilfoyle, *City of Eros: New York City, Prostitution, and the Commercialization of Sex, 1790–1920* (New York, 1992), p. 253.

32. Luc Sante, *Low Life: Lures and Snares of Old New York* (New York, 1991), pp. 247–49.

33. Gilfoyle, *City of Eros*, chapter 12.

34. Quoted in Erie, *Rainbow's End*, p. 10. For Tammany see also Gustavus Myers, *The History of Tammany Hall* (New York, 1971, originally 1917); Oliver Allen, *The Tiger: The Rise and Fall of Tammany Hall* (New York, 1993).

35. See Thomas N. Brown, *Irish American Nationalism* (Philadelphia, 1966).

36. Daniel Czitrom, "Underworlds and Undergods: Big Tim Sullivan and Metropolitan Politics in New York, 1889–1913," *Journal of American History* 78 (Sept. 1991): 536–58.

■

37. Kenneth S. Chern, "The Politics of Patriotism: War, Ethnicity, and the New York Mayoral Campaign, 1917," *New York Historical Society Quarterly* 63 (Oct. 1979): 300–301 and 307.

38. Mary Brown, "Italian Immigrants and the Catholic Church in the Archdiocese of New York, 1880–1950," PhD. diss., Columbia University, 1987, pp. 115–18 and 155.

39. Sister Marie De Lourdes Walsh, *The Sisters of Charity of New York, 1809–1959*, Vol. 3 (New York, 1960), chapter 7; Bernadette McCauley, " 'Who Shall Take of Our Sick,' Roman Catholic Sisterhoods and Their Hospitals, New York City, 1850–1930," PhD diss., Columbia University, 1992, p. 81.

40. McCauley, " 'Who Shall Take Care of Our Sick,' " pp. 127–29

41. Walsh, *Sisters of Charity*, pp. 3–6.

42. Ibid., pp. 90–91

43. Gary R. Mormino and George E. Pozzetta, *The Immigrant World of Ybor City* (Urbana, 1987), chapter 1.

44. For conditions in Europe see John Bodnar, *The Transplanted: A History of Immigrants in Urban America* (Bloomington, 1985), chapter 1; Philip Taylor, *The Distant Magnet: European Emigration to USA* (New York, 1971), chapters 2–3.

45. Gerald Sorin, *A Time for Building: The Third Migration, 1880–1920* (Baltimore, 1992), pp. 23 and 33; Ronald Sanders, *Shores of Refugee: A Hundred Years of Jewish Emigration* (New York, 1988), chapters 1–2.

46. Quoted in Howard Sachar, *A History of the Jews in America* (New York, 1992), p. 119.

47. Taylor, *The Distant Magnet*, chapter 4.

48. Quoted Sachar, *A History of the Jews in America*, p. 127.

49. Ibid., chapter 8.

50. U.S. Commission on Immigration, Vol. 31, *The Children of Immigrants in Schools* (Washington, 1911), p. 612.

51. U.S. Immigration Commission, *Immigrants in Cities*, Vol. 26–27, part 1 (Washington, 1911), p. 168.

52. See Richard Lieberman, "Social Change and Political Behavior: The East Village of New York City, 1880–1905," PhD diss., New York University, 1976, chapter 2.

53. Marie Sabsovich Orenstein, "The Servo-Croats of Manhattan," *The Survey* 29 (Dec. 7, 1912): 277.

54. Louis Pink, "The Magyar in New York," *Charities* 13 (Dec. 3, 1904): 262–63.

55. Thomas Capek, Jr., *The Cech (Bohemian) Community of New York* (San Francisco, 1969, originally 1921), p. 20.

56. Michael Contopoulos, "The Greek Community of New York City: Early Years to 1910," PhD diss., New York University, 1972, chapters 3–4.

57. Charles Moskos, *Greek Americans: Struggle and Success* (Englewood Cliffs, 1980), pp. 23–24.

58. Sister Adele Dabrowski, "A History and Survey of the Polish in Brooklyn Community," MA thesis, Fordham University, 1946, pp. 78–79 and 152.

■

59. Capek, *The Cech Community*, pp. 23–24.

60. Quoted in Eileen Boris, *Home Work: Motherhood and the Politics of Industrial Homework*, p. 27.

61. Schneider, *Trade Unions and Community*, pp. 64–65.

62. Moskos, *Greek Americans*, pp. 24–25; and Contopoulos, "The Greek Community," chapter 6. The number of Greek women increased after 1910, but men still outnumbered women 2.8 to 1 in 1930.

63. Orenstein, "The Servo-Croats of Manhattan, " p. 283.

64. For the ethnic press see Sally Miller ed., *The Ethnic Press in the United States: A Historical Analysis and Handbook* (Westport, Ct., 1987); Joshua Fishman et al., *Language Loyalty in the United States: The Maintenance and Perpetuation of Non-English Mother Tongues by American Ethnic and Religious Groups* ( The Hague, 1966).

65. Capek, *The Cech Community*, pp. 38–42.

66. Ibid.

67. Moskos, *Greek Americans*, pp. 23–24.

68. Theodore Saloutos, *The Greeks in the United States* (Cambridge, 1964), p. 79.

69. Moskos, *Greek Americans*, pp. 31–33.

70. Orenstein, "The Servo-Croats of Manhattan," p. 283.

71. Gregory Orfalea, *Before the Flames: A Quest for the History of Arab Americans* (Austin, 1989), pp. 75–78.

72. Lucius Hopkins Miller, *Our Syrian Population: A Study of the Syrian Communities of Greater New York* (San Francisco, 1968, originally 1902), p. 18.

73. Philip and Joseph Kayal, *The Syrian-Lebanese in America: A Study in Religion and Assimilation* (Boston, 1975), pp. 87–88.

74. Orfalea, *Before the Flames*, p. 767; Harriet D. Bodemer, "The Syrian Colony in Brooklyn," MA thesis, Fordham University, 1943, pp. 47–48; WPA Files, "Arabs in New York"; and Miller, *Our Syrian Population*.

75. The 1882 ban was temporary, but it was extended in subsequent years and finally repealed in 1943. Then China was granted a small immigration quota. Certain classes of Chinese could still come to America, and ways were found to get around the ban to permit "paper sons" (supposed sons of Chinese-American citizens) to emigrate to America. But in general the limits imposed severe restrictions on Chinese immigration. See Ronald Takaki, *Strangers from a Different Shore: A History of Asian Americans* (Boston, 1989), pp. 416–18.

76. Ibid., pp. 251–52.

77. Louis Winnick, *New People in Old Neighborhoods: The Role of New Immigrants in Rejuvenating New York's Communities* (New York, 1990), p. 95.

78. Ibid., pp. 77–78, 84, and 85.

79. David Mauk, "The Colony That Rose from the Sea: The Norwegians in the Red Hook Section of Brooklyn, 1850–1910," PhD diss., New York University, 1991, chapters 2–3.

80. Ibid., pp. 327–28.

81. Ibid., p. 454 and chapter 8.

82. Seth Scheiner, *Negro Mecca: A History of the Negro in New York City, 1865–1915* (New York, 1965), p. 221.

■

83. Calvin Holder, "The Causes and Composition of West Indian Immigration to New York City, 1900–1952," *Afro-Americans in New York Life and History* 11 (Jan. 1987): 8–17.

84. Philip Kasinitz, *Caribbean New York: Black Immigrants and the Politics of Race* (Ithaca, 1992), pp. 24–25, 33–35, and 41–52.

85. Quoted in Seth Scheiner, "The New York City Negro and the Tenement, 1880–1910," *New York History*, 45 (Oct. 1964): 306.

86. Scheiner, *Negro Mecca*, pp. 16–20.

87. Quoted in Osofsky, *Harlem*, p. 14.

88. Ibid., pp. 46–52.

89. Ibid., pp. 147–48; Connolly, *A Ghetto Grows in Brooklyn*, pp. 26–29; Marsha Hunt Hiller, "Race Politics in New York City, 1890–1930," PhD diss., Columbia University, 1972, pp. 36–50.

90. Osofsky, *Harlem*, pp. 41–42.

91. Ibid., pp. 95–100, 86–87; George Haynes, *The Negro at Work in New York City: A Study of Economic Progress* (New York, 1968, originally 1912), pp. 25–26.

92. Mary Ovington, *Half a Man: The Status of the Negro in New York* (New York, 1960, originally 1911), p. 88.

93. Quoted in Osofsky, *Harlem*, p. 166.

94. Haynes, *The Negro in New York*, chapter 4; Ovington, *Half a Man*, chapter 4.

95. Haynes, *The Negro in New York*, pp. 61–65.

96. See ibid., part II, chapters 1–3. Haynes optimistically subtitled his book "A Study in Economic Progress," but his data revealed a more sobering picture. In some activities, like catering and barbering, blacks had lost their former white clientele. See Ovington, *Half a Man*, p. 108.

97. Ovington, *Half a Man*, pp. 112–37.

98. James Weldon Johnson, *Black Manhattan* (New York, 1968, originally in 1930), chapters 9–10.

99. For an account of the riot, see Osofsky, *Harlem*, pp. 46–52.

100. Quoted in ibid., p. 48.

101. Ibid., pp. 48–49.

102. For these statements see Frank Moss, *The Story of the Riot* (New York, 1969, originally 1900).

103. Quoted in Osofsky, *Harlem*, pp. 50–52.

104. Michael Goldstein, "Preface to the Rise of Booker T. Washington: A View from New York City of the Demise of Independent Black Politics, 1889–1912," *Journal of Negro History* 42 (Jan. 1977): 94–96.

105. Ibid., pp. 115–20; Scheiner, *Black Mecca*, pp. 127–28.

## Chapter 5. Jews and Italians in Greater New York City

1. Howard M. Sachar, *A History of the Jews in America* (New York, 1992), p. 141; Gerald Sorin, *A Time for Building: The Third Migration, 1880–1920* (Baltimore, 1992), pp. 42 and 63; Moses Rischin, *The Promised City: New York's Jews, 1870–1914* (Cambridge, Mass., 1962), p. 243; and Stephen F. Brumberg, *Going*

*to America, Going to School: The Jewish Immigrant Public School Encounter in Turn-of-the-Century New York City* (New York, 1986), p. 55.

2. Sachar, *A History of the Jews in America*, pp. 118–19, 121.

3. Quoted in Irving Howe, *World of Our Fathers* (New York, 1976), p. 75.

4. Gerald Sorin states, "Nearly 67 percent of gainfully employed Jewish immigrants who arrived between 1899 and 1914 possessed industrial skills—a much higher proportion than any other national group." *A Time for Building*, p. 75.

5. Howe, *World of Our Fathers*, p. 59. Thomas Kessner provides occupational data on Jewish immigrants arriving in the United states between 1895 and 1910. Among the most numerous of the 395,823 reported skilled workers were 145,272 tailors, 36,138 carpenters and joiners, 23,519 shoemakers, and 23,179 seamstresses. Thomas Kessner, *The Golden Door: Italian and Jewish Immigrant Mobility in New York City, 1880–1915* (New York, 1977), p. 33.

6. Howe, *World of Our Fathers*, p. 59.

7. Ibid., p. 62; Sachar, *A History of the Jews*, pp. 174–75. Despite the traditional high regard for learning among Jews and emphasis upon reading demanded by their religion, the illiteracy rate among Jewish immigrants between 1899 and 1910 was 26 percent. This figure includes women, for whom education was not considered essential in *shtetl* society. Also, literacy was defined by immigration authorities to include writing as well as reading. In traditional religious schooling the teaching of writing was considered of secondary importance to that of reading. Brumberg, *Going to America, Going to School*, p. 29; Kessner, *The Golden Door*, pp. 40–41.

8. Sorin, *A Time for Building*, pp. 38, 39, 249–50. Travelling as families, the Jews also arrived with more older people than most other immigrant groups. Howe, *World of Our Fathers*, p. 58.

9. Rischin, *The Promised City*, pp. 76 and 78.

10. Ibid., pp. 76 and 106–7.

11. Howe, *World of Our Fathers*, p. 257.

12. Rischin, *The Promised City*, p.94.

13. Howe, *World of Our Fathers*, pp. 69 and 149.

14. Sachar, *A History of the Jews*, p. 141.

15. Rischin, *The Promised City*, pp. 92–94; Sorin, *A Time for Building*, pp. 70–71.

16. Howe, *World of Our Fathers*, pp. 130–32; Sachar, *A History of the Jews*, p. 214; and Rischin, *The Promised City*, pp. 92–93.

17. Quoted in Howe, *World of Our Fathers*, p. 131.

18. Ibid., pp. 131–32; Rischin, *The Promised City*, p. 93.

19. Brumberg, *Going to America, Going to School*, p. 54.

20. Quoted in Sachar, *A History of the Jews*, p. 125.

21. Selma C. Berrol, "In Their Image: German Jews and the Americanization of the *Ost Juden* in New York City," *New York History* 63 (Oct. 1982): 421–22.

22. Rischin, *The Promised City*, pp. 101–103; Howe, *World of Our Fathers*, pp. 230–35.

■

23. Howe, *World of Our Fathers*, pp. 230–35; Leonard Dinnerstein, "Education and the Advancement of American Jews," in Bernard J. Weiss ed., *American Education and the European Immigrant, 1840–1940*, (Urbana, Illinois, 1982), pp. 44–60.

24. Rischin, *The Promised City*, pp. 103–4.

25. Howe, *World of Our Fathers*, p.98.

26. Quoted in Sachar, *A History of the Jews*, p. 164. The Dillingham Commission was the common name for the United States Immigration Commission.

27. Ibid., p. 170; Howe, *World of Our Fathers*, p. 133; and Sorin, *A Time for Building*, p. 84.

28. Howe *World of Our Fathers*, pp. 133–35; Sachar, *A History of the Jews*, pp. 193–96; and Sorin, *A Time for Building*, pp. 214–18. For a thorough, scholarly, and vivid account of the Kehillah see Arthur A. Goren, *The Kehillah Experiment, 1908–1922* (New York, 1970).

29. See Goren, *The Kehillah*.

30. Howe, *World of Our Fathers*, p. 185. The best account of the *landsmanshaftn* is Daniel Soyer, "The Jewish *Landsmanshaftn* (Hometown Societies) of New York," PhD diss., New York University, 1993.

31. Sachar. *A History of the Jews*, pp. 197–98.

32. Rischin, *The Promised City*, p. 105.

33. Sachar, *A History of the Jews*, p. 133. Though initiated and, at the outset, run primarily by eastern European Jews, money from uptown German Jews helped sustain HIAS.

34. Rischin, *The Promised City*, p. 106.

35. Sachar, *A History of the Jews*, p. 198.

36. Ibid., p. 143.

37. Quoted in Howe, *World of Our Fathers*, p. 79.

38. Quoted in ibid.

39. Only in the fruit and vegetable wagon trade, dominated by Greeks and Italians, were the Jews outnumbered. Rischin, *The Promised City*, p. 56.

40. Ibid., pp. 56–58; Sorin, *A Time for Building*, p. 77. Rischin informs us that the rising cost of sugar led to the replacement of soda water by seltzer as "the staple beverage of Yiddish New York." Ibid., p. 58.

41. Kessner, *The Golden Door*, pp. 9–10.

42. Sorin, *A Time for Building*, p. 74.

43. Ibid.; Sachar, *A History of the Jews*, p. 145.

44. Kessner, *The Golden Door*, p.19.

45. Rischin, *The Promised City*, p. 245; Sorin, *A Time for Building*, p. 114.

46. Kessner, *The Golden Door*, p. 57.

47. Quoted in Howe, *World of our Fathers*, p. 83.

48. Sorin, *A Time for Building*, pp. 114–15; Sachar, *A History of the Jews*, p. 182.

49. Rischin, *The Promised City*, p. 178.

50. Ibid., pp. 176–83.

51. Howe, *World of Our Fathers*, p. 292.

52. Sorin, *A Time for Building*, pp. 115, 118, 119.

■

53. For union activity see Melvyn Dubofsky, *When Workers Organize* (Amherst, 1968).

54. Quoted in Howe, *World of Our Fathers*, p. 298. See also Dubofsky, *When Workers Organize*, pp. 49–58; Susan A. Glenn, *Daughters of the Shtetl: Life and Labor in the Immigrant Generation* (Ithaca, 1990), pp. 167–69. "Striking workers demanded a 52-hour workweek, paid overtime, the abolition of fines and inside subcontracting, and union recognition. . . . [The] union called an end to the strike on Feb. 15. Many of the workers returned to their shops without any concession from employers, but others succeeded in winning all or some of their demands." Glenn, *Daughters of the Shtetl*, p. 169.

55. Bonnie Mitelman, "Rose Schneiderman and the Triangle Fire," *American History Illustrated* (July 1981): 38–47.

56. Rischin, *World of Our Fathers*, p. 256; Sorin, *A Time for Building*, p. 131. 1909 also saw the Amalgamated Clothing Workers of America formed under the leadership of Sidney Hillman. Together with the International Ladies' Garment Workers, established in 1900, it provided a powerful and enduring labor federation for the needle trades. Sorin, *A Time for Building*, p. 128.

57. Sorin, *A Time for Building*, p. 118.

58. Berrol, "In Their Image," pp. 423–24.

59. Sorin, *A Time for Building*, p. 192.

60. In 1913, Tammany loyalist Aaron Jefferson Levy became the majority leader of the state Assembly. Rischin, *The Promised City*, p. 230.

61. Ibid., pp. 228–33; Sachar, *A History of the Jews*, p. 176.

62. Sachar, *A History of the Jews*, pp. 76–78.

63. Rischin, *The Promised City*, p. 166.

64. Ibid., p. 133.

65. Ibid., 233–34; Sorin, *A Time for Building*, pp. 220–23; and Sachar, *A History of the Jews*, pp. 204–5.

66. Rischin, *The Promised City*, p. 35; Sorin, *A Time for Building*, pp. 25–26, 174, 220; and Sachar, *A History of the Jews*, p. 189.

67. Quoted in Sorin, *A Time for Building*, p. 175.

68. Jeffrey S. Gurock, "A Stage in the Emergence of the Americanized Synagogue among East European Jews: 1890–1910," *Journal of American Ethnic History* (Spring 1990): 7, 23.

69. Brumberg, *Going to America, Going to School*, p. 70. A survey of Orthodox synagogues in 1917 revealed that only 23 percent employed rabbis and only 13 percent provided religious schools. Sachar, *A History of the Jews*, pp. 190–91.

70. Howe, *World of Our Fathers*, p. 197.

71. Rischin, *The Promised City*, p. 148. Galician and Hungarian Jews appointed their own Chief Rabbi in 1892, Joshua Segal. The following year Rabbi Hayim Vidrowitz, recently arrived from Moscow, declared himself "Chief Rabbi of America." Howe, *World of Our Fathers*, p. 195.

72. Gurock, "Americanized Synagogue," p. 7.

73. Sorin, *A Time for Building*, pp. 184–87; Howe, *World of Our Fathers*, pp. 197–200.

■

74. Quoted in Brumberg, *Going to America, Going to School*, p. 13.

75. Selma Berrol, "Public Schools and Immigrants: The New York City Experience," in Bernard J. Weiss ed., *American Education and the European Immigrant*, p. 32. See also Selma Berrol, *Immigrants at School: New York City, 1898–1914* (New York, 1978).

76. Quoted in Sydney Stahl Weinberg, "Longing to Learn: The Education of Jewish Immigrant Women in New York City, 1900–1933," *Journal of Ethnic History* (Spring 1989): 119.

77. Berrol, "Public Schools and Immigrants," pp. 36–37. See also Alan Kraut, *Silent Travelers: Germs, Genes, and the "Immigrant Menace"* (New York, 1994), pp. 228–32.

78. Quoted in Weinberg, "Longing to Learn," p. 119.

79. Ibid., pp. 108–9.

80. Howe, *World of Our Fathers*, p. 281; Leonard Dinnerstein, "Education and the Advancement of American Jews," in Bernard J. Weiss (ed.), *American Education and the European Immigrant* p. 50. Jewish students represented approximately 20 percent of all-female Hunter College's enrollment during this period. Ibid.

81. Up to 1903 compulsory attendance laws permitted students to leave school at age twelve or upon completion of the fifth grade. That year the age was raised to fourteen and the grade to six; in 1913 the age/grade requirement was upped to sixteen and eight. However, the laws were not vigorously enforced. Many children left school at age nine or ten. Of all children entering public schools in 1913 only one-third reached the eighth grade. Berrol, "Public Schools and Immigrants," pp. 36–38; Weinberg, "Longing to Learn," pp. 110, 115–16.

82. Sorin, *A Time for Building*, p. 106; Berrol, "Public Schools and Immigrants," p. 39.

83. Dinnerstein, "Education and the Advancement of American Jews," p. 49.

84. Weinberg, "Longing to Learn," pp. 121, 113; Howe, *World of Our Fathers*, p. 238.

85. Quoted in Dinnerstein, "Education and Advancement of American Jews," pp. 49–50.

86. Sorin, *A Time for Building*, pp. 102–3; Sachar, *A History of the Jews*, p. 201; and Howe, *World of Our Fathers*, p. 543.

87. Howe, *World of Our Fathers*, pp. 520, 523; Sachar, *A History of the Jews*, pp. 202–3.

88. Quoted in Sorin, *A Time for Building*, p. 120.

89. Dinnerstein, "Education and the Advancement of American Jews," p. 47; Weinberg, "Longing to Learn," p. 114.

90. Quoted in Sorin, *A Time for Building*, p. 103; Sachar, *A History of the Jews*, p. 204.

91. Every letter, whether printed in the paper or not, received a reply from either Cahan or the column editor, S. Kornbluth. Sachar, *A History of the Jews*, pp. 204–5.

■

92. There were between 250 and 300 coffee shops on the Lower East Side by 1905. Rischin, *The Promised City*, p. 142; Sachar, *A History of the Jews*, p. 200.

93. Howe, *World of Our Fathers*, pp. 417–28; Sachar, *A History of the Jews*, pp. 205–8.

94. The newly arrived challengers, collectively named *Di Yunge* (the Young Ones), disillusioned by the failure of the 1905 Russian uprising, foreswore didacticism in literature. Howe, *The World of Our Fathers*, pp. 428–32; Sachar, *A History of the Jews*, p.208.

95. Ibid., p. 210.

96. Quoted in ibid., p. 213.

97. Sorin, *A Time for Building*, p. 99.

98. Howe, *World of Our Fathers*, pp. 460–64.

99. Quoted in Sachar, *A History of the Jews*, p. 211

100. Ibid., pp. 211–12; Howe, *World of Our Fathers*, p. 480.

101. Sorin, *A Time for Building*, pp. 100–101.

102. Thomas Kessner describes New York's ghetto as a "mobility launcher." Kessner, *The Golden Door*, p. 174.

103. George Pozzetta, "The Italians of New York City, 1890–1914," PhD diss., University of North Carolina, 1971, p. 78.

104. Caroline Ware, *Greenwich Village, 1920–1930* (New York, 1977, first published 1935), pp. 152–57.

105. Pozzetta, "The Italians of New York City," pp. 105–7.

106. Ibid., p. 104.

107. Italians along with the Irish provided the bulk of the 7,700 laborers who built the city's first subway from City Hall to 145th Street and Broadway (1901–1904). Clifton Hood, *722 Miles: the Building of the Subways and How They Transformed New York* (New York, 1993), p. 85.

108. Pozzetta, "The Italians of New York City," p. 94; Donna Gabaccia, "Little Italy's Decline: Immigrant Renters and Investors in a Changing City," in David Ward and Olivier Zunz eds., *The Landscape of Modernity: Essays on New York City, 1900–1940* (New York, 1992), p. 247.

109. Robert Orsi, *The Madonna of 115th Street: Faith and Community in Italian Harlem, 1880–1950* (New Haven, 1985), p. 14.

110. Ibid., pp. 14–17.

111. Anthony L. LaRuffa, *Monte Carmelo: An Italian-American Community in the Bronx* (New York, 1988). pp. 17–18.

112. Pozzetta, "The Italians of New York City," pp. 332–38.

113. Ibid., p. 85.

114. Donna Gabaccia, *From Sicily to Elizabeth: Housing and Social Change Among Italian Immigrants, 1880–1930* (Albany, 1984), p. 54; Report of the U.S. Immigration Commission, *Immigrants in Cities*, Vol. 26 (Washington, 1911), p. 16.

115. Kate Claghorn, "The Foreign Immigrant in New York City," *Industrial Commission*, Vol. 15 (Washington, 1908), p. 474.

116. Ibid., p. 472.

117. Orsi, *The Madonna*, p. 29.

■

118. Jacob Riis, *How the Other Half Lives: Studies Among the Tenements of New York* (New York, 1971, originally 1890), p. 56.

119. See ibid., pp. 43–59 and 148–63.

120. Orsi, *The Madonna*, p. 31.

121. See Thomas Pitkin, *The Black Hand: A Chapter in Ethnic Crime* (Totowa, N.J., 1977); Humbert Nelli, *The Business of Crime: Italians and Syndicate Crime in the United States* (New York, 1976), chapter 4.

122. Nelli, *The Business of Crime*, pp. 97–99.

123. Claghorn, "The Foreign Immigration in New York City," p. 474.

124. Pitkin, *The Black Hand*, chapter 5.

125. Kessner, *The Golden Door*, pp. 44–53.

126. Ibid., p. 52.

127. Ibid., pp. 51–52 and 55.

128. Ibid., p. 57.

129. Pozzetta, "The Italians of New York City," pp. 339–41.

130. Miriam Cohen, *From Workshop to Office: Two Generations of Italian Women in New York City, 1900–1950* (Ithaca, 1993), p. 41.

131. Ibid., pp. 42–44.

132. Ibid., pp. 60–64.

133. Immigration Commission, "Immigrants in Cities," p. 200.

134. Ibid., p. 83.

135. Quoted in ibid., p. 141.

136. Ibid., pp. 152–64.

137. Kessner, *The Golden Door*, pp. 71–86.

138. Cohen, *From Workshop to Office*, pp. 118–20. See also Sister Mary Fabian Matthews, "The Role of the Public School in the Americanization of the Italian Immigrant Child in New York City, 1900–1914," PhD diss., Fordham University, 1966.

139. Matthews, "The Role of the Public School," pp. 97–98.

140. Cohen, *From Workshop to Office*, p. 121.

141. Pozzetta, "The Italians of New York City," pp. 356–57.

142. Ibid., pp. 358–59.

143. Ibid. pp. 359–63 and 351–54.

144. Kessner, *The Golden Door*, chapter 5.

145. Ibid., pp. 118–19.

146. Quoted in David Katzman and William M. Tuttle, Jr., eds., *Plain Folk* (Urbana, 1982), p. 12.

147. Thomas Kessner, *Fiorello H. La Guardia and the Making of Modern New York* (New York, 1989), pp. 30–40 and chapter 11.

148. Donna Gabaccia, *Militants and Migrants: Rural Sicilians Become American Workers* (New Brunswick, 1988), pp. 127–45.

149. Pozzetta, "The Italians of New York City,," pp. 252–66, 243–428.

150. Ibid., pp. 231–32.

151. Ibid., pp. 237–38.

152. Ibid., p. 267.

■

153. Mary Brown, "Italian Immigrants and the Catholic Church in the Archdiocese of New York, 1880–1950," PhD diss., Columbia University, 1987," p. 49.

154. Denise DeCarlo, "The History of the Italian *Festa* in New York City, 1880's to the Present," PhD diss., New York University, 1990, p. 47.

155. Ibid., p. 47.

156. Quoted in Ana Maria Diaz-Stevens, *Oxcart Catholicism on Fifth Avenue* (Notre Dame, 1993), p. 75.

157. Ibid.

158. Pozzetta, "The Italians of New York City," pp. 269–79.

159. Richard Gambino, *Blood of My Blood* (Garden City, 1975), p. 212.

160. Brown, "Italian Immigrants," pp. 221–26.

161. Pozzetta, "The Italians of New York City," pp. 295–303.

162. Brown, "Italian Immigrants," pp. 225–26.

163. Pozzetta, "The Italians of New York City," pp. 277–89.

164. Brown, "The Italians," pp. 320–37.

165. Mary Elizabeth Brown, *From Italian Villages to Greenwich Village: Our Lady of Pompei, 1892–1992* (New York, 1992), pp. 37–41.

166. Ibid., pp. 64–67.

167. Ibid., chapter 5.

## Chapter 6. Ethnic New Yorkers from the Great War to the Great Depression

1. Carl Wittke, *German-Americans and the World War* (Columbus, 1936), p. 33.

2. Phyllis Keller, *States of Belonging: German-American Intellectuals and the First World War* (Cambridge, 1979), pp. 139–61.

3. Wittke, *German Americans and the World War*, pp. 130 and 136.

4. Frederick Luebke, *Bonds of Loyalty: German Americans and World War I* (Dekalb, Ill., 1974), p. 231.

5. Quoted in Susan Canedy, *America's Nazis* (Menlo Park, 1990), p. 12.

6. WPA Files, (New York City Archives), "The Germans of New York City."

7. Anita Rapone, *The Guardian Life Insurance Company, 1860–1920: A History of a German-American Enterprise* (New York, 1987), pp. 143–55.

8. Luebke, *Bonds of Loyalty*, p. 249.

9. Quoted in Alter F. Landesman, *Brownsville: The Birth, Development and Passing of Jewish Community in New York* (New York, 1969), pp. 287–88.

10. Ibid., p. 288. Despite such criticism, Hillquit received 28 percent of the votes. For his account see Morris Hillquit, *Loose Leaves From a Busy Life* (New York, 1934), pp. 180–210.

11. For the anarchist opposition to the American invasion of Russia see Richard Polenberg, *Fighting Faiths: The Abrams Case, the Supreme Court, and Free Speech* (New York, 1987).

12. Marion Casey, "The Rising Tide," *Irish Echo*, Apr. 17–23, 1991.

13. John Patrick Buckley, *The New York Irish: Their View of American Foreign Policy, 1914–1921* (New York, 1976), especially chapters 2–3.

14. For a thorough treatment of the immigration restrictions of the 1920s, see

■

John Higham, *Strangers in the Land: Patterns of American Nativism, 1860–1925* (New Brunswick, N.J., 1988), chapter 11.

15. The newspaper still claimed a circulation of 80,000 as late as 1939. James M. Bergquist, "The German-American Press," in Sally Miller ed., *The Ethnic Press in the United States: A Historical Analysis and Handbook* (Westport, Ct., 1987), p. 151.

16. Quoted in WPA Files, "The Germans." For the declining German community of Greenwich Village, see Caroline Ware, *Greenwich Village, 1920–1930: A Comment on American Civilization in the Post-War Years* (New York, 1935), pp. 231–33.

17. For the impact of the subways, see Clifton Hood, *722 Miles: The Building of the Subways and How They Transformed New York* (New York, 1993).

18. Richard Plunz, *A History of Housing in New York City: Dwelling Type and Social Change in the American Metropolis* (New York, 1990), p. 122.

19. Ibid., pp. 123–24.

20. Quoted in Jill Jonnes, *We're Still Here: The Rise, Fall, and Resurrection of the South Bronx* (Boston, 1986), pp. 51–56.

21. Ira Rosenwaike, *Population History of New York City* (Syracuse, 1972), p. 133.

22. Thomas Kessner, *Fiorello La Guardia and the Making of Modern New York* (New York, 1989), p. 3.

23. Rosenwaike, *Population History*, p. 94.

24. Lloyd Ultan and Gary Hermalyn, *The Bronx in the Innocent Years, 1890–1925* (New York, 1985), p. xiii.

25. Marion R. Casey, "Twentieth Century Irish Immigration to New York City: The Historical Perspective," *New York Irish History* 3 (1988): 25–26.

26. Marion Casey, "Bronx Irish: An Example of Internal Migration in New York City, 1900–1950," PhD seminar paper, New York University, May, 1989.

27. Peter J. Donaldson, "A Life in the City," *America* 147 (Oct. 16, 1982): 205–206.

28. William O'Dwyer, *Beyond the Golden Door* (New York, 1987), pp. 90–91.

29. Casey, "The Bronx Irish," p. 16.

30. Deborah Dash Moore, *At Home in America: Second Generation New York Jews* (New York, 1981), pp. 19–20.

31. Landesman, *Brownsville*, p. 95.

32. Quoted in Egon Mayer, *From Suburb to Shtetl: The Jews of Boro Park* (Philadelphia, 1979), pp. 21–23.

33. Ibid., p. 24.

34. Moore, *At Home*, pp. 37–38.

35. Ibid., p. 42.

36. For an excellent discussion of this neighborhood's development as a Jewish community see Selma C. Berrol, "Manhattan's Jewish West Side," *New York Affairs* 10 (Winter 1987): 13–31.

37. Jeffrey Gurock, *When Harlem Was Jewish, 1870–1930* (New York, 1979), chapter 6.

■

38. Robert Orsi, *The Madonna of 115th Street: Faith and Community in Italian Harlem* (New Haven, 1985), pp. 14–19 and 42.

39. Rosenwaike, *Population History*, p. 167.

40. David Ment and Mary Donovan, *The People of Brooklyn* (New York, 1980), pp. 69–71; Ralph Foster Weld, *Brooklyn Is America* (New York, 1967, originally published in 1950), pp. 137–40.

41. Seth Scheiner, *Negro Mecca: A History of the Negro in New York City, 1865–1920* (New York 1965), p. 221.

42. Gilbert Osofsky, *Harlem: The Making of a Ghetto, Negro New York, 1890–1930* (New York, 1966), pp. 77–80. See also Gurock, *When Harlem Was Jewish*.

43. Osofsky, *Harlem*, pp. 82–86.

44. Ibid., pp. 92–104.

45. Quoted in ibid., pp. 106–7.

46. Ibid., pp. 105–6, 109–10, and 113–18.

47. James Weldon Johnson, *Black Manhattan* (New York, 1968), p. 3.

48. For the Harlem renaissance, see Nathan Huggins, *Harlem Renaissance* (New York, 1971).

49. For a harsh view of these neighborhoods, see Claude McKay, *Home to Harlem* (New York, 1940), pp. 23–28,

50. For the Garvey movement see Judith Stein, *The World of Marcus Garvey: Race and Class in Modern Society* (Baton Rouge, 1986).

51. Harold X. Connolly, *A Ghetto Grows in Brooklyn* (New York, 1977), pp. 52–58.

52. Ibid., p. 58.

53. Ibid., pp. 58–75.

54. Osofsky. *Harlem*, pp. 136–41.

55. Ronald Bayor, *Neighbors in Conflict: The Irish, Germans, Jews, and Italians of New York City, 1929–1941* (Urbana, 1988, 2nd edition), pp. 22–23.

56. Moore, *At Home*, p. 95.

57. Ibid., pp. 96.

58. *Irish Voice*, Nov. 12, 1991.

59. Joshua Freeman, *In Transit: The Transport Workers Union in New York City, 1933–1966* (New York, 1989), pp. 26–28; Bayor, *Neighbors in Conflict*, p. 23.

60. Freeman, *In Transit*, pp. 26–29.

61. Quoted in Ruth Jacknow Markowitz, *My Daughter, the Teacher: Jewish Teachers in the New York City Schools* (New Brunswick, N.J., 1993), p. 15.

62. For Mitchell see Edwin R. Lewinson, *John Purroy Mitchell: Boy Mayor of New York* (New York, 1965). Mitchell was also Irish, though not a Tammany candidate.

63. Warren Moscow, *What Have You Done For me Lately? The Ins and Outs of New York City Politics* (Englewood Cliffs, 1967), pp. 119–20.

64. See Jeffrey Gerson, "Building the Brooklyn Machine: Irish, Jewish and Black Political Succession in Central Brooklyn, 1919–1964," PhD diss., CUNY, 1990.

■

65. Charles Green and Basil Wilson, *The Struggle for Black Empowerment in New York City* (New York, 1989), p. 7.

66. For vaudeville and ethnic culture in New York see Robert Snyder, *The Voice of the City: Vaudeville and Popular Culture in New York* (New York, 1989).

67. Quoted in Peter Levine, *Ellis Island to Ebbets Field: Sport and the American Jewish Experience* (New York, 1992), p. 89.

68. Quoted in Steven Riess, *Touching Base: Professional Baseball and American Culture in the Progressive Era* (Westport, 1980), p. 189.

69. Levine, *From Ellis Island to Ebbets Field*, chapters 6–7.

70. Jerre Mangione and Ben Morreale, *La Storia: Five Centuries of the Italian American Experience* (New York, 1992), p. 379.

71. Levine, *From Ellis Island to Ebbets Field*, chapters 2–4.

72. Bernie Bookbinder, *City of the World* (New York, 1990), p. 172.

73. Ibid., p. 172. See also Levine, *From Ellis Island to Ebbets Field*, chapter 8, for Jewish fighters especially.

74. Moore, *At Home*, pp. 95–97; Sherry Gorelick, *City College and the Jewish Poor: Education in New York, 1880–1924* (New Brunswick, N.J., 1981), chapter 5.

75. Anti-Semitism in education and jobs will be discussed again in chapters 7 and 8.

76. Henry Feingold, *A Time for Searching: Entering the Mainstream, 1920–1945* (Baltimore, 1992), pp. 126–27.

77. Quoted in Miriam Cohen, *From Workshop to Office: Two Generations of Italian Women in New York City, 1900–1950* (Ithaca, 1993), p. 145.

78. Ibid.

79. *Journal of Retailing* 8 (Oct. 1932): 92–93.

80. Irving Howe, *A Margin of Hope* (New York, 1982), pp. 1–2.

81. Bayor, *Neighbors in Conflict*, pp. 17–18.

82. Cohen, *From Workshop to Office*, p. 145.

83. Ibid., chapter 5.

84. Gerald Meyer, *Vito Marcantonio: Radical Politician* (Albany, 1989), pp. 10–11.

85. WPA, *The Italians of New York* (New York, 1938), pp. 171 and 174–76.

86. Steve Corey, "The New York City Sanitation Department," PhD seminar paper, New York University, May, 1989.

87. Quoted in Kessner, *La Guardia*, p. 358.

88. Jenna Weissman Joselit, *Our Gang: Jewish Crime and the New York Jewish Community, 1900–1940* (Bloomington, 1983), chapter 6.

89. Ibid., pp. 140–56.

90. Quoted in ibid., p. 146.

91. Ibid., chapter 7.

92. Mark Haller, "Bootleggers and American Gambling, 1920–1950," in Commission on the Review of the National Policy Towards Gambling, *Gambling in America: Appendix I* (Washington, 1976), p. 109.

93. Alan Block, *East Side-West Side: Organizing Crime in New York, 1930–1950* (New Brunswick, N.J., 1983), pp. 183–89; Humbert Nelli, *The Business of Crime: Italians and Syndicate Crime in the United States* (New York, 1976), p. 109.

■

94. Block, *East Side-West Side*, pp. 225–27 and 246–49.

95. Nelli, *The Business of Crime*, pp. 193–95.

96. Cheryl Greenberg, *Or Does It Explode? Black Harlem in the Great Depression* (New York, 1991), chapter 2.

97. Ibid.; Larry Greene, "Harlem in the Great Depression, 1928–1936," PhD diss., Columbia University, 1979.

98. Greenberg, *Or Does It Explode?*, pp. 27–28.

99. J. Raymond Jones, *The Harlem Fox* (Albany, 1990), p. 46.

100. Quoted in Greenberg, *Or Does It Explode?* p. 64.

101. George Furniss, "The Political Assimilation of Negroes in New York City, 1870–1965," PhD diss., Columbia University, 1969, pp. 195–97; Michael Goldstein, "Race Politics in New York City, 1890–1930," PhD diss., Columbia University, 1973, pp. 213–14.

102. Ira Katznelson, *Black Men, White Cities: Race, Politics, and Migration in the United States, 1900–1930, and Britain, 1948–1968* (New York, 1973), pp. 70–73 and 84–85; Marsha Hunt Hiller, "Race Politics in New York City, 1890–1930," PhD diss., Columbia University, 1972, pp. 231–53 and 324–71.

103. Goldstein, "Race Politics," pp. 214–27, 303; Robert Fogelson, *Big-City Police* (Cambridge, 1977), pp. 124–25.

104. Goldstein, "Race Politics," pp. 315–23, 328–30.

105. Greenberg, *Or Does It Explode?* p. 95.

106. See Hiller, "Race Politics," pp. 33–50 and 57–80 for an excellent discussion of Brooklyn politics.

107. Connolly, *A Ghetto*, pp. 99–100 and 102–10.

108. Virginia Sanchez Korrol, *From Colonia to Community: The History of Puerto Ricans in New York City, 1917–1948* (Westport, Ct., 1983), p. 13.

109. Joseph Fitzpatrick, *Puerto Rican Americans: The Meaning of Migration to the Mainland* (Englewood Cliffs, 2nd edition, 1987), pp. 38–40.

110. Meyer, *Vito Marcantonio*, pp. 145–47.

111. Ronald Takaki, *Strangers from a Different Shore: A History of Asian Americans* (Boston, 1989), pp. 242–45 and 250–51.

112. WPA Files, "The Chinese Population in New York."

113. The history of the hand laundry and the union it spawned is covered in Renqiu Yu, *"To Save China, To Save Ourselves": The Chinese Hand Laundry Alliance of New York* (Philadelphia, 1992).

114. Mitziko Sawada, "Dreams of Change: The Japanese Immigrant to New York City, 1891–1924," PhD diss., New York University, 1985, chapter 7.

115. WPA Files, "The Koreans in New York."

116. Joan Jensen, *Passage from India: Asian Indian Immigrants to North America* (New Haven, 1988), pp. 19 and 168.

117. New York State Advisory Committee to the U.S. Commission on Civil Rights, *The Forgotten Minority: Asian Americans in New York City* (1977), p. 14.

118. WPA Files, "The Indonesians in New York."

119. Ibid.

120. WPA, *The Italians of New York*, pp. 224–25.

■

121. Howe, *Margin of Hope*, p. 2.

122. Jenna Weissman Joselit, *New York's Jewish Jews: The Orthodox Community in the Interwar Years* (Bloomington, 1990), p. 2.

123. Ibid., pp. 119–21.

124. Ibid., chapters 4 and 5.

125. Ibid., p. 147.

126. Moore, *At Home*, p. 77.

127. Ibid., chapter 6.

128. See Orsi's excellent book, *The Madonna of 115th Street.*

129. *New York Times*, July 4, 1991.

130. Mary Brown, "Italian Immigrants and the Catholic Church in the Archdiocese of New York, 1880–1950," PhD Diss., Columbia University, 1987, pp. 334–57.

131. See Casey, "The Bronx Irish."

132. Ment and Donovan, *The People of Brooklyn*, pp. 61–63. See also Christen T. Jonassen, "The Norwegians in Bay Ridge: A Sociological Study of an Ethnic Group," PhD diss., New York University, 1947.

133. Ment and Donovan, *The People of Brooklyn*, pp. 66–69.

134. WPA, *New York Panorama* (New York, 1938), pp. 106–7.

135. Ibid., pp. 107–9.

136. Ibid., pp. 109–15.

137. Kessner, *La Guardia*, p. 155.

## Chapter 7. A Time of Trial

1. Peter M. Rutkoff and William B. Scott, *New School: A History of the New School for Social Research* (New York, 1986), chapter 5.

2. For a general discussion of the Washington Heights community, see Steven M. Lowenstein, *Frankfurt on the Hudson: The German-Jewish Community of Washington Heights, 1933–1938* (Detroit, 1989).

3. Walter Iaacson, *Kissinger: A Biography* (New York, 1992), p. 34.

4. Ibid., p. 35.

5. Barbara Blumberg, *The New Deal and the Unemployed: The View from New York City* (Lewisburg, 1979), p. 17.

6. David Schneider and Albert Deutsch, *The History of Public Welfare in New York State, 1867–1940* (Montclair, N.J., 1969), p. 296.

7. Miriam Cohen, *From Workshop to Office: Two Generations of Italian Women in New York City, 1900–1950* (Ithaca, 1993), p. 97.

8. Robert Orsi, *The Madonna of 115th Street: Faith and Community in Italian Harlem, 1880–1950* (New Haven, 1985), p. 43.

9. Quoted in Howard Sachar, *A History of the Jews in America* (New York, 1992), p. 429.

10. Alfred Kazin, *A Walker in the City* (New York, 1951), pp. 38–39.

11. New York State Temporary Commission on the Condition of the Colored Urban Population, *Second Report* (Albany, 1939), pp. 32–37.

12. Larry Greene, "Harlem in the Great Depression, 1928–1934," PhD diss.,

■

Columbia University, 1979, pp. 98–146 and 431–46; Cheryl Greenberg, *Or Does It Explode?: Black Harlem in the Great Depression* (New York, 1991), chapter 3.

13. New York State Temporary Commission, *Second Report*, p. 37.

14. For the relief situation, see Greene, "Harlem in the Great Depression," chapter 8; and Greenberg, *Or Does It Explode?*, chapter 6.

15. Greenberg, *Or Does It Explode?*, pp. 181–86; Harold X. Connolly, *A Ghetto Grows in Brooklyn* (New York, 1977), pp. 117–23. See also the conditions described in Mayor La Guardia's Commission on the Harlem Riot of March, 1935, *Complete Report* (New York, 1969).

16. Peter Kwong, *Chinatown, N.Y.: Labor and Politics, 1930–1950* (New York, 1979), pp. 55–56.

17. Ronald Bayor, *Neighbors in Conflict: The Irish, Germans, Jews, and Italians of New York City, 1929–1941* (Urbana, 1988), pp. 10–14.

18. Quoted in Blumberg, *The New Deal and the Unemployed*, pp. 17–18.

19. Beth Wenger, "Ethnic Community in Economic Crisis: New York Jews and the Great Depression," PhD diss., Yale University, 1992, p. 25.

20. Cohen, *Workshop to Office*, pp. 162–65.

21. Wenger, "Ethnic Community in Economic Crisis," p. 22.

22. Ibid.

23. Cohen, *Workshop to Office*, p. 155; Wenger, "Ethnic Community in Economic Crisis," chapter 1.

24. Sachar, *A History of the Jews*, pp. 428–29; Wenger, "Ethnic Community in Crisis," chapters 3–4.

25. For the impact of the depression, see Mary Brown, "Italian Immigrants and the Catholic Church in the Archdiocese of New York, 1880–1950," PhD diss., Columbia University, 1987.

26. William Welty, "Black Shepherds: A Study of Leading Negro Clergymen in New York City, 1900–1940," PhD diss., New York University, 1969.

27. Greenberg, *Or Does It Explode?* pp. 58–61.

28. Ibid., p. 59.

29. Wenger, "Ethnic Community in Economic Crisis," p. 201. See also Schneider and Deutsch, *The History of Public Welfare*, chapters 16–17.

30. George J. Lankevich and Howard B. Furer, *A Brief History of New York City* (Pt. Washington, N.Y., 1984) p. 224.

31. Quoted in Greenberg, *Or Does It Explode?*, pp. 42–43.

32. Roger Waldinger, "The Ethnic Politics of Municipal Jobs," Institute of Industrial Relations, UCLA, Apr., 1993, p. 16.

33. Quoted in Thomas Kessner, *Fiorello La Guardia and the Making of Modern New York* (New York, 1989), pp. 228–29.

34. Ibid., p. 236.

35. Ibid., pp. 237–53.

36. Arthur Mann, *La Guardia: A Fighter Against His Times, 1882–1933* (New York, 1959), pp. 156–57.

37. Chris McNickle, *To Be Mayor of New York* (New York, 1993), pp. 32–40; Arthur Mann, *La Guardia Comes to Power 1933* (Philadelphia, 1956), chapters

■

5–6; and Charles Green and Basis Wilson, *The Struggle for Black Empowerment in New York City* (New York, 1989), p. 7. The percent of civil service jobs obtained by competitive examination went from 55 to 75 percent between 1935 and 1939.

38. Kessner, *La Guardia*, pp. 287–90.

39. Ibid., pp. 194–96.

40. Quoted in ibid., p. 575.

41. Ibid., pp. 432–44.

42. George Furniss, The "Political Assimilation of Negroes in New York City, 1870–1965," PhD diss., Columbia University, 1969, pp. 291–329; Thomas M. Henderson, "Harlem Confronts the Machine: The Struggle for Local Autonomy and Black District Leadership," *Afro-Americans in New York Life and History* 3 (July 1979): 51–68.

43. Greene, "Harlem in the Great Depression," p. 116.

44. Ibid., pp. 431–78; Greenberg, *Or Does It Explode?* chapter 5.

45. Greene, "Harlem in the Great Depression," pp. 323–50.

46. Kessner, *La Guardia*, pp. 299–304; Robert Caro, *The Power Broker* (New York, 1975), chapters 23–24.

47. Kessner, *La Guardia*, pp. 320–42; Caro, *The Power Broker*, pp. 610–13.

48. Caro, *The Power Broker*, pp. 489–94, 510–14, and 557–60. For the issue of discrimination in New Deal projects, including employment, see Greenberg, *Or Does It Explode?* pp. 153–63.

49. Robert P. Ingalls, *Herbert H. Lehman and New York's Little New Deal* (New York, 1975), p. 131.

50. Irving Bernstein, *Turbulent Years: A History of the American Workers, 1933–1941* (Boston, 1970), p. 84.

51. Ibid., p. 89.

52. For the teachers see Marjorie Murphy, *Blackboard Unions: The AFT and the NEA, 1900–1980* (Ithaca, 1990), p. 135; Diane Ravitch, *The Great School Wars, New York City, 1805–1973* (New York, 1974), pp. 236–39. The drop in immigration enabled the city to ease crowding in the schools and reduce class size.

53. Joshua B. Freeman, "Catholics, Communists, and Republicans," in Michael Frisch and Daniel Walkowitz eds., *Working-Class America: Essays on Labor, Community and Society* (Urbana, 1983), pp. 256–75.

54. For the TWU see Joshua Freeman, *In Transit: The Transport Workers in New York City, 1933–1966* (New York, 1989), especially chapters 9 and 11.

55. Ibid., especially chapter 6; Kessner, *La Guardia*, pp. 460–61.

56. Kwong, *Chinatown N.Y.*, pp. 61–67; Renqui Yu, *"To Save China, To Save Ourselves": the Chinese Hand Laundry Alliance of New York* (Philadelphia, 1992), chapter 2.

57. Nathan Glazer, *The Social Basis of American Communism* (New York, 1961), pp. 116–17 and 138–40. The few thousand communists in New York represented one third to one half of the party's national membership.

58. Kessner, *La Guardia*, p. 408.

■

59. Ibid., pp. 408–19; McNickle, *To Be Mayor of New York*, p. 37.

60. For a discussion of the American Labor Party and Vito Marcantonio see Gerald Meyer, *Vito Marcantonio: Radical Politician* (Albany, 1989).

61. Henry Feingold, *A Time for Searching: Entering the Mainstream, 1920–1945* (Baltimore, 1992), p. 68.

62. Ibid., pp. 69–71.

63. Bayor, *Neighbors in Conflict*, p. 29.

64. Frank Kingdom, "Discrimination In Medical Colleges," *American Mercury* 56 (Oct., 1945): 394; Walter R. Hart, "Anti-Semitism in N.Y. Medical Schools," ibid., 65 (July 1947): 56.

65. Bayor, *Neighbors in Conflict*, p. 28.

66. Ruth Jacknow Markowitz, *My Daughter, the Teacher: Jewish Teachers in the New York City Schools* (New Brunswick, N.J., 1993), pp. 15 and 18–30.

67. Bayor, *Neighbors in Conflict*, pp. 26–27 and 33–40; McNickle, *To be Mayor of New York*, pp. 32–40.

68. Bayor, *Neighbors in Conflict*, pp. 59–63.

69. Kessner, *La Guardia*, p. 521.

70. Bayor, *Neighbors in Conflict*, p. 65.

71. The Federal Writers' Project, *WPA Guide to New York City* (New York, 1939), pp. 251–52.

72. Bayor, *Neighbors in Conflict*, pp. 65–76, covers the growing anti-Nazi sentiment among German Americans.

73. Quoted in ibid., p. 78.

74. John Diggins, *Mussolini and Fascism: The View from America* (Princeton, 1972), pp. 134–37, 303–4, and 346–48. Anarchists like Carlo Tresca had always been vehemently anti-Fascist and foes of Mussolini.

75. Bayor, *Neighbors in Conflict*, pp. 78–86.

76. William Scott, *The Sons of Sheba's Race: African-Americans and the Italo-Ethiopian War, 1935–1941* (Bloomington, 1993), chapter 9.

77. Ibid., chapter 11; Mark Naison, *Communists in Harlem During the Great Depression*, (Urbana, 1983), pp. 157, 262–63, and 195–96.

78. Allen Guttmann, *The Wound in the Heart* (New York, 1962), chapter 3; Bayor, *Neighbors in Conflict*, pp. 87–97.

79. Bayor, *Neighbors in Conflict*, pp. 97–107.

80. Quoted in ibid., p. 156.

81. Joseph A. Wytrawal, *Poles in American History and Tradition* (Detroit, 1969), pp. 386–87.

82. Yu, *"To Save China, To Save Ourselves,"* chapter 4.

83. Mayor La Guardia's Commission, *Complete Report*, pp. 7–9.

84. Ibid., p. 18.

85. Ibid., p. 11. For the Communist party in Harlem in the 1930s, see Naison, *Communists in Harlem*.

86. See Mayor's Commission, *Complete Report*.

87. Greenberg, *Or Does It Explode?* chapters 7–8.

88. The Pulaski Day parade of 1943, for example, featured signs and banners

■

urging support for the Polish-American division of the National War Fund. *New York Times*, Oct. 11, 1943.

89. Richard Lingeman, *Don't You Know There Is a War On? The American Home Front, 1941–1945* (New York, 1970), p. 331.

90. For the response to the Holocaust see David Wyman, *The Abandonment of the Jews: America and the Holocaust, 1941–1945* (New York, 1984).

91. *New York Times*, Dec. 12, 1941.

92. Ibid., Oct. 13, 1942.

93. Ibid., Dec. 8, 1941.

94. Ibid., Oct. 16, 1942.

95. Greenberg, *Or Does It Explode?* pp. 198–200; Blumberg, *The New Deal and the Unemployed*, pp. 268–69.

96. Greenberg, *Or Does It Explode?* pp. 202–7.

97. Ibid., pp. 204–6.

98. Gordon Bloom, F. Marion Fletcher and Charles Perry, *Negro Employment in Retail Trade* (Philadelphia, 1972), p. 40.

99. Ibid., p. 42.

100. Blumberg, *The New Deal and the Unemployed*, pp. 268–69; Greenberg, *Or Does It Explode?* p. 199.

101. For the riot see Dominic Capeci, Jr., *The Harlem Riot of 1943* (Philadelphia, 1977).

102. Ibid., pp. 136–41.

103. Dominic J. Capeci, Jr., "Fiorello H. La Guardia and the Stuyvesant Town Controversy of 1943," *New York Historical Society Quarterly* 62 (Oct. 1978): 292.

104. Ibid., p. 295.

105. Ibid., pp. pp. 5–10. See also Arthur Simon, *Stuyvesant Town, U.S.A.: Pattern for Two Americas* (New York, 1970).

## Chapter 8. A Better Time

1. For the struggle against discrimination see Herman D. Bloch, *The Circle of Discrimination: An Economic and Social Study of Black Man in New York* (New York, 1969); Louis Ruchames, *Race, Jobs and Politics: The Story of the FEPC* (New York, 1953); and Milton R. Konvitz, *A Century of Civil Rights* (New York, 1961).

2. For the CCHR see Gerald Benjamin, *Race Relations and the New York City Commission on Human Rights* (Ithaca, 1974).

3. Konvitz, *A Century of Civil Rights*, pp. 197–201 and 225–28.

4. Quoted in Leonard Dinnerstein, "Anti-Semitism in America, 1945–1950," *American Jewish History* 71 (Sept. 1981): 138–39.

5. Ibid., pp. 139–40.

6. Leonard Dinnerstein, *Uneasy at Home: Anti-Semitism and the American Jewish Experience* (New York, 1987), p. 51.

7. U.S. Equal Employment Opportunity Commission, *Discrimination in White Collar Employment*, Hearings, New York City, Jan., 1968, pp. 667–79.

8. *New York Times*, June 29, 1986.

■

9. Howard Sachar, *A History of the Jews in America* (New York, 1992), pp. 649–50.

10. New School for Social Research, *New York's Jewish Poor and the Jewish Working Class* (New York, 1972), pp. 13–18.

11. Quoted in ibid., pp. 26–28.

12. Richard Gambino, *Blood of My Blood: The Dilemma of Italian-Americans* (Garden City, N.Y., 1975), pp. 265–68.

13. United Irish Counties Community Action Bureau, *The Needs of the American-Irish Community in the City of New York* (New York, 1975).

14. Dennis Clark, "The Irish in the American Economy," in P.J. Drudy ed., *The Irish in America: Emigration, Assimilation and Impact* (London, 1985), pp. 241–44.

15. See John Cooney, *An American Pope: The Life and Times of Francis Cardinal Spellman* (New York, 1984), pp. 101–2.

16. See John Mollenkopf, "The Postindustrial Transformation of the Political Order in New York City," in John Mollenkopf ed., *Power, Culture, and Place: Essays on New York City* (New York, 1988), pp. 230–41.

17. Quoted in Chris McNickle, *To Be Mayor of New York*, (New York, 1993), p. 169.

18. Quoted in ibid.

19. Ibid., chapters 8–9.

20. Theodore Lowi, *At the Pleasure of the Mayor* (New York, 1964), fig. 8.2.

21. For a defense of his regime, see Salvatore J. La Gumina, *New York at Mid-Century: The Impellitteri Years* (New York, 1992).

22. The best coverage of New York politics during these years is McNickle, *To Be Mayor of New York.*

23. See Cooney, *The American Pope*, for a critical view of Spellman.

24. Nathan Glazer and Daniel Moynihan, *Beyond the Melting Pot: The Negroes, Puerto Ricans, Irish, Jews and Italians of New York City* (Cambridge, 1970, 2nd edition), p. lvii.

25. *New York Times*, Mar. 9, 1968.

26. Martin Shefter, *Political Crisis, Fiscal Crisis: The Collapse and Revival of New York City* (New York, 1985), pp. 115–17; Joan Weitzman, *City Workers and Fiscal Crisis: Cutbacks, Givebacks and Survival: A Study of the New York Experience* (New Brunswick, N.J., 1979), pp. 1–2 and 10.

27. Lowi, *At the Pleasure*, fig. 8.2

28. Mark H. Maier, *City Unions: Managing Discontent in New York City* (New Brunswick, N.J., 1987), chapter 2.

29. Ibid., chapters 3–4.

30. David R. Eichenthal, "Changing Styles and Strategies of the Mayor," in Jewel Bellush and Dick Netzer, eds., *Urban Politics* (Armonk, N.Y., 1990), p. 70.

31. Shefter, *Political Crisis/ Fiscal Crisis*, pp. 115–19. For the organizing drives see Maier, *City Unions.*

32. Quoted in Joshua Freeman, *In Transit: The Transport Workers Union in New York City, 1933–1966* (New York, 1989), p. 335.

■

33. Jonathan Reider, *Canarsie: The Jews and Italians of Brooklyn Against Liberalism* (Cambridge, 1985), p. 15.

34. Ibid., pp. 15–19.

35. Gerald Sorin, *The Nurturing Neighborhood: the Brownsville Boys Club and the Jewish Community in America, 1940–1990* (New York, 1990), p. 168.

36. *New York Times*, May 31, 1989. By 1989 Co-op City was only a third Jewish.

37. For Staten Island see Nadia H. Youssef, *Population Dynamics on Staten Island: From Ethnic Homogeneity to Diversity* (New York, 1991).

38. Quoted in *New York Times*, Jan. 24, 1985.

39. Quoted in *The Record* (Bergen County, N.J.), May 31, 1989. See also Anthony L. LaRuffa, *Monte Carmelo: An Italian-American Community in the Bronx* (New York, 1988).

40. *New York Times*, May 27, 1973. See also David Reimers, "New York's Irish 1945–1990: An Overview," in Ron Bayor and Tim Meagher eds., *The Irish of New York City* (forthcoming).

41. See Caro, *The Power Broker* (New York, 1975), for a critical assessment of the influence of Moses.

42. Ira Rosenwaike, *A Population History of New York City* (Syracuse, 1972), p. 131. No official census was made in the late 1960s but experts said the city peaked at slightly more than 8 million then. The official high was 7,895,000 recorded in the 1970 census.

43. Paul Ritterbrand and Steven M. Cohen, "The Social Characteristics of the New York Area Jewish Community, 1981," *American Jewish Year Book, 1984*, pp. 128–29.

44. Joseph Palisi, "The Brooklyn Navy Yard," in Rita Miller, ed., *Brooklyn USA: The Fourth Largest City in America* (Brooklyn, 1979), pp. 119–24.

45. Louis Winnick, *New People in Old Neighborhoods: The Role of Immigrants in Rejuvenating New York's Communities* (New York, 1990), pp. 88–89.

46. Quoted in Will Anderson, "The Breweries of Brooklyn: An Informal History," in Miller, *Brooklyn USA*, p. 134. In recent years a few small breweries have opened again in the city.

47. Quoted in James Rubin, "The Brooklyn Dodgers and Ebbets Field—Their Departure," in Miller, *Brooklyn USA*, p. 170.

48. Louis Winnick, "Letter from Sunset Park," *NY: The City Journal* 1 (Winter 1991): 79.

49. Dept. of City Planning, *The Newest New Yorkers* (New York, 1992), p. 27.

50. United States Commission on Displaced Persons, *The DP Story: The Final Report of the United States Commission on Displaced Persons*, (Washington, D.C., 1952), p. 244; Lyman White, *300,000 New Americans: The Epic of a Modern Immigrant-Aid Society* (New York, 1957), pp. 316–19; Leonard Dinnerstein, *American and the Survivors of the Holocaust* (New York, 1982), p. 288; and Administrator of the Refugee Relief Act of 1953, *Final Report*.

51. Solomon Poll, *The Hasidic Community of Williamsburg: A Study in the Sociology of Religion* (New York, 1969), pp. 12–19 and 29–31. For a sympathetic pic-

■

ture of the Hasidim see Liz Harris, *Holy Days: The World of a Hasidic Family* (New York, 1985). A comprehensive account is Jerome Mintz, *Hasidic People: A Place in the New World* (Cambridge, 1992).

52. *New York Times*, Mar. 8, 1989.

53. Ibid., May 2, 1989.

54. Ibid., July 7, 1986; Mar. 8, 1989. See Poll, *Hasidic Community*, for a general discussion of Williamsburg's Hasidim and Mintz, *Hasidic People* for Crown Heights.

55. Dept. of City Planning, *The Newest New Yorkers*, p. 52. For an account of the new immigration law, see David M. Reimers, *Still the Golden Door: The Third World Comes to America* (New York, 1985), chapter 3.

56. Figures are based on the annual reports and *Statistical Yearbooks* of the Immigration and Naturalization Service (INS) and Dept. of City Planning, *The Newest New Yorkers*, p. 52.

57. Data is based on annual reports and *Statistical Yearbooks* of INS.

58. *New York Times*, Mar. 11, 1973.

59. Susan Jacoby, "A Dream Grows in Brooklyn," *New York Times Magazine*, Feb. 23, 1975.

60. Quoted in *New York Times*, Sept. 4, 1991.

61. Guiseppe Fortuna, "Recent Italian Immigrants in Queens, New York," PhD. diss., City University of New York, 1983, pp. 41–43 and 150–51.

62. Ibid., pp. 151–52; Jacoby, "A Dream Grows."

63. Elizabeth Bogen, *Immigration in New York* (New York, 1987), p. 38.

64. The Hellenic American Neighborhood Action Committee, Inc., *The Needs of the Growing Greek-American Community in the City of New York* (New York, 1974), pp. 13–21. In the early 1980s Greek organizations put the city's figure at 450,000. See *New York Times*, Mar. 13, 1984.

65. Ibid., pp. 41–48. See also Anna Veglery, "The Integration of Post-1945 Greek Immigrants to New York," PhD diss., Fordham University, 1987; Charles Moskos, *Greek Americans* (New Brunswick, N.J., 1989), pp. 54–56.

66. *New York Times*, Mar. 14, 1989.

67. *Newsweek*, July 7, 1980, p. 26.

68. Veglery, "Post-1965 Greek Immigrants," pp. 178–79 and 219–23.

69. Dept. of City Planning, *The Newest New Yorkers*, p. 52; P. J. Drudy, "Irish Population Change and Emigration Since Independence," in Drudy ed., *The Irish in America*, pp. 73–78; annual reports of the Immigration and Naturalization Service.

70. *New York Times*, Feb. 18, 1969; and May 27, 1973.

71. Philip Kasinitz, *Caribbean Immigrants: Black Immigrants and the Politics of Race* (Ithaca, 1992), pp. 131–35; Michel S. Laguerre, *American Odyssey: Haitians in New York City* (Ithaca, 1984), pp. 21–24.

72. Glenn Hendricks, *The Dominican Diaspora* (New York, 1974), pp. 53–70 and 75–83.

73. Bernard Wong, *Chinatown: Economic Adaptation and Ethnic Identity of the Chinese* (New York, 1982), p. 8.

74. Joseph Fitzpatrick, *Puerto Rican Americans* (Englewood Cliffs, 1987), pp. 14–27; Glazer and Moynihan, *Beyond the Melting Pot*, pp. 91–98.

75. An excellent discussion of the division can be found in Michael Lapp, "The Migration Division of Puerto Rico and Puerto Ricans in New York City, 1948–1969," in William Pencak, Selma Berrol, and Randall Miller eds., *Immigration to New York* (Philadelphia, 1991), pp. 198–214.

76. Fitzpatrick, *Puerto Rican Americans*, pp. 52–58.

77. Ibid., chapter 5.

78. Ibid., pp. 117–35.

79. For hints of this reasoning see Glazer and Moynihan, *Beyond The Melting Pot*; Oscar Handlin, *The Newcomers: Negroes and Puerto Ricans in a Changing Metropolis* (Garden City, 1962).

80. See, for example, U.S. Commission on Civil Rights, *Puerto Ricans in the Continental United States, An Uncertain Future* (Washington, 1976); Lloyd Rogler and Rosemary Santana Cooney, *Puerto Rican Families in New York City: An Intergenerational Process* (Maplewood, N.J., 1984).

81. For the early period see Angelo Falcon, "Puerto Rican Politics: 1860s to 1945," in James Jennings and Mote Rivera, eds., *Puerto Rican Politics in Urban America* (Westport, Ct., 1984), pp. 15–42.

82. See the essays in Jennings and Rivera eds., *Puerto Rican Politics in Urban America*.

83. Rosenwaike, *Population History*, pp. 139–42.

84. After 1970, migration from the South slowed, and in some years the flow was reversed with more blacks moving south than coming north. *New York Times*, June 11, 1989; Report of the Twentieth Century Fund on the Future of New York City, *New York World City* (Cambridge, 1990), pp. 63–65.

85. For a discussion of black politics in New York City see Charles Green and Basil Wilson, *The Struggle for Black Empowerment in New York City* (New York, 1989).

86. Edwin Lewinson, *Black Politics in New York City* (New York, 1974), pp. 88–89.

87. Ibid., pp. 144–59. For Jones's story see John C. Walter, *The Harlem Fox: J. Raymond Jones and Tammany, 1920–1970* (Albany, 1989).

88. Harold Connolly, *A Ghetto Grows in Brooklyn* (New York, 1977), pp. 162–67 and 174–80.

89. Lewinson, *Black Politics in New York City*, pp. 86–87.

90. See Kasinitz, *Caribbean New York*, pp. 207–23 for the early years of West Indian politicians.

91. Mayor's Commission on Black New Yorkers, *Report on Black New Yorkers* (New York, 1988), p. 93. A number of mayors, dating to the 1950s, had issued orders about nondiscrimination in municipal hiring.

92. *New York Times*, Aug. 31, 1984; Nov. 18, 1985; and Nov. 1, 1987.

93. Ibid., Nov. 1, 1987.

94. Lewinson, *Black Politics*, pp. 180 and 182–84.

■

95. Ibid., pp. 180–82 and 184–86. See also Walter Thomas, "The Integration of the Negro in the New York City Fire Department," *Amsterdam News*, Apr. 23, 1966.

96. Mayor's Commission, *Black New Yorkers*, pp. 208–12.

97. *New York Times*, Sept. 16, 1968 and June 7, 1990.

98. *Ibid.*, July 17, 1989.

99. For black theater and musicals in early 20th century New York City see James Weldon Johnson, *Black Manhattan* (New York, 1968), chapters 9 –11 and 14–17. For some of the difficulties confronting blacks and especially Paul Robeson, see Martin Duberman, *Paul Robeson* (New York, 1988), pp. 43–67.

100. Duberman, *Paul Robeson*, p. 125.

101. *New York Times*, Jan. 8, 1955.

102. U.S. Congress, House, Subcommittee on Study of Monopoly Power of the Committee on the Judiciary, *Organized Baseball*, Hearings, 82nd Congress, 1st sess., Part 6, pp. 483–85. For the black leagues see Jules Tygiel, *Baseball's Great Experiment: Jackie Robinson and His Legacy* (New York, 1983); Robert Peterson, *Only the Ball Was White* (New York, 1984), p. 123.

103. See Tygiel, *Baseball's Experiment*, for a discussion of the slow progress of desegregation, especially chapters 11 and pp. 224–26, 244–45 and 295–99.

104. Ibid., p. 335.

105. Bloch, *The Circle of Discrimination*, pp. 49–78.

106. Ibid., pp. 49–56.

107. U.S. Equal Employment Opportunity Commission, *Discrimination in White Collar Employment*, Hearings, New York City, Jan., 1968, pp. 557–664.

108. CCHR, *Bias in the Building Industry: An Updated Report, 1963–1967* (1967). See also Bloch, *Circle of Discrimination*, pp. 125–50; Report of the New York Advisory Committee, "Discrimination in the Building Trades: The New York City Case," in Walter Fogel and Archie Klingartner eds., *Contemporary Labor Issues* (Belmont, Ca., 1966), pp. 288–95.

109. For the role of the churches see Green and Wilson, *The Struggle for Black Empowerment*.

110. Benjamin, *Race Relations*, 173–77; *Amsterdam News*, Aug. 25, 1962, July 20, 1963, July 27, 1963, Oct. 12, 1963, and Nov. 23, 1963.

111. For Malcolm X, see Bruce Perry, *Malcolm X: The Life of a Man Who Changed Black America* (Tarrytown, N.Y., 1981).

112. Mayor's Commission, *Black New Yorkers*, pp. 54 and 91. The Mayor's Commission based its conclusions on a 1982 study by the Community Service Society of New York City.

113. Freeman, *In Transit*, pp. 28 and 152.

114. Maier, *City Unions*, p. 40.

115. Bernard Bellush and Jewel Bellush, *Union Power in New York: Victor Gotbaum and District Council 37* (New York, 1984), especially chapters 9–11; *Amsterdam News*, May 1, 1965.

116. For 1199 see Leon Fink and Brian Greenberg, *Upheaval in the Quiet Zone:*

*A History of the Hospital Workers's Union 1199* (Urbana, 1989).

117. Connolly, *A Ghetto Grows in Brooklyn*, pp. 133–34.

118. Flora Davidson, "City Policy and Housing Abandonment: A Case Study of New York City, 1965–1973," PhD. diss., Columbia University, 1979, pp. 20–23.

119. *New York Times*, Aug. 27, 1989.

120. Ibid., July 5, 1992. In July 1992 the New York City Housing Authority admitted that it had been steering African Americans to segregated units.

121. Caro, *The Power Broker*, especially chapter 41. For a particularly harsh view of Moses, liberals, and New York development during these years, see Joel Schwartz, *The New York Approach: Robert Moses, Urban Liberalism and the Redevelopment of the Inner City* (Columbus, 1993).

122. See Robert S. McElvaine, *Mario Cuomo* (New York, 1988), chapter 6.

123. Estelle Gilson, "What Hope for the Homeless People? *Columbia* 14 (Mar. 1989): 15. See also Michael A. Stegman, "Housing," in Charles Brecher and Raymond Horton, eds., *Setting Municipal Priorities, 1988* (New York, 1987), pp. 197–219.

124. City Commission on Human Rights (CCHR), *Arson, Vandalism and Other Racially Inspired Violence in New York City* (Dec. 8, 1972), p. 6.

125. Quoted in *New York Times*, Mar. 13, 1989. See also Douglas S. Massey and Nancy A. Denton, "Segregation in U.S. Metropolitan Areas: Black and Hispanic Segregation Along Five Dimensions," *Demography* 26 (Aug. 1989): 388.

126. Benjamin, *Race Relations*, pp. 100–104 and 230–35.

127. Mayor's Commission, *Black New Yorkers*, pp. 130–32 and 148–59.

128. Diane Ravitch, *The Great School Wars: New York City, 1805–1973* (New York, 1974), chapters 23 and 24.

129. Ibid., pp. 280–84. The Allen report did recommend changes to foster desegregation, but little actual racial integration resulted from these steps.

130. Mayor's Commission, *Black New Yorkers*, p. 128; *New York Times*, Sept. 22, 1987.

131. Mayor's Advisory Panel on Decentralization of the New York City Schools, *Reconstruction for Learning* (New York, 1967), pp. 1–2, 4–5, and 73–75.

132. Ravitch, *Great School Wars*, chapters 31–33.

133. David Lavin, Richard Alba and Richard Silberstein, *Right Versus Privilege: The Open-Admissions Experiment at the City University of New York* (New York, 1981), pp. 1–5.

134. *Amsterdam News*, Apr. 11, 1964.

135. Lavin, Alba and Silberstein, *Right Versus Privilege*, pp. 9–20.

136. *New York Times*, Dec. 2, 1989.

137. For the 1964 riot see Fred C. Shapiro and James W. Sullivan, *Race Riot New York 1964* (New York, 1964).

138. Woody Kline, *Lindsay's Promise: The Dream That Failed* (New York, 1970), pp. 204–6.

139. Shefter, *Fiscal Crisis*, pp. 111–16. For a good account of Lindsay, see Charles Morris, *The Cost of Good Intentions: New York City and the Liberal Experiment, 1960–1975* (New York, 1980), pp. 56–81.

■

140. *New York Times*, Nov. 8, 1971.

141. For the vote on the referendum see David Abott, et al., *Police, Politics and Race: The New York City Referendum on Civilian Review* (New York, 1969).

### Chapter 9. Truly a Global City

1. Dept. of City Planning, *The Newest New Yorkers* (New York, 1992), pp. 5–6. For the 1990 law, see David Reimers, *Still the Golden Door: The Third World Comes to America* (New York, 1991, 2nd ed.), chapter 8. About 100,000 undocumented aliens applied for amnesty in New York City under the terms of the 1986 Simpson-Rodino Act. For 1992 figures see *New York Times*, June 13, 1993.

2. *New York Times*, Sept. 2, 1993.

3. Dept of City Planning, *The Newest New Yorkers*, chapter 2; John Mollenkopf, *A Phoenix in the Ashes: The Rise and Fall of the Koch Coalition in New York City Politics* (Princeton, 1992), p. 58.

4. *Daily News*, Dec. 10, 1990.

5. *New York Times*, Sept. 15, 1985; Aug. 22, 1988.

6. Ibid., Aug. 22, 1988; *Daily News*, Dec. 10, 1990.

7. Evelyn Mann and Joseph J. Salvo, "Characteristics of New Hispanics in New York City: A Comparison of Puerto Ricans and Non-Puerto Ricans." Paper presented to the annual meeting of the Population Association of America (1984); *New York Times*, Sept. 1, 1990.

8. City of New York, *Annual Report on Hispanic Concerns* (New York, 1986), p. 1.

9. *New York Times*, Sept. 1, 1992; Dept. of City Planning, *The Newest New Yorkers*, pp. 33 and 61.

10. Patricia Pessar, "The Dominicans: Women in the Household and the Garment Industry," in Nancy Foner, ed., *New Immigrants in New York* (New York, 1986), pp. 104–105; Glenn Hendricks, *Dominican Diaspora* (Ann Arbor, 1974), chapter 4; *New York Times*, Nov. 17, 1986; Dec. 8, 1992; and Dec. 13, 1992.

11. Pessar, "Dominican Women," pp. 106–107.

12. Sherri Grasmuck and Patricia Pessar, *Between Two Islands: Dominican International Migration* (Berkeley, 1991), chapter 7.

13. Roger Waldinger, *Through the Eye of the Needle: Immigrants and Enterprise in New York's Garment Trades* (New York, 1986), chapter 6.

14. See Diana Balmori, *Hispanics in the Construction Industry in New York City, 1960–1982* (New York, 1983).

15. *New York Times*, Nov. 19, 1986.

16. Linda Chavez, *Out of the Barrio: Toward a New Politics of Hispanic Assimilation* (New York, 1991), pp. 150–51.

17. Quoted in *New York Times*, July 13, 1992.

18. Ibid., July 7, 8 and 9, 1992.

19. Ibid., June 3, 1991.

20. Ibid. This was part of eight excellent articles by *Times* reporter Sara Rimer.

21. Ibid., Sept. 4, 1993.

■

22. Ibid., Aug. 25, 1993.

23. Quoted in ibid., July 31, 1990; May 19, 1991.

24. Ibid., June 10, 1987.

25. *The Record* (Bergen County, N.J.), Mar. 26, 1990.

26. Daily News, *New York's New World* (New York, 1991), p. 26; Dept. of City Planning, *The Newest New Yorkers*, pp. 38–40.

27. Philip Kasinitz, *Caribbean New York* (Ithaca, 1992), pp. 54–67. The pre-World War II center of West Indian culture was Harlem with an important group in Brooklyn.

28. *New York Times*, June 3, 1988.

29. Ibid., Sept. 6, 1993.

30. Quoted in ibid.

31. Kasinitz, *Caribbean New York*, pp. 105–6; *New York Times*, Jan. 24, 1992.

32. Data on West Indian employment is drawn from Philip Kasinitz, *Caribbean New York*, chapter 3; Dept. of City Planning, Office of Immigrant Affairs, *Caribbeans in New York City* (New York, 1985), p. 4.

33. Kasinitz, *Caribbean New York*, pp. 104 and 176–78. Data on family incomes can be found on p. 178.

34. Ibid., chapter 5; Linda Basch, "The Vincentians and Grenadians: The Role of Voluntary Associations in Immigrant Adaptation to New York City," in Nancy Foner, ed., *New Immigrants in New York*, pp. 159–94.

35. See Kasinitz, *Caribbean New York*, chapter 5 for a discussion of Carnival.

36. Michel Laguerre, *American Odyssey: Haitians in New York City* (Ithaca, 1984), pp. 93–95 and 105–106.

37. *New York Times*, Feb. 13, 1986; Mar. 25, 1986. For events in 1991 and 1992 see ibid., Oct. 12, 1991; Sept. 3, 1992.

38. Susan Buchanan Stafford, "Language and Identity: Haitians in New York City," in Elsa Chaney and Constance Sutton eds., *Caribbean Life in New York City* (New York, 1987), pp. 202–18. See also Nina Glick-Schiller, et al, "All in the Same Boat? Unity and Diversity in Haitian Organizing in New York," in ibid., pp. 182–201.

39. *New York Times*, July 17, 1986.

40. Ibid., Feb. 7, 1989; Dept. of City Planning, Office of Immigrant Affairs, *Asians in New York City: A Demographic Summary* (1988), pp. 3–4; and 1990 US Census Data, Summary Tape File 1, New York City.

41. Peter Kwong, *The New Chinatown* (New York, 1987), pp. 39–41.

42. Hong Kong as a colony of Great Britain had a quota of only 600 until 1986, when it was increased to 6,000. The 1990 act raised it again.

43. Prices did drop during the recession beginning in 1989. *New York Times*, Dec. 25, 1986; Dec. 6, 1992.

44. Ibid., Nov. 19, 1988. See Hsiang-Shui Chen, *Chinatown No More: Taiwan Immigrants in Contemporary New York* (Ithaca, 1992), for the Queens settlement.

45. *New York Times*, Sept. 13, 1987.

46. Louis Winnick, *New People in Old Neighborhoods* (New York, 1990), chapter 7.

47. Kwong, *The New Chinatown*, pp. 60–67.

■

48. *New York Times*, Mar. 21, 1991; Mar. 23, 1992.

49. For a discussion of Chinese business generally see Chen, *Chinatown No More*.

50. This discussion of the garment industry is based on Waldinger's excellent *Through the Eye of the Needle*, chapters 6 and 7.

51. Quoted in *New York Times*, May 30, 1990.

52. For unionization among the women see, Xiaolon Bao, " 'Holding Up More Than Half the Sky' ": A History of Women Garment Workers," PhD diss., New York University, 1991.

53. Waldinger, *Through the Eye*, chapter 9.

54. For the problems of the so-called model minority, see *New York Times*, Mar. 20, 1990; *Newsday*, Jan. 29, 1990; and Kwong, *The New Chinatown*, pp. 70–74.

55. Samuel G. Freedman, *Small Victories: The Real World of a Teacher, Her Students and Their High School* (New York, 1990), pp. 26–28.

56. *New York Times*, Feb. 7, 1989; Feb. 26, 1989; New York City Planning Commission, *Manhattan Bridge Area Study: Chinatown* (New York, 1979), pp. 31–32; and *Newsday*, July 3, 1990.

57. *New York Times*, May 19, 1994.

58. Quoted in *New York Times*, Mar. 4, 1989. See the comments by Police Officer Andrew Siano who patrolled for 38 years in Chinatown before his retirement in 1990 in ibid., May 28, 1990. See also ibid., July 31, 1990; Oct. 16, 1990. For expansion into Queens see Frederic Dannen, "Revenge of the Green Dragons," *New Yorker*, Nov. 16, 1992.

59. Kwong, *The New Chinatown*, chapter 6; Betty Lee Sung, "Gangs in New York's Chinatown," in Gerry Lim ed., *The Chinese American Experience: Paper from the Second National Conference on Chinese American Studies* (1984); *New York Times*, Jan. 4, 1988; Apr. 12, 1992 and July 22, 1992; and Ko-lin Chin, *Chinese Subculture and Criminality: Non-traditional Crime Groups in America* (Westport, 1990). See also Gwen Kinkead, *Chinatown* (New York, 1992).

60. Kwong, *The New Chinatown*, pp. 129–36.

61. Illsoo Kim, *New Urban Immigrants: The Korean Community of New York City* (Princeton, 1981), chapter 5.

62. Ibid., chapter 4. See also Illsoo Kim, "The Koreans: Small Business in an Urban Frontier," in Nancy Foner ed., *New Immigrants in New York* (New York, 1987), chapter 8.

63. *Crain's New York Business*, May 21, 1990.

64. *New York Times*, May 22, 1990; Kim, *New Urban Immigrants*, chapter 5; and *Daily News*, "New York's New World," p. 40.

65. *New York Times*, May 22, 1990; Kim, *New Urban Immigrants*, chapter 6; and *Daily News*, "New York's New World," pp. 39–40.

66. *Daily News*, "New York's New World," p. 40.

67. *New York Times*, Dec. 30, 1976; *Filipino Reporter*, July 12, 1972.

68. A survey based on the 1970 census reveal a wide distribution of Filipinos in New York City. See *Filipino Reporter*, Oct. 15, 1974. Many Asian medical professionals lived near the hospitals that employed them.

■

69. *New York Times*, June 11, 1991.

70. For Indian organizations see Maxine Fisher, *The Indians of New York City: A Study of Immigrants from India* (New York, 1980), chapters 4 and 7.

71. *Filipino Reporter*, Apr. 9–15, 1976; Feb. 8–14, 1980; and May 20–16, 1988.

72. For a profile of Asian Indians see M.C. Madhavan, "Indian Emigrants; Numbers, Characteristics, and Economic Impact," *Population and Development Review*, 11 (Sept. 1985): 457–81. See also Fisher, *The Indians of New York City*, pp. 11–12.

73. For this "brain drain" see U.S. Congress, House, Committee on Science and Technology, Science Policy Study Background Rept. No. 9. *Demographic Trends and the Scientific and Engineering Work Force*, 99th Cong., 2d sess. (1986).

74. *Daily News*, "New York's New World," pp. 23–24.

75. Quoted in *New York Times*, Jan. 12 1992.

76. Ibid., Oct. 10, 1991.

77. Ibid., Aug. 17, 1991.

78. Ibid., Feb. 11, 1984.

79. Ibid., Dec. 8, 1982; May 10, 1985; and Elizabeth Bogen, *Immigration in New York* (New York, 1987), pp. 131–33.

80. *New York Times*, May 24, 1984.

81. Ibid., July 7, 1988.

82. *Amsterdam News*, Oct. 8, 1988; Nov. 12, 1988; and Dec. 10, 1988.

83. *New York Times*, May 17, 1990.

84. Quoted in ibid., Sept. 7, 1990; Sept. 23, 1990.

85. Ibid., Jan. 31, 1991; Feb. 11, 1991.

86. Ibid., Oct. 26, 1992.

87. For Iranian professionals see Abdolmaboud Ansami, *Iranian Immigrants in the United States: A Case Study of Dual Marginality* (New York, 1988).

88. *New York Times*, Jan. 12, 1992.

89. For a detailed look at young Yemeni men working in Brooklyn restaurants, see Shalom Staub, *Yemenis in New York City: the Folklore of Ethnicity* (Philadelphia, 1989).

90. For figures on Arab immigration and church affiliation see Gregory Orfalea, *Before the Flames* (Austin, 1988), pp. 314–18.

91. *New York Times*, July 14, 1989.

92. Ibid., May 3, 1989; May 4, 1993; and May 7, 1993.

93. Ibid., Apr. 16, 1991.

94. Ibid., Oct. 3, 1992; May 4, 1993.

95. Quoted in ibid., June 6, 1992.

96. Ibid., Sept. 30, 1992.

97. Bogen, *Immigrants in New York*, p. 38; City Planning Dept., *The Newest New Yorkers*, p. 46.

98. See Moshe Shokeid, *Children of Circumstances: Israeli Emigrants in New York* (Ithaca, 1988), for the Israelis.

■

99. *New York Times*, Aug. 15, 1985.

100. 41,000 Colombian-born persons were counted in the 1980 census, and 84,000 in the 1990 census. For the larger estimate see Saskia Sassen-Koob, "Formal and Information Associations: Dominicans and Colombians in New York," in Chaney and Sutton, eds., *Caribbean Life in New York City*, pp. 280–81.

101. *Daily News*, "New York's New World," p. 38.

102. *New York Times*, May 25, 198; Aug. 27, 1990.

103. Ibid., Jan. 7, 1985; Feb. 15, 1985; May 15, 1985; Jan. 15, 1989; and Dept. of City Planning, *The Newest New Yorkers*, pp. 48–9.

104. *New York Times*, Nov. 10, 1985; Feb. 19, 1986; and July 31, 1986.

105. New York Association for New Americans, *News* (1986–1987); *New York Times*, Mar. 21, 1989.

106. Jennifer Barber, "The Soviet Jews of Washington Heights," *New York Affairs* 10 (Winter 1987): 34–43; *New York Times*, Feb. 21, 1987; and Feb. 9, 1992. A comprehensive account of the Soviets is Fran Markowitz, *A Community in Spite of Itself: Soviet Jewish Emigres in New York* (Washington, 1993).

107. *New York Times*, Feb. 21, 1987; Markowitz, *A Community*, chapters 3–4.

108. Quoted in *New York Times*, Aug. 11, 1990.

109. Quoted in ibid., June 17, 1990.

110. Ibid., June 29, 1986. Rising crime rates appeared to be a problem in Brighton Beach. See Lydia S. Rosner, *The Soviet Way of Crime: Beating the System in the Soviet Union and the U.S.A.* (North Hadley, MA, 1986); *Maclean's*, 96 (June 20, 1983): 6–7.

111. *New York Times*, Oct. 21, 1968.

112. Dept. of City Planning, *The Newest New Yorkers*, p. 50; Center for Migration Studies, *Scope* (Spring, 1992), p. 7; and *New York Times*, June 13, 1993.

113. Laws passed in 1986 and 1990 favored Ireland; as a result, for example, 3,000 Irish legally settled in New York in 1992.

114. Quoted in *New York Times*, Aug. 13, 1990.

115. *The Record* (Bergen County, N.J.), Oct. 30, 1988.

116. *Irish Voice*, Dec. 8, 1988. See also Mary Corcoran, "Ethnic Boundaries and Legal Barriers: The Labor Market Experience of Undocumented Irish Workers in New York City," paper given at conference on the new immigration at the College of Staten Island in Apr., 1988; study by Linda Dowling Alemida in *Irish Voice*, Mar. 16, 1991.

117. *New York Times*, Oct. 16, 1988.

118. Ibid., Apr. 9, 1993.

119. See Mollenkopf, *A Phoenix in the Ashes* and Chris McNickle, *To Be Mayor of New York* (New York, 1933), chapters 10–12 for politics after 1970.

120. *New York Times*, Nov. 4, 1993.

121. Leonard Dinnerstein and David Reimers, *Ethnic Americans* (New York, 1988), p. 160.

122. Edward S. Shapiro, *A Time for Healing: American Jewry since World War II* (Baltimore, 1992), pp. 97 and 116–22.

123. *New York Times*, Aug. 1, 1986.

■

124. Quoted in ibid.

125. Ibid.

126. *New York Times*, June 10, 1992. See also Abraham Burstein, Office of Economic Research, Human Resources Administration), *Welfare Recipency in Predominately White Areas in New York City* (New York, 1974). Data for the 1991 study were limited, which prompted some critics to say that the figures were not reliable. In addition, the census had reported a lower figure for 1990, indicating that the 1991 study reflected New York's deep recession.

127. *New York Times*, Aug. 11, 1991.

128. Ibid., June 3, 1991.

129. Quoted in ibid., Oct. 16, 1990.

130. Quoted in ibid., Aug. 27, 1992.

131. Ibid., Nov. 20, 1989.

132. Ibid., July 30, 1990.

133. Lou Winnick, "Letter from Sunset Park," *NY The City Journal* 1 (Winter 1991): 76; *New York Times*, Sept. 15, 1985.

134. *New York Times*, May 25, 1987.

135. Quoted in ibid., Mar. 17, 1991.

136. James Berguist, "The German-American Press," in Sally Miller ed., *The Ethnic Press in the United States* (Westport, 1987), p. 153.

137. Quoted in *New York Times*, Sept. 15, 1985.

138. See Paul Spickard, *Mixed Blood: Intermarriage and Ethnic Identity in Twentieth-Century America* (Madison, 1989).

139. *New York Magazine*, Vol. 14 (June 29, 1981), p. 17.

140. Ibid., p. 19.

141. *New York Times*, May 1, 1986.

142. Ibid., Dec. 12, 1982; Ida Susser, *Norman Street: Poverty and Politics in an Urban Neighborhood* (New York, 1982), pp. 22–29; and Judith Noel DeSena, "The Dynamics of Neighborhood Defense: A Sociological Account of Greenpoint, Brooklyn," PhD. diss., City University of New York, 1985, p. 43.

143. Quoted in *New York Times*, June 22, 1984.

144. Ibid., Sept. 15, 1985. Another Polish paper, *Nowy Swiat*, had ceased publication when the number of New York Polish readers fell sharply just after World War II.

145. *Daily News*, Dec. 10, 1990.

146. *New York Times*, Dec. 7, 1972.

147. See David Reimers, "The New York Irish, An Overview, 1945–1992," Ronald Bayor and Timothy Meagher (eds.), *The New York Irish* (forthcoming).

148. John Cardinal O'Connor and Mayor Edward I. Koch, *His Eminence and Hizzoner: A Candid Exchange* (New York, 1989).

149. Quoted in *New York Times*, Sept. 22, 1991.

150. Egon Mayer, *From Suburb to Shtetl: The Jews of Boro Park* (Philadelphia, 1979), p. 135.

151. See Steven M. Cohen, *American Assimilation or Jewish Revival?* (Bloomington, Indiana, 1988).

■

152. See Richard D. Alba, *Italian Americans: Into the Twilight of Ethnicity* (Englewood Cliffs, N.J., 1985).

153. Nathan Glazer and Daniel Moynihan argued in their influential *Beyond the Melting Pot* (1969) that ethnic groups in New York City change over time, but are held together by political, social, and economic needs.

154. *New York Times*, May 1, 1990, May 3, 1990; and Michael Stone, "What Really Happened in Bensonhurst," *New York*, Vol. 22 (Nov. 6, 1990), p. 48. The city-wide drop out rate of Italian Americans was estimated to be 20 percent, but in Bensonhurst, it was 30 percent.

155. Stone, "What Really Happened," p. 48. See also John DeSantis, *For the Color of His Skin: The Murder of Yusuf Hawkins and the Trial of Bensonhurst* (New York, 1991).

156. Quoted in *New York Times*, Dec. 28, 1993.

157. City of New York, *Hispanic Concerns*. While Hispanics made up about 20 percent of the city's population in 1987, they accounted for only about 10 percent of municipal employees. An early retirement program for the city's public school principals in 1991 did lead to an increase in Hispanics in those position. *New York Times*, Oct. 8, 1991.

158. See Equal Employment Opportunity Committee of New York, *Equal Employment Opportunity in New York City Government, 1977–1987* (Oct., 1988).

159. *New York Times*, Nov. 18, 1988; Apr. 11, 1989 and Apr. 13, 1989. The actual drop rate was not known and studies differed. See Clara Rodriguez, *Puerto Ricans Born In the U.S.A.* (Boston, 1989), pp. 121–24; Rosa M. Torruellas, "The Failure of the New York Public Educational System to Retrain Hispanic and Other Minority Students," *Centro Newsletter* (June 1986), pp. 3–6.

160. Rodriguez, *Puerto Ricans*, pp. 121–22; *New York Times*, Aug. 21, 1986 and Apr. 13, 1989. By the late 1980s about 110,000 of the city's 900,000 public school pupils were reported to be deficient in English, 70 percent of whom were Hispanic. Yet 40 percent of these children were receiving no bilingual instruction. By 1993 the city's public schools enrolled more than one million students, with a growing proportion of immigrants having English deficiencies. *New York Times*, Apr. 16, 1993.

161. Carlos Rodriguez-Fraticelli, "Higher Education Task Force Retrospective," *Centro*, Vol. 2 (Summer 1989): 25–26; Rodriguez, *Puerto Ricans*, pp. 121–24. No accurate dropout rates exist, but all students of this subject agree that they are highest among Puerto Ricans.

162. Ibid., p. 28. Hostos Community College also accounted for over half of the total Puerto Rican faculty in the community colleges.

163. Emanuel Tobier, *The Changing Face of Poverty: Trends in New York City's Population in Poverty, 1960–1990* (New York, 1984), pp. 38 and 42–47.

164. Fitzpatrick, *Puerto Rican Americans*, pp. 95–101; Rodriguez, *Puerto Ricans*, pp. 30–42; and *New York Times*, Dec. 28, 1993.

165. *New York Times*, Sept. 27, 1992. In September 1994, Puerto Rican Roberto Ramirez was elected chairman of the Democratic Party in the Bronx, the first Hispanic to hold that position in any of the state's counties. However, the

■

power of the Bronx Democratic machine is a shadow of what it was in the days of bossess Ed Flynn and Charles Buckley. Just a year earlier it failed to carry the borough for Ramirez in his unsuccessful bid for the citywide post of public advocate. Ibid., Oct. 1, 1994.

166. Charles Green and Basil Wilson, *the Black Struggle for Empowerment* (New York, 1989), pp. 98–101; *New York Times*, Mar. 31, 1987; and Apr. 2, 1989.

167. *New York Times*, Nov. 9, 1989. There are excellent accounts of the Dinkins election and recent politics in New York in Asher Arian, et al., *Changing New York City Politics* (New York, 1991); Mollenkopf, *A Phoenix in the Ashes*, chapter 7; and McNickle, *To Be Mayor of New York*, chapter 12.

168. CCHR, *City Layoffs: The Effect on Minorities and Women* (Apr. 1976).

169. Mayor's Commission on Black New Yorkers, *Report on Black New Yorkers* (New York, 1988), p. 93; Roger Waldinger, *The Ethnic Politics of Municipal Jobs* (Institute of Industrial Relations, University of California, 1993), p. 47. Blacks also worked in state and federal government offices in the city, although total employment in those sectors was considerably less than that of the city.

170. *New York Times*, Nov. 1, 1987; Aug. 4, 1992.

171. Waldinger, *Ethnic Politics*, p. 47.

172. Mayor's Commission, *Black New Yorkers*, p. 93. A number of mayors, dating back to the 1950s, had issued orders about nondiscrimination in municipal hiring. See also Waldinger, *Ethnic Politics*.

173. Mayor's Commission, *Black New Yorkers*, p. 137; *New York Times*, May 14, 1994.

174. Mollenkopf, *A Phoenix in the Ashes*, p. 66.

175. *New York Times*, June 7, 1990.

176. Ibid., June 8, 1992.

177. See Thomas Bailey, "Black Employment Opportunities," in Charles Brecher and Raymond Horton, eds., *Setting Municipal Priorities, 1990* (New York, 1989), pp. 80–116.

178. Mayor's Commission, *Black New Yorkers*, pp. 19–30; Emanuel Tobier with Walter Stafford, "People and Income," in Charles Brecher and Raymond Horton, eds., *Setting Municipal Priorities, 1983* (New York, 1982), pp. 54–83. The rate of unemployment for white New Yorkers was 3.1 percent in 1987, but over 8 percent for blacks. United States Dept. of Labor, *News (Middle Atlantic Regional Office)*, Dec. 14, 1987.

179. *New York Times*, Aug. 14, 1988; Tyler, "A City Divided: A Tale of Three Cities, Upper Economy, Lower—and Under," *Dissent* (Fall 1987): 468; and Tobier, *The Changing Face of Poverty*, p. 83.

180. *New York Times*, Mar. 5, 1989.

181. Mayor's Commission, *Black New Yorkers*, p. 80.

182. *New York Times*, June 10, 1992.

183. Ibid., Mar. 6, 1984.

184. Mayor's Commission, *Black New Yorkers*, pp. 128–30.

185. *New York Times*, Dec. 5, 1988.

186. Ibid., Aug. 17, 1993; Sept. 2, 1993.

■

187. Ibid., Apr. 5, 1993. Earlier reports on these schools were mixed. See ibid., May 15, 1994.

188. David Lavin, Richard Alba, and Richard Silberstein, *Right Versus Privilege: The Open-Admissions Experiment at the City University of New York* (New York, 1981), chapter 5; Mayor's Commission, *Black New Yorkers*, pp. 12–14 and 193.

189. For the impact on the 1975 crisis on blacks and Puerto Ricans see Rodriguez-Fraticelli, "Higher Education Task Force," p. 25.

190. Ibid., pp. 28 and 31. Black faculty were also cut during the 1975 crisis.

191. Tobier, *The Changing Face of Poverty*, p. 38; *New York Times*, Feb. 28, 1989. It remained about the same in 1991. Ibid., June 10, 1992.

192. For a discussion of poverty see Tobier, *The Changing Face of Poverty*.

193. *New York Times*, July 9, 1989; July 13, 1989.

194. Ibid., July 15, 1989; July 14, 1992.

195. For Canarsie, see Jonathan Reider, *Canarsie: The Jews and Italians of Brooklyn Against Liberalism* (Cambridge, 1985). Mayor David Dinkins finally created an appointed civilian board in 1993, which Rudolph Giuliani said would be revaluated after one year.

196. See Charles Hynes, *Incident at Howard Beach: The Case for Murder* (New York, 1990).

197. *New York Times*, Aug. 28, 1989. See also DeSantis, *For the Color of His Skin*, for coverage of the incident.

198. For attitudes among blacks in Jews just after the Ocean Hill-Brownsville dispute see Louis Harris and Bert Swanson, *Black-Jewish Relations in New York City* (New York, 1970).

199. *New York Times*, Aug. 21, 1991; Nov. 18, 1992; Nov. 26, 1992; Nov. 30, 1992; Dec. 3, 1992; Dec. 5, 1992; Dec. 6, 1992; Dec. 18, 1992; and *Amsterdam News*, Aug. 24, 1991. For the background of the Crown Heights dispute see Jerome Mintz, *Hasidic People: A Place in the World* (Cambridge, 1992), chapters 13, 22 and 27.

## *Afterword*

1. *New York Times*, Mar. 17, 1988.

2. For an examination of resurgent ethnicity see Mary C. Waters, *Ethnic Options: Choosing Identities in America* (Berkeley, 1990).

3. *New York Times*, Oct. 18, 1993.

■

*Selected Reading*

Our sources are indicated in the footnotes. Listed below are accessible and readable secondary accounts of the main periods in New York City's racial and ethnic history.

### General

Allen, Oliver E. *New York New York: A History of the World's Most Exhilarating—Challenging City*. New York, 1990.

Glazer, Nathan and Moynihan, Daniel Patrick. *Beyond the Melting Pot: The Negroes, Puerto Ricans, Irish, Jews and Italians of New York City*. Cambridge, 1963.

Lankevich, George J. and Furer, Howard B. *A Brief History of New York City*. Port Washington, N.Y., 1984.

Rosenwaike, Ira. *Population History of New York City*. Syracuse, 1972.

■

## Colonial Era

Archdeacon, Thomas J. *New York City, 1664–1710: Conquest and Change*. Ithaca, 1976.

Butler, Jon. *The Huguenots in America: A Refugee People in New World Society*. Cambridge, 1983.

Davis, T. J. *A Rumor of Revolt: The "Great Negro Plot" in Colonial New York*. New York, 1985.

Goodfriend, Joyce. *Before the Melting Pot: Society and Culture in Colonial New York City, 1664–1730*. Princeton, 1992.

Marcus, Jacob Rader. *Early American Jewry: The Jews of New York, New England and Canada, 1649–1794*. 2 vols. Philadelphia, 1951.

McManus, Edgar. *Negro Slavery in New York*. Syracuse, 1966.

White, Shane. *Somewhat More Independent: The End of Slavery in New York City, 1770–1810*. Athens, 1991.

## Nineteenth and Early Twentieth Centuries

Allen, Oliver E. *The Tiger: The Rise and Fall of Tammany Hall*. New York, 1993.

Bernstein, Iver. *The New York City Draft Riots: Their Significance for American Society and Politics in the Age of the Civil War*. New York, 1990.

Dolan, Jay. *The Immigrant Church: New York's Irish and German Catholics, 1815–1865*. Notre Dame, 1983.

Ernst, Robert. *Immigrant Life in New York City, 1825–1863*. New York, 1979.

Ewen, Elizabeth. *Immigrant Women in the Land of Dollars: Life and Culture on the Lower East Side, 1890–1925*. New York, 1985.

Gabaccia, Donna R. *From Sicily to Elizabeth Street: Housing and Social Change Among Italian Immigrants, 1880–1930*. Albany, 1984.

Glenn, Susan. *Daughters of the Shtetl: Life and Labor in the Immigrant Generation*. Ithaca, 1990.

Gordon, Michael A. *The Orange Riots: Irish Political Violence in New York City, 1870 and 1871*. Ithaca, 1993.

Goren, Arthur. *New York Jews and the Quest for Community: The Kehillah Experiment, 1908–1922*. New York, 1970.

Gurock, Jeffrey. *When Harlem Was Jewish, 1870–1930*. New York, 1979.

Hammack, David. *Power and Society: Greater New York at the Turn of the Century*. New York, 1982.

Henderson, Thomas M. *Tammany Hall and the New Immigrants*. New York, 1976.

Howe, Irving. *World of Our Fathers*. New York, 1976.

Kessner, Thomas. *The Golden Door: Italian and Jewish Immigrant Mobility in New York City, 1880–1915*. New York, 1977.

Nadel, Stanley. *Little Germany: Ethnicity, Religion, and Class in New York City, 1845–1880*. Urbana, 1990.

Osofsky, Gilbert. *Harlem: The Making of A Ghetto, Negro New York, 1890–1930*. New York, 1966.

Ravitch, Diane. *The Great School Wars: New York City, 1805–1973*. New York, 1974.

■

Rischin, Moses. *The Promised City: New York's Jews, 1870–1914*. Cambridge, 1962.

Schneider, Dorothee. *Trade Unions and Community: The German Working Class of New York City, 1870–1900*. Urbana, 1994.

Scheiner, Seth M. *Negro Mecca: A History of the Negro in New York City, 1865–1920*. New York, 1965.

Sorin, Gerald. *A Time for Building: The Third Migration, 1880–1920* (The Jewish People in America, vol. 3). Baltimore, 1992.

Spann, Edward K. *The New Metropolis: New York City, 1840–1857*. New York, 1981.

Stott, Richard B. *Workers in the Metropolis: Class, Ethnicity and Youth in Antebellum New York City*. Ithaca, 1990.

### Since World War I

Bayor, Ronald H. *Neighbors in Conflict: The Irish, Germans, Jews and Italians of New York City, 1929–1941*. Urbana, 1987.

Blumberg, Barbara. *The New Deal and the Unemployed: The View from New York City*. Lewisburg, 1979.

Chen, Hsiang-Shui. *Chinatown No More: Taiwan Immigrants in Contemporary New York*. Ithaca, 1992.

Cohen, Miriam. *Workshop to Office: Two Generations of Italian Women in New York City, 1900–1950*. Ithaca, 1993.

Connolly, Harold X. *A Ghetto Grows in Brooklyn*. New York, 1977.

Fitzpatrick, Joseph P. *Puerto Rican Americans: The Meaning of Migration*. Englewood Cliffs, 1987.

Foner, Nancy ed.. *New Immigrants in New York*. New York, 1987.

Freeman, Joshua B. *In Transit: The Transport Workers Union in New York City, 1933–1966*. New York, 1989.

Grasmuck, Sherri and Pessar, Patricia R. *Between Two Islands: Dominican International Migration*. Berkeley, 1991.

Green, Charles and Wilson, Basil. *The Struggle for Black Empowerment in New York City*. New York, 1989.

Greenberg, Cheryl Lynn. *"Or Does It Explode?" Black Harlem in the Great Depression*. New York, 1991.

Joselit, Jenna Weissman. *New York's Jewish Jews: The Orthodox Community in the Inner War Years*. Bloomington, 1990.

Kasinitz, Philip. *Caribbean New York: Black Immigrants and the Politics of Race*. Ithaca, 1992.

Kessner, Thomas. *Fiorello H. La Guardia and the Making of Modern New York*. New York, 1989.

Kim, Illsoo. *New Urban Immigrants: The Korean Community in New York City*. Princeton, 1981.

Kwong, Peter. *The New Chinatown*. New York, 1987.

Lowenstein, Steven M. *Frankfurt on the Hudson: The German-Jewish Community of Washington Heights, 1933–1983: Its Structure and Culture*. Detroit, 1989.

■

Markowitz, Ruth Jacknow. *My Daughter, the Teacher: Jewish Teachers in the New York City Schools*. New Brunswick, 1993.

McNickle, Chris. *To Be Mayor of New York* (New York, 1993).

Mollenkopf, John Hull. *A Phoenix in the Ashes: The Rise and Fall of the Koch Coalition in New York City Politics*. Princeton, 1992.

Moore, Deborah Dash. *At Home in America: Second Generation New York Jews*. New York, 1981.

Rieder. Jonathan. *Canarsie: The Jews and Italians of Brooklyn Against Liberalism*. Cambridge, 1985.

Rodriguez, Clara E. *Puerto Ricans Born in the U.S.A.*. Boston, 1989.

Shokeid, Moshe. *Children of Circumstances: Israel's Emigrants in New York*. Ithaca, 1988.

Sleeper, Jim. *The Closest of Strangers: Liberalism and the Politics of Race in New York*. New York, 1990.

Sutton, Constance and Chaney, Elsa eds.. *Caribbean Life in New York City: Sociocultural Dimensions*. New York, 1987.

Tricarico, Donald. *The Italians of Greenwich Village: The Social Structure and Transformation of an Ethnic Community*. New York, 1984.

Waldinger, Roger D. *Through the Eye of the Needle: Immigrants and Enterprise in New York's Garment Trade*. New York, 1987.

Winnick, Louis. *New People in Old Neighborhoods: The Role of New Immigrants in Rejuvenating New York's Communities*. New York, 1990.

■

# Index

*Abendzeitung*, 83
Abolitionism, 30–31, 53, 57, 75–76, 89; *see also* Manumission
Abraham (butcher), 122
Abyssinian Baptist Church, 110, 181, 190
Academy of the Sacred Heart, 98
Accidental deaths, 60
Adenoid removal, 130
Adler, Felix, 80
Adler, Jacob, 134
*Advice to Irish Girls in America* (Nun of Kenmare), 60–61

Affirmative action programs, 215–16; *see also* Open admissions policy
Afghans, 239
African Americans, 262
—colonial era, 15, 30
—antebellum era, 53–58, 62, 272n104
—Civil War era, 73–74, 275n54
—late 19th-early 20th centuries, 95, 109–13, 158–60, 282n96
—1920s, 157, 167–69
—1930s, 176, 179–80, 184; communism and, 187; Italians and, 190; La Guardia and, 183; Moses and, 185

—World War II era, 194–95
—1945–70: 198, 214–24; in the
  Bronx, 155, 205, 215; influx of, 206;
  occupations of, 200, 203; politics
  and, 201
—1970–94: 226, 250, 251–57; Arab
  Muslims and, 239; Hasids and, 249;
  Housing Authority and, 303*n*120;
  Koreans and, 235, 238; occupations
  of, 312*n*169; politics and, 243,
  251–52; reverse migration by,
  302*n*84; West Indians and, 230
African American women: antebellum
  era, 54; early 20th century, 111;
  1920s, 167; 1930s, 179, 184; World
  War II era, 194, 195; 1945–70: 219;
  1970–94: 256
African Free Schools, 56–57
African Methodist Church, 56
Africans, 240–41
African slaves, *see* Slavery
Afro-American Realty Company, 158
AIDS (disease), 256
Aid societies, *see* Organizations
Aid to Dependent Children (ADC),
  251, 256
Ailey, Alvin, 223
Air migration, 212
Airports, 184
Albanians, 245
Albany, 2, 4, 268*n*11
Alcohol consumption, *see* Beer indus-
  try; Drinking establishments; Tem-
  perance legislation
Aldermen, 18
Alexander Avenue, 154
Alien and Sedition Acts, 35
Allen, James, Jr., 222, 304*n*129
Allen, Richard, 56
*Allgemeiner Arbeitbund*, 86
*Allgemeine Zeitung*, 83
Allied Powers, 149, 150, 151, 190
Amalgamated Clothing Workers'
  Union, 124, 143, 185, 187, 285*n*56
American Anti-Slavery Society, 57

American Federation of Labor, 99
American Federation of State, County,
  and Municipal Employees, 203, 219
American Jewish Congress, 188, 198
American Labor Party, 186, 187
American League, 207
American Protective Association, 50
American Republican Party, 71
American Revolution: German mer-
  cenaries in, 34; Irish immigration
  and, 33; population lost in, 31; reli-
  gious freedom and, 32; Shearith
  Israel and, 28; slavery and, 30
*The American Weekly*, 149–50
*Amerikai Magyar Nepszava*, 174
*Amerikanisher Arbeitbund*, 86
Amsterdam (Netherlands), 2, 6, 8
*Amsterdam News*, 223
Anarchism, 144, 151
Ancient Order of Hibernians, 98
Anderson, Marian, 217
Andros, Edmund, 18, 20, 21, 27,
  266*n*78
Anglican Church: disestablishment of,
  32; Dutch membership in, 21, 23;
  Huguenots and, 24, 25, 26; Natural-
  ization Act and, 27; *see also* Episco-
  palian churches
Anglo-American Free Church of St.
  George the Martyr, 49
Anglo-Dutch War (1652–54), 13
*Annual Report on Hispanic Concerns*, 227
Anshe Chesed (synagogue), 81, 82
Anti-Defamation League, 199
Antin, Mary, 103
Antiochian Orthodox Church, 239
Anti-Semitism, 261; colonial era, 8;
  late 19th-early 20th centuries, 97,
  103, 118, 126; 1920s, 156, 164;
  1930s, 188, 190–91; World War II
  era, 198; 1945–70: 214; *see also*
  Holocaust
Anti-slavery movement, *see* Aboli-
  tionism
Apartment houses, *see* Housing

Apparel industry, *see* Garment industry
Arabic-speaking Jews, 117
Arabs, 107, 238–39
*Arbeitbund*, 86
*Arbeiter Union* (newspaper), 87
*Arbeiter Zeitung*, 123
Arditi, Luigi, 51
Armenians, 241
Arson, *see* Fires
Arthur, Chester, 56
Artificial flower/feather industry, 141, 142
Artisans, 26, 34, 38, 39, 86
Asbestos, 255
Asch, Sholem, 134
Ashantis, 240
Ashkenazic Jews, 8, 26, 27, 80–81, 114
Asian Indians, 171, 229, 232, 235, 236–37
Asians: late 19th century, 108; early 20th century, 152; 1920s, 167, 170–71; 1945–70: 210, 212; 1970–94: 230, 248, 307*n*68
ASPIRA (organization), 213, 251
Association for Improving the Condition of the Poor, 43–44
Association of Guardians, 216
Astor, John Jacob, 37
Astoria, 47, 88, 210, 247
Astor Place Opera House, 51
Astor Place Riot (1849), 62, 273*n*16
Athletics, *see* Sports
Atlantic Avenue, 239
*Atlantis* (newspaper), 106
*Aufbau* (newspaper), 177
*Die Aurora* (newspaper), 79
Austro-Hungarian Empire, 102
Avenue B, 76

Baden (Germany), 85
Badillo, Herman, 214, 251
Bahai Iranians, 238
Baker, George (Father Divine), 181
Balkan Wars, 107
Baltimore, 36, 207

Bangladeshi, 237
Banking industry, 199, 243, 244, 254; *see also* Financial industry
Barbers, 51, 54, 140, 282*n*96
Barker, James, 71
Bars, *see* Drinking establishments
Barsimon, Jacob, 9
Baseball: amateur, 133, 162–63, 228; professional, 153, 163, 166, 207, 217, 228
Basketball, 163, 217
Bath houses, *see* Public bath houses
Battle, Samuel J., 111
Battle of Gettysburg, 73
Battle of the Boyne, 49, 65
Bavarians, 77, 276*n*70
Bayard, Nicholas, 21, 266*n*81
Bayor, Ronald, 188
Bay Ridge, 232, 247
Beame, Abe, 202, 243
Bedford-Stuyvesant: early 20th century, 159–60, 167, 169; 1930s, 180; 1945–70: 219, 220; 1970–94: 229
Beer gardens, 83–84
Beer industry, 207, 300*n*46
Bellevue Hospital, 45
Belmont, August, 37, 90
Belmont (Bronx), 205
Benevolent associations (unions), 203–4
Benevolent organizations, *see* Organizations
Benny, Dopey, 166
Bensonhurst, 209, 249–50, 257, 310*n*154
Berkovitch, Boris, 199
Berrol, Selma, 125
Bible, 68, 71
Bilingual instruction, 311*n*160
Bingham, Theodore, 119–20
"Bintel Brief" (newspaper column), 133
Bismarck, Otto von, 80, 91
Black Americans, *see* African Americans

■

"Black Hand" (crime), 139, 140
Black Muslims, 218–19
Bloomingdale, *see* Upper West Side
Blumstein, L. M., 179, 184
B'nai B'rith (organization), 82
B'nai Jeshurin (synagogue), 81
Boarders, 139, 270*n*61; *see also*
  Lodgers
Boardinghouses, 46, 270*n*61
Bodegas, 227
Bohemians, *see* Czechs
Bolshevik Revolution, 174
Bolsheviks, 151
Bombay, 117
Bonrepos, David de, 25–26
Bootblacks, 51, 106
Bootleggers, 166, 167
Born to Kill (gang), 235
Boro Park, 156, 172, 208, 249
Boss Cabinetmakers (organization), 87
Boston, 20, 36
Botta, Vicenzo, 51
Bovshover, Yosef, 133
Bowery, 76
Bowery B'hoys (gang), 62, 63
Boxing, 163–64
Boycotts, 184, 189, 194, 238
Boyne Day, 49, 65
Brace, Charles Loring, 44
Brady, James T., 73
Brazil, 8–9, 12
Breweries, 207, 300*n*46
Bribery, *see* Corruption
Bridges, 97, 178
Brighton Beach, 241, 309*n*110
Britain: capital from, 37; colonial
  claims of, 2, 3; Dutch relations with,
  9, 13, 17, 18, 264*n*23; German mer-
  cenaries of, 34; Hong Kong under,
  232, 306*n*42; Huguenots and, 24,
  25; India under, 171; Irish animosity
  toward, 62, 74, 100, 205, 273*n*16;
  New Amsterdam vs., 12, 15, 16;
  New York under, 16–32; packet
  service to, 36; population of, 39;
  Protestant ascendancy in, 49; in
  World War I, 151
British immigrants, 33, 48–49, 84, 96,
  269*n*25; *see also* English immigrants;
  Irish immigrants
British Parliament, 26–27
Broad Street, 265*n*62
Bronx: anti-Semitism in, 191; blacks
  in, 155, 179, 205, 215; construction
  in, 153–54, 195; demographic
  changes in, 204- 5; high schools in,
  131; Hispanics in, 155, 205; Irish in,
  99, 155, 173, 242; Italians in, 136,
  137; Jews in, 117, 156, 157, 165,
  171–73; Koreans in, 236; politics in,
  243, 311*n*165; socialists in, 125;
  Thais in, 237; *see also* East Bronx;
  South Bronx; West Bronx
Bronx Co-op City, 205
Bronx Science High School, 222
Brooklyn: development of, 204; ferry
  service to, 56; jobs lost in, 207–8;
  neighborhoods of, 205; population
  of, 154, 269*n*18, 269*n*22; racial
  changes in, 219–20
—Arabs, 107, 239
—Asians, 171
—blacks: colonial era, 28; antebellum
  era, 55, 57; late 19th-early 20th centuries, 109, 110, 159–60, 169,
  305*n*27; 1945–70: 215; 1970–94:
  229, 230, 257
—Catholics, 102
—Chinese, 232, 235
—Germans: antebellum era, 47, 48,
  78–80; late 19th-early 20th
  centuries, 97, 152, 276*n*74
—Greeks, 211
—Irish, 60
—Italians: late 19th-early 20th centuries, 136, 137; 1920s, 157–58, 161,
  167; 1945–70: 209; 1970–94:
  249–50, 310*n*154
—Japanese, 170
—Jews: late 19th-early 20th centuries,

117, 172; 1920s, 156, 157, 161;
1970–94: 240, 241, 249, 257,
309*n*110
—Koreans, 238
—Norwegians, 109, 174, 246, 247,
260
—Poles, 50, 105–6, 247
—Puerto Ricans, 212
—Scandinavians, 108, 247
Brooklyn Army Terminal, 207
Brooklyn Bridge, 97
Brooklyn College, 189
Brooklyn Diocese, 248
Brooklyn Dodgers (baseball team),
163, 207, 217, 218
*The Brooklyn Eagle* (newspaper), 207
Brooklyn Heights, 48, 156
Brooklyn Navy Yard, 169, 170, 194,
207
*Brooklyn Tablet* (newspaper), 188
Brown, Lee, 243, 252
Browne, John, 8
Brownson, Orestes A., 69, 71
Brownsville: early 20th century, 117;
1920s, 156, 161; 1930s, 178–79;
1945–70: 204, 219, 222–23
Bruce, Herbert, 215
Buchanan, James, 89
Buckley, Charles, 201, 311*n*165
Budapest, 183
Buddhists, 236, 237
Buffalo *Commercial Advertiser*, 275*n*49
Building crews, *see* Construction
workers
Building projects, *see* Housing; Public
works
Bukovian Jews, 121
Bundists, 115, 116, 124
Bundy, McGeorge, 222
Burghership rights, 11, 14; *see also*
Civil rights
Burmese, 237
Burns, George, 162
Business cycles, *see* Economic
conditions

Businesses, 206, 218; Afghan, 239;
black, 111, 112, 167, 216, 253;
German, 87; Italian, 166, 190; Jew-
ish, 121–22, 162, 164; Protestant,
199, 243; West Indian, 229–30; *see
also* Commerce; Industrialization;
Retail trade
Butler, Jon, 5
Button manufacture, 106
Byrd, William, 23
Byrnes, Thomas, 100

Cacchione, Peter Vincent, 187
Cafes, *see* Coffeehouses
Cahan, Abraham, 132–33, 286*n*91
Calabrians, 205
California, 108, 247
Calvinist Dutch, 2, 3–5, 24
Calvinist French, *see* Huguenots
Calvinist New Englanders, 37
Cambodians, 238
Cameron, Simon, 72
Canada, 102
Canarsie (Brooklyn), 204, 244, 256
Canarsie Indians, 4
Cantor, Eddie, 162
Cantor, Jacob, 126
Carew, Rod, 228
Caribbean area, 176–77, 211–12, 214,
227–31
*Carib News*, 230
Carnegie Hall, 217
Carnera, Primo, 190
Carolinas, 109
Caro, Robert, 185
Car service vehicles, 230
Carver Federal Savings and Loan
Association, 253
Casey, Marion, 155
Castle Garden, 41, 137
Castro, Fidel, 228
Catering, 282*n*96
Catholic Charities (organization), 181
Catholic Church, *see* Roman Catholic
Church

■

Catholic Club, 98
Catholic Protectory of New York, 44
Celler, Emanuel, 152
Central Americans, 228
Central Federated Union, 99
Central Powers, 151
Cesnola, Luigi Palma de, 51
Charities, 173, 181–82, 243–44, 249
Charity Organization Society, 147, 181
Chase Manhattan Bank, 244
Chateaubriand, François René, Viscount de, 34
Chicago, 93, 94
Childcare, 242; *see also* Domestic workers
Children: black, 15; Bohemian, 106; Chinese, 233; Depression era, 181; homeless, 44; Italian, 141, 142–43; Jewish, 116, 131–32; Puerto Rican, 214, 251; *see also* Schools
Children's Aid Society, 44, 95, 181
Chi Luu, 238
Chinatown: 19th century, 52, 108; 1920s, 170; 1970–94: 232, 233, 234, 237
Chinatown Planning Council, 235
Chinese: 19th century, 52, 107–8, 262, 281*n*75; 1930s, 180, 186, 191; World War II era, 212; 1970–94: 227, 231–35, 245
Chinese Consolidated Benevolent Association, 108, 170, 186, 235
Chinese Exclusion Act, 212
Chinese Hand Laundrymen Alliance, 186
Chisholm, Shirley, 215
Chmielnicki Cossacks, 8
Cholera, 45, 101
Christian Arabs, 107, 239
Christian Front, 191
Christian holidays, 239
Christian Iranians, 238
Christian Koreans, 236
Christian slaves, 28

Christmas, 109, 146
Churches, *see* Religious denominations
Church of England, *see* Anglican Church
Church of Our Lady of Mount Carmel, 173, 231
Church of the Lady of Perpetual Help, 107
Cigar manufacture, 106, 169
Citizens' Association of New York, 43
Citizen's Protective League, 112
City College of New York, 213, 238; basketball at, 163; Jewish students at, 130, 164, 192; white students at, 223
City University of New York, 213, 254; black students at, 255; Jewish students at, 131; open admissions policy at, 200, 223, 251, 255; Puerto Rican students at, 251
Citywide Citizens' Committee, 194
Civilian review board proposal, 224, 256, 313*n*195
Civil rights: colonial era, 10–11, 14, 26, 27, 30; 19th century, 57, 110
Civil Rights Act (1873), 110
Civil rights movement, 218–19; *see also* Affirmative action
Civil service, 182, 183, 189, 295*n*37; *see also* Municipal employees
Civil War: black civil rights and, 57; draft riots in, 55, 72- 73; immigration and, 39; Irish participation in, 72; Italian participation in, 51; labor-management relations and, 87; uniforms manufactured for, 85; volunteer units in, 52; F. Wood campaign and, 89
Civil Works Administration (U.S.), 185
Claghorn, Kate, 140
Clara de Hirsch Home for Working Girls, 119
Clark, Una, 229

Classis (Dutch Reformed Church), 5, 6–7, 9, 10

Clergy, 57, 80; *see also* Rabbis; Roman Catholic clergy

Cleveland Indians (baseball team), 228

Clothing industry, *see* Garment industry

Club Avanti, 144

Cocaine, 256

Cockran, W. Bourke, 98

Coffeehouses, 107, 133, 211, 286*n*92

Cohalan, Daniel F., 151

Cohen, Miriam, 142

Cold War, 187, 208

Cole, Bob, 111

Collective bargaining, 203

College of Staten Island, 244

College of the City of New York, *see* City College of New York

College Point, 87–88

Colleges and universities: anti-Semitism in, 188, 198; black students at, 223; Catholic, 98–99; Chinese students at, 234; discrimination by, 198–99; Italian students at, 200; Jewish graduates of, 164; prestigious, 254; *see also* Community colleges; Municipal colleges

Colombian Civic Center, 240

Colombians, 240, 308*n*100

Colored Orphan Asylum, 73

Columbia University, 164, 188, 199, 244

Columbus Day Rally, 193

Commerce, 3, 17, 18, 31; *see also* Businesses; Merchants; Retail trade

*Commercial Advertiser* (Buffalo), 275*n*49

*Commercial Advertiser* (New York), 35

Commission Against Discrimination (N.Y.S.), 198, 218

Commission on Immigration (Dillingham Commission), 104, 105, 119, 138, 141

Committee for Ethiopia, 190

Common School Act (1894), 110

Communicable diseases, 40, 41, 55, 59; *see also* Cholera; Yellow fever

Communism: Cuban, 228; Depression era, 184, 186–87, 192, 296*n*57; Fourierist, 86; German American, 84, 86, 87; Polish, 242; Soviet, 174

Communist Club, 86

Community colleges, 255

Community organizations, *see* Organizations

Community Service Society, 244

Compulsory Education Act (1895), 96

Compulsory military service, 39; *see also* Draft riots (1863)

Concourse Plaza Hotel, 153–54

Condom distribution, 248

Coney Island, 154, 170

Congregation K'hal Adath Jeshurun, 177

Congress of Racial Equality, 218

Connolly, Harold, 219–20

Connolly, Richard ("Slippery Dick"), 65

Conrad Poppenhusen Enterprise Works, 87–88

Conscription Act (1863), 73

Conservative Jews, 129, 172, 208

Constitution (U.S.), 53, 57, 72

Constitution Day, 106

Construction projects, *see* Housing; Public works

Construction workers, 153, 200; black, 179, 218, 219; Irish, 154, 242, 287*n*107; Italian, 143, 157, 287*n*107; Norwegian, 174

Contagious diseases, *see* Communicable diseases

Cooke, Terence J., 202, 248

Cooper, James Fenimore, 51

Cooperative production, 86, 87

Cornish, Samuel, 57

Corona, 221

Corresca, Rocco, 144

*Corriere della Sera* (newspaper), 143

Corrigan, Michael A., 147

■

Corruption: antebellum era, 71, 76; early 20th century, 99–100, 166; 1930s, 182–83, 184; 1945–70: 220
Cosmopolitan Soccer League, 245
Cossacks, 8
Coughlin, Charles E., 190–91
Council of Revision (N.Y.S.), 35
Council on Hygiene (N.Y.C.), 42, 43
Crack cocaine, 256
Craftsmen, 26, 34, 38, 39, 86
Creole language, 229, 231
Crèvecoeur, Jean de, 22
Crime, 256; Chinese, 234–35; German, 75; Italian, 120, 139–40, 166–67; Jewish, 119–20, 166, 309*n*110; *see also* Corruption; Illegal aliens; Violence
Croatians, 105, 106, 107
Cromwell, Oliver, 17
Croton Aqueduct, 45
Croton Reservoir, 137, 205
Crown Heights: 1920s, 161; 1945–70: 208, 219; 1970–94: 229, 249, 257
Cubans, 228
Cuccinello, Tony ("Chick"), 163
Cuddihy family, 200
Cultural enterprises, *see* Entertainment industry; Organizations
Cultural leaders, *see* Intellectuals
Cuomo, Mario, 221, 243
Curacao, 9
Custom house, 90
*Cymro American* (newspaper), 48
Cyprus, 210, 211
Czechs: 19th century, 105, 106, 107; World War II era, 192, 193; 1970–94: 242

Daille, Pierre, 24
Daily, Thomas, 248
*Daily Mirror*, 163, 172
*Daily News*, 73, 163, 172
*Daily News* (*Dowy Dziennick*), 247
*Daily Plebian*, 69
Dakota (apartment house), 157

Dance halls, 134
Dance Theater of Harlem, 223
Dandradj, Salvador, 11
*Dauphine* (ship), 1
Davis, Benjamin, 195
Dead Rabbits (gang), 62
Dearie, John C., 243
Death rate, 40, 45, 55
"The Decline of Protestantism and Its Causes" (J. Hughes), 70
De Lancey, Stephen, 25
Delaware River, 11
*Delnicke Listy*, 106–7
Demo, Antonio, 147
Democratic Party: American Labor Party and, 187; blacks and, 113, 168, 184, 215; in the Bronx, 311*n*165; Dinkins-Koch primary and, 252; Germans and, 76, 88, 89, 90; Hillquit and, 127; Irish and, 63–66, 71, 100, 200, 274*n*19; Italians and, 144, 201–2; Seward and, 68
*Demokrat* (newspaper), 83
Department stores, 165, 179, 184
Depressions, 86, 123, 157, 269*n*24; *see also* Fiscal crisis (1975); Great Depression
DeSapio, Carmine, 201
Desegregation, *see* Segregation
*Deutscher Verein*, 97
*Deutsches Volksecho* (newspaper), 189
Devoy, John, 100, 151
De Witt Clinton High School, 166
Dickens, Charles, 45, 55
Dillingham Commission (Immigration Commission), 104, 105, 119, 138, 141
DiMaggio, Joe, 163
Dinkins, David, 239; black-Korean conflict and, 238; Brown and, 243; civil review board and, 313*n*195; on ethnic "mosaic," 261; mayoral campaigns of, 252
Discrimination, *see* Racism
Diseases, *see* Communicable diseases

Displaced Persons Acts (1948, 1950), 208
Dissenters (English Protestants), 24
District Council 37, 219
Divine, Father (G. Baker), 181
Dockhands, *see* Longshoremen
Dodgers (baseball team), 163, 207, 217, 218
Dolan, Jay, 66, 69, 274*n*274
Domestic workers, 269*n*25; black, 54, 111, 158, 161, 167, 179; Irish, 60–61, 98, 161; West Indian, 230; *see also* Childcare
Dominicans: antebellum era, 34, 35, 37; 20th century, 211–12, 227–28, 245
Dominion of New England, 20
Dongan, Thomas, 19, 20–21, 23, 27, 32
Dongan Charter (1686), 267*n*100
Douglass, Frederick, 56
Downstate Medical Center, 218
*Dowy Dziennick*, 247
Draft riots (1863), 55, 72–73, 276*n*60
Drinking establishments, 95, 99; German, 83–84; Irish, 61, 64, 83, 242; Scottish, 48; *see also* Temperance legislation
Drisius, Samuel, 6
Drug traffic, 227–28, 235, 256
Dubinsky, David, 124, 187
Dubois, John, 34, 66
Dudley, Joseph, 20, 266*n*78
Dutch Americans, 37
Dutch East India Company, 2, 3
Dutch Jews, 8, 9, 10
Dutch New York, *see* New Amsterdam
Dutch Protestants, 2, 3–5, 24
Dutch Reformed Church: under British rule, 17, 19, 20, 21; Classis of, 5, 6–7, 9, 10; English language and, 22; French Church and, 24, 25, 26; German Protestants and, 79; integrative role of, 16; Jews and, 9,

27; Lutherans and, 7; Walloons and, 3; West India Company and, 6
Dutch States General, 2, 3, 17, 18
Dutch Surinam, 9
Dutch Town, see *Kleindeutschland*
Dutch West India Company, *see* West India Company (Netherlands)
Dutch West Indies, 14
Duvalier regime, 211, 231

East Bronx, 165, 171–73
Easter, 109
Eastern European immigrants, 96, 102, 108, 116; 1920s, 174; 1970–94, 242
Eastern European Jews, 114–16, 261; capitalism of, 125; at CCNY, 131; German Jews and, 118–20, 124, 126; HIAS and, 284*n*33; industrial skills of, 115–16, 283*n*5; mobility of, 156; organizations of, 120–21; prosperity of, 162; religious practices of, 127–29; teaching profession and, 188; on West Side, 157; *see also* Hasidic Jews
Eastern Parkway, 230
Easter Rebellion (1916), 151
East Harlem: Haitians in, 231; housing in, 138; Jews in, 151, 154; Puerto Ricans in, 169, 212, 214, 245; *see also* Italian Harlem
East India Company (Netherlands), 2, 3
East Indians, 171, 229, 232, 235, 236–37
East New York, 220, 254
East Side, 47, 50, 105; *see also* Lower East Side
East Village, 247
Economic conditions: colonial era, 25, 31; 19th century, 48, 72, 81, 85–86, 115; World War II era, 193–94; 1945–70: 197- 98; 1970–94: 250, 253; *see also* Depressions; Fiscal crisis (1975); Poverty; Wages

Economic Opportunity Office (U.S.), 200
Edelstadt, David, 133
Edict of Nantes (1685), 24
Education, *see* Schools
Educational Alliance, 118–19
Egypt, 210
E. H. Kress and Company, 191–92
Eighth Ward, 271*n*72
El Al Moving Company, 240
Elections:
—19th century: blacks and, 53; Germans and, 90; Irish and, 64, 68; national, 72; nativism in, 69–70, 71; 87
—early 20th century, 126–27, 151, 168
—1930s, 183
—1940s, 187
—1945–70: 201–2, 215
—1980s, 252
—*see also* Politics
Elevated trains, *see* Street railways
Eleventh Ward, 47, 74
Elizabeth I, Queen of England, 17
Elizabeth Street, 138
Ellis Island, 104; Castle Garden and, 41; fire at, 278*n*2; Italians at, 137–38; Jews at, 115, 121; La Guardia at, 183; opening of, 94
Elmhurst, 240
Elore Hungarian Players, 174
El Salvador, 228
Emancipation Proclamation, 72
Embargo Act (1807), 36
Empire Foundation, 261
Employment, *see* Occupations
England, *see* Britain
English immigrants:
—Dutch colonial era, 7–8
—British colonial era: Dutch culture and, 18, 19–20, 23; Huguenots and, 25; labor shortage of, 14, 28; slavery and, 15, 28–31; on Staten Island, 24
—antebellum era, 37, 49

English language: British immigrants and, 48; Bronx Jews and, 171–72; Chinese immigrants and, 234; Dutch colonists and, 21, 22; evening study of, 131; Indochinese immigrants and, 238; in Jewish sermons, 128, 129, 172; municipal employment and, 99; official status of, 247; Puerto Ricans and, 213; schoolchildren and, 96, 130, 311*n*160
English Protestants, 24, 67
English women, 7
Enlightenment, the, 81, 82
Enoch, May, 112
Entertainment industry: early 20th century, 101, 111–12, 134, 162; 1945–70: 216–17, 223–24; *see also* Movies; Music; Sports; Theater
Entrepreneurs, *see* Businesses
Epidemics, *see* Communicable diseases
Episcopalian churches, 26, 49, 56; *see also* Anglican Church
Equal Employment Commission (U.S.), 218
Erie Canal, 36
Ethical Culture Society, 80
Ethiopia, 190, 240
European Americans, 243, 246–47, 250
European drama, 134
European immigrants: colonial era, 2, 12, 13–14, 28, 31; antebellum era, 37, 39, 47; Civil War era, 52; early 20th century, 152; 1920s, 171; 1945–70: 208; 1970–94: 226, 241; *see also* Eastern European immigrants; Southern European immigrants, *etc.*
European Jews, 8–9, 81, 82, 192–93
European municipalities, 14
European Protestants, 11, 260
European revolutions (1848), 81; *see also* Forty-Eighter republicans
European wars, 36
Exogamous marriages, *see* Marriages
Extortion, 234

■

Fabbri, E. P., 51
Factory production, *see* Industrialization
Fair Employment Practices Committee, 194
*Familienblätter*, 83
*Farbands*, 121
Farley, James, 187
Farley, John, 147
Farmers, 39, 48, 102
Fascism, 176, 189, 190, 193, 297*n*74
Father Divine (G. Baker), 181
*Faust* (Goethe), 84
Federal . . . , *see* United States . . .
Federation of Colombian Organizations, 240
Federation of Jewish Philanthropies, 178, 199, 206
Feingold, Henry, 164
Fernandez, Joseph, 251
Ferry service, 56
Festivals, 147, 173
Fidelio (organization), 97
Fieldston, 156
Fifteenth Amendment, 53
Fifth Avenue Bus Company, 194
Filipino Community Center of New York, 236
Filipinos, 171, 235, 236, 307*n*68
Filling stations, 237
Fillmore, Millard, 71
Financial industry, 36–37, 94, 244; *see also* Banking industry
Finnish Aid Society, 174
Finns, 108, 174
"Finn Town," 108
Fire fighters, 46, 62, 168, 184, 216
Fires, 29; Ellis Island, 278*n*2; "Great" (1858), 46; Happy Land Night Club, 229; Triangle Shirtwaist Company, 96, 125
First Anglo-Dutch War (1652–1654), 13
First Avenue trolley, 137
First Ward, 47

First World Zionist Congress (1897), 127
Fiscal crisis (1975): Beame and, 202; blacks and, 253–54, 312*n*190; education and, 251, 254–55; municipal employment and, 203, 252; municipal services and, 256; Puerto Ricans and, 250; white exodus and, 206
Fishman, Rafail, 241
Fitzgibbon, Irene, 44
Five Points, 44–45, 50, 53
Flatbush, 48, 229, 238
Flemings, 2
Flour monopoly, 266*n*77
Flour Riot (1837), 62
Flower vendors, 228
Flushing, 7–8, 87, 232, 236
Flushing Remonstrance, 7–8
Flynn, Edward J., 187, 200–201, 215, 311*n*165
Food, 241
Food industry, 122; *see also* Grocers; Restaurants
Football, 217
Ford, Henry, 166
Ford, Patrick, 100
Fordham, 155
Fordham College, 98–99
Fordham University, 200, 205
Foreign languages, *see* Languages
Forest, Edwin, 62
Forest Hills, 221
Fort George (Fort Amsterdam), 19, 20, 24
Fort Greene, 169
Fort New Amsterdam, 4
Fort Orange, 4, 5
Forty-Eighter republicans, 39; animosity towards, 75; German pastors and, 80; Prussian monarchy and, 91; Republican Party and, 89; *Turnvereine* and, 84
*Forverts* (newspaper), 132–33, 171, 172, 188; on Harlem, 117; letters to, 133, 286*n*91; on movie houses, 134;

■

90th anniversary of, 246; on World War I, 151
Fourier, Charles, 86
Fourteenth Ward, 136
Fourth Ward, 44, 47
Francis I, King of France, 1
Franco, Francisco, 191
Franco-Prussian War, 91
Frankfurt (Germany), 177
Franks, Jacob, 27
Fraternal organizations, *see* Organizations
Fraunces, Samuel, 54
Fraunces Tavern, 54
Free blacks, *see* African Americans
Freedom of conscience, *see* Religious tolerance
*Freedom's Journal*, 57
Freeman, Rhoda, 272*n*104
Free Sons of Israel (organization), 82
Freethinkers (*Frei Gemeinden*), 80
Frémont, John C., 89
*French and American Gazette*, 34
French Church, 24, 25, 26
French colonialism, 3
French exploration, 1
French immigrants: 17th century, 19–20, 23; 18th century, 33, 34, 35, 53; antebellum era, 50
French language, 229, 231
French Protestants, *see* Huguenots; Waldensians
French Revolution, 34
French-speaking Catholics, 66
French-speaking Dutch (Walloons), 2, 3–5, 24
Friendly Sons of Saint Patrick (organization), 34, 59–60
Friends (Quakers), 7–8, 10, 27, 32
Friends of Irish Freedom (organization), 100
Fuchs, Lawrence H., 66, 91
*Fulton* (frigate), 207
Funk Silk Mill, 87
Fur trading, 2, 4, 12

Fur workers, 210
Fusionist Party, 126

Gabaccia, Donna, 138
*Gaelic American* (newspaper), 100, 106, 151
Gaelic Athletic Association, 173, 242
Gaelic Society, 98
Gaine, Hugh, 35
Galamison, Milton, 218
Galician Jews, 114, 116, 121, 285*n*71
Gambino, Richard, 146, 200
Gangs, 61–63, 133, 191, 234–35
Garcia, Robert, 214, 251
Garibaldi Guard, 51
Garment industry: antebellum era, 36, 61; Civil War era, 85; late 19th-early 20th centuries, 94–95, 115, 122–25, 140, 141, 142; 1945–70: 207; 1970–94: 227, 233–34; *see also* Tailoring
Garvey, Marcus, 159, 215
Gas stations, 237
Gates Avenue Association, 160
*Gazette Française*, 34
General Pulaski Day, 106, 191, 297*n*88
General Theological Seminary, 56
Gennaro Gardenia Company, 173
Gentlemen's Agreement (1907), 170
"Gentlemen's canal," 265*n*62
George, Henry, 126
George Washington Bridge, 178, 206, 227–28
German-American Bund, 189, 191, 193
German-American Fire Insurance Company, 87
German Americans, 260
—late 19th-early 20th centuries: Eastern European Jews and, 116, 117; in Harlem, 158; Italians and, 99, 136; labor movement and, 277–278*n*10; politics and, 101; prosperity of, 96–97, 160

■

—World War I era, 149–51, 152
—1920s, 245
—1930s, 160–61, 189
—World War II era, 193
—1945–70: 206
—1970–94: 245
German Catholics, 77–79, 276*n*74;
  bigotry against, 75; Irish and, 66;
  language and, 76; temperance and,
  276*n*73; on Upper West Side, 157
German Central Book Store, 189
German Democratic Union Party, 89
German Empire, *see* Germany
German Hospital and Dispensary, 150
Germania Life Insurance Company,
  150
Germania Ultra Marine Works, 87
German immigrants:
—18th century, 33, 34
—19th century, 41–42, 74–92,
  271*n*69, 276*n*73; blacks and, 53;
  Civil War and, 52; Democratic Party
  and, 66; Metropolitan Police vs., 63;
  neighborhoods of, 47–48; "New
  Immigrants" and, 96, 102; politics
  and, 64; sex ratio among, 60
—1920s, 154
German Jews, 261
—colonial era, 8
—19th century, 81–82, 85, 277*n*83
—late 19th–early 20th centuries: Eastern European Jews and, 118–20,
  122–23, 124, 126; HIAS and,
  284*n*33; philanthropy of, 173; prejudice against, 97; public schools and,
  129, 188
—1920s, 157
—1930s, 177
—1970–94: 245
German language, 76, 82, 88, 133,
  150–51
German Lutherans, 6–7, 79
German Polyclinic, 150
German Protestants, 77, 79–80, 97
German Reform Party, 90

German Savings Bank, 87
German Society, 34–35, 41, 52
German women, 61, 74–75, 101
German Workers Club, 189
Germany: 19th century, 76, 80, 91;
  World War I era, 150, 152; 1930s,
  183, 189, 190, 191, 193; World War
  II era, 192, 198
Gettysburg, Battle of, 73
Ghanaians, 240
Giants (baseball team), 153, 217, 218
Gilfoyle, Timothy J., 100
Gimbel's Department Store, 194
Gitletz (baseball fan), 162
Giuliani, Rudolph, 243, 252, 313*n*195
Glazer, Nathan, 310*n*153
Glorious Revolution (1688), 20, 21
Gold, Michael, 156
Golden, Harry, 128
Goldfogle, Henry, 126
Gomez, Estaban, 1–2
Gomez, Lewis, 27
Goodfriend, Joyce, 16, 265*n*60
Gordin, Jacob, 134
Gordon, Waxy, 166
Gotbaum, Victor, 203, 219
Government agencies: Chinese
  recourse to, 235; construction aided
  by, 184–85, 204; discrimination
  banned by, 261; housing programs
  of, 220, 221; immigrant processing
  by, 40; progressive reformers and,
  95; *see also* Municipal government;
  United States government
Government employees, 216,
  253, 312*n*169; *see also* Municipal
  employees
Governor's Island, 4
Grace, William R., 65–66
Gracie, Archibald, 37
Gradual Manumission Act (1799), 53
Graft, *see* Corruption
Grand Concourse, 156, 172–73,
  204–5
Grape prices, 102

■

Great Britain, *see* Britain
Great Depression, 176–92; Catholic relief in, 181, 202; in Harlem, 167; housing construction and, 178, 204; Jewish migration and, 156; Puerto Rican immigration and, 169, 176; J. Walker and, 175
Great Fire (1858), 46
Great Hunger (Ireland), 74
Great Migration (1910–20), 158
Greek Orthodox Church, 107, 174
Greeks: 19th century, 50, 105, 106; early 20th century, 281n62, 284n39; 1920s, 174; 1945–70: 209, 210–11; 1970–94: 247, 301n64
Greek-speaking Jews, 117
Greek War for Independence, 50, 105
Greeley, Horace, 69
Green, Richard, 253
Greenberg, Cheryl, 194
Greenberg, Hank, 163
Greengrocers, 226, 235–36, 238, 284n39
Greenpoint, 105–6, 247
Greenwich House, 147
Greenwich Village, 101, 136, 147, 173
Grocers, 284n39; Dominican, 227; German, 85; Irish, 155; Italian, 51; Korean, 226, 235–36, 238
Grog shops, *see* Drinking establishments
Guardian Life Insurance Company, 150
Guatemala, 228
Guild restrictions, 26
Gunther, Godfrey, 89–90
Gurock, Jeffrey S., 129
Guyanese, 229

Haitians, 53, 211, 230–31
Hale, Shelton, 181
"Half freedom," 15, 29
*Half Moon* (ship), 2
Haller, Mark, 167

Hamburg (Germany), 34
Hamid, Abdul, 184
Hamilton, Alexander, 22
Hamilton Ferry, 137
Hand laundries, 170, 180, 186, 232
Hannover (Germany), 85
Hanrahan, Frank, 155
Hansbury, Lorraine, 223
Happy Land Night Club, 229
Harlem: abandoned buildings in, 220; businesses in, 216; early, 42; politics in, 215; racial conflict in, 191–92, 194–95, 224, 238
—blacks: early 20th century, 158–59, 168; 1920s, 157, 167; 1930s, 179–80, 181, 184, 185; 1945–70: 219
—Germans, 97
—Italians, *see* Italian Harlem
—Jews, 117–18, 156
—West Indians, 109, 305n27
—*see also* East Harlem; West Harlem
Harlem Hospital, 168, 184, 192
Harlem Property Owners' Improvement Corporation, 158
Harlem Renaissance, 159, 160
*Harmonie* (organization), 97
Har Moriah Hospital, 121
Harper, James, 71
*Harper's Weekly*, 72, 74
Harris, Arthur, 112
Hasidic Jews, 208–9, 249, 261
Havemeyer, William, 90
Hawaii, 170
Hayes, Patrick, 173, 181, 202
Haynes, George, 111, 282n96
*Hazzanim*, 27
Health facilities, *see* Hospitals
Hearst, William Randolph, 126, 127, 132
Hebrew Free Loan Society, 121
Hebrew Immigrant Aid Society, 121, 284n33
Hebrew language, 82, 172
Hebrew Orphan Asylum, 119

*Heere Gracht*, 265n62
Hellenic American Neighborhood
Action Committee, 211
Hellenic immigrants, *see* Greeks
Hell's Kitchen, 98
Henry Henning Guards, 79
Henry Street Settlement, 95
Heroin traffic, 235, 256
*Herold* (newspaper), 152; see also
*Staats-Zeitung und Herold*
Higher education, *see* Colleges and
universities
Highland Guards, 48
High schools: late 19th-early 20th
centuries, 95, 98, 102, 131; 1930s,
180; 1945–70: 221–22; *see also* Spe-
cial high schools
Hillis, Newell Dwight, 150
Hillman, Sidney, 124, 187, 285n56
Hillquit, Morris, 126, 133, 151,
289n10
Hindu Temple, 236
Hirschbein, Peretz, 134
Hispanics, 227–29; in the Bronx, 155,
205; on City Council, 252; educa-
tion of, 222; Koch and, 243; Kore-
ans and, 235; occupations of, 200,
203, 311n157; Pakistanis and, 238;
in Ridgewood, 245; West Indians
and, 230; white poverty and, 244; in
Woodside, 248; *see also specific groups,*
*e.g., Puerto Ricans*
Hitler, Adolf, 189, 191, 193
Hoffmann, John T., 65
Hogs, 45
Holidays, 239
Holland (kingdom), *see* Netherlands
Holland (province), 3
Holocaust, 172, 192–93, 208
Holy Agony Church, 169
Holy Trinity Church (Catholic), 78
Holy Trinity Church (Orthodox), 107
Homelessness, 44, 177–78
Homosexuals, 248, 256
Hondurans, 229

Hong Kong, 231, 306n42
"Hoovervilles," 177
Hospitals: Catholic, 101–2; German,
150; Jewish, 121; private, 219; pub-
lic, 167, 194
Hospital Workers Union 1199: 219
Hostos Community College, 251,
311n162
Household workers, *see* Domestic
workers
Housing: late 19th-early 20th
centuries, 138, 139; 1920s, 153, 156,
157, 160; 1930s, 178; World War II
era, 194, 195; 1945- 70, 197, 204;
1970–94: 256; *see also* Boarders;
Landlords; Lodgers; Public housing
projects; Rents; Tenement houses
Howard Beach, 257
Howe, Irving, 115–16, 124, 162–
63, 165
*How the Other Half Lives* (Riis), 139
Hudson, Henry, 2
Hudson River, 1, 2, 11, 56
Hudson Valley, 17
Hughes, John, 66–70, 101; German
Catholics and, 77, 78; on poor Irish,
60; on slavery, 72
Hughes, Mary Angela, 101
Hugo Funk Silk Mill, 87
Huguenots, 23–26, 28, 32; descen-
dants of, 37; in East Ward, 22; New
Englanders and, 19–20
Hungarians: Jewish, 114, 116, 285n71;
La Guardia and, 183; neighborhoods
of, 105, 116; scrap-metal drive
and, 193
Hunter, Robert, 29
Hunter College, 164, 189, 213,
286n80
Hunter College High School, 221
Hutchinson, Anne, 7
Hylan, John, 153, 161, 168

I. B. Kleinert Rubber Company, 87
Illegal aliens, 226, 304–305n1; Central

■

American, 228; Chinese, 233; Irish, 242; Israeli, 240; Senegalese, 241; West Indian, 230
Illegal drug traffic, 227–28, 235, 256
Illiteracy, 283*n*7
*Illustrierte Welt* (periodical), 83
*Illustrierte Zeitung*, 83
Immigration Commission (Dillingham Commission), 104, 105, 119, 138, 141
Impellitteri, Vincent, 201–2
Independent League, 127
Independent Order B'rith Abraham, 121
Independent Yiddish Artists Company, 134
India Day Parade, 236
Indians, *see* Asian Indians; Native Americans
Indo-American Association, 171
Indochinese, 237–38
Indonesians, 171
Industrial accidents, 60
Industrial Commission (U.S.), 140
Industrialization: constraints upon, 94; European, 39, 102; garment industry and, 123; Irish immigration and, 70; politics and, 64; trade union movement and, 87; *see also* Manufacturing industries
Infectious diseases, *see* Communicable diseases
Infrastructure, *see* Public works
Inquisition, 9
Integration, *see* Segregation
Intellectuals, 185; German, 75; Italian, 51; Jewish, 116, 133, 134, 177, 187; *see also* Professionals
Interborough Rapid Transit, 155, 160, 186
Intermarriages, *see* Marriages
International Ladies' Garment Workers' Union, 124, 185, 285*n*56; American Labor Party and, 187; Chinese and, 233; Italians and, 143

International Longshoremen's Union, 187
International Workingmen's Association, 87
Intervale Jewish Center, 245
Intolerance, *see* Tolerance
Intravenous drug users, 256
Inwood, 155
Iranians, 238
Ireland, 49, 100, 186, 205
Irish Americans, 260
—late 19th-early 20th centuries, 97–101; blacks and, 110, 112; corruption and, 166; Italians and, 136, 143, 157, 287*n*107; Jews and, 116, 117; politics and, 143, 161; prosperity of, 160
—World War I era, 151–52
—1920s, 164, 167, 173
—1930s, 164, 186, 189, 191
—1945–70: 200–201, 205, 206, 218, 219
—1970–94: 243, 244, 247–48, 252
Irish Arts Center, 248
Irish Catholic Benevolent Union, 98
Irish Catholics, 260; economic status of, 59–60, 98–99; Orangemen vs., 49–50; politics and, 65, 274*n*19; Redemptionist missions and, 78; self-identity of, 67; on Upper West Side, 157
*Irish Echo* (newspaper), 242
Irish Emigrant Society, 41, 52
Irish immigrants:
—18th century, 33, 34, 35
—19th century, 41–42, 59–74, 91, 140; blacks and, 53, 55, 58, 62, 272*n*104; Chinese and, 52; Germans and, 75, 85–86, 88–89; health of, 45; neighborhoods of, 47, 271*n*69; "new" immigrants and, 96, 102, 135, 137; occupations of, 270–271*n*66, 273*n*5; religious conflicts among, 49–50; sex ratio among, 273*n*4

—1920s, 154, 155, 173
—1945–70: 211
—1970–94: 230, 242, 247, 248, 309*n*113
Irish Protestants, 49–50, 65
Irish Repertory Theater, 248
Irish Republican Army, 205, 248
Irish 69th Regiment, 72, 73, 151–52
Irish women, 135, 273*n*4; in child-care, 242; Chinese men and, 52; in domestic work, 60–61, 75, 98; education of, 98; employment of, 161; labor movement and, 99; in nursing, 161, 188; in school teaching, 160
*Irish World* (newspaper), 100, 151
Irving Trust Company, 244
Isaacs, Stanley, 195
Islamic revolution (1979), 238
Israel, 238, 249
Israeli Jews, 240, 249
Italian Americans, 261
—late 19th-early 20th centuries, 157–58, 165–67, 287*n*107
—1920s: Americanization of, 171; baseball and, 163; boxing and, 163–64; crime and, 166–67; culture of, 173; in East Harlem, 154; politics and, 161, 162
—1930s: blacks and, 190; education of, 180; municipal employment of, 189; politics and, 183, 184, 187
—World War II era, 193
—1945–70: in construction industry, 218; declining numbers of, 206; education of, 199–200; municipal employment of, 202–3; in outer boroughs, 204–5, 205; politics and, 201–2
—1970–94: achievements of, 244; blacks and, 256; Dominicans and, 227; education of, 310*n*154; ethnicity of, 249–50; Koreans and, 235; politics and, 243, 252
Italian fascism, 176, 189, 190, 193, 297*n*74

Italian government, 143
Italian Harlem: late 19th-early 20th centuries, 137, 138, 139; 1920s, 154, 157, 173; 1930s, 157, 165, 178, 180; World War II era, 193; 1970–94: 231, 245; *see also* Little Italies
Italian immigrants: 19th century, 50–52; early 20th century, 120, 135–48, 284*n*39; 1945–70: 209–10
Italian School, 51
Italian Socialist Federation, 144
IV drug users, 256
Ives-Quinn Law (1945), 198, 217

Jack, Hulan, 215
Jackson Heights, 154, 240
Jacksonian democracy, 64
*Jägercompagnie*, 79
Jamaicans, 229
James II, King of England, 18, 20, 21, 27, 49
Japan, 191, 196
Japanese, 170, 192, 237
Jennings, Elizabeth, 56
Jesuit priests, 21
Jewish Big Brothers and Sisters (organization), 119
*Jewish Communal Register*, 115
*Jewish Daily Forward*, see *Forverts* (newspaper)
Jewish holidays, 239
Jewish Holocaust, 172, 192–93, 208
*Jewish King Lear* (Gordin), 134
Jewish language, *see* Yiddish language
Jewish Maternity Hospital, 121
Jewish National Workers' Alliance, 121
Jewish Prisoners Aid Society, 119
Jewish Theological Seminary, 129
Jewish women, 116, 172; education of, 130, 131, 133, 164–65, 189, 283*n*7; in garment industry, 123, 124–25; at Hunter College, 286*n*80; in teaching profession, 160, 164, 188–89; in Triangle

■

Shirtwaist fire, 96, 125 Jews, 261
—colonial era, 8–11, 22, 26–28, 32,
267*n*104
—antebellum era, 80–82, 277*n*83
—late 19th-early 20th centuries,
114–35, 136; in garment industry,
94–95, 115, 122–25, 140, 142; in
Harlem, 137, 158; at Hunter College, 286*n*80; industrial skills of,
115–16, 283*n*4-5; Italians and, 140,
144, 145, 148
—World War I era, 151
—1920s, 156–57, 172; baseball and,
162–63; boxing and, 163–64; crime
and, 166, 167; in East Bronx,
171–73; in East Harlem, 154; occupations of, 164, 165; politics and,
161–62; prosperity of, 162–63
—1930s, 172; Communist Party and,
186–87; education of, 180; German,
177; municipal employment of, 189;
politics and, 183, 184; relief for,
181, 182
—World War II era, 192–93
—1945–70: declining numbers of,
206; Hasidic, 208–9; minority workers and, 219; municipal employment
of, 202–3; occupations of, 199;
in outer boroughs, 204–5; politics
and, 201
—1970–94: 249; blacks and, 257;
Dinkins and, 252; German, 243–44;
Iranian, 238; Israeli, 240; Soviet,
241–42
—*see also* Anti-Semitism; *specific sects
(e.g., Orthodox Jews) and ethnic groups
(e.g., Russian Jews)*
Jitney buses, 230
Jogues, Isaac, 5–6, 31
John Paul II, Pope, 247
Johnson, Alvin, 177
Johnson, Edward, 168
Johnson, James Weldon, 159
Johnson, J. Rosamund, 111–12
Johnson, Lyndon, 202, 224

Jolson, Al, 162
Jones, J. Raymond, 167, 215
Jones' Wood, 84
Joselit, Jenna, 172
Joseph, Jacob, 128–29
Judeo-Spanish language, 117

Kalm, Peter, 22, 27
Kapoor brothers, 237
*Katholische Kirchenzeitung*, 79
*Katholische Volksblatt*, 79
Kazin, Alfred, 178–79
Kehillah, 120
Kellor, Frances, 96
Kelly, "Honest John," 89, 90
Kelly, Raymond, 243
Kessner, Thomas, 140, 175, 283*n*5,
287*n*102
K'hal Adath Jeshurun (synagogue), 177
Kieft, Willem, 12
Kieft's War, 12
King James Bible, 68, 71
Kings County, *see* Brooklyn
Kishinev pogrom (1905), 126
Kissinger, Henry, 177
*Kleindeutschland*, 47; borders of, 76,
276*n*67; decline of, 97, 152; enter-
tainment in, 84; Jews in, 82, 116;
occupations in, 85; particularism in,
77, 91; producer cooperatives in, 86;
Republican rallies in, 89
Kleinert Rubber Company, 87
Knights of Labor (union), 140
Know Nothing Party, 72, 275*n*49,
275*n*51
Kobasniuk Travel Inc., 247
Kobrin, Leon, 134
Koch, Ed, 243, 248, 252, 257
Koreans, 171, 226, 232, 235–36
Kornbluth, S., 286*n*91
Kress and Company, 191–92
Krupp, Alfred, 88
Kuhn, Fritz, 189
Kunz Mill, 87
Kwong, Peter, 180, 232

■

Labor Day Carnival, 230
Labor movement: blacks and, 54; Chinese and, 233; civil rights movement and, 219; in construction industry, 218; *Forverts* and, 133; Germans and, 84, 85–86, 87, 88, 277–78*n*103; Great Depression and, 185–86; Irish and, 99; Italians and, 140–41, 143; Jews and, 123–25, 140, 143; Kehillah and, 120; municipal employees and, 203–4; in shipping industry, 208
Labor racketeering, 167
"Lace curtain Irish," 98, 154–55, 200
Ladino language, 117
Lager beer, 83
La Guardia, Fiorello, 183–84; Harlem riot and, 192; House seat of, 144; Irish electorate and, 200; mayoral campaigns of, 162, 187, 201; National Origins Act and, 152; race relations and, 195; TWU and, 186
La Guardia Airport, 184, 185
Lakeview Home for Jewish Unwed Mothers, 119
Landis, Kenesaw Mountain, 153
Landlords: antebellum era, 39, 42; late 19th–early 20th centuries, 102, 158–59, 160; 1930s, 178; 1945–70: 220; *see also* Real estate business
*Landsmannschaften*, 84, 91
*Landsmanshaftn*, 120–21, 124, 128
Languages, 5–6; *see also* Bilingual instruction; *specific languages*
Laotians, 238
Latin America, 102
Latinos, *see* Hispanics
Laundries, 170, 180, 186, 232
Laurelton, 221, 256
Law firms, 243
Law schools, 188
Lazzeri, Tony, 163
League of Nations, 190
Lebanon, 238
LeFrak, Samuel, 199

Legal Rights Association, 56
Lehrman Institute, 261
Leisler, Jacob, 20–21
Lemlich, Clara, 125
Lenox, Robert, 37
Lenox Avenue Subway Line, 158
Lenox Hill Hospital, 150
Leonard, Benny, 164
Levantine Jews, 116–17
Levy, Aaron Jefferson, 285*n*60
Lewis, Reginald, 253
Leyden (Netherlands), 3
Liberal Party, 187
Liberty Bonds, 150
Libraries, 131–32, 223–24
*Liederkranz* (organization), 97
Lief Erikson Day, 109
Lincoln, Abraham, 72, 126
Lincoln Center for the Performing Arts, 220
Lincoln Tunnel, 178
Lindsay, John V., 201, 204, 221, 224
Literacy, 283*n*7
Little Germany, see *Kleindeutschland*
Little Italies, 50, 136, 205; anti-fascism in, 193; Chinese in, 232, 245; middle classes in, 143; Petrosino murder and, 139; regionalism in, 138; unemployment in, 178; *see also* Italian Harlem
Little *Norge*, 109
Little Scandinavia, 232
Liverpool (England), 37
Local loyalties, 77, 79, 91, 138
Local organizations, *see* Organizations
Lodgers, 111, 139; *see also* Boarders
Loews Corporation, 199
London, Meyer, 127, 133
Long Island: Canarsie Indians on, 4; colonization of, 12; commutation from, 206; Germans on, 80; Poles on, 247; religious refugees on, 7; slaves on, 29; Treaty of Hartford and, 264*n*23
Longshoremen: 19th century, 55, 75,

140–41; early 20th century, 165;
1920s, 158, 167; 1945–70: 207–8
Louis, Joe, 190
Louis Philippe, King of the French, 34
Low, Seth, 101, 126
Lower East Side, 11; late 19th-early
20th centuries, 105, 116–35, 172,
286*n*92; 1920s, 156, 171; 1970–94:
232, 245; *see also* East Village; *Klein-
deutschland*
Lower West Side, 107
Lubavitch Hasidim, 208, 209
*Lucerna* (newspaper), 106
Lutherans, 6–7, 8, 10, 32, 79

McCarthy, Joseph, 202
McClellan, George, 153
McCloskey, John, 67, 146
*McClure's Magazine*, 119
McDonnell, James Francis, 200
McGill, William J., 244
McGuire, Robert J., 244
McInerney, Monica Maria, 102
McKee, Joseph V., 183
McKeon, Douglas E., 243
McLarnin, Jimmy ("Baby Face"), 164
McManus, Edgar, 265*n*59
McQuade, James A., 182–83
Macready, William, 62, 273*n*16
Madison Square Garden, 186, 189, 193
Mafia, 139
Magnes, Judah, 120
Magyars, *see* Hungarians
Malcolm X, 219
Mancuso, Gus ("Blackie"), 163
Manhattan: blacks in, 55, 109, 110;
Catholics in, 21, 78, 102, 276*n*74;
Chinese in, 52; draft riots in, 73;
ferry service to, 56; Germans in, 48,
78, 80, 97, 276*n*74; ghetto proposed
for, 11; Haitians in, 231; high
schools in, 131; Hudson exploration
of, 2; Irish in, 60, 99, 155; Italians in,
136; Jews in, 117, 157, 191; land
prices in, 17; Minuit purchase of, 4;

"new" immigrants in, 104; piano
manufacture in, 88; population of,
154; socialists in, 125; subway devel-
opment and, 153; Verrazano sighting
of, 1; Walloons in, 4–5; *see also* East
Side; West Side
Manhattan Bridge, 97
Manhattan College, 99
Manufacturers Hanover Trust Compa-
ny, 199
Manufacturing industries: 19th centu-
ry, 36, 94, 278*n*4; 1930s, 178;
1945–70: 207; 1970–94: 250,
253–54
Manumission, 15, 28, 30; *see also* Abo-
litionism
Maranos, 8
Marcantonio, Vito, 165–66, 187
Marian devotion, 78
Mariel Boat Lift (1980), 228
Maronite Catholics, 239
Marriages: colonial era, 16, 22, 25;
19th century, 77, 109, 276*n*70;
1930s, 181; 1970–94: 246, 249
*Il Martello* (newspaper), 144
Marx brothers, 162
Marxism, *see* Communism
Mary II, Queen of England, 20
Maryland, 14, 109
Matzos manufacture, 122
Mauk, David, 108
Maxwell, William H., 129
May, Cornelius Jacobsz, 3–4
May, Michael, 78
Mayer, Egon, 249
May Laws (Russia: 1882), 103
Mayors, 18, 302*n*91, 312*n*172
Medical facilities, *see* Hospitals
Medical professionals, 235, 236, 240,
307*n*68; *see also* Nurses; Physicians
Medical schools, 188
Megapolensis, Dominies Johannes, 6,
9, 10
Merchants: Dutch colonial era, 2;
British colonial era, 17, 18, 20, 21,

■

25; 19th century, 36, 37, 50, 51; *see also* Commerce; Retail trade
Merchant Tailors' Association, 87
Meredith, James, 223
Merzbacher, Leo, 82
Methodists, 49, 56, 236
Metropolitan Life Insurance Company, 195
Metropolitan Museum of Art, 51
Metropolitan Opera Company, 151, 217
Metropolitan Police, 62–63, 274*n*17
Mexicans, 228
Michaelius, Domine Jonas, 6
Middle classes, 206; black, 167, 223, 253, 254, 256; German, 96–97, 160, 162; Irish, 98, 154–55, 200; Italian, 143; Jewish, 162, 172; Puerto Rican, 250
Middle Easterners, 116–17, 238–40
*Mikvahs*, 172
Military service, *see* Compulsory military service
Miller, Douglas T., 70
Miller, Edwin, 199
*Minerva* (ship), 34
Ministers, *see* Clergy
Ministry Act (1693), 21
Minuit, Peter, 4
*Minyans*, 245
Missions, 43, 78, 146, 147
Mitchell, Arthur, 223
Mitchell, John Purroy, 101, 151, 161, 291*n*62
Mohawk Indians, 5
Moore, Deborah Dash, 156, 160, 172–73
Moore, Fred, 169
Moravian churches, 26
Morgan, J. P., 51
Morgan Guaranty Trust, 199
Moriarty, Annie, 99
Mortality, 40, 45, 55
Moses, Robert, 184–85, 195, 206, 220
Mosques, 239

Most Holy Redeemer Church, 77, 78–79
Mott Haven, 155
Movies, 95, 134, 162, 187–88
Moynihan, Daniel, 310*n*153
Mozart Hall, 89
Mugavero, Francis J., 248
Mulberry Bend, 138, 139, 157, 173
Municipal colleges, 180; *see also* City University of New York; Community colleges
Municipal employees: 19th century, 71, 90; early 20th century, 99, 111, 140, 160, 168; 1930s, 182, 184, 189, 192; 1945–70: 202–3, 215–16, 219, 302*n*91, 312*n*172; 1970–94: 250, 252–53, 311*n*157; *see also* Civil service
Municipal government, 14, 220, 267*n*100; *see also* Mayors; New York City Council; Tammany Hall
Municipal hospitals, 167, 194
Municipal Lodging House, 177
Municipal Police, 62–63, 274*n*17
Municipal politics, *see* Politics
Municipal services: antebellum era, 45–46; Progressive era, 95; 1930s, 182, 192; 1945–70: 208; 1970–94: 256, 261; *see also specific services, e.g., Fire fighters; Public schools; etc.*
Municipal unions, 203–4
Murder Inc., 166, 167
Murray family, 200
Music, 111–12, 217; German, 83, 84; Irish, 173; Italian, 140; *see also* Opera
Muslims, 238, 239
Mussolini, Benito, 183, 189, 190, 193, 297*n*74
Mutual aid societies, *see* Organizations

Nadel, Stanley, 77, 82, 85
Nannies, *see* Childcare
Napoléon I, Emperor of the French, 81
Narcotics traffic, 227–28, 235, 256
Nast, Thomas, 72

■

National Association for the Advancement of Colored People, 218
National Basketball Association, 217
National Committee for the Relief of Sufferers by Russian Massacres, 126
National Desertion Bureau, 119
National League, 207
National Origins Act (1924), 152, 170
National Urban League, 95, 160, 179, 181
National War Fund, 297*n*88
Nation of Islam, 218–19
Native American Democratic Association, 71
Native Americans: Dutch and, 4, 11–12, 15; Germans and, 75; Hudson and, 2; Jogues and, 5; slaves and, 29
Nativism, 50, 69–70, 71, 75, 89; *see also* Racism
Naturalization Act (1740), 26–27
Nazi Germany, *see* Germany
Neau, Elias, 29
Needle trade, *see* Garment industry
Negro Ensemble Company, 223
Neighborhood organizations, *see* Organizations
Netherlands: British relations with, 9, 13, 17, 18; colonial prosperity and, 12; Hudson and, 2; Huguenots and, 25; Jewish immigration to, 11; religious tolerance in, 6; slave trade and, 14
*Die Neue Zeit* (newspaper), 83, 277*n*101
New Amsterdam, 2–18, 23, 27, 28, 259–60; Jews in, 8–11, 114, 267*n*104; slavery in, 14–15, 265*n*59; Treaty of Hartford and, 264*n*23
New Amsterdam Council, 11
Newark, 184, 224
New Deal, 179–80, 185, 187, 190, 220
New England: migration from, 7, 19, 37; New Netherland trade with, 12, 13; Pilgrims in, 3; *see also* Dominion of New England

"New Immigration," 51, 96, 102, 104
"New Irish," 230, 242, 247, 248, 309*n*113
New Jersey, 84, 104, 206, 207, 227–28
New Netherland: British seizure of, 16; fur trade in, 2; Jews in, 10, 11; religious refugees in, 7–8; under Stuyvesant, 12–14, 17; Walloons in, 3, 4–5
New Orange, 18
New School for Social Research, 177
Newspapers, 106–7, 172, 226, 246; black, 230; eastern European, 174; French, 34; German, 79, 83, 87, 91, 97, 151, 246; Greek, 211; Irish, 98, 100, 151; Italian, 144, 145, 190, 193; Slavic, 247; Yiddish, 132–33, 188, 209
Newsstands, 237
*Newsweek*, 211
New York and Harlem Railroad, 42
New York Association for Improving the Condition of the Poor, 51–52, 95, 181–82
New York Bank for Savings, 61
New York Central *Verein*, 79
New York Cigarmakers Union, 87
New York City Ballet, 223
New York City Bias Investigation Unit, 238
New York City Board of Education, 131, 185, 222, 251, 253
New York City Board of Estimate, 161
New York City Board of Health, 45, 169
New York City Board of Higher Education, 223
New York City Chancellor of Education, 255
New York City Collective Bargaining Law (1967), 203
New York City College, *see* City College of New York

New York City Commission on Human Rights, 198, 218, 221

New York City Commission on the Year 2000: 221

New York City Common Council, 27, 68

New York City Council: antebellum era, 65; World War II era, 195; 1945–70: 198–99, 202; 1970–94: 229, 239, 252

New York City Council on Hygiene, 42, 43

New York City Department of City Planning, 226

New York City Department of Hospitals, 168

New York City Detective Bureau, 100

New York City Health Department, 45, 169

New York City Housing Authority, 303*n*120

New York City Kehillah, 120

New York City Magistrate's Court, 119

New York City Mayor's Slum Clearance Committee, 220

New York City Welfare Department, 182

*New Yorker Socialistischer Turnverein*, 84

*New Yorker Staats-Zeitung*, 96, 97, 106; circulation of, 152, 289*n*15; German Democrats and, 89, 90; influence of, 83; on World War I, 150; see also *Staats-Zeitung und Herold*

*New York Evening Post*, 131–32

New York Foundling Hospital, 44

New York *Gazette*, 34

New York Giants (baseball team), 153, 217, 218

New York Know Nothing Party, 71

*New York Magazine*, 247

New York Manumission Society, 30, 53, 56–57

New York Omnibus Company, 194

*New York Panorama* (WPA), 174

New York Public School Society, 57, 67–68

New York 69th Regiment, 72, 73, 151–52

New York Society for the Information and Assistance of Persons Emigrating from Foreign Countries, 35

New York State Board of Commissioners of Emigration, 41

New York State Bureau of Labor Statistics, 123

New York State Census, 47, 138

New York State Commission Against Discrimination, 198, 218

New York State Constitutional Convention (1821), 64

New York State Council of Revision, 35

New York State Legislature: Assemblymen of, 65, 168, 169, 229, 285*n*60; black members of, 252; Board of Commissioners of Emigration and, 41; civil rights and, 58; collective bargaining and, 203; German Society and, 35; Metropolitan Police and, 63; schools and, 68, 95, 110; slavery and, 29, 30; welfare reforms of, 96

New York State "Peoples University," 131

New York Stock Exchange, 94, 244

New York Telephone Company, 194

*New York Times*: on anti-fascism, 193; on blacks, 110; on Chinese, 52; on Dominicans, 228; German Democrats and, 90; on Irish, 244, 260; on Italians, 137–38; on Jews, 245

New York University, 51, 164, 199, 244

*New York Utiset*, 174

New York Yankees (baseball team), 153, 163, 217, 228

*New Yorske* (newspaper), 106

Nicaragua, 228

■

Nicolls, Richard, 16, 17
Nielsen, Emil, 108–9
*Nieu Nederlandt* (ship), 3
Nigerians, 240
Ninfo, Salvaroe, 143
Ninoy Aquino Movement, 236
Nixon, Richard, 224
*Nordisk Tidende* (*Norway Times*), 106, 108–9, 174, 246
*North American Review*, 119
Northern Aid Committee, 248
Northern European immigrants, 38, 50, 102
Northern Ireland, 205, 248
Norwegian-American Seamen's Association, 109
Norwegians: 19th century, 108–9; 1920s, 174; 1980s, 232; 1990s, 246, 247, 260
*Novoye Russkoye Slovo* (newspaper), 247
*Nowy Swiat* (newspaper), 106, 310*n*144
Nun of Kenmare, 60–61
Nuns, *see* Roman Catholic nuns
Nurses: black, 168, 192, 194; Irish, 161, 188; West Indian, 230

*Obrana* (newspaper), 107
Occupations, 106, 200, 206–8; black, 54, 110–11, 167, 179, 282*n*96, 312*n*169; Chinese, 52; Dominican, 211–12; Dutch, 13; Eastern European Jewish, 115–16, 283*n*4, 283*n*5; German, 74, 85, 161; German Jewish, 81; Haitian, 231; Irish, 97–98, 99, 161, 270–271*n*66, 273*n*5; Israeli, 240; Italian, 51, 140, 142, 143, 209–10; Jewish, 26, 27, 81, 199; Syrian, 107; *see also* Businesses; Municipal employees; Professionals; Skilled labor; Unemployment; Wages; White collar workers
Ocean Hill, 222
O'Connor, Charles, 72

O'Connor, John J., 248
O'Dwyer, Paul, 244
O'Dwyer, William, 155, 198, 201
Office workers, *see* White collar workers
Old Brewery, 44–45
"Old Immigration," 38, 96, 135, 162, 260
Olechowski, Christopher, 247
Oliva, L. Jay, 244
Omnibuses, 42
Opdyke, George, 36, 89
Open admissions policy, 200, 223, 251, 255
Opera, 51, 134, 151, 217
"Operation Bootstrap," 212
Orange, House of, 18
Orangemen, 49–50, 65
Order of United American Mechanics, 50
O'Reilly, Leonora, 99
Organizations, 41, 52; German, 84, 97; Irish, 98; Italian, 145; Jewish, 82, 115, 118–19, 120–21, 242; Puerto Rican, 213
Organized labor, *see* Labor movement
"Orient Express" (subway line), 232
Orsi, Robert, 139, 173, 178
Orthodox churches, *see* Antiochian Orthodox Church; Greek Orthodox Church
Orthodox Jews: 19th century, 81; early 20th century, 120, 127, 129, 172, 285*n*69; 1930s, 177; 1970–94: 249; *see also* Hasidic Jews
Osofsky, Gilbert, 160
Ostvang, Tjoralv, 246
Ottendorfer, Oswald, 83, 89–90, 96–97
Ottoman Empire, 105, 117; *see also* Turkey
Our Lady of Mount Carmel Church, 173, 231
Our Lady of Pompei Parish, 147
Ovington, Mary, 95, 111

■

Packet service, *see* Shipping
*Padroni*, 137, 140
Pakistanis, 237, 238
Pale of Settlement (Russia), 103, 115, 116, 118, 120
Palmer Raids (1919), 151
Palmieri, Peter C., 244
Palmo, Ferdinand, 51
Pan Aryan Association, 171
Panics, *see* Depressions
Parkchester housing project, 195
Parking rules, 239
Park Slope, 156
Parochial schools: antebellum era, 69, 95; late 19th-early 20th centuries, 98, 102, 147; 1920s, 173; 1945–70: 222; 1980s, 248
Particularism, 77, 79, 91, 138
Passover matzos, 122
Patrolman's Benevolent Association, 216
Patti, Alavatore, 51
Payton, Philip, Jr., 158
Pearl button manufacture, 106
Pearl Harbor, 193
Peasants, 39, 48, 102
Pecse, Francesco, 209
Peddlers, 121–22, 140, 228, 241
Peiret, Pierre, 24, 25
Pennsylvania Station, 167
People's Republic of China, 231
"Peoples University," 131
People's Washing and Bath Establishment, 43
Pernicone, Carole, 60, 270*n*61
Perry, Nick, 229
Perry family, 37
Peru, 65–66
Petrosino, Joseph, 139
Phelan, John J., Jr., 244
Philadelphia, 36, 56, 71, 268*n*11
Philanthropies, 173, 181–82, 243–44, 249
Philipsburg Manor, 13
Philipse, Frederick, 13, 266*n*81

Physicians, 121, 154, 167, 168, 192
Piece work, 123
Pilgrims, 3
Pinski, David, 134
Pittsburgh, 94
*Plattdeutsche Post*, 91
*Plattdeutscher Volksfest* (1875), 85
Plunkitt, George Washington, 100
Plymouth Congregational Church, 150
Poetry Society of America, 150
Pogroms, 103, 118, 126
Police force: antebellum era, 46, 62–63, 274*n*17; early 20th century, 99–100, 111, 112–13, 139, 140; 1920s, 166; 1930s, 168, 184, 191; World War II era, 194–95; 1945–70: 216, 224; 1970–94: 228, 235, 241, 243, 244, 252; *see also* Civilian review board proposal; New York City Bias Investigation Unit; New York City Detective Bureau
Polish Americans, 167, 191, 192, 200, 247
Polish Catholics, 50, 105–6, 146
Polish Democratic Club, 50
Polish immigrants, 50, 105–6, 242
Polish Jews, 8
Polish National Home, 105
Polish occupation (1939), 191
Political corruption, *see* Corruption
Politics, 200–202, 243; blacks and, 167–69, 184, 214–15, 251- 52; Germans and, 75–76, 88–89; Huguenots and, 25; Irish and, 63–66, 99–101, 125, 143, 161; Italians and, 144; Jews and, 26, 125–27, 132; Puerto Ricans and, 214, 251; West Indians and, 229; *see also* Elections; Government agencies
Polo Grounds, 217
Pope, Generoso, 190, 193
Poppenhusen, Conrad, 85–86, 88
Poppenhusen Institute, 88
Port Authority, 253

■

Porters, 167
Portugal, 9, 12
Portuguese Jews, 8, 80, 114
Post offices, 111
Potato blight, 39
Potofsky, Jacob, 124
Poverty, 43, 45; black, 181, 224, 244, 255–56, 262; Bohemian, 106; Chinese, 234; Dominican, 227; German, 74; Haitian, 211; Irish, 59–60, 61, 98; Italian, 135, 141; Puerto Rican, 251, 256, 262; white, 244; *see also* Homelessness
Powell, Adam Clayton, Jr., 184, 190, 195, 214, 218
Powell, Adam Clayton, Sr., 110, 181
Pownall, Thomas, 22
Presbyterians, 22, 48, 236
Press, *see* Newspapers
Priests, *see* Roman Catholic clergy
Principals, 311*n*157
Private businesses, *see* Businesses
Private hospitals, 219
Private philanthropies, 173, 181–82, 243–44, 249
Private schools, *see* Schools
Privies, 46
Producer cooperatives, 86, 87
Produce stores, 226, 235–36, 238, 284*n*39
Professionals, 94; Asian Indian, 237; black, 54, 111, 112; Chinese, 232, 233, 234; Italian, 145; Jewish, 131, 164, 177, 188, 199; *see also* Intellectuals; Medical professionals
Progress (organization), 97
Progressive movement, 95, 98
Progressive Party, 126
*Il Progresso* (newspaper), 145, 190, 193
Prohibition, 63, 166, 167
*Il Proletario* (newspaper), 144
*Promineti*, 145
Property taxes, 90
Prostitution, 61, 99–100, 108, 110, 119

Protestant Episcopal Church, *see* Episcopalian churches
Protestant missions, 43, 146, 147
Protestant religion: British immigrants and, 48; Catholic children and, 44, 67–68; J. Hughes on, 70; Leislerite defense of, 20; Redemptionist missions and, 78
Protestants, 98, 199, 243; Dutch, 2, 3–5, 24; English, 24, 67; European, 11, 260; French (*see* Huguenots; Waldensians); German, 77, 79–80, 97; Irish, 49–50, 65; Korean, 236; *see also specific denominations*
Prussia, 88, 91
Prussian immigrants, 79, 85
Public bath houses, 43; see also *Mikvahs*
Public colleges, *see* Municipal colleges
Public employees, *see* Government employees; Municipal employees
Public hospitals, 167, 194
Public housing projects, 185, 220–21, 224
Public life, *see* Politics
Public schools:
—antebellum era, 57, 68–69
—late 19th-early 20th centuries, 95–96, 104, 133, 286*n*81; blacks and, 110; Italians and, 142; Jews and, 128, 129–31
—1930s, 185, 296*n*52
—1945–70: 222–23
—1970–94: blacks and, 253, 256, 257; Catholic Church and, 248; fiscal crisis and, 254–55; Hispanics and, 311*n*160; Puerto Ricans and, 250–51
—*see also* High schools; New York City Board of Education; Principals; Teachers
Public School Society, 57, 68
Public transportation, *see* Transit systems
Public welfare, 96, 179, 182, 251, 256

■

Public works, 136–37; 1920s, 153; 1930s, 178, 179–80, 184- 85; 1945–70: 218
Puerto Rican Day Parade, 230
Puerto Rican Family Institute, 213
Puerto Rican Forum, 213
Puerto Rican Legal Defense and Education Fund, 213
Puerto Ricans: early 20th century, 169; 1920s, 167; 1930s, 176; 1945–70: 198, 212–14, 220, 223, 227; 1970–94: 250–51, 253, 256, 262, 311*n*161
Puerto Rico Migration Division, 212–13
Pulaski Day, 106, 191, 297*n*88
Pulitzer, Joseph, 132
Pullman porters, 167
Puritans, 37
Pushcart operators, 122

Quakers, 7–8, 10, 27, 32
Quarantines, 40
Queens (borough), 7, 153, 154, 204, 221; blacks, 229, 253, 256; Chinese, 232, 235; Colombians, 240; Dominicans, 227; Filipinos, 236; Germans, 47, 87–88, 152, 245; Greeks, 210, 247; Haitians, 231; Irish, 155, 205, 211, 242, 247–48; Israelis, 240; Italians, 209; Koreans, 235; Mexicans, 228; Pakistanis, 238
Queens College, 200
Queens-Midtown Tunnel, 178
Quill, Mike, 186, 187, 203–4
Quinn, John, 98

Rabbis, 128, 129; Eastern European, 115, 285*n*71; Hasidic, 209; Orthodox, 285*n*69
Racism, 262
—antebellum era, 53–54, 55–56, 58, 62
—late 19th century, 107–8, 109–13
—World War II era, 195–96, 212

—1945–70: 198, 214, 224; in baseball, 217; in business, 218; in housing, 221; in municipal hiring, 302*n*91, 312*n*172
—1970–1994: 226, 230–31, 238, 250, 261
—*see also* Anti-Semitism; Nativism; Segregation
Radicalism, 76, 115, 116, 144; *see also* Anarchism; Communism; Forty-Eighter republicans
Radio, 173, 187
*Radost* (newspaper), 107
Raffeiner, Johann Stephen, 78
"Rag Pickers' Paradise," 74
Railway porters, 167
Railways, 103, 109; *see also* Street railways; Subway system
*A Raisin in the Sun* (Hansbury), 223
Ramadan, 239
Ramirez, Manny, 228
Ramirez, Roberto, 311*n*165
Rampler, Gabriel, 79
Rattle Watch, 11
Rau, Jes, 245
Reagan administration, 221
Real estate business, 143, 162, 199; *see also* Landlords; Rents
Recife (Brazil), 8–9, 10, 12
Reconstruction Era, 57
Red Caps (porters), 167
Redemptionist missions, 78
Red Hook, 209
Reformed Dutch Church, *see* Dutch Reformed Church
Reformed Presbyterian Church, 48
Reform Jews: 19th century, 81, 82; 20th century, 127, 128, 129, 172, 208
Regional loyalties, 77, 79, 91, 138
Relief funds, 96, 179, 182, 251, 256
Religious denominations: colonial era, 5–6, 19, 23, 31; antebellum era, 56; Civil War era, 80; early 20th century, 110; 1930s, 181; 1945–70: 218

■

Religious festivals, 147, 173
Religious holidays, 239
Religious philanthropies, 173, 181–82, 243–44, 249
Religious schools: Catholic (*see* Parochial schools); Jewish, 27- 28, 128, 172, 177, 285*n*69; Muslim, 239
Religious tolerance: in Netherlands, 6; in New Netherland, 3, 11; in New York, 27, 32, 38–39
Rensselaer family, 13–14
Rents: antebellum era, 43, 46, 90; early 20th century, 110, 111, 160; 1930s, 178, 179; World War II era, 194; 1945–70: 206
Republican Party: blacks and, 57, 113, 167–68; Corresca and, 144; Germans and, 76, 83, 88, 89; Hillquit and, 127; Jews and, 126
Restaurants, 161; Afghan, 239; Asian Indian, 236; Chinese, 180, 233; Filipino, 236; *see also* Catering; Coffeehouses
Retail trade, 194; *see also* Department stores; Merchants; Peddlers
Return migration, 116, 136, 144, 302*n*84
Revolutionary republicans, *see* Forty-Eighter republicans
Revolutionary War, *see* American Revolution
Revolutions of 1848, *see* European revolutions (1848)
Richmond, Julia, 130
Rickey, Branch, 217
Ridder, Victor, 189
Ridgewood, 245
Riis, Jacob, 139
Riots: 1837: 62; 1844: 71; 1849: 62, 273*n*16; 1863: 55, 72–73, 276*n*60; 1871: 49–50, 65; 1900: 112–13; 1905: 113; 1935: 190- 91; 1943: 194–95; 1964: 224; 1991: 257; 1992: 228; *see also* Slave rebellions
Rischin, Moses, 116, 127, 284*n*40

Riverside, 156
Rivington Street, 162
Roberts, Lillian, 203, 219
Robeson, Paul, 217
Robinson, Jackie, 217
Rodeph Shalom (synagogue), 82
Roman Catholic Church: colonial era, 20–21, 24, 32; 19th century, 44, 66–71, 101–2, 145–47, 274*n*36; 20th century, 147–48, 202; World War I era, 151; 1920s, 173; 1930s, 188, 191; 1945–70: 213; 1970–94: 231, 236, 240, 248
Roman Catholic clergy, 73; German, 76, 78; Irish, 145–46, 173; Italian, 145, 146, 147, 173; Jesuit, 21
Roman Catholic Germans, *see* German Catholics
Roman Catholic Irish, *see* Irish Catholics
Roman Catholic nuns, 44, 101–2; Bavarian, 78; Irish, 60, 147; Italian, 173
Roman Catholic Poles, 50, 105–6, 146
Roman Catholic schools, *see* Parochial schools
Romanian immigrants, 245
Romanian Jews, 114, 116
Roosevelt, Franklin, 182, 187, 190, 193
Roosevelt, Theodore, 126
Rosenberg, Charles, 45
Rosenfeld, Morris, 133
Ross, Barney, 164
Rothschild, House of, 37
Rothstein, Arnold, 166
Rou, Louis, 25
Royal Society (London), 23
"Runners," 40–41
Ruppert, Jacob, 85, 153
Russia, 151; *see also* Pale of Settlement (Russia); Soviet Union
Russian Jews, 114–15, 116, 241; in Amsterdam, 8; in garment industry, 123; intellectual life of, 133; persecu-

■

tion of, 103; politics and, 126; *see
also* Soviet Jews
Russian Revolution (1905), 124,
287*n*94
Russian Revolution (1917), 174
*Russkoe Slovo* (newspaper), 106
Russwurm, John, 57
Ruth, Babe, 153
Ryan, Joseph P., 187
Ryan, Thomas Fortune, 98

Sabbath observance, 127; *see also* Sun-
day observance
Sailors, 108–9, 171
St. Andrew's Society, 41, 52
*St. Charles* (ship), 9, 11
St. David's Day, 49
St. David's Society, 49
St. Demetrios Greek Orthodox
Church, 211
St. Francis of the Fields Church, 78
St. Francis Xavier College, 99
St. George's Church, 23
St. George's Society, 41, 49, 52
St. George's Ukrainian Catholic
Church, 247
St. George the Martyr Church, 49
St. John Nam Church, 236
St. Johns College, 98–99
St. Joseph *Verein*, 79
St. Nicholas's Church, 78
St. Patrick's Cathedral, 63, 67, 274*n*35
St. Patrick's Club, 98
St. Patrick's Day Parade, 230, 248
St. Patrick's School, 102
St. Paul's Church, 23
St. Philip's Protestant Episcopal
Church, 56, 181
Saints' festivals, 147, 173
St. Stanislaus's Church, 50, 105
St. Vincent's Hospital, 101
Saloons, *see* Drinking establishments
Salvador, 228
Sambuca (Italy), 138
Samuel Kunz Mill, 87

San Antonio River, *see* Hudson River
Sanitation, *see* Sewer system; Street
cleaning
Sanitation workers, 140, 166, 203, 216
San Juan Hill, 110, 113, 158
Santo Dominicans, *see* Dominicans
Saratoga Springs, 99
Sardi, Vincent, 173
Sardi's Restaurant, 173
Satmar Hasidim, 208, 209
Scandinavians, 6–7, 108–9, 247
Schaefer, Ferdinand Maximilian, 84, 85
Schleswig-Holstein, 6
Schneider, Dorothee, 75
Schneiderman, Rose, 96, 125
Schomburg Library, 223–24
Schools, 67–68, 164–65; black, 29,
56–57; Jewish, 27–28, 128, 172, 177,
285*n*69; Muslim, 239; *see also* Col-
leges and universities; Parochial
schools; Principals; Public schools;
Teachers
Schorenstein, Hyman, 161
Schrafft's restaurants, 161
*Schützenvereine*, 84
Schuyler, George, 167
Schuyler family, 13
*Schwabbisches Wochenblatt*, 91
Scottish Guard, 48
*Scottish Patriot* (newspaper), 48
Seabury, Samuel, 182
Seamen, 108–9, 171
Sedition Act (1918), 151
Segal, Joshua, 285*n*71
Segregation: in education, 110, 222,
256; in housing, 221, 256, 303*n*120
Self-employed, *see* Businesses
Seltzer, 284*n*40
Selyns, Hendricus, 21
Senegalese, 241
Sephardic Jews, 8, 114, 261
Sephardic rite, 27, 81
Servants, *see* Domestic workers
Servo-Croatian immigrants, 105, 106,
107

■

Settlement houses, 95, 144–45, 147

Seventeenth Ward, 47, 63

Seward, William Henry, 68, 71

Sewer system, 45, 46

Shakespeare, William, 130

Shanker, Albert, 222

Shannon, William, 61

Sharkey-Brown-Isaacs Act, 221

Shaw, Samuel, 31

Shearith Israel (synagogue), 27–28, 81

Sheriffs, 18

Shipping: 19th century, 36, 39–40, 140; early 20th century, 93- 94, 103–4; 1920s, 174; World War II era, 193–94; 1945–70: 208; *see also* Longshoremen; Sailors

Shoeblacks, 51, 106

Shoemakers, 85

*Shokets*, 28

*Shtetl* dwellers, 115, 116, 120, 283*n*7

Siano, Andrew, 307*n*58

*Siberia* (Adler and Gordin), 134

Sicilians, 138, 139, 144

Sikh Day Parade, 236

Sikhs, 236

Silverberg, Dadja, 128

Simkhovitch, Mary Kingsbury, 147

Simpson-Rodino Act (1986), 305*n*1

Singh, Parmjit, 237

Sisters of Charity, 44, 101, 102

Sisters of St. Dominic, 78

Sixth Ward: boarders in, 46, 270*n*61; elections in, 63; ethnic distribution in, 47; exodus from, 99; family units in, 60; mortality in, 45; occupations in, 270–271*n*66, 273*n*5; overcrowding in, 44; saloons in, 61; school board of, 69

Skilled labor, 51, 74, 85, 161, 209; *see also* Artisans; White collar workers

"Slave markets" (Bronx), 179

Slave rebellions, 29–30, 34, 53, 267*n*119

Slavery: colonial era, 14–15, 28–31, 265*n*59; antebellum era, 53, 54;

Civil War era, 72; *see also* Abolitionism; African Americans; Manumission

Slum clearance, 220

Smith, Alfred E., 153–54, 161

Smith, William, 29

Soccer, 244–45

Social Democratic Party, 115

Socialism, 90; *Forverts* and, 132, 133; Italians and, 144; Jews and, 125, 128; Kehillah and, 120; *New Yorker Socialistischer Turnverein* and, 84; trade union movement and, 87, 88, 123, 124; World War I and, 151; *see also* Communism

Socialist Party, 126, 127, 144

*Social Justice* (periodical), 190

Social organizations, *see* Organizations

Social Party, 87

*Social Register*, 97

Social welfare, *see* Philanthropies; Public welfare

Social work, 203; *see also* Settlement houses

Society for the Propagation of the Gospel in Foreign Parts, 25, 29

Society for the Protection of Italian Immigrants, 145

Society of Friends (Quakers), 7–8, 10, 27, 32

Soda water, 122, 284*n*40

Sons of Italy (organization), 145, 190

Sorge, Frederick, 87

Sorin, Gerald, 283*n*4

South Africans, 240

South Bronx, 212, 214, 220, 245

South Brooklyn, 171

Southeast Asians, 231, 237

Southern European immigrants, 96, 102, 108, 116, 174

Southern Italy, 250

Southern states, 72, 109, 176, 214, 302*n*84

South Koreans, 236

■

Sovern, Michael, 244
Soviet immigrants, 174, 247
Soviet Jews, 241–42, 249, 309n110;
    see also Russian Jews
Soviet Union, 191, 239, 242; see also
    Russia
Spain, 1–2, 6, 169
Spanish-American War, 169
Spanish Civil War, 191
Spanish Jews, 8, 80, 114
Spanish language, 213, 214
Spanish-Portuguese Synagogue
    (Shearith Israel), 27–28, 81
Spanish-speaking immigrants, see
    Hispanics
Spanknobel, Heinz, 189
Spann, Edward K., 42
"Spartan Band," 65
Special high schools, 221–22, 234,
    254, 255
Spellman, Francis, 181, 202, 248
*La Spia* (Arditi), 51
Sports, 173, 217–18; see also specific
    sports
*The Spy* (Cooper), 51
*Staats-Zeitung und Herold*, 189, 245,
    246; see also *New Yorker Staats-
    Zeitung*
Stadttheater, 84
Stansell, Christine, 61
State . . . , see New York State . . .
Staten Island: colonial era, 5, 12, 24,
    25–26; antebellum era, 40, 41;
    1945–70: 201, 204, 205, 209;
    1970–94: 232
Statue of Liberty, 104
Steamships, 36, 40, 56, 103–4
Steiner, Edward, 103
Steingut, Irwin, 161
Steinmeyer, Ferdinand, 32
Steinway, Henry Englehard, 85
Steinway, William, 88, 90,
    277–278n103
Stern, Leonard, 244
Stevedores, see Longshoremen

Stewart, Alexander T., 37
*Stimme des Volkes* (newspaper),
    277n101
Stock brokers, see Financial industry
Stott, Richard B., 38, 39, 64, 269n25
Stouffer's restaurants, 161
Straus, Oscar, 126
"Street arabs," 44
Street cleaning, 239
Street gangs, 61–63, 133, 191, 234–35
Street railways, 42, 55–56, 112, 137
Street riots, see Riots
Street vendors, 121–22, 140, 228, 241
Strikes, 124–25, 140, 143, 278n103,
    284–285n54
"Strivers' Row," 159
Stuyvesant, Peter: final report by, 17;
    Jews and, 9–10, 11; Lutherans and,
    6–7; municipal council of, 14;
    Quakers and, 7–8; surrender by, 16
Stuyvesant High School, 222
Stuyvesant Polyclinic, 150
Stuyvesant Town, 195
*The Subterranean* (newspaper), 65
Suburbanization, 206
Subway system, 153, 155, 158,
    287n107; see also Interborough
    Rapid Transit
Suffrage, see Elections
Sugar Hill, 159
Sugar prices, 284n40
Sullivan, Tim, 100–101
Sunday observance, 86, 89, 101; see
    also Sabbath observance
Sunset Park, 174, 207–8, 232
Surinam, 9
Sutton, Percy, 215
"Sweatshop poets," 133
Sweatshops, 94–95, 123, 233
Sweeney, Peter, 61, 65
Synagogues: 19th century, 81, 82;
    20th century, 128, 129, 285n69;
    1920s, 173; 1930s, 172, 181; 1970s,
    204
Syrian Jews, 117

■

Syrian Ladies Aid Society, 107

Tailoring, 85, 86, 122
Taiwanese, 231, 232
Talleyrand, Charles Maurice de, 34
Tammany Hall:
—19th century: Germans and, 76, 88, 89, 90; *Harper's Weekly* and, 73; Irish and, 63–66, 71–72; Italians and, 144
—early 20th century, 113; Irish and, 99, 100, 101, 161; Jews and, 126, 127
—1920s, 162, 166, 167, 168
—1930s, 182, 190, 215
—1945–70: 202
Task system, 123
Taverns, *see* Drinking establishments
Taylor, John, 158
Teachers, 257; black, 57, 110, 255, 312*n*190; Depression era, 182, 185; Irish, 99, 101, 160; Italian, 173; Jewish, 160, 164, 188–89, 203, 222–23; Puerto Rican, 311*n*162; white, 253; *see also* Principals
Telephone operators, 194
Temperance legislation, 86, 89, 276*n*73; *see also* Prohibition
Temple Emanu-El, 81, 82
Tenderloin District, 98, 110, 112, 158
Tenement House Laws, 44, 95, 123, 139
Tenement houses, 42–43, 55, 60, 121–22, 165
Tenth Ward, 47, 117, 122
Terracciano, Anthony P., 244
Thais, 237
Theater, 187, 217; German, 84; Greek, 174; Italian, 173; Yiddish, 127, 134–35, 162, 188; *see also* Movies; Opera
Thirty Years War, 8
Tieman, Daniel, 63
Tisch, Lawrence and Preston, 199
Tishman, Julius, 199
TLC Group, Inc., 253

Tobacco business, 12, 55; *see also* Cigar manufacture
Tolerance, 2, 23, 259, 261; *see also* Religious tolerance
Tompkins Square Park, 76, 85
Tong wars, 234–35
Trade, *see* Commerce
Trade associations, 87
Trades, *see* Occupations
Tradesmen, *see* Merchants
Trade unions, *see* Labor movement
Transit systems: 19th century, 42, 55–56, 58, 157; early 20th century, 97, 112, 160; 1930s, 160–61, 179, 186; World War II era, 194; 1945–70: 204, 205–6, 219; *see also* Subway system
Transport Workers Union, 186, 194, 219
Treaty of Hartford (1650), 264*n*23
Treaty of Versailles (1919), 151
Tresca, Carlo, 144, 297*n*74
Triangle Shirtwaist Company, 96, 125
Triborough Bridge, 178
Trinity Church, 19, 22
*Trojan Senator* (ship), 138
Trolleys, *see* Street railways
Tunnels, 178
Tuoti, Giuseppe, 143
Turkey, 210, 211; *see also* Ottoman Empire
*Turnvereine*, 84, 89
Tweed, William Marcy ("Boss"), 63, 65
Tweed Ring, 65, 74, 90
Typhoid fever, 46

Ukrainians, 174, 247
Undocumented aliens, *see* Illegal aliens
Unemployment: 1893: 123; 1930s, 177–78, 180, 181; 1970–94: 254, 312*n*178
Union labor, *see* Labor movement
Union League Club, 51, 58
United Cabinetmakers (union), 87

■

United Civic League, 168
United Federation of Teachers, 222–23
United Hebrew Trades (union), 123, 125
United Irish Counties Association, 248
United Provinces, *see* Netherlands
United States Bureau of the Census, 206
United States Civil Works Administration, 185
United States Congress: blacks in, 252; Chinese immigration and, 108; Dillingham Commission and, 105; Greek community and, 211; House members of, 65, 144, 183, 187, 215; immigration restrictions of, 139, 152, 229; 1906 elections for, 126; Puerto Ricans in, 214, 251
United States Constitution, 53, 57, 72
United States Equal Employment Commission, 218
United States Federal Bureau of Investigation, 192
United States Federal Emergency Relief Administration, 180
United States Federal Equal Opportunity Employment Commission, 199
United States government: antipoverty programs of, 213; Ellis Island and, 104; German-American Bund and, 189, 193; housing and, 185, 220, 221; Italian contract labor and, 137
United States Immigration Commission, 104, 105, 119, 138, 141
United States Industrial Commission, 140
United States Navy, 195
United States Office of Economic Opportunity, 200
United States War Department, 150
United States Work Projects Administration (Works Progress Administration), blacks and, 194; Moses and, 185; surveys by, 152, 166, 170, 171, 174
United Synagogues of America (organization), 129
Universal Negro Improvement Association, 159
Universities, *see* Colleges and universities
University Heights, 155
University of Mississippi, 223
Upper West Side, 42, 157, 172, 212
"Uptown" Chinese, 232, 233, 234
Urban League, 95, 160, 179, 181
Urban renewal, 220
Utopianism, *see* Radicalism

Van Cortland, Stephen, 21, 266*n*81
Van Cortland Manor, 13
Van Cortlandt Park, 242
Vaudeville, 111, 134, 162
Veiller, Lawrence, 95
Velazquez, Nydia M., 251
*Vereine*, 84, 97
Verhulst, Willem, 4
Verrazano, Giovanni da, 1, 2
Verrazano Bridge, 205
Victoria, Queen of England, 49
Vidrowitz, Hayim, 285*n*71
Viereck, George Sylvester, 149–50
Vietnamese Chinese, 234–35, 237–38
Vietnam War, 202
Ville de Bonheur (Haiti), 231
Violence, 238, 249, 250, 256–57; *see also* Riots; Slave rebellions
Virginia: black migration from, 109; New Netherland and, 12, 13; slavery in, 14, 15; Walloons and, 3
Vlasto, Solon, 106
Vocations, *see* Occupations
*Volksfests*, 85
*Volks-Zeitung*, 83
Volpe, Edmond L., 244
Voluntary organizations, *see* Organizations

■

Volunteer fire companies, 62
Voting, *see* Elections
Voting Rights Act (1970), 215

Wages, 70; black, 111; Bohemian, 106; Irish, 60; Italian, 142; Jewish, 123
Wagner, Richard, 151
Wagner, Robert, 201, 203
Waldensians, 5
Waldinger, Roger, 182
Wald, Lillian, 95
Walker, Dixie, 217
Walker, George, 111
Walker, Jimmy, 174–75; election of, 161, 162; Harlem Hospital and, 168; layoffs by, 182; resignation of, 183
Walloons, 2, 3–5, 24
Wall Street, 36–37, 94
Walsh, Mike, 65
War Brides Act, 212
Ward, Benjamin, 243, 252
Ward's Island, 41
War for Greek Independence, 50, 105
War of 1812, 36
War on Poverty programs, 224
Warsaw Pact nations, 242
Washington, George, 54
Washington Heights, 117, 177, 227, 245
Wassenaer, Nicolaes van, 3
Water supply, 43, 45, 103; *see also* Croton Reservoir
Waxman, Harry and Sidney, 204
Weitling, Wilhelm, 86
Welfare programs, 96, 179, 182, 251, 256
Welsh, 48–49, 269n27
West Bronx, 154
Westchester County, 137, 205, 206
Western European immigrants, 38, 102
Western states, 44, 108, 170
West Friesland, 3
West Harlem, 138
West India Company (Netherlands): charter of, 3; development plans of, 4; Dutch Reformed Church and, 19; English conquest and, 17; New Orange and, 18; propaganda of, 13; Recife under, 9; slavery and, 14–15; tolerance of, 6, 7, 8, 10, 11, 259
West Indies: black migration from, 109, 215, 229–30, 305n27; Jews in, 9; return migration to, 177; slavery in, 14, 30
Westinghouse Science Scholarships, 234, 254
West Side, 50, 105, 152, 157, 236; *see also* Lower West Side; Upper West Side
Weydemeyer, Joseph, 86, 277n101
Wheat prices, 102
Whig Party, 68, 71, 83
White collar workers, 94; black, 218; Depression era, 180; German, 96; Irish, 161; Italian, 165; Jewish, 164, 165; *see also* Professionals
White, Douglas H., 221
White, Stanford, 159
William III, King of England, 20, 21, 49
Williams, Bert, 111
Williamsburg: Germans in, 47, 77, 78; Jews in, 156, 172, 208; Poles in, 50, 105–6
Williamsburg Bridge, 97
"Will You Love Me in September as You Do in May?" (J. Walker), 175
Wilson, Woodrow, 126
Winchevsky, Morris, 133
Winnick, Louis, 207–8
Wise, Stephen, 124, 128
*Witte Paert* (ship), 14
Women: black (*see* African American women); Chinese, 108, 233; Czech, 106; Dominican, 227; English, 7; German, 61, 74–75, 101; Greek, 281n62; Irish (*see* Irish women); Italian, 141–42, 164, 165, 173, 210; Jewish (*see* Jewish women); Norwe-

gian, 108, 109; Puerto Rican, 213, 251; Syrian, 107; West Indian, 230; white, 244; *see also* Prostitution; Roman Catholic nuns
Women's Trade Union League, 99, 124
Wong, Bernard, 212
Wood, Benjamin, 73
Wood, Fernando, 62–63, 89–90
Woodlawn, 155
Woodside, 155, 205, 242, 247–48
Work, *see* Occupations
Workers' League, 86
Workmen's Circle, 121, 124, 125
Work Projects Administration, *see* United States Work Projects Administration (Works Progress Administration)
World Series (1919), 166
World War I, 136, 148, 149–52, 169, 260
World War II, 169, 191, 192–96, 198
World Zionist Congress (1897), 127

Xavier Club, 98

Yale University, 201
Yankees (baseball team), 153, 163, 217, 228

Yankee Stadium, 153, 217
Yellow fever, 59
Yeshivas, 172, 177
Yeshiva University, 181
Yiddish language: courses on, 119; in East Bronx, 171; foreign words in, 133; in garment industry, 123; Hasidim and, 209; lectures in, 131; on Lower East Side, 116
Yiddish movies, 134, 187–88
Yiddish newspapers, 132–33, 188, 209
Yiddish theater, 127, 134–35, 162, 188
*Yidisher Amerikaner* (newspaper), 132
*Yidisher Tageblatt*, 132, 188
*Yidisher Velt* (newspaper), 132
YMCA (W. 53d St.), 110
York, Duke of, *see* James II, King of England
Yorkville: 19th century, 42, 48, 91; early 20th century, 97, 152; 1930s, 189; World War II era, 193
Young Israel movement, 129
Yugoslavs, 245; *see also* Croatians
*Di Yunge* (Russian Jews), 133, 287n94

Zeckendorf, William, 199
Zionism, 115, 116, 127